D1242309

Intelligence and Personality

*Bridging the Gap in Theory
and Measurement*

Intelligence and Personality

Bridging the Gap in Theory and Measurement

Edited by

Janet M. Collis
University of Plymouth

Samuel Messick
Educational Testing Service

2001

LAWRENCE ERLBAUM ASSOCIATES, PUBLISHERS
Mahwah, New Jersey   London

The final camera copy for this work was prepared by the editors
and therefore the publisher takes no responsibility for consistency
or correctness of typographical style. However, this arrangement
helps to make publication of this kind of scholarship possible.

Lawrence Erlbaum Associates, Inc., Publishers
10 Industrial Avenue
Mahwah, New Jersey 07430

Cover design by Kathryn Houghtaling Lacey

Library of Congress Cataloging-in-Publication Data

Intelligence and personality : bridging the gap in theory and measurement / edited by
Janet M. Collis, Samuel Messick.
    p. cm.
   Includes bibliographical references and index.
   ISBN 0-8058-3166-5 (alk. paper)
    1.   Personality and intelligence—Congresses. I. Collis, Janet M. II. Messick, Samuel.

BF698.9.I6 I55 2001
153.9—dc21

                    99-058492

Books published by Lawrence Erlbaum Associates are printed on acid-free paper,
and their bindings are chosen for strength and durability.

Printed in the United States of America
10 9 8 7 6 5 4 3 2 1

CONTRIBUTORS

John W. Berry
Queen's University
Ontario, Canada

Peter Borkenau
Martin Luther University
Halle-Wittenberg, Germany

Lyn Corno
Teachers College
Columbia University, USA

Noel Entwistle
University of Edinburgh, UK

Adrian Furnham
University College
London, UK

Peter Gollwitzer
University of Konstanz, Germany

Jan-Eric Gustafsson
University of Göteborg, Sweden

Joop Hettema
Tilburg University,
The Netherlands

Willem K. B. Hofstee
University of Groningen,
The Netherlands

Sidney H. Irvine
University of Plymouth, UK

Arthur R. Jensen
University of California, USA

Paul Kline
University of Exeter, Devon, UK

David F. Lohman
The University of Iowa, USA

Samuel Messick
Educational Testing Service, USA

David N. Perkins
Harvard University, USA

Lawrence A. Pervin
Rutgers University, USA

Anna Piotrowska
University of Warsaw, Poland

Bernd Schaal
University of Konstanz, Germany

Ulrich Schiefele
University of Bielefeld, Germany

Robert J. Sternberg
Yale University, USA

Jan Strelau
University of Warsaw, Poland

Shari Tishman
Harvard University, USA

Bogdan Zawadzki
University of Warsaw, Poland

Moshe Zeidner
University of Haifa, Israel

CONTENTS

List of Contributors   v

Preface   xi
Janet M. Collis

**PART I: INTELLIGENCE IN RELATION
TO TEMPERAMENT AND CHARACTER**

Chapter 1   3
Spearman's Hypothesis
Arthur R. Jensen

Chapter 2   25
On the Hierarchical Structure of Ability
and Personality
Jan-Eric Gustafsson

Chapter 3   43
Intelligence and Personality: Do They Mix?
Willem K. B. Hofstee

Chapter 4   61
Temperament and Intelligence: A Psychometric Approach
to the Links Between Both Phenomena
Jan Strelau, Bogdan Zawadzki, and Anna Piotrowska

Chapter 5   79
Issues in the Definition and Measurement of Abilities
David F. Lohman

Chapter 6   99
Issues in the Measurement of Temperament and Character
Peter Borkenau

Chapter 7   113
Ability and Temperament
Paul Kline

PART II: INTELLIGENCE AND CONATION

Chapter 8   121
Conative Individual Differences in Learning
Lyn Corno for R. E. Snow

Chapter 9   139
How Goals and Plans Affect Action
Peter M. Gollwitzer and Bernd Schaal

Chapter 10   163
The Role of Interest in Motivation and Learning
Ulrich Schiefele

Chapter 11   195
Challenges and Directions for Intelligence and Conation:
Integration
Moshe Zeidner

PART III: INTELLIGENCE AND STYLE

Chapter 12   217
Learning Styles and Cognitive Processes in Constructing
Understanding at the University
Noel Entwistle

Chapter 13   233
Dispositional Aspects of Intelligence
David N. Perkins and Shari Tishman

Chapter 14   259
Style in the Organization and Defense of Cognition
Samuel Messick

Chapter 15   273
Self-Concept and Status as Determinants of Cognitive Style
Sidney H. Irvine

Chapter 16   289
Test-Taking Style, Personality Traits, and Psychometric Validity
Adrian Furnham

PART IV: INTELLIGENCE AND PERSONALITY IN CONTEXT

Chapter 17   307
Persons in Context: Defining the Issues, Units, and Processes
Lawrence A. Pervin

Chapter 18   319
Contextual Studies of Cognitive Adaptation
John W. Berry

Chapter 19   335
Personality in Context, Control, and Intelligence
Joop Hettema

Chapter 20   347
Successful Intelligence: Understanding What Spearman Had Rather Than
What He Studied
Robert J. Sternberg

Author Index   375
Subject Index   385

PREFACE

Janet M. Collis

This volume emanates from the second in a series of symposia entitled the Spearman Seminars. The idea was conceived by Sidney Irvine in 1993, when the first Spearman Seminar took place in Plymouth, England, and gave rise to the book *Human Abilities: Their Nature and Measurement*. The contributors were some of the most outstanding researchers in the field of ability measurement and several of them were invited to return to Plymouth in 1997 to contribute to the next seminar and to the production of this book. The theme for the second meeting was deliberately chosen to broaden into issues of personality as well as ability, but more important to attempt to bridge the historical divide between these two domains. Leading contributors from Europe, North America, and the Middle East have attempted to address these issues, and the result is a remarkable collection of work that embraces the interfaces of intelligence and personality: style, structure, process, and context.

PART I: INTELLIGENCE IN RELATION TO TEMPERAMENT AND CHARACTER

In the opening chapter, Jensen commends the importance of a dual approach to the study of intelligence; both psychometric and factor analytic approaches (which emphasize individual differences) and experimental approaches (which stress common designs, features, and functions of the brain) are crucial to the understanding of intelligence. He discusses what he terms *Spearman's hypothesis*—an observation made by Spearman that the size of group differences between White and Black subjects on different tests is a function of the g loading of each test. Jensen reports several tests of Spearman's hypothesis by exploring the relationship between g loadings and standardized White-Black differences, resulting in significant correlations that are not diminished when controlling for socioeconomic status and that appear in both standard psychometric tests and elementary cognitive tests. Gustafsson provides a comprehensive discussion of several hierarchical models of cognition and personality with their accompanying theories, examining in particular bottom-up and top-down approaches. Alternative views on the existence or otherwise of a general factor tends to influence the support of a particular hierarchical model. Through application of confirmatory factor analysis to a classical study (Holzinger & Swineford, 1939), Gustafsson showed that this approach is most appropriate for research on hierarchical models. The discussion is extended to include the relationship between ability and personality, where evidence of overlap between the two domains suggests that hierarchical models of ability may benefit from the examination of the variance attributed to personality factors.

The debate on hierarchical approaches is continued by Hofstee, who gives an interesting account of attempts to assess maximal personality and typical intelligence but concludes that the concepts are problematic for a variety of reasons. A more promising outcome might be achieved by blending personality and stylistic intellect. To that end, Hofstee introduces a hierarchical model, with a new notion of personality (the p-factor) as a parallel to the established g-concept. He shows that the p-factor encompasses stylistic intellect and other personality factors and may well represent Competence or Coping. Identification of five hierarchical levels yields several patterns of stylistic intellect, and Hofstee emphasizes the usefulness of setting stylistic intellect within the context of personality rather than within the domain of maximal intelligence tests.

Strelau, Zawadski, and Piotrowska examine the relationship between various measures of intelligence and temperament by paying particular attention to temperamental characteristics related to arousal. They conclude that a psychometric exploration of these links shows that not all intellectual characteristics are related to temperament. The relationship between fluid intelligence and temperament may be a function of developmental stages because the roles of fluid and crystallized intelligence are dependent on life stages. Strelau, et al. also consider that the strength of the relationship between emotionality and intelligence may be affected by the perceived stressfulness of the intelligence tasks given. Finally, the finding that crystallized intelligence is related to a temperament factor labeled sensitivity to environment reinforces Strelau et al.'s proposal that temperament may affect the interaction between genetically determined intelligence potential and the environment, thereby influencing the development of crystallized intelligence.

Lohman compares and contrasts the approaches associated with differential and experimental psychology and emphasizes that both approaches make valuable contributions to the study of abilities because they offer different perspectives on the study of variation. Four definitions of ability are reviewed and Lohman concludes by supporting Snow's (1994) suggestion that a definition of abilities must include influences of the environment—the situated view of abilities. This encompasses the influences of affect, volition, and context, as well as opportunity and ability.

Borkenau investigates the consequences of the use of judgmental data on the measurement of personality, conducting studies where the amount and type of information available to judges is controlled to test models of the judgment process. The ensuing moderate correlations suggest that dissimilar conclusions are reached from the same information systems and that the level of consensus among judges (in equivalent information conditions) is not diminished by reducing the amount of information given. Borkenau proposes that consensus might be reduced by a lack of shared meaning systems. This was confirmed by a study showing a lack of consensus among judges in prototypicality ratings of behavior, despite high retest stability within judges. A further study in which judges assigned activities to behavior-descriptive categories showed that using multiple prototypicality codes (rather than one activity–one category conditions) resulted in closer correspondence between online behavior records and retrospective frequency ratings of the same behavior.

Finally, Kline focuses on the structure of personality and ability and that relation, noting that the observed weak correlations between the two may reflect the variation in item type. He cites evidence that does, however, suggest closer relations between the two domains. Kline's critique of the five-factor theory account of personality includes the suggestion that the Openness factor may represent intelligence as well as personality. Kline also links Openness with the authoritarian personality, which is also related to intelligence, and recommends that this historically important concept, being absent from current accounts of personality, should be revisited.

PART II: INTELLIGENCE AND CONATION

Corno begins this section by describing recent developments in conative individual differences, including a taxonomy of conative aptitudes. She discusses the interaction between learning environments and conation. The important distinction between motivation and volition is emphasized, along with the interaction between conation, cognition, and treatment to determine individual differences in learning.

Gollwitzer and Schaal give a comprehensive account of types of goal theories. In particular, they discuss the Rubicon model of action phases as an additional attempt to explain differences between motivation (goal choice) and volition (goal implementation). From this model, the importance of mindsets appropriate to each phase is highlighted, together with contrasts between goal intentions and implementation intentions. Gollwitzer and Schaal emphasize the relevance of current goal theories for educators and students alike and advise the encouragement of goal-setting and goal regulation strategies along with teaching. They stress the influence of both teachers' and students' own implicit theories of goal setting and the promotion of goals with a positive outcome focus to enable a better likelihood of goal attainment.

Schiefele examines the role of interest and motivation in academic learning, first by distinguishing between the two concepts. He regards motivation as a specific mental state and interest as a relatively stable, stored belief set. Interest predetermines intrinsic motivation and is probably the core condition of intrinsic motivation to learn. Schiefele reports that interest is related to different measures of text learning in different ways and controlling for prior knowledge and ability reveals that interest and cognitive factors contribute independently to text learning. In addition, the functional state of the learner (in particular the measurement of arousal), appears to significantly mediate the effects of interest on text learning.

Zeidner underlines the theme in all of the chapters on the role of conation. He discusses the links, both conceptual and empirical, between intelligence and conation and the possible future directions that research in both fields could pursue, together with issues that are relevant to the potential integration of the two constructs. Improved understanding of such integration is believed to be crucial to the theoretical underpinning of real-world behavior.

PART III: INTELLIGENCE AND STYLE

Entwistle describes the interaction of cognitive and conative processes in learning with student perceptions of assessment procedures. Learning outcomes are viewed as a function of stylistic preference, approach to studying, awareness of targets, motivational approach, and suitable response to task demands. Entwistle commends the notion of composite concepts, perhaps like a disposition to learn or understand, that appear to capture real-life experiences of learning. Interviews with students that describe such experience are offered in support of this notion, whereas factor analyses of self-reports show the covarying nature of approaches to studying, stylistic preferences, academic success, and understanding. Perkins and Tishman also argue for the role of disposition in intelligence and propose that intelligent behavior encompasses sensitivity to circumstance, inclination to engage, and ability to perform. The first two components, sensitivity and inclination, constitute thinking disposition and may account for the gap between ability to perform in a certain way and the actual occurrence of such performance on a given occasion. Studies in the conduct of thinking suggest that low sensitivity (poor detection of thinking shortfall) may be primarily responsible for processing difficulties.

Messick examines the relationship between two particular cognitive styles of attention scanning and four defensive styles. Cognitive styles affect the organization and control of cognitive processes, whereas defensive styles are related to the organization and control of intrusion in cognitive processing.

Messick reports that the defensive styles are characterized by their modes of attentional behavior. Orientation to one or another cognitive style of attentional scanning appears to predispose to a particular defensive style. If cognitive styles do serve as organizers of defensive styles, then it still remains to determine what underlies the development of cognitive styles.

Irvine raises the issue of how style might best be measured, echoing Messick's (1996) recommendation that style could be measured in non normative ways. He emphasizes the persistence of styles long after the termination of conditions that shaped particular stylistic development. Irvine's conclusions, supported by the findings of four studies, are that styles are not universal; style may be a cultural variable that is determined in part by what is taught and learned in school and by the conditions under which learning takes place. Irvine also concludes that self-concepts can determine successful performance. The work styles that emerge from self-concepts appear to be successfully defined by both ipsative and normative measures.

Furnham focuses on three aspects of test-taking style that he believes are consistent, stable, and potentially useful trait measures. The first style, which is the time taken to complete a test, appears to be linked to neuroticism. A second style, indecisiveness, which is reflected in the use of "can't decide" options on a response scale and has also been found to be related to neuroticism and may of course be linked to test-taking speed. Research covering the third style of faking or socially desirable responding is far more extensive, and social desirability has often been regarded as a consistent, stable trait in its own right. Furnham concludes that because these test-taking styles appear to be stable and related to personality traits, there may be a relationship between personality and ability as measured by test scores. This will depend, to some extent, on the nature of the ability test and its particular properties. Differences may occur when comparing tests requiring speed versus accuracy, sustained versus brief attention demands, and the relative importance of test outcome.

PART IV: INTELLIGENCE AND PERSONALITY IN CONTEXT

In Part IV, four authors offer different approaches to the study of context and its acknowledged influence on both intelligence and personality. Pervin argues that the study of personality should incorporate the identification of consistencies across individuals and the organization of various parts into a functioning system. Although acknowledging the crucial role of context, he suggests that there may be regularities present in the way the system functions. It may, therefore, be more fruitful to focus on aspects of the system itself, especially the principles of its functioning to identify such regularities that could be independent of context. The emphasis, therefore is placed on change or adaptation brought about by processes of functioning rather than the highly idiosyncratic perceptions of situations and contexts.

Contextual effects as a result of cultural variation are described by Berry; competences are seen as being inextricably linked to the demands of the culture in which they develop. Assessment without understanding of cultural factors may be inappropriate or misleading. One alternative approach to the study of culture and cognition is to identify the style of processing rather than the amount, and Berry explores possible differences in cognitive style, using cultural variations as predictors.

In attempting to identify the conditions under which consistency and inconsistency occur, Hettema proposes that the exertion of different types of control over the environment may be important. An information-processing model of control is offered to account for consistency in intelligence, where primary control is dominant and actively shapes the environment. When primary control ceases to be dominant, secondary control affects cognitive processes, resulting in internal adaptation to the environment and subsequent inconsistency in person situation interactions.

In the final chapter, Sternberg continues the theme of a restrictive view of intelligence and argues for the concept of successful intelligence: the ability to adapt to, shape, and select environments for the successful pursuit of goals. He contrasts this with conventional concepts of intelligence that may only identify some types of intelligent individuals. He discusses how this new concept of intelligence might be a more effective predictor of success beyond school performance and shows how it can encompass the role of personal values in success and allow for cultural differences in the definition of intelligence. The components of successful intelligence are those described by Sternberg's triarchic theory and studies reported here show that matching instructional style to triarchic abilities results in more successful learning and performance.

ACKNOWLEDGMENTS

Many people contributed to the organization of the seminar and the production of the book. Wendy Tapsfield, Gill Butland, and Ann Jungeblut worked hard to ensure the success of the meeting, and advice and support from Paddy Tapsfield was gratefully received. Thanks are also due to Geoff Payne, the former Dean of Human Sciences at the University of Plymouth, and Ernest Anastasio, Executive Vice President of ETS, Princeton, who enthusiastically supported the seminar financially. I am particularly indebted to Kathy Howell at ETS who worked unstintingly and meticulously to prepare publication materials.

It is with great sadness that I report the death of Samuel Messick in October, 1998. A scholar of international repute with an outstanding research record, Sam was the driving force behind the second Spearman seminar and the coeditor of these proceedings.

I hope this book will also serve as a fitting tribute to four key contributors to the seminar series. Hans Eysenck, who was to deliver the Spearman lecture, died in September 1997. Dick Snow, whose work is represented in this volume by Lyn Corno, died in December 1997, after a long illness. Ann Jungeblut, who served as the co-director of the second Spearman seminar, died in August, 1998. Finally, Paul Kline, a seminar discussant and contributor to this volume died in September 1999. Each, in their own particular and unique way will be missed and remembered with fondness and respect.

Janet Collis
University of Plymouth

REFERENCES

Holzinger, K. J., & Swineford, F. (1939). A study in factor analysis: The stability of a bi-factor solution. *Supplementary Educational Monographs, No. 48*. Chicago: Department of Education, University of Chicago.

Messick, S. J. (1996). Bridging Cognition and Personality in Education: The Role of Style in Performance and Development. *European Journal of Personality, 10*, 353-376.

Snow, R. E. (1994). Abilities in academic tasks. In R. J. Sternberg & R. K. Wagner (Eds.), *Mind in Context: Interactionist perspectives on human intelligence* (pp. 3-37). Cambridge, UK: Cambridge University Press.

PART 1

INTELLIGENCE IN RELATION TO TEMPERAMENT AND CHARACTER

1

Spearman's Hypothesis

Arthur R. Jensen
University of California

This occasion is a pleasure and a privilege for me, because Charles Edward Spearman (1863–1945) occupies a high position in my personal pantheon of pioneers in the history of psychology. Along with Sir Francis Galton and Edward Lee Thorndike, Spearman is one of my few heroes, at least in the behavioral sciences. Indeed, my book on the *g*-factor (Jensen, 1998) is dedicated to the memory of Spearman.

My pleasure is diminished, however, by my disappointment and deep regret that Professor Hans Eysenck, who was originally invited to give The Spearman Address, has had to curtail his activities for a time because of a serious illness, and I wish him well.[1] I have known Eysenck for 41 years, initially having done a 2-year Post-doc with him, way back in the mid-1950's. Some years later, I spent my first sabbatical year from Berkeley at Eysenck's lab. My time with Eysenck, I must say, was among the most valuable experiences in my life and there is no one else to whom I feel more indebted professionally. As the leading exponent of the London School of differential psychology founded by Galton and Spearman, Eysenck's presence at this Spearman Seminar is greatly missed.

If Eysenck were with us, I imagine that an important part of his message would include a concern he expressed in a passage he wrote about Spearman's thought in his book *The Structure and Measurement of Intelligence* (Eysenck, 1979):

> The isolation of a psychometric and factor analytic work from the experimental and theoretical tradition of psychology has had many unfortunate consequences, which were foreseen by Spearman, who insisted on the dual psychological study of intelligence: the psychometric study of individual differences, and the experimental study of the general laws of intellectual functioning. It is unfortunate that his successors embraced wholeheartedly the psychometric method, and disregarded the experimental method. It is only recently that the

---

[1] Professor Eysenck died on September 5, 1997 at age 81 (Jensen, 2000).

process of unification has begun, and our success in gaining a proper understanding of intelligence depends very much on the continuation of this unification. (p. 29)

Now, 18 years later Eysenck's statement deserves repetition because the conceptual confusion between these two domains mentioned by Eysenck still exists. It is especially evident in the two liveliest and most promising branches of behavioral science—experimental cognitive psychology and cognitive neuroscience. My reading in these fields and discussion with scientists working in them has revealed a conceptual confusion that simply should not be allowed to persist. It is the result of a failure to recognize the essential distinction implied by Spearman's notion of the dual nature of the study of intelligence, or what he preferred to call mental abilities. This confusion, in fact, has led some of the scientifically most respectable cognitive psychologists and neuroscientists to ignore or dismiss Spearman's major theoretical contribution, even his empirical work, and much of the research that has sprung from Spearman's ideas in the half-century since he died in 1945.

Modern brain science, with its emphasis on many highly specialized functions of various neural processes and anatomically distinct modules that process different classes of information, would seem to contradict the existence of a general mental ability, or Spearman's g. Some, indeed, argue that the findings of modern neuroscience contradict the existence of a small number of very broad group factors and are incompatible with any hierarchical theory of mental abilities. A few experimental psychologists and neuroscientists pooh-pooh factor analysis altogether, viewing it as merely a kind of hocus pocus numerology or pseudoscience. The essence of this rejection lies in the confusion between two conceptually distinct aspects of what we may call cognitive abilities.

What are these dual aspects conceived by Spearman? On the one hand, there are the neural mechanisms, what might be called the essential design features of the brain or its basic operating principles. These features make possible such mental functions as perception, discrimination, attention, learning, memory, and reasoning—all of the conceptually distinguishable aspects of information processing that we subsume under the term intelligence. In the light of what we now know about mammalian evolution and human evolution in particular, it is most unlikely that there are any differences among living *Homo sapiens* in the essential design features of the brain or in its basic operating principles. At this level of analysis involving neural mechanisms, modules, and the like, it is most unlikely that there are any intraspecies differences among biologically normal human beings, which includes all humans without major gene defects, chromosomal anomalies, or neurological damage due to trauma or disease.

On the other hand, there are conspicuous individual differences in the behavioral manifestations of these design features of the brain. It is only these individual differences that are dealt with in psychometrics and factor analysis. Without reliable individual differences, of course, correlational analysis or factor structure would be meaningless. Further, it is known from research in behavioral genetics and from the correlations between psychometric test scores and various measures of individual differences in physical brain variables—such as brain size, evoked potentials, glucose metabolic rate, and intracellular pH level—that psychometric variance is not exclusively the product of different learning experiences. Rather, it is known that it has a substantial biological basis that interacts with, and in large part determines, experiential differences.

The biological basis of individual differences most probably does not reside in the design features and operating principles of the brain. These are common to every biologically normal member of the species *Homo sapiens*. Although these design features are the principal subject matter of research in cognitive neuroscience, they reveal only half of the picture.

Here I wish to emphasize the hypothesis that the biological basis of individual differences is distinct from and, as it were, superimposed upon, the species-common brain mechanisms, modules, and the like, that make possible the various functions that are generally viewed as constituting intelligence. I would suggest also that the biological basis of individual differences has been on a different evolutionary time track from the species-common neural basis of cognitive functions. As a crude analogy, consider the many makes of gas-powered automobiles. Although they all operate according to the principles of the internal combustion engine, they show differences in variables such as horsepower, maximum speed, fuel efficiency, and the like because of quantitative differences in the number and cubic capacity of the cylinders, the tolerance and lubrication of the moving parts, the octane rating of the gas, and the like. Electric cars and steam engine cars, with their quite different operating principles, are analogous to different species or genera.

In this dual view of the neurophysiology of mental ability, consisting of the design features of the brain on the one hand and individual differences on the other, there is no conflict at all between the aims and findings of cognitive neuroscience and the structure of individual variation in abilities as represented by factor analysis. Both realms of phenomena are proper grist for research and are essential for a comprehensive science of human abilities. And both are biological as well as behavioral.

The biological basis of individual differences could reside in quantitative variation in neural structures, such as the number or density of neurons, the number of their synapses, and the amount of dendritic arborization. Among individuals, there is also quantitative variation in extraneural structures such as the degree of myelination of the axons, the richness of glial cells, nerve conduction velocity, glucose metabolic rate, the chemical neurotransmitters, and other elements of brain chemistry, such as intracellular pH level, all acting more or less generally throughout the central nervous system.

If the operating efficiency of the brain's functional mechanisms were all more or less homogeneously affected by individual variation in any one or more of these superimposed quantitative features, individual differences in various mental abilities would, of course, be positively correlated with one another in the population. A hierarchical factor analysis would reveal the g factor, as was originally hypothesized by Galton (1869) and discovered empirically by Spearman (1904), (Jensen, 2000).

However, it is not yet known which properties of the brain cause the positive correlations among virtually all cognitive abilities where there are individual differences and that give rise to the phenomenon that Spearman labeled g. But this, too, is a question that goes beyond psychometrics and factor analysis and will be fruitful territory for neuroscientists, provided they come to realize that it is both conceptually and physically distinguishable from the brain's species-characteristic operating principles. It may well be possible to discover the biological basis of g sooner (and more easily) than to discover the neurological mechanisms that mediate all of the diverse information processing functions that make up what is referred to as "intelligence" (Jensen, 1997).

Spearman realized clearly that research on these two aspects of mental ability is two distinct tasks. Intelligence consists of all of the cognitive functions attributed to it. The existence of the g-factor, on the other hand, depends on the empirically established phenomenon of positive correlations among all of the measurable behavioral attributes and manifestations of intelligence. Failure to recognize this critical distinction between intelligence and g is a roadblock to discovering the biological basis of g.

Discovering the biological bias of g, which was virtually impossible with the technology of Spearman's time, was nevertheless Spearman's greatest wish, the ultimate outcome of the line of research he initiated. He stated that the final understanding of g ". . . must come from the most profound and detailed direct study of the human brain in its purely physical and chemical aspects" (p. 403).

Although Spearman was generally regarded as Britain's leading psychologist during the latter part of his career and was accorded such distinguished recognition as Fellowship in the Royal Society and honorary membership in the United States National Academy of Sciences, I believe his stature has steadily grown in the 5 decades since his death. In noting the many citations of Spearman's work in my extensive reading of the literature on mental ability over the years, I have gained the impression that behavioral scientists have shown a steadily increasing interest in an appreciation of Spearman.

To determine if my subjective impression has any objective validity, I recently asked the Institute for Scientific Information (ISI), which produces the Science Citation Index (SCI) and the Social Science Citation Index (SSCI), to provide me a citation count on Spearman's work in every 5-year interval during the half-century since his death, that is, from 1945 to 1995. Figure 1.1 shows a plot of these citations.

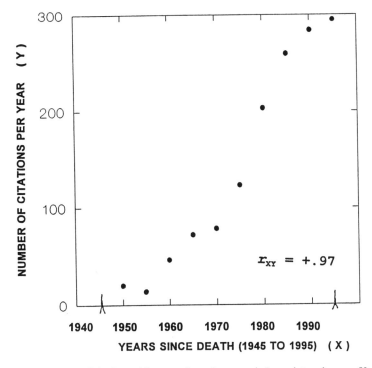

FIG. 1.1. Number of citations of Spearman's works per each 5-year interval over a 50-year period after his death.

There is a correlation of +0.97 between the number of Spearman citations and the number of years since his death. This confirms my initial impression. Skinnerians might better appreciate Figure 1.2, which shows the same data presented as a cumulative record. It forms a perfect, positively accelerated growth curve. The ISI informed me that the frequency of citations of Spearman's cited works, just since his death, places them at the 99.98th percentile of all works ever cited at least once in the Citation Index. While serving on faculty search committees, I have heard it claimed that a good prognosis for a better-than-average career in research is the candidate's having independently published a journal article even before doing the PhD dissertation. Well, Spearman published two articles 2 years before getting his PhD (in Wundt's lab), and both articles are still frequently cited in recent years. One is a true landmark in the history of our field and is frequently cited right up to the present day—93 years since the appearance of his famous 1904 article in the *American Journal of Psychology*.

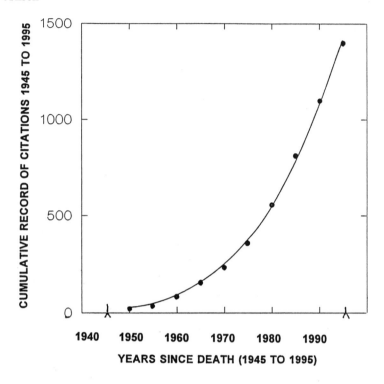

FIG. 1.2. A cumulative frequency distribution of Spearman citations during the 50 years following his death.

This is indeed exceptional. As a rule, the number of citations of the vast majority of psychologists who are ever cited at all, even the very famous ones, rapidly dwindles to near zero after their death.

What is responsible for this increasing interest in Spearman's work? It is known, of course, that he made a number of important contributions—several statistical methods (which now are frequently used but seldom cited), as well as empirical and theoretical discoveries and formulations. He is usually regarded as the inventor of factor analysis (although that is a historically complicated claim) and he is certainly the acknowledged father of what we now call "classical test theory." But with the overshadowing ascendance of item response theory (IRT) in the last 20 years, it is unlikely that the increasing interest in Spearman reflects his historic role in the development of classical test theory. That appears now to be past history. Judging from his works that are the most frequently cited in the modern literature, particularly his most famous work, *The Abilities of Man* (1927), it is clear that the renewed interest in Spearman is due to the increasing recognition of the importance of the *g* factor, often and appropriately referred to as Spearman's *g*.

The present interest in g now extends far beyond its origins in psychometrics and factor analysis (Jensen, 1987b). Discussions are now focused largely on its physiological basis (Jensen, 1997) on the one hand and on its broad societal implications on the other (Gottfredson, 1997).

Probably more present-day psychologists have read and cited *The Abilities of Man* than was true of Spearman's contemporaries. There are good reasons for this. Besides being one of the great classics of psychology that also deals with issues that are very much alive today, it is a wellspring of ideas, questions, suggestions, hypotheses, and embryonic findings regarding phenomena that invite further research—research that is highly relevant to contemporary problems in differential psychology.

Spearman's own empirical research was always theory-driven but usually with small-scale studies by today's standards, and results were typically tentative and seldom sufficient for firm establishment of the points he argued. These were often left at a stage best viewed as either untested or inconclusively tested hypotheses. Yet Spearman's scientific genius was such that when his ideas and findings were later studied on a larger and more rigorous scale than was feasible in his time, they have usually panned out empirically, just as he would have predicted. One example is the theory he dubbed the "law of diminishing returns," in which he hypothesized, in effect, that if the normal distribution of general ability, or g, in the population is split at the median, the average of the correlations among diverse tests (and hence their g loadings) would be larger for the lower half of the distribution than for the upper half. In other words, the demands of various mental tasks reflect g to a greater degree in individuals of below-average ability than in individuals of above-average ability. The higher the level of g, the less the amount of g variance in any given test. At the higher levels of ability, some of the g variance is replaced by various group factors or by task specificity. If true, this is an interesting phenomenon that needs to be explained by any comprehensive theory of intelligence. Quite recently, large-scale and methodologically elegant studies by Detterman and Daniel (1989) and by Deary and Pagliari (1991), Deary et al. (1996), established Spearman's so-called law as a genuine psychological phenomenon. These investigators have provided their own theoretical explanations of Spearman's law, and these, too, invite further empirical tests.

Another example of delving further into one of Spearman's ideas is the work I have done during the past decade or so on what I have dubbed "Spearman's hypothesis." Because Spearman himself never presented it as a formal hypothesis, a few people have objected to my crediting it to Spearman. So whenever I say Spearman's hypothesis, I hope you visualize these words in quotation marks.

But I should begin my story by telling you how I discovered Spearman's hypothesis in the first place and why I was eager to pursue it empirically.

Back in the 1970s, when I became especially interested in the question of test bias with respect to the well-known Black–White IQ difference, I found it virtually impossible to explain the very considerable variation in the mean Black–White differences on various cognitive tests. I had noted that the group differences were markedly smaller on tests of rote learning and short-term memory than on tests more typical of those found in conventional IQ tests. I formalized these observations in my so-called Level I–Level II theory (Vernon, 1981). This was really just the empirical generalization that tasks requiring little or no transformation of the input information (called Level I ability) in order to arrive at the output showed little or no difference between races or social classes. The larger racial and social-class differences existed on tests to the degree that they required transformation or mental manipulation of the input in order to arrive at the correct output (called Level II ability). This effect was clearly evident in the two most similar subtests of the Wechsler Intelligence Scale–Forward Digit Span and Backward Digit Span. These two tasks require different amounts of transformation or mental manipulation of the input. In large representative samples, I found that the mean Black–White difference was reliably twice as large for Backward as for Forward Digit Span (Jensen & Figueroa, 1975). As this finding did not readily lend itself to an explanation in terms of cultural bias or in terms of any other theory I knew of except my Level I–Level II notion, I kept thinking about it.

Then one day while rereading *The Abilities of Man* (Spearman, 1927) in preparation for a new course I was about to teach titled "Theories of Intelligence," I came across the idea that guided a good deal of my subsequent research. Although I had read *Abilities* some 20 years earlier at Eysenck's suggestion (while I was doing my Post-doc under him), I had either overlooked or completely forgotten the passage that this time around jumped right off the page and gave me pause. It was just one of Spearman's many casual conjectures, as it was not based on anything that could be called hard evidence, and he never did anything more with it.

Spearman had suggested that the variable magnitude of the mean Black–White difference on various tests was a direct function of the respective test's *g* loading. Here, I thought, was the essential phenomenon that would explain, in much broader, more fundamental terms, the specific psychometric phenomena that gave rise to my Level I–Level II formulation. I immediately realized that it was probably only a special case of the more general hypothesis proposed by Spearman and which I later formalized as "Spearman's hypothesis." This discovery appealed to me, because the great many different and often incompatible ad hoc cultural-type hypotheses I had seen in the literature to explain the Black-White differences on each and every particular type of test (or specific test item) might be explained by a single and simple hypothesis—Spearman's hypothesis. If the hypothesis were true, it would mean that before we could understand the nature of the Black-White difference on cognitive tests, we would first have to understand the nature of g itself.

I factor-analyzed my Wechsler data on large samples of Black and White children and found exactly what Spearman conjectured—that Backward Digit Span had about twice the g loading as Forward Digit Span, just as the Black-White standardized mean difference on Backward Digit Span was about double that on Forward Digit Span. It was at that point that I formalized Spearman's hypothesis and began testing it on a wide variety of psychometric tests administered to large representative samples of the American White and Black populations (Jensen, 1985a, 1985b, 1985c, 1987a).

My empirically testable formulation of Spearman's hypothesis and the alternative hypothesis are shown in Figure 1.3.

At the top is the "strong form" of the hypothesis, which states that the size of the difference on various tests is solely a function of the tests' differing g loadings (Δ_g); no group factor (A,B,C) independent of g enters into the mean difference. In the middle is the weak form of the hypothesis, which states that the largest part of the difference is g but allows that one or more group factors (Δ_{non-g}) enters into the mean difference. The contra hypothesis states that there is no Black–White difference in g but only in one or more of the group factors, or possibly in test specificities, which would imply uncorrelated unique racial-cultural biases in each test on which there is a Black-White difference.

The most straightforward method for testing the hypothesis is shown in Figure 1.4. A battery of diverse tests, A, B, C, and so forth obtained on large representative samples of Blacks and Whites is factor analyzed separately within each group. This insures that no aspect of the between-groups variance can enter into the factor structure. The column vector of each of the various tests' g loadings (in either group), here labeled g_x is correlated with the column vector composed of the standardized mean differences between the groups on each test, here labeled D. A nonparametric test of the null hypothesis is performed, based on the Spearman rank-order correlation between these two vectors. The nonparametric rank correlation usually differs only slightly from the Pearson r but the nonparametric statistic is preferable, as its standard error requires no assumptions about the form of the distribution of either of the two correlated vectors.

The hypothesis is not testable unless the vector of g loadings is highly congruent across the racial groups, as indicated by a congruence coefficient of at least .95. The hypothesis assumes, of course, that one and the same g- factor exists in both groups. The data fully bear this out. The average congruence coefficient in all of the independent data sets studied so far is + .995; that is, virtual identity of the g factor in the Black and White samples. This high degree

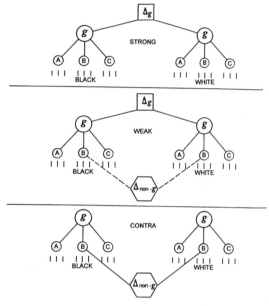

FIG. 1.3. Diagrammatic representation of the strong and weak forms of Spearman's hypothesis and the contra-hypothesis in terms of the factor structure of nine supposed tests (vertical lines) giving rise to three first-order group factors A, B, C, and a g factor, for both black and white groups. The mean W-B difference is represented by Δ, with its subscript indicating that one (or more) factor(s) that enter into it. Dashed lines signify a weaker relationship of the factor to Δ than do solid lines. In the contra hypothesis, test specificity (of any number of the tests) could also contribute to the Δ_{non-g}.

of similarity warrants averaging each test's g loadings across groups, thereby increasing the reliability of the tests' g loadings.

Because the reliability of each test affects both its g loading and the magnitude of the standardized mean group difference, and because the various tests in a battery have different reliability coefficients, it is necessary to demonstrate that the correlation between the g and D vectors is not the result of the heterogeneity of the various tests' reliability. The most rigorous control is to partial out the column vector composed of the tests' reliability coefficients. This is, of course, an extremely severe test, making it difficult to reject the null hypothesis because the N on which the correlation r_{gD} (with reliability partialled out) is based is not the subject sample size, but rather on the number of tests, which is only about 10 to 12 tests in most studies. For the partialled correlation, the degrees of freedom is $N - 3$. Hence, if anything, the cards are stacked against rejecting the null hypothesis. The subject sample size is important. The larger it is, the better, because it affects the reliability of each test's g loading and of the D value on each test.

$$\text{Test } (x) \qquad g_x \qquad \bar{D} = (\bar{X}_W - \bar{X}_B)/\bar{\sigma}$$

Test (x)	g_x	$\bar{D} = (\bar{X}_W - \bar{X}_B)/\bar{\sigma}$
A	.85	.73
B	.80	.75
C	.76	.65
D	.71	.70
E	.60	.62
F	.55	.58
G	.53	.50
H	.49	.55
I	.40	.40
J	.35	.25
ETC.	.30	.20

$$r_{g\bar{D}}$$

FIG. 1.4. The method of correlated vectors, whereby the column vector of various tests' g loadings (g_x) is correlated with the column vector of mean group differences (D). The correlation between the two vectors is r_{gD}.

Let me summarize the results obtained from 17 independent data sets derived from a total of 171 psychometric tests (with 149 different tests) obtained from samples of 45,000 Blacks and 245,000 Whites. Figures 1.5 and 1.6 summarize these studies. So that all of the data points from the 17 independent studiescould be represented in one graph, I have expressed the g loadings and the mean differences in standardized form based on each study. Figure 1.5 shows the scatter diagram when the g loadings are derived from the data for the Black samples. The correlation (Pearson r) is + .57. Figure 1.6 show the results based on the g loadings of the White samples.

The correlation is + .62. Partialling out the effect of test reliability has no significant effect on these results. If one combines the sgnificance levels (i.e. p values) of the correlation obtained in each of the independent studies, the null hypothesis can be rejected at $p < 10^{-10}$.

It is worth noting that the prediction made by Spearman's hypothesis is borne out at an early age, as shown in a study of preschoolers averaging 3 years of age

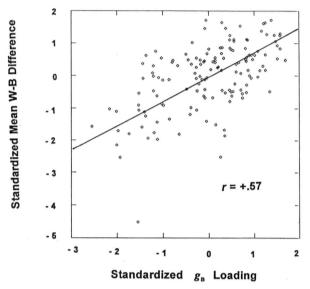

FIG. 1.5. Scatter diagram of the correlation (r_{gD}) between the g loadings and the standardized mean W-B differences (D) on 149 different psychometric tests, with the g loadings based on data from Black samples ($N = 45,000$).

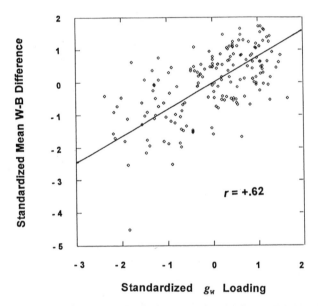

FIG. 1.6. Scatter diagram of the correlation (r_{gD}) between the g loadings and the standardized mean W-B differences (D) on 149 difference psychometric tests, with the g loadings based on data from White samples ($N = 245,000$).

The question has been raised whether the phenomenon predicted by Spearman's hypothesis is mainly a result of the average difference in socio-economic status (SES) between Blacks and Whites. To investigate this, samples of 86 matched pairs of Black and White fourth graders, matched on a standard scale of SES as well as on age, sex, and school, were tested on both the Wechsler Intelligence Scale for Children–Revised (WISC–R) and the Kaufman Assessment Battery for Children (K–ABC) —constituting a total of 24 diverse subtests (Naglieri & Jensen, 1987). As can be seen in Figure 1.7 controlling SES did not diminish the correlation between g and D.

A few critics have mistakenly supposed that Spearman's hypothesis is just a kind of tautology, predicting a statistical artifact as a mathematically inevitable consequence of the machinations of factor analysis (Jensen, 1992a, 1992b). But this is quite obviously false, of course, because the correlation matrix is factor analyzed separately for each group and, therefore, cannot possibly contain any information about the means or standard deviations of the variables or the mean differences between groups. In computing correlations, all of the variables are either standardized or rank-ordered, thereby absolutely eliminating all information about group means or mean differences between groups. If, then, the g factor extracted from the correlation matrix is significantly related to group mean differences, as we find in the tests of Spearman's hypothesis, this finding cannot possibly be a mere statistical artifact or a tautology. Rather, it is indeed a wholly genuine empirical phenomenon.

In fact, it is not universally true that all groups that differ, on average, in their overall score on a test battery will necessarily conform to Spearman's hypothesis. Large samples of Whites and Indians in the public schools in South Africa were found to differ almost 1 standard deviation (0.96σ, to be exact) on an IQ test consisting of 10 diverse subtests. But when Spearman's hypothesis was tested on these groups, the correlations between g loadings and standardized mean differences was only +.08 (Lynn & Owen, 1994). The corresponding correlation based on the same test battery applied to Whites and Blacks was +.62.

Do we find Black–White differences on group factors independent of g? The answer is yes, which means that we must reject the strong form of Spearman's hypothesis. Tests that are loaded on a spatial visualization factor quite consistently fall significantly above the regression line predicted by tests' g loadings. Tests loaded on a short-term memory factor fall *below* the g regression line. That is to say, that when the two racial groups are statistically equated on g, Whites, on average, perform better than Blacks on spatial tests and Blacks perform better than Whites on memory tests. These effects, however, are quite small compared to the effect of g, which in the combined studies accounts for at least four times as much of the variance between groups as does all of the significant non-g group factors combined. In controlling for g, there generally appears to be no Black–White difference at all on a verbal factor that is loaded small compared to the effect of *g*, which in the combined studies accounts for at least four times as much of the variance between groups as does all of the significant non-*g* group factors combined. In controlling for *g*, there generally appears to be no Black–White difference at all on a verbal factor that is loaded on tests such as vocabulary, similarities, sentence completion, verbal analogies, and paragraph comprehension. Test specificity, or whatever is left over after all the significant factors (i.e., the number of principal components with eigenvalues > 1) have been extracted (minus measurement error) is negatively correlated (about -.40) with the Black–White difference. The effect of test specificity, therefore, slightly diminishes the mean difference between groups on any particular test. This finding disproves the hypothesis that the group difference is due to some cultural factor specific to each test.

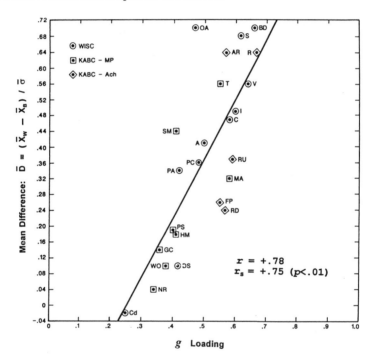

FIG. 1.7. Mean B–W differences (expressed in units of the average within-groups standard deviation) on WISC-R and K-ABC subtests as a function of each subtest's loadings on *g*. WISC-R subtests: I-Information, S-Similarities, A-Arithmetic, V-Vocabulary, C-Comprehension, DS-Digit Span, PC-Picture Completion, PA-Picture Arrangement, BD-Block Design, OA-Object Assembly, Cd-Coding.

K-ABC Mental Processing (MP) subtests: HM-Hand Movements, GC-Gestalt Closure, NR-Number Recall, T-Triangles, WO-Word Order, MA-Matrix Analogies, SM-Spatial Memory, PS-Photo Series; K-ABC Achievement (Ach) subtests: FP-Faces and Places, AR-Arithmetic, R-Riddles, RD-Reading/Decoding, RU-Reading/Understanding.

If Spearman's hypothesis is true, why are these correlations that serve as the statistical test of Spearman's hypothesis not larger than the values of r that we are typically found? The answer is sampling error. The method of correlated vectors used to test the hypothesis allows a lot of play for the three main sources of sampling error. First, there is the usual sampling error in the correlations from which g is extracted and, of course, the standard error of the mean difference between groups on each test. Second, there is the fact that g, being a latent variable, is never represented perfectly by any particular battery of tests given to any particular sample of the population. Then there is psychometric sampling error; that is, the estimate of g obtained from any particular collection of diverse tests is not perfectly correlated with the g obtained from every other collection of tests. (The average correlation of g–factor scores across quite different random samples of tests is about .85). Third, most of the standard test batteries on which Spearman's hypothesis has been tested were devised as intelligence or aptitude tests, which means the test constructors aimed for tests with quite substantial g saturations, so there is a restriction of variance among the various subtests' g loadings. Because each g loading has some sampling error, when the magnitudes of the factor loadings are bunched very close together, their observed rank order is a less reliable indicator of their true rank order. The same applies to the sizes of the mean group difference, D, of each subtest and the imperfect reliability of their rank order due to their sampling error and restriction of variance.

Although the previous sources of attenuation affect the test of Spearman's hypothesis, they are theoretically not at all intrinsic to it. I have shown that when the standard deviation of the g loadings and the standard deviation of the group differences, D, are entered into a multiple regression equation to predict the correlations between g and D across 12 independent studies, the multiple R turns out to be +.46. In other words, more than one–fifth of the variance in the tests of Spearman's hypothesis (that is, the values of the correlation r_{gD} across different studies) is attributable to attenuating effects that are theoretically not intrinsic to Spearman's hypothesis. If all of these attenuating effects were taken into account, as in a meta-analysis, the true value of r_{gD} would probably approach .90. But it would not be much higher as the strong form of the hypothesis has been rejected because of the slight but real group differences in the spatial and memory factors, independent of g.

Does Spearman's hypothesis apply only to conventional psychometric tests, or is it manifested as well in quite different types of cognitive tasks? To investigate this, I have turned to the simplest type of what cognitive psychologists refer to as elementary cognitive tasks (ECTs; Jensen, 1993b). Performing these tasks is so simple that the only reliable measures of individual differences must be obtained chronometrically as the median reaction time (RT) and movement time (MT), both averaged over a number of trials, and the trial-to-trial intraindividual variability of RT and MT, measured by the standard deviation of a person's RT (or MT) across a number of trials (RTSD or MTSD). Many previous studies have shown that these measures have some low to moderate correlation with IQ (Jensen, 1982, 1987c, 1992a).

One study, based on 800 White and Black pupils in grades 4 to 6, measured three ETCs, as shown in Figure 1.8. The console in the upper left measures simple RT. Subjects are always told that this is a test of their speed of reaction and that they should react as fast as they can without hitting the wrong button. The subject begins by pressing the Home Button (lower black dot); a preparatory signal (beep) sounds, and after a random interval of 1 to 4 seconds, the green light (crossed circle) goes on. The subject releases the Home Button and presses the button (circle) that turns off the light. RT is the interval between the onset of the light and the subject's releasing the Home Button; MT is the interval between releasing the Home Button and touching the button that turns off the light.

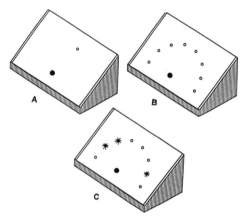

FIG. 1.8. The subject's response console for (A) SRT, (B) CRT, (C) DRT (odd man out). The black dot in the lower center of each panel represents the *home* button. The open circles, 6 inches from the home button, are green, underlighted translucent push-buttons. In the SRT and CRT conditions (i.e., A and B), only one button lights up on each trial; on the DRT task, three buttons light up simultaneously on each trial, with unequal distances between them (shown in C), the remotest button from the other two being the odd man out, which the subject must touch.

The response console is 13 in. by 17 in., painted flat black, and tilted at a 30° angle. At the lower center is the home button (black, 1 in. diameter), which the subject depresses with the index finger while waiting for the reaction stimulus. The small circles represent translucent pushbuttons (green, ½ in. diameter, each at a distance of 6 in. from the home button); each button can be lighted independently. Touching a lighted button turns off the light. A test trial begins with the subject depressing the home button (black dot); 1 sec. Later, a preparatory stimulus (beep) of 1 sec. duration occurs; then, after a 1 to 4 sec. random interval, one of the translucent buttons lights up, whereupon the subject's index finger leaves the home button and touches the lighted button. RT is the interval between a light–button going on and the subject's lifting the index finger from the home button; MT is the interval between releasing the home button and touching the underlighted button.

The second test is Choice RT (upper right). The procedure is exactly the same as previously, except that one out of 8 lights goes on, randomized over trials. Because of the uncertainty as to which light will go on, the RT is considerably longer for this task than for Simple RT.

The third task is still more complex (lower center). It is the oddity problem called the Odd Man Out, in which three lights go on simultaneously, two of them always closer together than the third (Frearson & Eysenck, 1986). The three lights all go out simultaneously only if the subject touches the "odd-graders, as the overall mean RT for the total sample in my study is only about seven tenths of a second. (Error responses were not averaged into the score; every subject had 36 error-free trials).

Each of these three tasks yielded four variables (RT, MT, RTSD, and MTSD); hence, 12 variables in all. Estimates of their g saturations were obtained by correlating each variable with Raven's Standard Progressive Matrices, one of the most purely and highly g-loaded psychometric tests. The rank-order correlation between the estimated g loadings of each of the 12 chronometric variables and the standardized mean White–Black differences on each of these variables is +.79 ($p < .01$), shown in Figure 1.9. (The Pearson r = +.81).

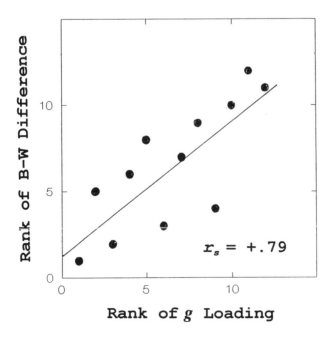

FIG. 1.9. The scatter diagram of the rank-order correlation between the rank order of the ECT g loadings and the rank order of the mean standardized B–W differences on each of the ECTs.

A second study (Jensen, 1993b) in this vein was done using three quite different elementary tasks in which RT, MT, RTSD, and MTSD were measured. The tasks, presented on a computer monitor, required binary (YES or NO) responses to single-digit addition, subtraction, and multiplication problems, for example, 2 + 4 = 6 or 2 + 2 = 5, which are answered by pressing either the YES or the NO buttons on the response console, as shown in Figure 1.10.

These tasks were intended to measure the subject's speed of access to over–learned information stored in long-term memory. These number facts had already been well–learned by all of the 4th to 6th grade pupils in the study, each of whom scored 100% correct when the same items were administered as a paper-and-pencil test. As before, the g saturations of each of the 12 chronometric variables were estimated by their correlations with the Raven Standard Progressive Matrices. Spearman's hypothesis was again confirmed–the correlation between the column vector of estimated g loadings and the parallel vector of standardized mean Black–White differences was $r + .73$; partialling out the vector of reliability coefficients of the chronometric variables lowered the r to $+.70$ ($p < .05$).

To determine whether Spearman's hypothesis applies to a different racial group, the procedures of the previous study were exactly replicated on groups of Chinese-Americans and non-Hispanic Whites in Grade 4 to 6 (Jensen & Whang, 1994). The correlation between the chronometric variables' column vector of g loadings and the parallel vector of the Chinese–White standardized mean differences was $r = -.93$ and $r_s = -.90$ ($p < .01$); the direction of the correlation is the opposite to that in the Black–White studies. That is, the more g loaded the chronometric task, the larger the Chinese–White difference in favor of the

FIG. 1.10. A binary response console (6½ in. X 10 in.) used in all ECTs that call for a binary response (Yes–No, True–False, Same–Different, etc.). The push-buttons are all 1 inch in diameter. The lower one is the home button, which the subject depresses with the index finger until the reaction stimulus occurs. On each trial, the subject responds by pressing either the left or right button, here labeled YES and NO. (The magnetized labels can be quickly and easily changed). The programmed reaction stimuli appear on a computer monitor directly behind the response console.

Chinese–Americans, whose responses were faster (relative to Whites) the greater the variable's *g* loading. To the best of my knowledge, no one has yet looked at Asian–White differences on conventional psychometric tests as a function of their *g* loadings. From the study just mentioned, however, I would predict that one should find the reverse of Spearman's hypothesis for Black–White differences.

Finally, I should point out that I have applied the same method of correlated vectors that was used to test Spearman's hypothesis to discover the relationship of *g* to various nonpsychometric variables. I have examined the vector composed of the various tests' correlations with a given external variable in relation to the parallel vector of the tests' *g* loadings. The correlation between the two vectors is indicated by the values of *r* in Figure 1.11. The phenomena summarized here were presaged by Spearman's own assertion that *g* is essentially a biological phenomenon whose psychometric aspects must eventually be explained in physiological terms (Jensen, 1993a, 1997, 1998).

What I have called Spearman's hypothesis must now be regarded as an empirical fact rather than just hypothesis. I close with this plea: In attempting to explain the empirically established phenomenon first surmised by Spearman, which I have formalized and tested as Spearman's hypothesis, behavioral science has no more challenging task than to investigate the apparent clues to the biological correlates of Spearman's *g* such as those I have shown in Figure 1.11.

How psychology will meet this challenge is a test of whether it can deal with socially sensitive issues in the objective, analytical manner of the natural sciences, or in the final analysis can only rationalize popular prejudice or social ideology.

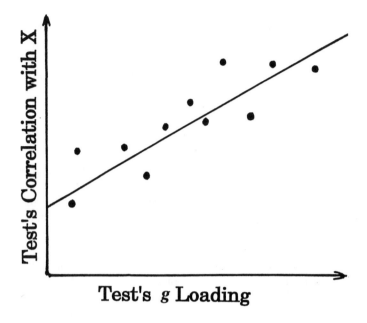

Variable X	r_{xg}
Spouse correlation	.90
Heritability	.60--.80
Inbreeding Depression	.80
Cerebral Glucose Metabolic Ra	-.79
Brain Intracellular pH	.63
Head Size	.60--.70
Choice & Discrimination RT	.70--.80
Average Evoked Potential	
Habituation-Amp.	.80
Waveform Complexity	.95

FIG. 1.11. A graphical illustration of the method of correlated vectors as applied to a number of psychometric tests' correlations with some nonpsychometric variable (X), whereby the tests' correlations with X are plotted as a function of the tests' g loadings. The correlation r indicates the degree of linear relationship between the two column vectors. Here are listed some of the nonpsychometric variables to which this method of correlated vectors has been applied, and the obtained correlation between the two vectors.

REFERENCES

Deary, I. J., Egan, V., Gibson, G. J., Austin, E., Brand, C. R., & Kellaghan, T. (1996). Intelligence and the differentiation hypothesis. *Intelligence, 23,* 105–132.

Deary, I. J., & Pagliari, C. (1991). The strength of *g* at different levels of ability: Have Detterman and Daniel rediscovered Spearman's "Law of Diminishing Returns"? *Intelligence, 15,* 247–250.

Detterman, D. K., & Daniel, M. H. (1989). Correlations of mental tests with each other and with cognitive variables are highest for low IQ groups. *Intelligence, 13,* 349–359.

Eysenck, N. J. (1979). *The structure and measurement of intelligence.* New York: Springer-Verlag.

Frearson, W. M., & Eysenck, H. J. (1986). Intelligence, reaction time (RT) and a new "odd-man-out" RT paradigm. *Personality and Individual Differences, 7,* 808–817.

Galton, F. (1869). *Hereditary genius: An inquiry into its laws and consequences.* London: Macmillan.

Gottfredson, L. S. (1997). (Guest editor). Intelligence and social policy. *Intelligence, 24,* 1–320.

Jensen, A. R. (1982). Reaction time and psychometric *g.* In H. J. Eysenck (Ed.), *A model for intelligence* (pp. 93–132). New York: Springer.

Jensen, A. R. (1985c). The nature of the Black–White difference on various psychometric tests: Spearman's hypothesis. *Behavioral and Brain Sciences, 8,* 193–219.

Jensen, A. R. (1985a). The Black–White difference in *g*: A phenomenon in search of a theory. *Behavioral and Brain Sciences, 8,* 246–263.

Jensen, A. R. (1985b). Humphrey's attenuated test of Spearman's hypothesis. *Intelligence, 9,* 285–289.

Jensen, A. R. (1987a). Further evidence for Spearman's hypothesis concerning the black–white differences on psychometric tests. *Behavioral and Brain Sciences, 10,* 512–519.

Jensen, A. R. (1987b). The *g* beyond factor analysis. In R. R. Ronning, J. A. Glover, J. C. Conoley, & J. C. Witt (Eds.), *The influence of cognitive psychology on testing* (pp. 87–142). Hillsdale, NJ: Lawrence Erlbaum Associates.

Jensen, A. R. (1987c). Individual differences in the Hick paradigm. In P. A. Vernon (Ed.), *Speed of information processing and intelligence* (pp. 101–175). Norwood, NJ: Ablex.

Jensen, A. R. (1992c). Spearman's hypothesis: Methodology and evidence. *Multivariate Behavioral Research,* 27, 225–234.

Jensen, A. R. (1992b). More on psychometric *g* and "Spearman's hypothesis". *Multivariate Behavioral Research, 27,* 257–260.

Jensen, A. R. (1992a). The importance of intraindividual variability in reaction time. *Personality and Individual Differences, 13,* 869–882.

Jensen, A. R. (1993a). Spearman's g: Links between psychometrics and biology. *Annals of the New York Academy of Sciences, 702,* 103–131.

Jensen, A. R. (1993b). Spearman's hypothesis tested with chronometric information-processing tasks. *Intelligence, 17,* 47–77.

Jensen, A. R. (1997). The neurophysiology of *g.* In C. Cooper & V. Varma (Eds.), *Processes in individual diferences* (pp. 107–124). London/NY: Routledge & Kegan Paul.

Jensen, A. R. (1998). *The g Factor.* Westport, CT: Praeger.

Jensen, A. R. (2000). Charles E. Spearman: The discoverer of *g.* In G. A. Kimble & M. Wertheimer (Eds.) *Portraits of pioneers in psychology,* Vol. IV (pp. 93-111). Washington, D. C.: American Psychological Association. Mahwah, NJ: Lawrence Erlbaum Associates.

Jensen, A. R. & Figueroa, R. A. (1975). Forward and backward digit span interaction with race and IQ: Predictions from Jensen's theory. *Journal of Educational Psychology, 67,* 882–893.

Jensen, A. R. & Whang, P. A. (1994). Speed of accessing arithmetic facts in long-term memory: A comparison of Chinese–American and Anglo–American Children. *Contemporary Educational Psychology, 19,* 1–12.

Lynn, R., & Owen, K. (1994). Spearman's hypothesis and test score differences between Whites, Indians, and Blacks in South Africa. *Journal of General Psychology, 12*, 27–36.

Naglieri, J. A. & Jensen, A. R. (1987). Comparison of Black–White differences on the Wisc-R and the K-ABC: Spearman's hypothesis. *Intelligence, 11*, 21–43.

Peoples, C. E., Fagan, J. F., III, & Drotar, D. (1995). The influence of race on 3-year-old children's performance on the Stanford-Binet: Fourth edition. *Intelligence, 21*, 69–82.

Spearman, C. (1904). General intelligence, objectively determined and measured. *American Journal of Psychology, 15*, 201–293.

Spearman, C. (1927). *The abilities of man: Their nature and measurement.* New York: MacMillan.

Vernon, P. A. (1981). Level I and Level II: A review. *Educational Psychologist, 16*, 45–64.

2

On the Hierarchical Structure
of Ability and Personality

Jan-Eric Gustafsson
University of Göteborg

Hierarchical models of individual differences include dimensions of different degrees of generality, from broad to narrow (e.g., Carroll, 1993; Gustafsson, 1988). Such models have proven extremely useful in research on cognitive abilities because they resolve the conflict between theorists who emphasize one general ability (e.g., Humphreys, 1985; Jensen, 1987; Spearman, 1927) and theorists who emphasize several specialized abilities (e.g., Gardner, 1985; Guilford, 1967; Thurstone, 1938) by allowing for both categories of abilities in the model. In personality research, too, the hierarchical approach has proven useful, particularly so as a tool to identify broad dimensions of personality (e.g., Cattell, 1965; Digman, 1990; McCrae & John, 1992).

Hierarchical modeling is still limited, with many unexplored problems and potentials. The number of empirical studies that rely on hierarchical modeling still is limited and when hierarchical techniques are applied, this is typically done in a simple, descriptive fashion with lower order factors serving as building blocks to define high-order factors. One reason for this is probably that hierarchical analysis is a rather complex endeavor and there is no general agreement as to how such analyses are best performed. But the hierarchical approach also poses many theoretically and practically interesting questions, which so far have not been explored to any great depth. One of these concerns relations between factors at different levels of a hierarchical analysis. Another concerns the relative advantages of different hierarchical approaches (Gustafsson & Undheim, 1996). Research on hierarchical structures of personality and cognitive ability has also, to a large extent, been conducted along parallel lines and as has been argued by Cattell (1987) and others much is to be gained if these lines of research are more tightly integrated.

The purpose of this chapter is to discuss some of the technical and methodological issues in hierarchical modeling of individual differences. The main focus is on understanding individual differences in cognitive abilities but it is argued that this goal is more easily attained if individual differences in personality are attended to as well.

SOME TECHNICAL ASPECTS OF HIERARCHICAL MODELING

There are, basically, three different ways in which a hierarchical model may be estimated: through principal component (or principal factor) analysis, through higher order factor analysis, and through nested-factor analysis.

Principal Factors

In a principal factor analysis, or in the highly similar principal components analysis (see Harman, 1967), the observed variables are transformed into new uncorrelated (orthogonal) variables in such a way that the first factor (or centroid) accounts for the largest proportion of the total variance, the second largest principal factor for the second largest proportion, and so on. Some researchers identify the general factor of a hierarchical model as the first principal factor in a matrix of intercorrelations between test performances (see e.g., Jensen, 1987). Because performance on different cognitive tests is typically positively correlated, all tests will be positively correlated with the first principal factor. The second and following principal factors tend to be bipolar: tests having both positive and negative loadings on them. These factors are often difficult to interpret, however, and often attention is restricted to the general factor only.

However, one serious problem with this approach is that the nature of the general factor varies as a function of which particular tests are included in the matrix (e.g., Horn, 1989; Thurstone, 1947). If there are many verbal tests, say, in one battery and many spatial tests in another battery, the first principal factors of these test batteries will define different general factors (see Thurstone, 1947).

Higher Order Factor Models

In order to solve the problem of invariance, Thurstone (e.g., 1947) proposed that a factorial solution should have a "simple structure" in the sense that each factor is associated with a subset of the observed variables and that each observed variable is influenced by only one or a few factors. This allows an invariant determination and interpretation of factors because when the simple structure criteria are satisfied, it is known both to which observed variables a factor is related and to which it is not. The simple structure criteria have been implemented in computer programs for exploratory factor analysis so that the solution is numerically optimized against these criteria, according to one of several different algorithms. The best approximation to simple structure is typically obtained when the factors are allowed to be correlated in an oblique solution.

A hierarchical model may then be constructed through factoring of correlations among the factors, using the same factor-analytic principles as when observed variables are analyzed. It may, for example, be hypothesized that a single "second-order" factor accounts for the intercorrelations among the factors. If a single factor cannot account for the correlations among the factors, one or more additional second-order factors may be introduced. Should we end up with several second-order factors, these may be correlated. To account for these correlations, a third-order factor may be introduced, and so on. Thus, with this approach, a hierarchy of factors is built up, starting from below with a large number of narrow first-order factors and ending at the top of the hierarchy with one, or a few, broad higher order factors. Gustafsson and Undheim (1996) thus characterized higher order (HO) factor analysis as a "bottom-up" procedure.

An example of a simple higher order model, which only involves six observed variables, three first-order (I, V, and S), and one second-order factor (G) is shown in Figure 2.1. In this model, the loading of I on G is assumed to be unity, so there is no residual variance in the first-order I-factor. For the other two first-order factors, there are residuals, however, that are labeled V' and S', respectively.

In an HO-model, there are no direct relations between the observed variables and the higher order factors. However, an HO-model may be transformed into a model with orthogonal factors, all of which are directly related to the observed variables (Schmid & Leiman, 1957).

Fitting of HO-models is the most frequently used procedure to estimate hierarchical models, and this may be done both with exploratory factor analytic and confirmatory factor analytic techniques. Thus, Carroll (1993), whose model is described in greater detail later this chapter, used higher order exploratory factor analysis to fit models with factors up to the third level. Gustafsson (1984), to take another example, fitted a confirmatory HO-model to a test-battery of 20 tests, which included 10 first-order factors, three second-order factors, and one third-order factor. There are different opinions, however, as to whether the exploratory approach is to be preferred because of its simplicity and large-scale applicability (Carroll, 1993; Spearritt, 1996) or whether the more powerful and precise confirmatory approach should be used. This issue is brought up later.

As has already been pointed out, there has, however, been a considerable reluctance to fit either exploratory or confirmatory HO-models. In addition to the technical problems involved in doing that, there are the problems of interpretation. These are well formulated by Gorsuch (1983):

> The understanding of primary factors is based upon interpretations of their relationships
> with the original variables. The interpretations are post hoc and subject to considerable

error. Interpretations of the second-order factors would need to be based on the interpretations of the first-order factors. Whereas it is hoped that the investigator knows the variables well enough to interpret them, the accuracy of interpretation will decrease with the first-order factors, will be less with the second-order factors, and still less with the third-order factors. (p. 245)

Nested-Factor Models

It is not necessary, however, to stack the factors on top of one another. The analysis may also start with the general factor and go down in a "top-down" approach. In the 1930s, Holzinger developed the bi-factor method (see Holzinger, 1944; Holzinger & Swineford, 1939) to allow extension of Spearman's (1904) "Two-Factor" theory into a "Three-Factor" theory or "Bi-Factor" theory. The essence of the bi-factor solution is that it includes a general factor, uncorrelated group factors, and unique factors. The bi-factor solutions can directly, and relatively simply, be computed from the correlation matrix. It does, however, require that the tests be brought together in groups before the analysis; in this sense, it is more similar to confirmatory factor analysis than to exploratory factor analysis. This technique was, however, rejected by Thurstone (1947) on the grounds that it does not agree with the simple structure principles, which is probably why it never became popular in U.S. research. It is, however, described in great detail in Harman's (1967) book on factor analysis.

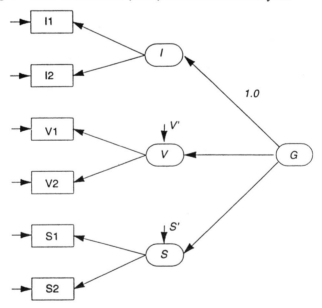

FIG. 2.1. A higher order model with three first-order abilities and one second-order ability.

In British research on abilities, however, a set of highly similar factoring techniques, namely hierarchical group-factor methods (see Vernon, 1950, 1961), was adopted as the standard procedure. These methods also yield a general factor, group factors, unique factors. In the British research, the structure of abilities has been described in such terms, as is described in greater detail later in this chapter.

Gustafsson and Balke (1993) introduced within the confirmatory framework a type of hierarchical model that is highly similar to the bi-factor model, which they called the nested-factor (NF) model. In an NF-model, orthogonal factors are allowed to span a broader or a more narrow range of observed variables. A general factor is typically fitted first, after which successively more narrow factors are fitted to the residual correlations. Holzinger's (1944) bi-factor model may thus be seen as a special case of an NF-model. In Figure 2.2, an NF-model is shown for the same six observed variables as were used to illustrate the HO-model:

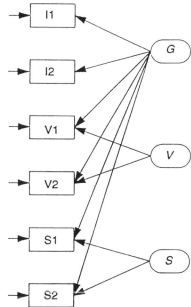

FIG. 2.2. A nested-factor model with one broad and two narrow factors.

In this model, the ability factors are all directly related to the tests. Because the G factor accounts for variance in the tests to which V and S are related, the narrow factors are residual factors in this model, too. In this model, there is no I' (or I) factor because the G-factor leaves no systematic variance unaccounted for in the two variables that measure the I-factor.

The HO- and NF-models carry the same substantive interpretation. Typically the numerical estimates of relations between observed variables and factors in an NF-model and a Schmid-Leiman (1957) transformed HO-model are highly similar. It may be noted, however, that the NF-model is more parsimonious than is the HO-model. Thus, in the NF-model in Figure 2.2 there are only three latent variables, whereas in the HO-model in Figure 2.1 there are four latent variables. This is, of course, because of the equivalence between G and I, which in the top-down NF-analysis causes the I-factor to vanish, whereas it remains in the bottom-up HO-analysis. However, the Schmid-Leiman transformation of the HO-model will reveal that the I-factor does not correlate with any test, so in this step, the results from the two models converge.

The fact that the NF-approach results in more parsimonious models with fewer latent variables can also be observed in empirical research. Gustafsson and Balke (1993) reanalyzed the Gustafsson (1984) study with an NF confirmatory model and found that a model with 10 orthogonal factors fitted the data at least as well as the original HO-model with 14 factors. This is because there were, in several instances, a perfect relationship between factors at different levels of the HO-model. The theoretically most interesting case was a relationship of unity between the third-order G-factor and the second-order factor Fluid intelligence (Gf), which thus caused the Gf-factor to vanish from the NF-model. Also, factors, which in the HO-model appeared as first-order factors, vanished. Thus, after the broad factor of General visualization (Gv) was introduced, the Flexibility of Closure (Cf) factor could not be identified; after G (or Gf) was introduced, the first-order Induction (I) factor vanished; and a first-order Verbal Achievement factor could not be found after the second-order Crystallized intelligence (Gc) was introduced. As has already been pointed out, these factors do not really exist in the HO-model either because all the variance in them is accounted for by higher order factors, but this is not so easily seen.

The Problem of Factorial Invariance

NF-models do not comply with the simple structure principles, so with reference to the problem of factorial invariance, this type of model was rejected by Thurstone and his followers (e.g., Mulaik, 1993). It was thus argued that the nature of the general factor will vary from study to study as a function of which tests are in the test battery. This certainly is a serious problem but it does not appear to be completely impossible to deal with, even in NF-models (Gustafsson, 1994).

Application of the simple-structure principle in HO-modeling does not solve the problem of identifying an invariant general factor either (see also Horn, 1989). This is, of course, because a truly general factor will have a relationship with every factor at the next lower level so that simple structure cannot be achieved. Thus, in HO-modeling too, the nature of the general factor will be influenced by the nature of the tests included in the test battery. Thurstone (1947) may have thrown out the g-factor baby with the technical bathwater when he insisted that the bi-factor method should be dismissed in favor of techniques that comply with the principles of simple structure.

One way to solve the problem of applying the simple structure criteria when studying the general cognitive factor is to add noncognitive variables to which the general factor does not have any relation, as has been recommended by Cattell (1971, 1987). This supplies what Cattell (1987) called "hyperplane stuff" and allows application of the simple-structure criteria. Unfortunately, however, it seems that Cattell is one of the few to have systematically combined measurement of cognitive and noncognitive variables on the same subjects, so there is only a limited number of studies available. However, the prolific contributions by Cattell (e.g., 1965, 1987) and his collaborators provide a rich source of information to which I return to later in this chapter.

It is quite interesting to note, however, that the results obtained in Gustafsson's (1984; see also Gustafsson, 1988; Undheim, 1981; Undheim & Gustafsson, 1987) study indicate that there may be a fortuitous empirical circumstance that may solve the invariance problem of the general factor even when only cognitive measures are available—namely the finding of a perfect relationship between G as a third-order factor and Gf as a second-order factor. This empirical finding implies, of course, that G is equal to Gf and because the latter may be invariantly identified with the simple-structure principle, it also follows that G will be invariantly identified. In NF-modeling, this corresponds to the situation where a certain group of tests is only related to the general factor and not to any narrow factor. In this case, the general factor is invariantly identified and may be interpreted in terms of what is common to this group of tests.

But this line of reasoning relies on the assumption that there is, indeed, such a perfect relationship between G and Gf. This conclusion has been challenged by, for example, Carroll (1996) and Spearritt (1996). Carroll said, "In my view it is possible that measures of Gf feature attributes that require specific skills in inductive and deductive reasoning that are not necessarily present in other measures of g" (p.15). This issue is brought up again, when the empirical results from research on the hierarchical structure of cognitive abilities has been reviewed.

Hierarchical Models of the Structure of Cognitive Abilities

With the publication of Carroll's (1993) book, the number of hierarchical analyses has increased dramatically. In his monumental study, Carroll presented reanalyses of almost every set of data collected in the history of research on the structure of cognitive abilities, along with a hierarchical model. Carroll called his model the "Three-Stratum Model" because the term *stratum* indicates a more absolute reference than does the technical term *order*. The problem is, of course, that a factor that, in one analysis, may appear at the second-order level just as well may appear in another analysis involving a smaller or a larger number of variables at the first- or third-order levels.

The three-stratum division corresponds to a classification of abilities in the categories narrow, broad, and general. The primary abilities of the kind identified by Thurstone (1938) and Guilford (1967) belong to the category of narrow abilities and Carroll identified some 70 such abilities (see Gustafsson & Undheim, 1996, for a brief summary). Carroll also identified 10 broad and general abilities, which are briefly characterized here:

Fluid Intelligence (Gf or 2F; in Carroll's notation, the stratum to which a broad ability belongs is indicated by a number in the factor label). In most studies, this factor dominates reasoning factors but also other factors such as those that involve visual–spatial processing have been found to have substantial relations with Gf. The factor thus involves difficult tasks of induction, reasoning, problem solving, and visual perception.

Crystallized Intelligence (Gc or 2C). This factor is also classified as belonging to the second stratum. First-order factors with high loadings on Gc tend to involve language and reading skills and declarative knowledge in wide areas. Factors involving numerical content also have been found to have substantial loadings on Gc but it should be observed that the tests measuring these abilities most often are verbal and that the numerical skills are acquired through processes of schooling, which tend to emphasize verbal means of communication. The Gc factor may thus be interpreted as a broad verbal factor.

General Memory and Learning (Gy or 2Y). Carroll identified a second-stratum memory factor, which spans narrow factors reflecting short-term acquisition of material. However, he also reported that there are strong indications of several second-order memory factors, even though the currently available evidence does not make it possible to identify these with precision.

Broad Visual Perception (Gv or 2V). This factor dominates narrow factors that involve manipulation of figural information. Carroll interpreted Gv as a general ability to deal with visual form, particularly when perception or mental manipulation is complex and difficult.

Broad Auditory Perception (Ga or 2U). According to Carroll, there is evidence for at least one broad auditory perception factor. This factor spans a broad range of narrow factors reflecting hearing acuity, discrimination of sound features, and musicality. Carroll hypothesized that an important component of Ga is the degree to which the individual can cognitively control the perception of auditory stimulus inputs.

Broad Retrieval Ability (Gr or 2R). This factor dominates a large set of narrow factors involving tasks designed to reflect originality and quickness of retrieving symbols. A central element in this factor seems to be the capacity to readily call up concepts, ideas, and names from long-term memory.

Broad Cognitive Speediness. The higher-order analyses conducted by Carroll yielded more than one factor involving speed. One factor (Gs or 2S) is involved in narrow factors involving relatively simple tasks administered under time constraints. Another factor (Gt or 2T) dominates various kinds of reaction-time tasks. A third factor (General Psychomotor Speed; Gp or 2P) is primarily concerned with the speed of finger, hand, and arm movements.

Most of the abilities identified by Carroll have also been found in other studies, although no other study matches the comprehensiveness and generality of Carroll's model. The concepts of fluid and crystallized ability were proposed by Cattell in the early 1940s. Cattell (1941) argued that there is not one general factor of intelligence but two. He labeled these fluid and crystallized intelligence. However, systematic empirical research on these factors was not reported until considerably later (e.g., Cattell, 1963; Horn & Cattell, 1966), when several broad, second-order, abilities were identified in higher order factor analytic studies. In addition to Gf and Gc, several other second-order factors were also identified such as Gv, Gs, and Gr (see Cattell, 1987).

Carroll's Three-Stratum model thus extends and unifies the tradition of research on higher order ability structures. But there is also a British tradition of research on hierarchical ability structure with results that partially overlap those achieved by Carroll and others working in the American tradition.

The first factor-analytic model was developed by Spearman (1904) under the name of the Two-Factor Theory. This model emphasized a single, general ability, but Spearman and his followers extended the model into a hierarchical theory with the G-factor at the apex, group factors below G, and specific factors at the lowest level. Many researchers contributed to this development, such as Burt (1949) and Spearman and Wynn Jones (1950), but the model created on the basis of a review of the literature by Vernon (1950; with a slightly revised and expanded version published in 1961) seems to have had most impact.

At the top of the Vernon model is Spearman's g-factor. The model also includes two major group factors: the verbal–numerical–educational (*v:ed*) factor and the practical–mechanical–spatial–physical (*k:m*) factor. Given the central position of Gf in the higher order model, it is interesting to note that there is no major group factor that represents reasoning abilities. However, according to Vernon (1961), this is because "reasoning ability is one of the commoner definitions of intelligence, and we would therefore expect, if we allow a g factor, that g would include the whole of the variance of reasoning factors" (p. 54). Thus, because the analysis has been done with a top-down approach, no factor corresponding to Gf is detected.

Given a sufficient number of tests, the major group factors may be subdivided into several minor group factors. Thus, the *v:ed* factor subdivides into different scholastic factors such as *v* (verbal) and *n* (number) group factors. For example, Vernon (1961) summarized several studies showing that different school subjects group together under narrow factors. Other minor group factors were also identified, such as Fluency (cf. Carroll's Gr) and Rote Memory (cf. Carroll's Gy). The *k:m* factor may be subdivided into minor groups such as perceptual, spatial, and mechanical abilities (it may be noted that the term *k* was early introduced in British research to represent a broad spatial–visualization factor, much like Gv.

In British research however, relatively little emphasis has been placed on the minor group factors. One reason for this is that the general factor and the broad group factors have played a much more central role in this tradition. Vernon (1961) theoretically also questioned the separate empirical existence of many of the primary factors because the variance in these factors may be accounted for in terms of the broad factors. He reviewed studies in several areas that demonstrate this is actually the case. For example, one study shows the Flexibility of Closure (Cf) variance to be entirely due to g and k (Vernon, 1961) which, incidentally, seems to agree with the finding by Gustafsson and Balke (1993) of a perfect relationship between Gv and Cf.

In comparison with the Carroll model, the Vernon model seems quite limited in scope and generality, which is partly a consequence of the fact that it has a much more limited empirical basis. The greater parsimony of Vernon's model is also a function of the fact that it has been derived from top-down analyses, in which the variance due to broad factors is removed from the more narrow factors. This not only causes fewer factors to appear but it also establishes links between factors at different levels, which in particular aid in the identification and interpretation of the broad factors. Of special interest in this regard is, of course, the finding that G is a reasoning factor, which does provide some support for Gustafsson's (1984, 1988) findings of equivalence between G and Gf.

The results and approaches of the British tradition are thus not superseded by the recent progress in higher order modeling; it seems, in contrast, that much would be gained if the top-down mode of analysis and thinking was applied to the Three-Stratum Model. That would allow a closer investigation of how many factors at each stratum are uniquely identifiable, and it would permit a closer analysis of the nature of the broad factors.

ALTERNATIVE APPROACHES IN ESTIMATING HIERARCHICAL MODELS: AN EXAMPLE

As has already been described, the Carroll Three-Stratum Model includes a general factor (G) at the third level as well as the Gf factor at the second level. However, although Carroll's results indicate that there is a slight tendency for Gf to be the second-stratum factor most highly related to G (see Carroll, 1993) there certainly is no basis for claiming that Carroll's results show a perfect relationship between Gf and G. Given the theoretical, methodological, and practical importance of this hypothesized relation of unity, it may be worthwhile to bring in some further empirical evidence and consider the methodological problems in estimating hierarchical models.

In a recent study, Gustafsson (2000) compared three different methods of analysis in a reanalysis of the 24 tests included in Holzinger and Swineford's (1939) classical study. The three analytical approaches were a confirmatory bottom-up approach, a confirmatory top-down approach, and an exploratory bottom-up approach. One purpose, in particular, of this study was to compare exploratory and confirmatory modes of analysis. This is because one possible interpretation of the different results obtained from the confirmatory models on the one hand and Carroll's analysis on the other, is that the intercorrelations among first- and second-order factors are underestimated in exploratory factor analysis. This is because, in exploratory analysis, there are small, nonsignificant loadings in every cell of the factor-loading matrix (except, of course, where there are salient loadings). These loadings tend to attenuate the estimates of the correlations between the factors. The degree of obliqueness of the solution may, furthermore, in almost all rotational methods be influenced by choice of different parameter values (e.g., the gamma parameter in Oblimin, and the k parameter in Promax) and with a more oblique solution, a better approximation to simple structure is typically obtained. However, the most oblique solution and the best approximation to simple structure is almost always obtained when the nonsalient loadings are fixed to zero, as is done in confirmatory factor analysis.

The Holzinger and Swineford test battery comprises 24 tests and most of these are close to tests still in use. The test battery was designed to measure abilities in five broad areas: spatial, verbal, memory, speed, and mathematical deduction. As it is discussed in greater detail by Gustafsson (2000), the tests represent a rather mixed bag of first-stratum factors, so it was hypothesized that the five hypothesized second-stratum factors Gv, Gc, Gy, Gs, and Gf would be identifiable as first-order factors. It was also hypothesized that there is a second-order G-factor, on which Gf has a standardized loading of 1.0.

The sample consisted of 301 seventh- and eighth-grade students from two Chicago schools. One school (The Grant-White Elementary School, $N = 145$) was suburban middle-class, in which most pupils had native English-speaking parents. The other school (Pasteur Elementary School, $N = 156$) was a Chicago school serving a working-class area. Many of the Pasteur parents were foreign born and many were still using their native language at home.

The hypothesized HO-model with five first-order factors, and one second-order factor is shown in Figure 2.3.

In the path-diagram, residuals in observed variables and in the first-order factors are shown as latent variables. The residual variables are assigned the labels of the corresponding dependent variable but with an ampersand added as a suffix (e.g., VISPER&). It should be observed that the hypothesized model includes no residual for Gf, which is, of course, an implication of the hypothesis of a perfect relationship between G and Gf.

In the first step an oblique five-factor model was fitted to the covariance matrix for the total sample. The X^2 goodness-of-fit test was highly significant, but descriptive measures of fit indicated that the originally hypothesized model fits well enough to be used in further modeling, even though there clearly is room for improvement of model fit. In the next step, several modifications were made.

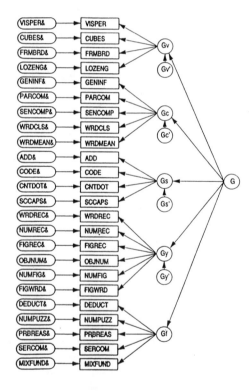

FIG. 2.3. The hypothesized higher order model for the Holzinger and Swineford data.

Some additional relations were thus introduced (see Gustafsson, 2000), and another latent variable (*Num*) also was introduced, with relations to several tests with numerical content. The modified model fits quite well, both for the pooled sample and for the separate samples.

In the next step of modeling, the G-factor was introduced into the models (i.e., both the original and the modified ones) as a second-order factor, without any further restrictions being imposed. In all cases, the loadings of Gf on G are close to unity and lower than unity for all the other factors. These results thus provide excellent support for the hypothesis that there is a perfect relationship between Gf and G, and it also seems that this result is quite robust over different samples and formulations of the first-order model.

As has already been mentioned, the confirmatory NF-model is very similar to the bi-factor method of factor analysis developed by Holzinger (1944). The

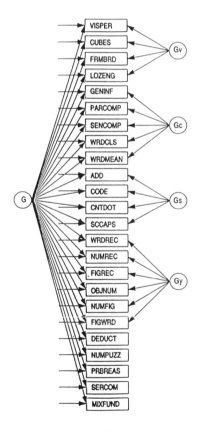

FIG. 2.4. The hypothesized nested-factor model for the Holzinger and Swineford data.

hypothesized pattern in this kind of model is one in which a general factor (G) has relations to all tests and narrow factors have relations to subsets of tests. If there is a perfect relation between Gf and G, this causes the Gf factor to vanish in this type of model because all the variance is accounted for by G. Figure 2.4 shows a path-diagram of the hypothesized NF-model.

In this model no Gf-factor is shown, which is equivalent to not showing any Gf-residual in Figure 2.3.

In the first step of modeling, the originally hypothesized model was fitted to the three samples. The fit was reasonably good and when the model was estimated without any Gf-factor, the fit remained at the same level. Thus, in a model that includes a G-factor, it is not possible to introduce a residual Gf-factor.

These reanalyses provide very good support for the results originally reported by Holzinger and Swineford (1939). They observed that their analysis failed to produce the hypothesized deductive factor and pointed out that: "While such negative results do not constitute proof, they cast doubt on the existence of a mathematical reasoning factor as distinct from the general factor. Indeed, the general factor may be just such a deductive factor as these tests were expected to measure" (p. 8). On the basis of interpretation of the factor loadings, Holzinger and Swineford arrived at the conclusion that "the general factor appears to be largely deductive in character—a reasonable assumption in view of the fact that inference and deduction would necessarily be the chief elements in a general factor such as that postulated by Professor Spearman" (p. 27).

As has already been pointed out, the Holzinger and Swineford study has been favorite material for illustrations of factor analytic techniques in text books and in research articles. There is little reason to review the results from all these studies but it may be worthwhile to select a few that demonstrate differences between the confirmatory techniques already applied and exploratory techniques.

Gorsuch (1983) illustrated second-order factor analysis through fitting one second-order factor to the correlation matrix between four oblique Promax-rotated (k = 4) factors fitted to the Holzinger and Swineford data. The loadings on the general factor varied between .65 and .78, from which result Gorsuch concluded, "The second-order factor is equally defined by each and every primary factor, and so represents general intellectual ability" (p. 245). The Numerical (deductive) factor has the lowest loading, so there is nothing in these results to suggest that reasoning would be more central in general intelligence than any other ability.

Gorsuch (1983) also presented the correlation matrix between the four first-order factors estimated with Promax-rotation with k set to 8, which does produce an even more oblique solution. Estimating a one-factor model from this matrix yields loadings that vary between .71 and .89, again with the lowest loading for the Numeric factor. With the k-parameter set to lower values, the loadings of the first-order factors on the second-order factor becomes lower and when k = 0, they vanish completely. Similar results may be obtained with other oblique methods of rotation, such as Oblimin (see e.g., Harman, 1967).

The results from the confirmatory HO-analysis, the confirmatory NF-analysis, and the original Holzinger and Swineford bi-factor analysis agree perfectly in showing unity between Gf and G. The exploratory HO-analyses presented here do not show this unity, however. This is most certainly due to the limitations inherent in exploratory factor analysis: not only are there uncertainties in the number of factors and the estimates of factor loadings but the amount of intercorrelation among the factors in an oblique solution may quite arbitrarily be determined by the researcher. Because these correlations determine the relative importance of lower and higher order factors, this makes exploratory factor analysis unsuitable for high order modeling.

Thus, to the extent that is possible, exploratory factor analysis should be avoided in research on hierarchical structures of individual differences. Given the amount of computational power and easy-to-use software for structural equation modeling that is now available (e.g., Arbuckle, 1997; Gustafsson & Stahl, 1997; Jöreskog & Sörbom, 1996), it should be possible to attack even the largest studies with confirmatory techniques. Carroll's (1993) reanalyses will also provide excellent starting points for the model-building that is an essential part of confirmatory factor analysis.

How Many Abilities Are There?

The most basic question about the structure of cognitive abilities concerns the number of abilities that should be distinguished. For both theoretical and practical reasons, a parsimonious account with a small number of abilities is to be preferred over one in terms of many abilities. The hierarchical approach offers good possibilities for parsimonious models of ability, but different hierarchical models differ greatly in this respect. Thus, models based the bottom-up approach, such as Carroll's Three-Stratum Model, tend to include a larger number of factors than models based on the top-down approach. The reason for this is that in a top-down approach, the broader factors extract variance from the narrow factors, which may cause the latter to vanish. One important task of future ability research will thus be to investigate which narrow ability factors should be ascribed separate existence and which should be discarded as merely being reflections of broader constructs. This will, hopefully, result in a considerable reduction of the somewhat bewildering array of broad and narrow ability constructs in the current literature. Such an endeavor may also provide a better basis for understanding the nature of the broad constructs.

But there is also another set of relations that should be attended to when investigating how many abilities should be identified and that is, of course, relations to personality constructs.

Cattell (e.g., 1987) was one of the few researchers who systematically studied relations between broad ability constructs and personality factors. His position was that several of the broad ability constructs, to a major extent—or even wholly—may be accounted for in terms of personality constructs.

One example is the second-stratum Gr dimension, in which fluency and quickness of retrieval from long-term memory seems central. Cattell (1987) argued that a substantial part of fluency may be traced to the temperament source trait Exuberance, which is characterized by, among other things, a high metabolism rate, fast reading tempo, fast speed of social judgment, "and other signs of an expansive temperament" (p. 446).

Cattell also demonstrated a striking overlap between a factor labeled Competitive Ego Strength and Gs. This personality factor "can add as much as half the variance to individual differences in success in, for example, social decisions, running mazes, checking simple sums at speed, etc." (p. 447).

Cattell's research offers many other examples of substantive overlap between personality and ability dimensions, but the examples cited are sufficient to demonstrate that a further simplification of hierarchical models of ability may be achieved if variance from personality factors are partialled out from both broad and narrow factors of ability.

Finally, research intended to establish links between personality and ability will provide opportunities for further investigations of hierarchical personality structures. In this field, also, quite profound differences may be seen between those who favor a bottom-up approach (e.g., Cattell, 1965) and those who favor a top-down approach (e.g., Eysenck, 1960; Costa & McCrae, 1995). Furthermore, the proliferation of personality dimensions seems to be even more of a problem than is the proliferation of ability dimensions. A program of research aiming to clarify overlap among broad and narrow dimensions both within and across the domains of personality and ability would thus seem most worthwhile.

REFERENCES

Arbuckle, J. L. (1997). *Amos User's Guide. Version 3.6.* Chicago: Small Waters Corporation.

Burt, C. (1949). The structure of the mind: A review of the results of factor analysis. *British Journal of Educational Psychology, 19,* 100–111, 176–199.

Carroll, J. B. (1993). *Human cognitive aililties.* Cambridge, England: Cambridge University Press.

Carroll, J. B. (1996). A three-stratum theory of intelligence: Spearman's contribution. In I. Dennis & P. Tapsfield (Eds.), *Human abilities: Their nature and measurement* (pp. 1–7). Mahwah, NJ: Lawrence Erlbaum Associates.

Cattell, R. B. (1963). Theory of fluid and crystallized intelligence: A critical experiment. *Journal of Educational Psychology, 54,* 1–22.

Cattell, R. B. (1965). *The scientific analysis of personality.* London: Penguin.

Cattell, R. B. (1971). *Abilities: Their structure, growth and action.* Boston: Houghton-Mifflin.

Cattell, R. B. (1987). *Intelligence: Its structure, growth and action.* New York: North-Holland.

Cattell, R. B. (1941. Some theoretical issues in adult intelligence testing. *Psychological Bulletin, 38,* 592.

Costa, P. T., Jr., & McCrae, R. R. (1995). Domains and facets: Hierarchical personality assessment using the Revised NEO Personality Inventory. *Journal of Personality Assessment, 64 Rom (1st ed.),* 21–50.

Digman, J. M. (1990). Personality structure: Emergence of the five-factor model. *Annual Review of Psychology, 41,* 417–440.

Eysenck, H. J. (1960). *The structure of human personality (2nd ed.)* London: Methuen.

Gardner, H. (1985). *Frames of mind: The theory of multiple intelligences.* New York: Basic Books.

Gorsuch, R. L. (1983). *Factor analysis (2nd ed.).* Hillsdale, NJ: Lawrence Erlbaum Associates.

Guilford, J. P. (1967). *The nature of human intelligence.* New York: McGraw-Hill.

Gustafsson, J.-E. (1984). A unifying model for the structure of intellectual abilities. *Intelligence, 8,* 179–203.

Gustafsson, J.-E. (1988). Hierarchical models of individual differences in cognitive abilities. In R. J. Sternberg, *(Ed.), Advances in the psychology of human intelligence, Vol, 4 (*pp. 35–71). Hillsdale, NJ: Lawrence Erlbaum Associates.

Gustafsson, J.-E. (1994). Hierarchical models of intelligence and educational achievement. In A. Demetriou & A. Efklides (Eds.), *Intelligence, mind and reasoning: Structure and development,* (pp. 45–73). New York: Elsevier.

Gustafsson, J.-E. (2000). *On the relation between fluid and general ntelligence: A reanalysis of the Holzinger and Swineford (1939) study.* Manuscript submitted for publication.

Gustafsson, J.-E., & Balke, G. (1993). General and specific abilities as predictors of school achievement. *Multivariate Behavioral Research, 28,* 407–434.

Gustafsson, J.-E., & Stahl, P. A. (1997). *STREAMS User's Guide,* Version 1.7. Mölndal, Sweden: Multivariate Ware.

Gustafsson, J.-E., & Undheim, J. O. (1996). Individual differences in cognitive functions. In D. Berliner & R. Calfee (Eds.), *Handbook of educational psychology (*pp. 186–242). New York: Macmillan.

Harman, H. H. (1967). *Modern factor analysis (2nd ed).* Chicago: The University of Chicago Press.

Holzinger, K .J. (1944). A simple method of factor analysis. *Psychometrika, 9,* 257–262.

Holzinger, K. J., & Swineford, F. (1939). A study in factor analysis: The stability of a bi-factor solution. *Supplementary Educational Monographs,* No. 48. Chicago: University of Chicago.

Horn, J. L. (1989). Models of intelligence. In R. L. Linn (Ed.), *Intelligence, measurement, theory and public policy* (pp. 29–73). Urbana: University of Illinois Press.

Horn, J. L., & Cattell, R. B. (1966). Refinement and test of the theory of fluid and crystallized intelligence. *Journal of Educational Psychology, 57,* 253–270.

Humphreys, L. G. (1985). General intelligence: An integration of factor, test and simplex theory. In B. B. Wolman (Ed.), *Handbook of intelligence, theories, measurements and applications* (pp. 201–224). New York: Wiley.

Jensen, A. R. (1987). The *g* beyond factor analysis. In R. R. Ronning, J. A. Glover, J. C. Conoley, & J. C. Witt (Eds.), *The influence of cognitive psychology on testing.* (pp. 87–142). Hillsdale, NJ: Lawrence Erlbaum Associates.

Jöreskog, K. G., & Sörbom, D. (1996). *LISREL 8 User's Reference Guide (2nd ed.).* Chicago: Scientific Software.

McCrae, R. R., & John, O. P. (1992). An introduction to the five-factor model and its applications. *Journal of Personality, 60,* 175–215.

Mulaik, S. A. (1993). Objectivity and multivariate statistics. *Multivariate Behavioral Research, 28,* 171–203.

Schmid, J., & Leiman, J. M. (1957). The development of hierarchical factor solutions. *Psychometrika, 22,* 53–61.

Spearman, C. (1904). "General intelligence," objectively determined and measured. *American Journal of Psychology, 15,* 201–293.

Spearman, C. (1927). *The abilities of man.* London: MacMillan.

Spearman, C., & Wynn Jones, L. (1950). *Human ability: A continuation of "The abilities of man."* London: MacMillan.

Spearritt, D. (1996). Carroll's model of cognitive abilities: Educational implications. *International Journal of Educational Research, 25(2),* 107–197.

Thurstone, L. L. (1938). Primary mental abilities. *Psychometric Monographs,* No.1.

Thurstone, L. L. (1947). *Multiple factor analysis.* Chicago: The University of Chicago Press.

Undheim, J. O. (1981). On intelligence II: A neo-Spearman model to replace Cattell's theory of fluid and crystallized intelligence. *Scandinavian Journal of Psychology, 22,* 181–187.

Undheim, J. O., & Gustafsson, J. E. (1987). The hierarchical organization of cognitive abilities: Restoring general intelligence through the use of linear structural relations (LISREL). *Multivariate Behavioral Research, 22,* 149–171.

Vernon, P. E. (1950). *The structure of human abilities.* London: Methuen.

Vernon, P. E. (1961). *The structure of human abilities (2nd ed.).* London: Methuen.

3

Intelligence and Personality: Do They Mix?

Willem K. B. Hofstee
University of Groningen, Netherlands

Intelligence and personality suffer from the salad-dressing syndrome. Certain dressings based on oil and vinegar form an unstable emulsion; they have to be shaken forcefully prior to usage, and, even so, they separate within seconds. Similarly, there seems to be little attraction between personality and intelligence. Over the past 6 years, they occur together in the title of a mere 25 publications. Moreover, only a handful of these (e.g., Ackerman & Heggestad, 1997; Goff & Ackerman, 1992) represent attempts at blending the two concepts. In most other cases, intelligence and personality variables occur in mere juxtaposition, for example, as separate predictors of performance or as characteristics of particular groups; finally, a number of studies deal with the influence of personality on intelligence or vice versa (e.g., Furnham, Forde, & Cotter, 1998; see also Saklofske & Zeidner, 1995) rather than mixing the two concepts.

This chapter confines itself to analyzing attempts at blending the concepts of intelligence and personality. On reviewing such attempts, I propose to assign them either to the domain of stylistic intellect—which, however, I argue to be a proper subset of personality—or to the domain of psychological intelligence, which belongs in the area of intelligence tests. Finally, I present an elaboration of stylistic intellect.

MAXIMAL AND TYPICAL BEHAVIOR

In psychometric reality, intelligence is measured by a person's maximal performance, whereas personality is usually judged on the basis of typical behavior. Thus, in practice, personality and intelligence are separated by a difference in approach. Cronbach (1949), who introduced the terms *typical* and *maximal* performance, did not even bother to define intelligence and personality apart from this distinction and simply subsumed them under the difference in method. How cogent is the distinction, and what may be learned from putting it to the test?

Maximal Personality. Attempts have been made to mix oil and vinegar. First, one may try to measure personality performance. This is the ability, capability, maximal-versus-typical, or skills approach to personality testing (for an overview, see Riemann, 1997), investigating an individual's capability to behave in a particular manner. This research tradition revives from time to time but has not made a lasting impact. On the basis of a series of empirical studies, Riemann (1997) concluded that personality capabilities have no added value over traits.

A first conceptual problem relies on concepts like "capacity for neuroticism" or, generally, a capacity to display socially undesirable behavior. Surely, one can think of rather remote or perverse examples where it pays to behave in a neurotic style. But mainly, such a combination of ability and deficiency is a literary figure of speech–an irony, a paradox, an oxymoron–rather than a psychological concept. The range of convenience of the capacity definition is limited to positive traits. As the personality domain is bipolar (Hofstee, 1990), the capacity definition is half applicable at best.

A further problem with the stage metaphor, which underlies the skills approach to personality, revolves about genuineness–for example, on observing a dictator behaving in a maximally friendly manner toward small children on the arm of their mothers. That behavior might count for the dictator's score on histrionic ability, but not even the children would experience a dictator as genuinely friendly. The emulsion separates: We witness an ability to perform in a friendly manner together with an unfriendly personality. Maximum performance, being purposeful behavior, seems to preclude interpretations in terms of personality.

Typical Intelligence. Converse to maximal personality, one may wish to assess typical intelligence. Assessed intelligence arose, for example, as a by-product of Sternberg's (Sternberg, Conway, Ketron, & Bernstein, 1981) research on lay definitions of intelligence (for an overview of such studies, see Angleitner & Ostendorf, 1993). Another, rather inadvertent and embarrassing development has been the fifth of the big five factors of personality, taking the shape of assessed intelligence, intellect, or intellectance in some studies (for an overview, see John, 1990), although other authors—most notably, Costa and McCrae (1992)—prefer to emphasize the difference between their Factor V and measured intelligence. A more purposeful approach is represented by Ackerman's (Ackerman & Heggestad, 1997; Goff & Ackerman, 1992) concept of typical intellectual engagement, assessed by a questionnaire with items like, "I prefer my life to be filled with puzzles I must solve." In the Goff and Ackerman (1992) study, typical intelligence correlated .7 with the Openness-to-Experience scale of the NEO-Personality Inventory (Costa & McCrae, 1992) after correction for unreliability of both scales, but other big-five factors also play a part: On adding Conscientiousness, Emotional Stability, and Disagreeableness as predictors, the attenuation-corrected multiple correlation rose to .9 (Rocklin, 1994).

What is the conceptual status of assessed typical intellect? First, it should be made sure whether it is empirically distinct from measured intelligence. That is not so obvious as would appear from the low observed correlations (see Ackerman & Heggestad, 1997) between the two. Taking rater idiosyncrasies into account, in addition to other sources of invalid variance, the proportion of construct-valid variance in questionnaires may be estimated at .4 (Hofstee, 1994). Gauging the valid proportion in an intelligence test at .8, the upper ceiling for a questionnaire-test correlation is below .6. Still, the reported correlations between measured and assessed intelligence reach only about halfway to that ceiling. Therefore, typical intellect is indeed different from IQ.

How do assessed and measured intelligence differ? First, by definition. Sternberg (Sternberg et al., 1981) has shown that lay concepts of intelligence—which operate in most assessment studies—are partly different from the way IQ is defined. Second, the difference may be in the extent to which people use their brains. A familiar picture is the underachieving genius. Motivational and temperamental factors (Goff & Ackerman, 1992) are supposed to make actual intelligence different from maximal intelligence. Are we therefore looking at a stable emulsion of intelligence and personality; namely, typical intellect? I have some conceptual reservations to offer.

In deciding whether to send a sprinter to the Olympic Games, a national committee may take an average of his or her speed over the last so many trials. But it would make no sense at all to consider the average typical speed of a candidate, which would be close to zero; the committee would average maxima. So typical running speed is, in fact, a typical maximum. Observed maxima are highly predictive of future maxima, which form the relevant criterion: The Olympic Committee is not interested in predicting future typical speed. Likewise, what is typical about intelligence are the peaks rather than the level of the plateau. In the Goff and Ackerman (1992) study, the validity of Typical Intellectual Engagement against both High School and University GPA was zero, whereas intelligence tests had validities up to .4. The logic of maximum performance is hard to beat. It is as old as the idea of putting persons or objects to the test, rather than observing their everyday behavior.

One may wonder why judgments of intellect do not seem to capture a person's performance peaks. One reason may be that these peaks are infrequent and need not occur in public settings. Another plausible explanation is that the human assessor is distracted by salient stylistic aspects like culturedness, or even looks, that hardly predict real-life problem solving. The lack of predictive validity, together with the close ties between assessed intellect and other stylistic aspects of personality (Rocklin, 1994; see also later this chapter), are adequately caught in the–purposely tongue-in-cheek–label of "stylistic intellect."

To anticipate an objection: There can be no doubt that assessments of stylistic intellect are valid against judgmental (as different from performance) criteria, like ratings of managerial success. They may even outperform intelligence tests in that respect, if the assessments can be made sufficiently reliable. The validity of stylistic intellect against managerial success comes close to a parallel-forms reliability, to the extent that managers are judged by their style rather than by their output, according to the adagium, "It ain't what you do but the way that you do it." On the one hand, such tendencies are a fact of life and there is no need to be prudish about them; certain aspects of temperament and character can make a person unfit for the job, whatever his or her measured intelligence. On the other hand, certain conceptual distinctions have to be maintained, on penalty of cynicism. Broadly speaking, tests and measurement serve to correct for naive impressions; part of the scientific heritage of psychometrics is the distinction between a person's reputation and his or her abilities.

Ostendorf (personal communication, September 11, 1997) pointed to the possibility of collecting ratings of pure intelligence—for example, using trait terms like Intelligent and Analytical—and predicted that such ratings will be better predictors of measured intelligence than are Openness to Ideas, Typical Intellectual Engagement, and the like. Although concurring with this prediction, I would nonetheless expect that the disattenuated correlation between assessed and measured intelligence would still be far from perfect, for the reasons given previously.

Conclusion. Differences in psychometric tradition may be indicative of something more fundamental rather than just historical. One may observe that psychologists measure intelligence by testing a person's limits, whereas personality is usually assessed as typical behavior. A creative scientific reaction to such a state of affairs is to construct a fourfold table and fill in the off-diagonal cells: maximal personality, typical intelligence. Sometimes the creative strategy works and novel concepts emerge. In other cases, the conceptual tie is reaffirmed and all we retain is a better understanding. This may be such a case. Maximal personality and typical intelligence appear to be contradictions in terms. Clarity would be served by adhering to Cronbach's (1949) distinction and defining personality, temperament, character, and the like as assessed typical behavior and intelligence, capabilities, and the like as tested maximal performance. "Personality test" is thus contradictory jargon, as many educated lay persons would be likely to agree. Another consequence is that "Intelligence B" (Eysenck & Eysenck, 1985), namely, daily life intelligence as assessed by others or self (as distinct from genotypic intelligence A and measured intelligence C) would belong in the area of personality, not intelligence.

PRACTICAL INTELLIGENCE—OR PERSONALITY?

Another alternative to the classical intelligence test, but different from the typical intelligence approach, is Sternberg's (Sternberg & Wagner, 1993; Sternberg, Wagner, Williams, & Horvath, 1995) concept of practical intelligence. For example, you are asked to imagine that you want to improve the sales of an inexpensive photocopier that is overstocked; would it be a good idea to stress its simplicity of use, tell the customer that only a few are left, and so on? Practical intelligence is an intriguing concept with many faces. The question here is about its place at the crossroads of intelligence and personality.

The temptation to consider this kind of test as a personality questionnaire is difficult to resist. The Lie-to-the-customer option, for example, is indistinguishable from items like Deceives people, Misrepresents the facts, and Abuses people's confidence that fall in the II-V- facet of the Five-Factor Personality Inventory (FFPI; Hendriks, 1997); that is, it would have a primary negative loading on Factor II, Agreeableness, and a secondary negative loading on V, Intellectual Autonomy. A scale consisting of such items would presumably represent a negative facet of practical intelligence (although it might be dreaded to have positive predictive validity in certain commercial settings where cheating on customers is judged socially desirable by superiors).

The questionnaire interpretation is reinforced by the way the test is scored. There is no objective criterion for whether the answers are right or wrong; they are pitted against expert consensus or common lore. But that is known to be a fallible criterion: Up through the Middle Ages, there was a consensus that the Earth was flat, and erroneous collective beliefs can be found even in this scientific age. By the operational definition of practical intelligence, a test of it could wholly consist of items keyed positive that are false by reasonably objective standards. Moreover, consensus may be grounded in values rather than facts. For example, it is common lore that it pays to be honest, but one would hesitate to put that proposition to the empirical test; it is mainly a self-fulfilling prophecy, as long as people adhere to it. Thus the familiar introduction to personality questionnaires would apply: "There are no right or wrong answers."

However, the pragmatics of administering this kind of test are quite different by virtue of its presentation as a test of intelligence. The implicit message to the participant is more like, "Your answers will be scored as more or less correct, although we have no objective way of scoring them. They will be judged by what people (e.g., experts) believe, presumably for good reasons." Assuming that participants are properly informed, they will see their task as to second-guess the scoring key. In this respect, the test of practical intelligence is very different indeed from an ordinary personality questionnaire. It amounts to administering a personality questionnaire under social-desirability instructions, thus: "For each item, find the most socially desirable option," instead of, "Choose the option that applies most to you."

The participant is thus faced with a test of maximal performance rather than a stylistic-intellect questionnaire. It would measure a particular kind of psychological intelligence; namely, the ability to predict what the test constructor had in mind, presumably for good reasons. Practical intelligence would correspond to differential success in socially desirable responses to a personality questionnaire on being challenged to do so; that is, success in predicting the social desirability values of the items. It would follow that one could take standard personality questionnaires, administer them with the instruction to respond in a maximally socially desirable manner, and have a practical-intelligence test. Although this is reminiscent of an early study by Messick (1960) on individual differences in social desirability, the implication is unorthodox: Differential socially desirable responding is almost universally considered as a nuisance variable and has even been denounced as a red herring (Ones, Viswesvaran, & Reiss, 1996). How can the positive validities of practical-intelligence tests (Sternberg & Wagner, 1993; Sternberg et al., 1995) be accounted for against the background of the overall lack of success of social-desirability scales as predictors, suppressors, or even moderators, as documented by Ones, Viswesvaran, and Reiss?

The answer may be simple: Social-desirability scales are questionnaire scales among others (see later this chapter) not tests of maximal performance, so nothing is to be learned from the comparison. Only if they—among other questionnaire scales—were administered under maximal-performance instructions ("Find the most socially desirable answer") would the comparison be relevant. Validation of such tests of psychological intelligence is an exciting research prospect.

Analytically, tests of practical intelligence do not represent a mixture of personality and intelligence any more than successful prediction of human behavior by psychologists would testify to their personality traits. Successful prediction of common sense or expert opinion, as in practical-intelligence tests, is indicative of an ability—albeit not of the kind that is covered by standard batteries. In opposition to analytical intelligence, it may be understood as a form of empirical intelligence: The ability to predict an empirical outcome; in this case, others' ratings of the social desirabilities of response options. Psychological intelligence would be part of the kind of social perceptiveness that is often attributed to females rather than males.

On a final note, practical intelligence as defined by Sternberg and Wagner (1993) cannot be tested as such. A constitutive element in the definition of practical intelligence is that the problems are not posed by others (i.e., test makers) but are encountered in real life and require recognition and formulation. By this definition, attempts to test someone's practical intelligence suffer from the original sin of psychometrics; that is, purposeful test construction and administration. Practical intelligence only exists in paradise, before the Fall. One may study practical intelligence in natural settings (Ceci, 1990). But its testing is internally contradictory.

THE INTERPLAY BETWEEN TRAITS

So far, the conclusion seems to be that intelligence and personality had better stay away from each other to avoid conceptual confusion. Surely, there is more to social success than just IQ, but that is no reason to construct mixtures. Sometimes one needs both a hammer and a screwdriver, but that is no reason to combine them into a single instrument. Just enter them into a multiple regression equation.

That attitude, however, would fail to do justice to a particular fascination, which may be called taxonomic. In everyday life, we are struck time and again by the interplay of personality traits, including stylistic intellect. For example, there are Intelligent and Unintelligent versions of Disagreeableness; there are separate concepts: Shrewdness for the Intelligent version and Callousness for the Unintelligent one (see Hofstee, De Raad, & Goldberg, 1992). This section is dedicated to trait structure. I do not cross the border between intelligence proper and personality; the interplay is between stylistic intellect—that is, intelligence before its emigration to the land of tests and measurement—and other personality traits like Extraversion, Agreeableness, Conscientiousness, and Emotional Stability. By drawing the latter into the picture, I expand on studies like the one by Angleitner and Ostendorf (1993) on the internal structure of stylistic intellect, using only ability items. For illustrative purposes, I lean heavily on Hendriks' (1997) doctoral dissertation on The Construction of the FFPI.

The p-Factor. While keeping measured intelligence and assessed personality (including stylistic intellect) apart, certain parallelisms in their structures may still be fruitfully considered. By virtue of their positive intercorrelations, intelligence tests find their place in the positive quadrant of an n-space. The number of dimensions depends on one's sense of parsimony and may vary anywhere between 1 and the number of variables; nowadays, there is a broad consensus (see Neisser et al., 1996) that it makes sense to take just one and call it g, as long as this does not preclude retaining additional principal components.

Essentially, this taxonomic conception may well be carried over to the domain of personality: Like measured intelligence, it may be analyzed at different levels. In this spirit, I first present an argument for a unidimensional conception of personality.

The large majority of personality traits, scored in a socially desirable direction, intercorrelate positively[1]; there is no question of natural orthogonality. Thus, they form a positive manifold just like intelligence variables. Their undesirable opposites form a negative manifold but after reflection, they fit in the positive quadrant. I propose to call their first principal component the (as distinct from Eysenck's, 1991, P) *p*-factor. What is its meaning?

One obvious interpretation is social desirability: The more socially desirable a trait is, the higher it may be expected to load on the first principal component. There is nothing against this interpretation as long as it is realized that social desirability is more than just an artifact of social perception. Some people are

---

[1] I considered this statement to be a truism, until one of my distinguished critics took issue with it; we decided to take a closer look. Of the correlations in a representative set of 225 trait adjectives used by Hendriks (1997), scored in socially desirable direction, over 80% appeared to be positive. Although this is less than would be expected among intelligence items, it is a sufficient base for a *p*-factor of personality. Note also that this procedure does not even maximize the proportion of positive correlations in the matrix.

more socially desirable than others (Hofstee & Hendriks, 1998): Different judges agree on target persons' scores on the first principal component and there can be no reasonable doubt that its heredity coefficient is as high as is usually found in traits.

More interesting, one may look at the variables that load highest on p. That would depend to some extent on the composition of the set of traits[2]. Hendriks (1997) presented a set of 914 personality-descriptive items that cover just about every corner of the domain. The highest-loading items on the first principal component are given in Table 3.1. An appropriate label for this component is Competence, in the sense of adequacy of reaction to situations. Notably, it is not a moral factor, as one might have expected; also, it would not be called mere social desirability. In this p-factor, stylistic intellect and other personality traits seem to be united in an evolutionary function: Adequate reaction to reality leads to survival. It remains to be seen whether this component replicates in other unselected sets of personality variables, for example, trait ratings. Half of the items in Table 3.1 come from an item file that was added with the purpose of overrepresenting intellect-related items. Another item set to be considered is Hendriks' (1997) FFPI consisting of a stratified sample of 100 items selected to cover the big-five factors. The highest-loading items on the first FFPI principal component are presented in Table 3.2. Here, the emphasis is more temperamental; an appropriate label would be Coping. Part of the shift from Competence to Coping may be explained by the fact that the FFPI items were selected to be easy to understand; many intellect-related items did not satisfy that criterion. Saucier (personal communication, August 6, 1997) obtained first principal components from sets of trait adjectives that have features of both Competence and Coping, so the truth may well be in the middle.

A notable precursor of the p-factor is Webb's (1915; see Deary, 1996) w-factor of personality, resulting from a procedure that is comparable to taking the first principal component of a broad set of personality items. Webb's w has been interpreted by later authors either in terms of Emotional Stability or Conscientiousness (Deary, 1996), to use the big-five labels; the blend of these two would amount to Steadiness (Hofstee, De Raad, & Goldberg, 1992). In Webb's days, a preference for unidimensional solutions may have been fostered by methodological restrictions. But the removal of those is not a valid reason to ignore the p-component. Next, I outline a flexible taxonomic procedure for analyzing data at different levels of complexity.

---

[2] With respect to measured intelligence, there is a meaningful substantive argument on the nature of the g-factor (see Chap. 2, this volume). In the present context, however, such an argument would be premature.

TABLE 3.1
Highest-Loading Items on the First Principal Component of an
Unselected Set of 914 Personality-Descriptive Items

Positive:	Knows what he or she is talking about
	Can handle situations
	Reacts adequately
	Carries tasks to a successful conclusion
	Is in touch with reality
Negative:	Talks nonsense
	Ducks responsibilities
	Misrepresents the facts
	Misjudges situations

A Hierarchy of Generalized Simplexes

The p-component may be viewed as the top trait in a sophisticated hierarchy. The second hierarchical level comes about by adding the second principal component and applying a rotation to positive manifold. Using positive and negative traits, the result is a gappy circumplex. The gaps are found mainly in the second and fourth quadrants containing ambivalent traits: traits that load in a socially desirable direction on one component and undesirable on the other (for examples, see Hofstee, De Raad, & Goldberg, 1992). They are far fewer in number than are straight traits (Hofstee, De Raad, Goldberg, 1992; Hofstee, Ten Berge, & Hendriks, 1998). Like negative capabilities, ambivalent traits may be highly inspiring to the literary mind. However, they tend to be psychometrically unreliable, presumably because they are interpreted positively in some rater target combinations and negatively in others. So, rather than retaining full circumplexes (as in Hofstee, De Raad, & Goldberg, 1992), I now propose a taxonomic model in the shape of an n-dimensional double cone, or an n-dimensional quadrant if negative traits are reflected.

TABLE 3.2
Highest-Loading Items on the First Principal Component of the FFPI

Positive:	Is sure of his or her ground
	Can stand a great deal of stress
	Looks at the bright side of life
	Acts comfortably with others
	Is able to see the best in a situation
Negative:	Is easily intimidated
	Invents problems for him or herself
	Fears for the worst
	Panics easily
	Is apprehensive about new encounters

With two dimensions, four[3] facets or segments of 30 degrees may be distinguished. Two of these have the orthogonal axes as their bisectrix and thus contain relatively factor-pure traits. The other two are in between, with bisectrices at 30 degrees and 60 degrees: One facet contains traits that have their primary loading on the first rotated component and a non-negligible secondary loading on the second; the other, vice versa. In this model, variables are represented by their projections on the closest facet bisectrix.

At the third level of the hierarchy, is a sphere quadrant (and its antipode). That structure may be abridged by considering only three planes (simplexes) that are formed by two axes at a time and by representing variables by their projection on the closest plane. Together, the abridged simplex contains 9 facets: three factor-pure facets, 3 x 2 blends. Hofstee, Ten Berge, and Hendriks (1998) showed that the structure of the FFPI at this third level is Eysenckian, featuring Emotional Stability, Extraversion, and an everyday version of Psychoticism as dimensions.

At the fourth level, there are 6 simplexes and 4 + (6 x 2) = 16 facets; at the fifth level in the hierarchy, there are 10 simplexes and 5 + (10 x 2) = 25 facets. I use the five-dimensional structure to illustrate the interplay between stylistic intellect and other personality components.

Blends of Stylistic Intellect and Personality. The Big Five factor most associated with intellect is Factor V, whose psychometric status, however, is dubious (De Raad, Perugini, & Szirmák, 1997; Hofstee, Kiers, DeRaad, Goldberg, Ostendorf, 1997). In Hendriks' (1997) materials, it emerges as

---

[3] Alternatively, the quadrant could be split into three segments of 30 degree, with bisectrices at 15 degree, 45 degree, and 75 degree, amounting to an oblique structure that might describe the data even better. I do not explore that possibility here.

Intellectual Autonomy. Table 3.3 contains the highest-loading items. The negative pole of this factor especially represents Heteronomy (subordination to authority from without) or, perhaps, External Locus of Control rather than lack of intellect. Also, there are indications that this Factor V correlates even less with measured intelligence than other versions of assessed intellect (McCrae, personal communication, August 30, 1997). Nonetheless, this factor can serve as a pivot around which other facets of stylistic intellect revolve. The simplexes that are formed by Factor V and the other four are given in Tables 3.4A to 3.4D. I+ to V+ designate factor-pure items; I+V+ designates items with a positive primary loading on I and a positive secondary loading on V, and so on.

Factor I, Extraversion, does not contribute a facet of stylistic intellect; the V+I+ blend contains Assertiveness. One might wonder if intellect would not blend more easily with introversion, but the pertinent ambivalent facets are virtually empty.

Factor II, Agreeableness, is much more fertile. The V+II+ facet contains Intellectual Curiosity. From its position in the five-space, it follows that assessed Intellectual Curiosity has a social connotation: One seeks to learn from others, rather than solitarily. This connotation is further emphasized in the II+V+ facet, in which Openness to ideas again, others' ideas—finds its place. In the Revised NEO Personality Inventory (Costa & McCrae, 1992), this connotation is absent as the Openness to Ideas facet scale has no loading on the Agreeableness factor. Probably the labels mean different things (unless one assumes that the American respondents were only open to their own ideas).

TABLE 3..3
Factor-Pure Items of FFPI-Factor V (Intellectual Autonomy)

V+	Can link facts together
	Thinks quickly
	Analyzes problems
	Wants to form his or her own opinions
	Counters others' arguments
V-	Follows the crowd
	Does what others do
	Copies others
	Agrees to anything
	Takes things lying down

TABLE 3.4A
Factor I (Extraversion) and Factor V

I+	V+I+
Loves to chat	Takes the initiative
Laughs aloud	Takes charge
Slaps people on the back	Meets challenges
I+V+	**V+**
Starts conversations	Can link facts together
Gets the party going	Thinks quickly
Expresses him or herself easily	Analyzes problems

I-	V-I-
Keeps apart from others	Lets others make the decisions
Avoids contacts with others	Waits for others to lead the way
Prefers to be alone	Blends into the crowd
I-V-	**V-**
Does not commit him or herself	Follows the crowd
Keeps him or herself uninvolved	Copies others
Sits alone by him or herself	Agrees to anything

TABLE 3.4B
Factor II (Agreeableness) and Factor V

II+	V+II+
Tolerates a lot from others	Likes to learn new things
Tries to prevent quarrels	Wants to understand things
Is willing to make compromises	Seeks explanations
II+V+	V+
Respects others	Can link facts together
Is open to ideas	Thinks quickly
Accepts people as they are	Analyzes problems
II-	V-II-
Imposes his or her will on others	Echoes what others say
Orders people around	Doesn't understand things
Uses others for his or her own end	Misjudges situations
II-V-	V-
Looks down on others	Follows the crowd
Speaks ill of others	Copies others
Deceives people	Agrees to anything

TABLE 3.4C
Factor III (Conscientiousness) and Factor V

III+	V+III+
Does things according to plan	Knows what he or she is talking about
Loves order and regularity	Uses his or her brains
Finishes tasks directly	Sees through problems

III+V+	V+
Likes to be well-prepared	Can link facts together
Does things in logical order	Thinks quickly
Works hard	Analyzes problems

III-	V-III-
Acts without planning	Talks nonsense
Makes a mess of things	Just lets things happen
Does things at the last minute	Gives up easily

III-V-	V-
Leaves his or her work undone	Follows the crowd
Neglects his or her duties	Copies others
Acts without thinking	Agrees to anything

TABLE 3.4D
Factor IV (Emotional Stability) and Factor V

IV+	V+IV+
Can take his or her mind off problems	Can handle complex problems
Readily overcomes setbacks	Decides things on his or her own
Is always in the same mood	Keeps things in hand

IV+V+	V+
Is sure of his or her grounds	Can link facts together
Keeps a cool head	Thinks quickly
Can stand a great deal of stress	Analyzes problems

IV-	V-IV-
Invents problems for him or herself	Will believe anything
Gets overwhelmed by emotions	Is easily intimidated
Has crying fits	Lets him or herself be used

IV-V-	V-
Panics easily	Follows the crowd
Is easily disturbed	Copies others
Is afraid of many things	Agrees to anything

Factor III, Conscientiousness, also mixes well with intellect. Facet III+V+ may be interpreted as Tight Intellect (Peabody & Goldberg, 1987). The V+III+ facet is virtually indistinguishable from the Competence factor in Table 3.1; its negative pole V-III- accommodates the Underachiever who (in addition to the items listed in Table 3.4C) Just lets things happen, Gives up easily, and Forgoes opportunities.

Factor IV, Emotional Stability, reintroduces the Coping component of Table 3.2, now in the shape of the IV+V+ facet; it would not count as a facet of stylistic intellect. The V+IV+ facet blends Coping and Intellectual Autonomy into the kind of Tough Intellect that would be expected in decision makers.

Thus, the generalized simplex approach yields several patterns of stylistic intellect, in addition to Intellectual Autonomy (V+); Intellectual Curiosity (V+II+) and Openness to Ideas (II+V+); Tight Intellect (III+V+) and Competence (V+III+); and Tough Intellect (V+IV+). Each of these have their own conceptual identity. They represent a pattern of traits that would be recognizable in a particular individual.

The status of these patterns of stylistic intellect is illustrative rather than exhaustive or even representative. Ostendorf (personal communication, September 11, 1997) re-analyzed data on 430 German trait terms including 128 ability items, constituting a Factor V that is clearly an Intellect factor. Its relevant mixtures with the other factors may be labelled as Creativity (V+I+), Spiritualness (I+V+), Artisticness (V+II+), Competence (V+III+), Ambitiousness (III+V+), and Erudition (V+IV+). Clearly, the facets are sensitive to differences in item pools, with the possible exception of Competence.

Considering stylistic intellect in the context of other personality variables uncovers many facets. The procedure helps to understand such everyday concepts by embedding them in an appropriate nomological network. The representation of stylistic intellect as a set of facets of personality should also make it easier to resist the temptation to transfer them to the domain of maximal performance intelligence tests, where they do not belong. Maximal wittiness tends not to be witty, maximal creativeness kills creativity, and maximal wisdom is rather unwise. Thus, the present approach also functions as a safeguard against attempts to inflate the domain of intelligence testing.

ACKNOWLEDGMENTS

I am indebted to A.A. Jolijn Hendriks for providing the materials used in Tables 3.1 and 3.2 and in Footnote 3.2, and to Alois Angleitner, Ian Deary, Adrian Furnham, Paul Kline, Paul van der Maesen de Sombreff, Jeff (R. R.) McCrae, Samuel Messick, Fritz Ostendorf, Lawrence A. Pervin, Rainer Riemann, and Gérard Saucier for their often extensive and thorough comments on an earlier version, leading to the present thoroughly revised text.

REFERENCES

Ackerman, P. L., & Heggestad, E. D. (1997). Intelligence, personality, and interests: Evidence for overlapping traits. *Psychological Bulletin, 121,* 219–245.

Angleitner, A., & Ostendorf, F. (1993). Zur Struktur von Fähigkeits- und Begabungsbegriffen in Selbst- und Bekanntenbeurteilungen [On the structure of capability and talent concepts in self and acquaintance ratings]. In H. Bauersfeld & R. Bromme (Eds.), *Bildung und Aufklärung: Studien zur Rationalität des Lehrens und Lernens* (pp. 1–32). Münster, Germany: Waxman.

Ceci, S. J. (1990). *On intelligence . . . more or less: A bioecological treatise on intellectual development.* Englewood Cliffs, NJ: Prentice Hall.

Costa, P. T., Jr., & McCrae, R. R. (1992). *Revised NEO personality inventory and NEO five factor inventory: Professional manual.* Odessa, FL: Psychological Assessment Resources.

Cronbach, L. J. (1949). *Essentials of psychological testing.* New York: Harper & Row.

Deary, I. J. (1996). A (latent) big five personality model in 1915? A reanalysis of Webb's data. *Journal of Personality and Social Psychology, 71,* 992–1005.

De Raad, B., Perugini, M., & Szirmák, Z. (1997). In pursuit of a cross-lingula reference structure of personality traits: Comparisons among five languages. *European Journal of Personality, 11,* 167-185.

Eysenck, H. J. (1991). Dimensions of personality: 16, 5 or 3? Criteria for a taxonomic paradigm. *Personality and Individual Differences, 12,* 773–790.

Eysenck, H. J., & Eysenck, M. W. (1985). *Personality and individual differences.* New York: Plenum.

Furnham, A., Forde, A., & Cotter, T. (1998). Personality and intelligence. *Personality and Individual Differences, 24,* 187-192.

Goff, M., & Ackerman, P. L. (1992). Personality-intelligence relations: Assessment of typical intellectual engagement. *Journal of Educational Psychology, 84,* 537–552.

Hendricks, A. A. J. (1997). *The construction of the five-factor personality inventory (FFPI).* Unpublished doctoral dissertation, University of Groningen, The Netherlands.

Hofstee, W. K. B. (1990). The use of everyday personality language for scientific purposes. *European Journal of Personality, 4,* 77–88.

Hofstee, W. K. B. (1994). Who should own the definition of personality? *European Journal of Personality, 8,* 149–162.

Hofstee, W. K. B., De Raad, B., & Goldberg, L. R. (1992). Integration of the big five and circumplex approaches to trait structure. *Journal of Personality and Social Psychology, 63,* 146–163.

Hofstee, W. K. B., Kiers, H. A. L., De Raad, B., Goldberg, L. R., & Ostendorf, F. (1997). Comparison of big-five structures of personality traits in Dutch, English and German. *European Journal of Personality, 11,* 15–32.

Hofstee, W. K. B., & Hendriks, A. A. J. (1998). The use of scores anchored at the scale midpoint in reporting people's traits. *European Journal of Personality, 12,* 219-228.

Hofstee, W. K. B., Ten Berge, J. M. F., & Hendriks, A. A. J. (1998). How to score questionnaires. *Personality and Individual Differences, 25,* 897-909.

John, O. P. (1990). The "Big Five" factor taxonomy: Dimensions of personality in the natural language and in questionnaires. In L. A. Pervin (Ed.), *Handbook of personality: Theory, and research* (pp. 66–100). New York: Guilford.

Messick, S. (1960). Dimensions of social desirability. *Journal of Consulting Psychology, 24,* 279–287.

Neisser, U., Boodoo, G., Bouchard, T. J., Jr., Boykin, A. W., Brody, N., Ceci, S. J., Halpern, D. F., Loehlin, J. C., Perloff, R., Sternberg, R. J., & Urbina, S. (1996). Intelligence: Knowns and unknowns. *American Psychologist, 51,* 77–101.

Ones, D. S., Viswesvaran, C., & Reiss, A. D. (1996). The role of social desirability in personality testing for personnel selection: The red herring. *Journal of Applied Psychology, 81,* 660–679.

Peabody, D., & Goldberg, L. R. (1987). Some determinants of factor structures from personality-trait descriptors. *Journal of Personality and Social Psychology, 57,* 552–567.

Riemann, R. (1997). *Persönlichkeit: Fähigkeiten oder Eigenschaften?* [Personality: Capabilities or traits?]. Pabst, Germany: Lengerich.

Rocklin, T. (1994). Relation between typical intellectual engagement and openness: Comment on Goff and Ackerman (1992). *Journal of Educational Psychology, 86,* 145–149.

Saklofske, D., & Zeidner, M. (Eds.). (1995). *International handbook of personality and intelligence.* New York: Plenum.

Sternberg, R. J., Conway, B. E., Ketron, J. L., & Bernstein, M. (1981). People's conception of intelligence. *Journal of Personality and Social Psychology, 41,* 37–55.

Sternberg, R. J., & Wagner, R. K. (1993). The g-ocentric view of intelligence and job performance is wrong. *Current Directions in Psychological Science, 2,* 1-5.

Sternberg, R. J., Wagner, R. K., Williams, W. M., & Horvath, J. A. (1995). Testing common sense. *American Psychologist, 50,* 912–927.

Webb, E. (1915). Character and intelligence. *British Journal of Psychology Monographs, 1*(3), 1-99.

4

Temperament and Intelligence: A Psychometric Approach to the Links Between Both Phenomena

Jan Strelau
University of Warsaw and Silesian University

Bogdan Zawadzki
Anna Piotrowska
University of Warsaw

Both temperament and intelligence are regarded as topics that belong to the psychology of individual differences, and it is not accidental that many recognized scholars in this field of psychology were involved in studying both phenomena. To give a few examples, consider Thurstone (1953), Guilford, Zimmerman, and Guilford (1976), Eysenck (1979), and Teplov (1964). Thurstone, the author of the concept of primary mental abilities, is known in temperament research as the author of the Thurstone Temperament Schedule (TTS; Thurstone, 1953). Guilford, who contributed to the field of intelligence by developing the well-known Model of the Structure of Intellect, is also the author of the Guilford–Zimmerman Temperament Schedule (GZTS; Guilford, Zimmerman, & Guilford, 1976). Both temperament inventories, TTS and GZTS, were for many years very popular assessment instruments applied in research and practice. One of the founders of contemporary research on temperament, Eysenck and Eysenck (1985), developed a three-dimensional model of intelligence. Although this model did not gain much popularity, it is worth mentioning that among the three dimensions that, according to Eysenck (1979) constitute the structure of intellect—mental processes, test material, and quality—the latter has a temperament component. Quality is composed of mental speed and error-checking and persistence has been considered one of the most basic temperament characteristics. Nowadays, there exists about a dozen temperament inventories (see Strelau, 1998) aimed at measuring this temperamental trait. In turn, Teplov (1964) is regarded as one of the pioneers of intellectual abilities and musical giftedness in Russia. But his main contribution consists of adapting and modifying Pavlov's typology of higher nervous activity to man and, together with Nebylitsyn (1972), Teplov (1964) developed a neo-pavlovian theory of temperament.

WHY IS IT REASONABLE TO SEARCH FOR LINKS BETWEEN TEMPERAMENT AND INTELLIGENCE?

Temperament and intelligence seem, for most contemporary researchers, to be phenomena rather isolated from each other. Because there is no agreement among scientists as to what intelligence is and the same is true for temperament, an unequivocal solution to this issue is hardly possible, if realistic at all. To reach an answer to this, both concepts—temperament and intelligence—need some explanation. For the purpose of this chapter, we consider *intelligence* to be a theoretical construct that refers to relatively stable internal conditions of humans, that determine the efficiency of behavior in which human-specific cognitive processes are involved (Strelau, 1992). Defined in such a way, intelligence is expressed as behavior that consists of solving tests aimed at measuring intellectual capacities.

In turn, *temperament* is basic, relatively stable personality traits that are present since early childhood, that occur in humans, and that have a counterpart in animals. The number of temperamental traits now identified is not far from 100. Therefore, we concentrate only on the traits with the biological basis that has been explained by referring to the concepts of arousal and/or arousability although the physiological or biochemical mechanisms to which these temperament characteristics refer are trait-specific (Strelau, 1994). In studies on adults and adolescents, extraversion, sensation seeking, activity, and the Pavlovian constructs—all of which belong to the most typical traits for the arousal-oriented approach to temperament—have been most often related to intellectual functioning.

There are at least two perspectives from which the links between intelligence and arousal-oriented temperamental traits may be viewed. One is based on the psychometric approach to intelligence that has its roots in Binet's (1911) view, according to which intelligence is expressed in complex mental functioning: The other perspective refer's to intelligence defined in terms of information processing. The belief that intelligence can be expressed in simple sensory processes was already present in Spearman's (1904) theory. For the purpose of this chapter, we chose the psychometric approach to demonstrate some links between temperament and intelligence.

To show the links between temperament and intelligence, we concentrate on so-called arousal-oriented temperament characteristics, such as Eysenck's (Eysenck & Eysenck, 1985) PEN factors, Zuckerman's (1994) sensation seeking, the Pavlovian properties of the central nervous system (CNS, Strelau, 1983), and the temperamental traits proposed by Strelau's (1996) regulative theory of temperament. These links are discussed from four different perspectives briefly described next.

Temperament May Modify the Result of Intelligence Tests

Psychometric-oriented researchers do not agree about the quality and quantity of components that are comprised by the notion of intelligence, varying from one (the Spearman g–factor) to over 100 (Guilford, 1967). In spite of these differences, they agree that complex cognitive processes such as memory, reasoning, and comprehension belong to the basic mental processes involved in solving intelligence tests.

It is known that completion of an intelligence test occurs in a situation that might be characterized as a highly stimulating demand. Some reasons why this situation is demanding are that: The individual solves tasks that are on or over the borderline of his or her mental capacities; infrequently, the outcome has far-reaching educational, social, or professional consequences; test performance is often accompanied by a feeling that a result below expectancies brings discredit in the eyes of others, and so forth. All of these factors, taken separately and especially when in interaction with each other, result in a stressful situation. Temperament characteristics that moderate the stimulative value of the situation by increasing or decreasing the intensity of stimuli might be regarded as variables that influence the result of test performance (Strelau, 1995). Such temperamental traits as extraversion, emotionality, sensation seeking, reactivity, or strength of the nervous system may be mentioned as candidates for these moderatory effects.

Such a point of view regarding potential links between intelligence and temperament allows us to interpret some spectacular results obtained in a study conducted by Lewowicki (1975). The Standard Raven test was administered to 1,820 fifth- to eighth-grade pupils recruited across Poland from 28 elementary schools. Their temperament was assessed by means of the Strelau Temperament Rating Scale, which allows for measurement of the three basic Pavlovian properties—strength of excitation, strength of inhibition, and mobility of nervous processes (Strelau, 1983). Among other variables, school achievement was measured by means of an educational test constructed by Lewowicki. This large-scale study showed that intelligence correlated .41 with strength of excitation and .33 with mobility of nervous processes, and both temperament characteristics predicted school achievement to a higher extent than psychometric intelligence (.52, .42, and .37 respectively). It is highly probable that the state of stress, present when intelligence tests and achievement tests were administered under the control of teachers, influenced the efficiency of performance. Strength of excitation and mobility of nervous processes may be regarded in this situation as moderators of the state of stress, which explains their links with intelligence and school achievement. Eysenck and Eysenck (1985), when summarizing the data in respect to efficiency of performance based on intellectual tests, underlined that the effect of the stimulative value of the situation is moderated by extraversion in such a way that "extraverts perform faster than introverts under relatively arousing conditions. Whereas introverts respond faster than extraverts when long and monotonous tasks are used" (p. 274).

TEMPERAMENTAL TRAITS MAY INFLUENCE THE INTERACTION BETWEEN THE GENETICALLY DETERMINED INTELLECTUAL POTENTIAL AND ENVIRONMENT

Some temperament characteristics—for example, sensation seeking, extraversion, strength of excitation, and activity (a tendency to undertake behavior of high stimulative value)—might be regarded as one type of variable that influence's the interaction between the individual's genetically determined intellectual potentials and the environment that results in the development of cognitive functions. Depending on the position that individuals occupy on these temperament dimensions, the moderatory effect may be different. It might be assumed that individuals who are prone to new experience and sensations open to the external world, tolerant for intensive stimulation, and are active, especially in the cognitive domain, have more possibilities and opportunities to get in contact with the surrounding world, with unknown and ambiguous situations and behaviors, when compared with persons representing opposite characteristics. This results, as a consequence, in higher cognitive stimulation when compared with persons who are resistant to new experiences and sensations, closed to the external world, avoid intensive stimuli, and who are passive. Such a view of the relationship between intelligence and temperament may be helpful in explaining several findings in the domain of intelligence-temperament relationships. For example, Zuckerman (1994) reported a study that showed that IQ measured in 138 high school students by means of the Wechsler Adult Intelligence Scale (WAIS) correlated significantly with experience seeking (.34), disinhibition (.19) boredom susceptibility (.21) and with the total score (.22) of the Sensation Seeking Scale (Form IV). A similar result was found in a sample of male drug abusers (Zuckerman, 1994), which shows that intelligence as measured by WAIS correlates positively with sensation seeking. The temperament –intelligence links may be specific, however, depending on which of the intelligence scales are taken into account. For example, a study conducted by Robinson (1985), although on a small sample of graduate and postgraduate students, has shown that whereas extraverts score higher on performance tests of the WAIS, introverts score higher on WAIS verbal tests. In general, it has to be repeated, after Eysenck and Eysenck (1985), that the results of the studies in which extraversion was correlated with intelligence measures are not unequivocal.

A study conducted by Ledzińska (1996) took a sample of 961 high school students and selected two groups, taking into account the highest ($N = 108$) and lowest ($N = 105$) scores from the Standard Raven test. It was shown that highly intelligent students scored significantly higher on the Strength of excitation and Mobility of nervous processes scales when compared with low-intelligent students. Temperament characteristics were measured with the Strelau Temperament Inventory (STI, Strelau, 1983).

TEMPERAMENT MAY INFLUENCE COPING WITH INTELLECTUAL DEMANDS ON THE BORDERLINE OF THE INDIVIDUAL'S CAPACITY

One of the basic postulates elaborated by developmental psychologists (Hunt, 1969; Vygotsky, 1960) says that optimal conditions for cognitive development occur when intellectual demands are on the borderline of the individual's capacity. This gives another perspective from which the links between temperament and intellect may be viewed.

One may hypothesize that performance of intellectual tasks, which are highly demanding in terms of effort expenditure (Schönpflug, 1986), and which are at the limits of the individual's "readiness" (Hunt, 1969) to internalize this intensive intellectual stimulation, is influenced by temperament characteristics taking part in moderating the level of arousal. Functioning on the borderline of the individual's capacity to cope with the intellectual demands is a stressful situation. It might happen that individuals resistant to intensive stimulation cope more efficiently with these demands than individuals not resistant to such stimulation. If so, one may assume that individuals characterized by a high level of arousability (e.g., introverts, sensation avoiders, highly reactive persons, individuals with a weak nervous system) will avoid intellectual tasks that are on the borderline of their readiness. As a consequence, this may lead to a lower intellectual development as compared with individuals who represent the opposite pole of these temperament dimensions. This speculative but theoretically grounded hypothesis, can hardly, if at all, be subject to empirical generalizations.

DIVERGENT THINKING, ONE OF THE MAIN COMPONENTS OF THE STRUCTURE OF INTELLECT, IS MODERATED BY TEMPERAMENTAL TRAITS

In extending the domain of intellectual characteristics to fluency and flexibility, the two components of divergent thinking that have been incorporated by Guilford (1967) to the structure of intellect, there are reasons to assume that these intellectual characteristics are related to some temperament traits. By *flexibility*, we mean the ability to generate highly varied and qualitative different ideas. By *fluency*, we mean the facility to generate a great number of related ideas (Guilford, 1967). On close inspection, we find they both share some features with Pavlov's mobility of nervous processes and with the behavioral equivalent as measured by the STI or the newly developed Pavlovian Temperament Survey (PTS; Strelau & Angleitner, 1994). Accordingly, mobility is perceived as the ability to switch as quickly as possible from one reaction (behavior) to another one adequately in response to changes in the surroundings. One may assume that a person scoring high on the Mobility scale will perform better in tasks aimed at measuring fluency and flexibility. The reason is that both forms of divergent thinking, although in a different way, are expressed in the individual's ability to switch as soon as possible from one concept or idea to another. A study was reported by Strelau (1977) in which a group of 112 university students (62 males and 50 females) were given Guilford's tests for measuring fluency and flexibility. Mobility was measured by the STI. This showed that semantic as well as figural fluency and flexibility correlate significantly (between .23 and .35) with mobility of the nervous system. However, when mobility was assessed in experimental settings by means of a method known as the "alteration of the signal value of applied stimuli" (see Strelau, 1983), this relationship did not come out. This result was replicated (Strelau, 1977) in a study in which slightly different fluency and flexibility tasks were applied to a group of 96 high school students (50 females and 46 males). The relationship of "temperament-divergent thinking" was especially expressed in women, with coefficients of correlation between .33 (for flexibility) and .40 (for fluency).

EMPIRICAL EVIDENCE REGARDING THE RELATIONSHIP BETWEEN TEMPERAMENT AND INTELLIGENCE

A preliminary study conducted in our laboratory by Piotrowska and Strelau (1994) resulted in lack of relationship between intelligence and temperament when both phenomena were measured by means of psychometric procedures. In this study conducted on 90 adult subjects (aged from 22 to 55, 39 females and 51 males), intelligence was measured by means of the Standard Raven Test and temperament was measured by a preliminary version of the Formal Characteristics of Behavior–Temperament Inventory (FCB–TI; Strelau & Zawadzki, 1993). Additionally, some other tests capturing different aspects of intelligence were applied, such as Aphorisms, Syllogisms, Fluency, Originality, Situations, and Faces. The data have shown that there is no relationship between intelligence as measured by the Standard Raven Test and temperament characteristics, and this finding emerged not only for the total sample but also when the sample was divided into subgroups, taking into account such criteria as age, sex, and educational level. The only link that was found persistently, independent of the way data were analyzed, was the relationship between fluency as measured by Guilford's (1967) Remote Consequences of Uncommon Events and temperament characteristics. Fluency correlated positively with such scales as Mobility, Endurance, and Activity and negatively with Perseveration and Emotional Reactivity.The rather pessimistic result in our search for a relationship between temperament and intelligence motivated us to conduct a study that, on the one hand, takes into account broader characteristics of intelligence and, on the other hand, comprises measures of temperament representing different conceptualizations although has a common denominator—all of them refer in a given way to the construct of arousal

Method

The study in which different measures of intelligence and related areas were applied, and in which several temperament inventories were administered was conducted on different samples. To make it clear which of the tests were administered, to the separate samples, we first describe the diagnostic tools for intelligence and temperament.

Measures of Intelligence and Temperament

For measuring fluid intelligence the Raven Progressive Matrices—Standard version (RPM–S) was administered in an authorized Polish adaptation (Jaworowska & Szustrowa, 1991). The APIS test constructed by Matczak, Jaworowska, Szustrowa, and Ciechanowicz (1995) was applied to measure crystallized intelligence. APIS is composed of eight scales aimed at measuring four following kinds of abilities: general reasoning (GR), verbal abilities (VA), spatial abilities (SA) and social abilities (SoA). Each of the four abilities is represented by two scales.

Four tests were administered for measuring different aspects of divergent thinking (Guilford, 1967): the Utility Test (UT) was used as a measure of verbal fluency (number of produced ideas), and both the Unusual Uses Test (UUT) and the Consequences of Unusual Events (CUE) test were applied to measure flexibility by taking into account the number of remote associations. In turn, the fourth measure of divergent thinking—originality—was taken by counting the number of statistically rare responses obtained in both UUT and CUE tests.

Additionally, to assess reasoning abilities, two tests based on Thurstone's (1943) measures of intelligence were administered—the Aphorisms Test (AT) and the Syllogisms Tests (ST). AT, which is composed of 11 tasks, is aimed at measuring verbal reasoning. In turn, the ST is composed of six tasks, allowing assessment of deductive reasoning as understood by Sternberg (1985). One more test—Faces (FT), constructed by Piotrowska, was applied to measure social intelligence. FT, which is composed of 15 female pictures illustrating a diversity of emotional stages, reminds one to some extent of Guilford's (1967) Facial Situations test.

In the domain of temperament, three inventories, representative of three approaches to temperament, were administered. The first, FCB–TI (Strelau & Zawadzki, 1993, 1995), was developed within the regulative theory of temperament (Strelau, 1996). FCB–TI is composed of the following scales: Briskness (BR), Perseveration (PE), Sensory sensitivity (SS), Emotional reactivity (ER), Endurance (EN) and Activity (AC). The PTS (Strelau & Angleitner, 1994) is aimed at measuring the theoretical constructs of the CNS as developed by Pavlov. PTS has three following scales: Strength of excitation (SE), Strength of inhibition (SI) and Mobility of nervous processes (MO). The Eysenck Personality Questionnaire–Revised (EPQ–R) is a Polish adaptation by Drwal and Brzozowski (1995). The three scales of EPQ–R–Psychoticism (P), Extraversion (E), and Neuroticism (N; with the Lie scale, L, added)—are most representative for measuring the traits as proposed by Eysenck's PEN theory (Eysenck & Eysenck, 1985).

Subjects

The study was conducted on four samples. Sample A was composed of 147 subjects aged from 20 to 55 ($M = 35.41$, $SD = 9.76$); among them were 72 females and 75 males. The following tests were administered to this sample: FCB–TI and the three tests of divergent thinking (UT, UUT, and CUE); also originality was measured on the basis of UUT and CUE data. To a part of this sample (A1), composed of 116 subjects (age: 20–55, $M = 36.87$, $SD = 7.91$, 64 females and 52 males), additional measures of intellectual functioning were applied: RPM–S, Piotrowska's FT, and tests aimed at measuring reasoning abilities (AT and ST).

Sample B comprised 201 subjects (79 females and 122 males) with ages 23 to 48 ($M = 26.55$, $SD = 5.60$). The following measures were applied: FCB–TI,

Guilford's tests of divergent thinking (UT, UUT, and CUE), APIS (GR, VA, SA, and SoA), and Piotrowska's FT. The EPQ–R was also administered to a subsample (B1) that included 145 subjects (aged 23–40, $M = 24.27$, $SD = 2.11$, 61 females and 84 males.)

Sample C included 112 fifteen-year old adolescents (60 females and 52 males) from a study conducted by Czerniawska. The following tests were applied: PTS, Guilford's tests of divergent thinking, and RPM–S.

Sample D comprised 195 high school and university students aged from 16 to 22 ($M = 18.51$, $SD = 1.10$), among them 57 females and 129 males (in case of 11 subjects, there was no information regarding sex and age). This study, in which FCB–TI and RPM–S were administered, was conducted by Cegλowski.

Results

Taking as a point of departure the three different arousal-oriented conceptualizations on temperament, we present the data by showing how the various measures of intelligent behavior are related to temperament constructs represented by the three temperament inventories: FCB–TI, PTS, and EPQ–R.

The FCB–TI, which allows for measuring traits as proposed by the regulative theory of temperament, is the only inventory to which all measures of intelligent behavior applied in our study were related. The data of this comparison are presented in Table 4.1.

Among the 96 coefficients of correlation collected from four different samples are 28 coefficients that suggest a possible relationship between temperament and characteristics of intelligent behavior, although no one of the statistically significant coefficients extends beyond .33. The Raven test correlates in both samples with perseveration (.18 & .19) and, in one sample, with sensory sensitivity (.30). Although the Total APIS score does not correlate with any of the six temperament scales, some of the separate APIS scales show briskness (.16) and exactly the same but reverse relationship (-.16) was found between these two abilities and emotional reactivity. Additionally, spatial ability is obtained with respect to sensory sensitivity (.16).

Most consistent are the data in which different aspects of divergent thinking are related to temperament. In both samples in which fluency was measured (UT), this intellectual characteristic correlates with briskness, endurance, and activity (from .18 to .31) and negatively with emotional reactivity (-.15, & -.16).

TABLE 4.1
Temperamental Traits Assessed by FCB-TI and Measures of Intelligent
Behavior (IB)

Measures of IB	Sample	FCB-TI					
		BR	PE	SS	ER	EN	AC
Raven	A1	-.04	.18**	-.06	-.10	.08	.14
Raven	D	.01	.19**	.30**	.10	-.04	-.06
APIS - Total	B	.11	.07	.12	-.14	.10	.02
APIS - GR	B	.00	.12	.04	-.04	.05	.01
APIS - VA	B	.16*	-.04	.13	-.16*	.10	.07
APIS - SA	B	.16*	.08	.16*	-.16*	.10	.03
APIS - SoA	B	-.02	.05	.02	-.02	.05	-.05
Aphorisms	A1	-.10	-.03	.08	.07	-.02	-.05
Syllogisms	A1	-.17	.11	-.20*	-.02	.03	.07
FT	A	-.21**	-.02	-.01	.08	-.33**	-.23**
FT	B	.10	-.02	.05	.02	-.08	-.03
UT	A	.23**	-.06	.11	-28**	.31**	.18**
UT	A	.26**	-.07	.08	-.15*	.18**	.24**
UUT	B	.13**	-.02	-.03	-.16*	.14*	.19**
CUE	B	.06	-.03	-.02	-27**	.12*	.27**
Originality	A	.05	-.01	.08	-.12	.17*	.12

Note:

* p < .05

** p < .01 (one-tailed test for divergent thinking, for the remaining ones - two-tailed test). BR = Briskness, PE = Perseveration, SS = Sensory sensitivity, ER = Emotional reactivity, EN = Endurance, AC = Activity, GR = General reasoning, VA = Verbal abilities, SA = Spacial abilities, SoA = Social abilities, FT = Faces test, UT = Utility test, UUT = Unusual uses test, CUE = Consequences of unusual events.

A similar consistency was obtained in respect to flexibility, which is related to the same temperament characteristics (except CUE in sample B) with comparable strength of links. Additionally, originality correlates with EN (.17). Among the remaining measures of intelligence, the Syllogisms Test correlates negatively with sensory sensitivity and the Faces Test, administered in two samples, shows only in sample A with negative correlations with BR, EN, and AC (from -.21 to -.33).

In only one sample (C), the Pavlovian temperament traits were related to measures of intelligence and divergent thinking. These data are presented in Table 4.2.

Table 4.2 shows that the Raven scores do not correlate with Pavlovian CNS properties as measured by PTS, whereas both measures of divergent thinking, the Utility Test and the Unusual Uses Test, show correlations with mobility of nervous processes (.35 & .38 respectively).

Also, only in one sample (B1) were the Eysenckian superfactors related to selected measures of intelligent behavior—APIS, divergent thinking scores, and Faces Test. The data are depicted in Table 4.3.

As can be seen, abilities as measured by the APIS, test which allows us to assess crystallized intelligence, do not show many links with the Eysenckian dimensions of temperament. With the exception of social ability, which correlates (unexpectedly) negatively with extraversion, the only significant correlations refer to psychoticism (see Table 4.3). Three of the five APIS scores correlate negatively with this Eysenckian dimension. The Faces test shows no correlation with PEN and the only dimension that is related to all three measures of divergent thinking is extraversion (from .21—UT to .32—UUT).

In the next step of our study, we wanted to get a more general picture of the relationships between ability and temperament variables. Therefore, we separately factor analyzed the temperament and ability scales. Analysis was performed on data obtained on subsample B1 ($n = 145$) in respect to which the largest number of temperament and intellectual ability variables was recorded.

The procedure of principal components with Varimax rotation was applied and the Cattellian scree-test was used to determine the number of factors.

TABLE 4.2
Temperamental Traits Assessed by PTS and Measures of
Intelligent Behavior (IB)

Measures Of IB	Sample	PTS		
		SE	SI	MO
Raven	C	-.05	-.01	.07
Utility Test	C	.11	-.05	.35*
Unusual Uses Test	C	.15	.00	.38*

Note:
* p < .01 (one-tailed test). SE = Strength of excitation, SI = Strength of inhibition, MO = Mobility of nervous processes.

TABLE 4.3
Temperamental Traits Assessed by EPQ-R and Measures of Intelligent
Behavior (IB)

Measures of IB	Sample	EPQ-R			
		P	E	N	L
APIS - Total	B1	-.23*	-.07	-.01	-.02
APIS - GR	B1	-.19*	-.09	.02	-.03
APIS - VA	B1	-.12	.08	-.08	-.01
APIS - SA	B1	-.25**	-.01	-.06	.01
APIS - SoA	B1	-.10	-.19*	.12	-.02
Faces Test	B1	.02	.07	.03	-.10
Fluency (UT)	B1	.11	.29*	-.01	-.14
Flexibility (UUT)	B1	.01	.32*	.00	-.11
Flexibility (CUE)	B1	.00	.21*	-.10	-.05

Note:
P = Psychoticism, E = Extraversion, N = Neuroticism, L = Lie scale; for remaining abbreviations
see Table 4.1.
$p < .01$ (one-tailed test).

In case of temperament scales, three factors were separated. Factor I, with highest loadings on such scales as Neuroticism, Emotional reactivity, and Perseveration was identified as Emotionality. Factor II, named Extraversion –activity has the highest loadings on Activity, Extraversion, and Briskness scales. Factor III, with highest loadings on the Sensory sensitivity scale and with reverse sign on the Psychoticism scale, was described as Sensitivity toward environment.

Factor analysis of scales measuring intelligent behavior resulted in two factors. Factor I was identified as Divergent thinking, with highest loadings on all three Guilfordian measures (UT, UUT, and CUE), and Factor II with highest loadings on three APIS scales (VA, SA, and GR). This factor was marked as Crystallized intelligence. The two social ability tests (SoA and FT) occupied different places in the factor solution and with very low (.28 on Factor I) or low (.41 on Factor II) loadings.

Subsequently, we correlated temperament scales with the two ability factors as well as with total abilities scores. The latter comprised a summary score of the three divergent thinking scales and the Total APIS score. The results of this analysis are depicted in Table 4.4.

TABLE 4.4
Correlations Between Temperament Scales and Ability
Factors and Scales

Temperament scale	Factor I	Factor II	UT + UUT + CUE	APIS (total)
E	0.32**	-0.04	0.32**	-0.07
N	-0.02	-0.03	-0.03	-0.01
P	0.03	-0.22*	0.04	-0.24**
BR	0.21*	0.25**	0.24**	0.18*
PE	0.03	0.05	0.01	0.10
SS	0.10	0.07	0.05	0.18*
ER	-0.14	-0.13	-0.15	-0.10
EN	0.23**	0.22*	0.25**	0.21*
AC	0.27**	-0.06	0.24**	-0.08

Note:
For explanation of Abbrevations see Tables 4.1 and 4.3.
*$p < 0.05$
** $p < 0.01$ (two-tailed).

The pattern of correlations shows that Factor I (divergent thinking) and the corresponding divergent thinking total score have significant relations with extraversion, briskness, endurance, and activity, with coefficients varying from .21 to .32. Factor II (crystallized intelligence) and the corresponding Total APIS score correlate negatively (-.22 & -.24) with the Psychoticism scale. Both briskness and endurance also correlate weakly with Factor II as they do with Factor I. Weak links occurred between the SS scale and the Total APIS score (18).

The scales referring to intelligent behavior were correlated with temperament factors. As seen in Table 4.5 the pattern of correlations is clear.

Factor I (emotionality) does not correlate significantly with any of the intellectual ability scales. Factor II (extraversion–activity) correlates significantly with the UT, UUT, and CUE scales and with the total divergent thinking score. Factor III (Sensitivity toward environment) correlates significantly with VA, SA , GR, and Total APIS scores reflecting Crystallized intelligence, but not with both social intelligence scales.

A similar picture was obtained when temperament factors were correlated with intellectual ability factors (see Table 4.6). The Emotionality factor does not correlate with any of the two ability factors. The Extraversion–activity factor correlates with the Divergent thinking factor, as does the factor labeled as Sensitivity toward environment with the Crystallized intelligence factor.

TABLE 4.5
Correlations between Ability Scales and Temperament
Factors

Scale	Factor I	Factor II	Factor III
SoA	0.05	-0.15	0.13
VA	-0.12	0.07	0.18*
SA	-0.10	-0.01	0.37**
GR	-0.00	-0.09	0.21*
UT	0.01	0.34**	0.06
UUT	-0.02	0.29*	0.03
CUE	-0.11	0.18*	0.06
FT	-0.01	0.08	0.02
APIS (Total)	-0.07	-0.06	0.33*
Divergent thinking (UT + UUT + CUE)	-0.05	0.32*	0.06

Note:
The description of intellectual ability scales is in Table 4.1
* $p < 0.05$,
** $p < 0.01$, (two-tailed).

TABLE 4.6
Correlations Between Ability and Temperament Factors

Ability/temperament factors	Factor I (Emotionality)	Factor II (Extraversion/ activity)	Factor III (Sensitivity to environment)
Factor I (Divergent thinking)	-0.02	0.32*	0.08
Factor II (Crystallized Intelligence)	-0.10	-0.02	0.27*

Note:
* $p < 0.01$ (two-tailed)

Discussion

Not all characteristics of intellectual behavior in this study were related to the three basic approaches to temperament. The relationships between temperament and measures of intelligent behavior (depending on which conceptualization of temperament is taken into account) cannot be fully drawn. The weakness of our study lies in the fact that the Raven test was not related to EPQ–R scales and the APIS was not related to PTS measures. Nevertheless, some general conclusions can be drawn from our data. The findings from our study might be summarized as follows:

- The links between a variety of psychometric measures of intellectual behavior and temperament characteristics, as represented by three different approaches, are rather weak although the frequency with which they have been stated is above chance.
- If there are correlations between intellectual abilities and temperament characteristics, the coefficients vary mostly from .20s to .30s.
- The relations between intellectual abilities and temperament are trait-specific and depend on what kind of measure is taken into account. Most generally, it might be concluded that:

1. The scales measuring different aspects of emotionality are not related to any ability factors.
2. The scales measuring different aspects of extraversion–activity are related only to divergent thinking factors and scales.
3. The scales measuring different aspects of sensitivity toward environment are related to crystallized intelligence factors and scales.
4. The scales measuring social intelligence are not related to temperament factors and scales.

Because fluid intelligence is strongly related to biological determinants of intelligence (Cattell, 1971; Jensen, 1993), there were reasons to expect that the Raven test would show some relationships to temperamental traits. These links should be especially evident with respect to the Pavlovian CNS processes (strength of excitation and mobility of nervous processes) as demonstrated by Ledzińska (1996) and Lewowicki (1975). Our data are negative or at least ambiguous and replicate the former finding by Piotrowska and Strelau (1994), who demonstrated a lack of relationship between the Pavlovian measures of temperament and fluid intelligence. It is known that fluid intelligence is strongly determined by developmental changes in the biological background (Cattell, 1971). One may expect that in earlier stages of life, when fluid intelligence plays the dominant role, the links between temperament and fluid intelligence will be stronger than in later developmental stages, when crystallized intelligence plays the dominant role. A study is needed that takes into account a life-span approach to the relationship: fluid intelligence–temperament.

One of the reasons why intelligence measures show some, albeit weak, correlations with selected temperament characteristics may be due to the fact that intelligence and arousal-oriented temperament dimensions have a common denominator–arousability. It has been argued by Robinson (1993, 1996) that the neurophysiological mechanism underpinning intelligence has much to do with cerebral arousability understood as the inherent reactivity of neural networks.

The fact that no relationship occurred between intelligent behavior as measured by RPM–S and APIS tests and measures of emotionality, such as neuroticism and emotional reactivity, suggests that performance of intelligence tasks was not regarded by subjects as being stressful. Many data collected in the literature show that emotionality and similar constructs are essential moderators of stress-inducing situations (Eysenck, 1983; Kagan, 1983; Strelau, 1995).

The data are most consistent where temperament characteristics were related to measures of divergent thinking. Both characteristics of intelligent behavior, fluency and flexibility, correlate with mobility of nervous processes, as stated earlier in Strelau's (1983) and Piotrowska and Strelau's (1994) studies. They also correlate in the range between .20s and .30s with extraversion and energetic characteristics measured by means of the FCB–TI, such as briskness, endurance, activity, and negatively with emotional reactivity. This finding can be explained if we consider that mental speed, to which fluency and flexibility undoubtlty refer (Stankov & Roberts, 1997), is causally related to level of arousal, which is a common denominator of the temperament characteristics mentioned previously.

The data derived from factor analysis are interesting in that they show that the factor labeled as Sensitivity toward environment and composed of psychoticism and sensory sensitivity is positively correlated (.27) with the factor identified as Crystallized intelligence, the latter being composed of the APIS scales. This finding is in favor of our hypothesis, which says that some temperament characteristics may be regarded as variables that influence the interaction between the individual's genetically determined intellectual potential and the environment that contributes to the development of crystallized intelligence. In individuals characterized as sensitive toward environment, the range of perceived stimuli seems to be broader and the ability to differentiate between exposed stimuli and experienced situations higher when compared. In individuals sensitive toward environment, crystallized intelligence may develop to a higher extent than in individuals representing opposite temperament characteristics.

Our data regarding the temperament–intelligence relationship contribute to the increase of doubts rather than enlarging the number of clear-cut findings. Extensive studies are needed to arrive closer to the understanding of links between temperament and intelligence if they exist at all, as we believe they do.

REFERENCES

Binet, A. (1911). Nouvelles recherches sur la mesure du niveau ntellectuel chez les enfants d'école. *L'Année Psychologique, 17*, 145–201.

Cattell, R. B. (1971). *Abilities: Their structure, growth, and action.* New York: Houghton Mifflin.

Drwal, R. L., & Brzozowski, P. (1995). Zrewidowany Inwentarz Osobowoœci H. J. Eysencka (EPQ–R) [Revised H. J. Eysenck Personality Questionniare (EPQ–R)]. In R. L. Drwal (Ed.), *Adaptacja kwestionariuszy osobowoœci* [Adaptation of personality inventories] (pp. 109–131). Warszawa: Wydawnictwo Naukowe PWN.

Eysenck, H. J. (1979). *The structure and measurement of intelligence.* Berlin: Springer-Verlag.

Eysenck, H. J. (1983). Stress, disease, and personality: The 'inoculation effect'. In C. L. Cooper (Ed.), *Stress research* (pp. 121–131). London: Wiley.

Eysenck, H. J., & Eysenck, M. W. (1985). *Personality and individual differences: A natural science approach.* New York: Plenum.

Guilford, J. P. (1967). *The nature of human intelligence.* New York: McGraw-Hill.

Guilford, J. S., Zimmerman, W. S., & Guilford, J. P. (1976). *The Guilford-Zimmerman Temperament Survey handbook: Twenty-five years of research and application.* San Diego, CA: Edits Publishers.

Hunt, J. M. V. (1969). *The challenge of incompetence and poverty: Papers on the role of early education.* Urbana: University of Illinois Press.

Jaworowska, A., & Szustrowa, T. (1991). *Podręcznik do Testu Matryc Ravena. Wersja Standard* [Manual of the Raven's Matrices Test: Standard version]. Warszawa: Pracownia Testów Psychologicznych PTP.

Jensen, A. R. (1993). Why is reaction time correlated with psychometric *g*? *Current Directions in Psychological Science, 7,* 53–56.

Kagan, J. (1983). Stress and coping in early development. In N. Garmezy & M. Rutter (Eds.), *Stress, coping and development in children* (pp. 191–216). New York: McGraw-Hill.

Ledzińska, M. (1996). *Przetwarzanie informacji przez uczniów o zróżnicowanym poziomie zdolności a ich postśpy szkolne* [Information processing in pupils differing in intelligence level and school achievements]. Warszawa: Oficyna Wydawnicza Wydziaču Psychologii Uniwersytetu Warszawskiego.

Lewowicki, T. (1975). *Psychologiczne różnice indywidualne a osiągnięcia uczniów* [Psychological individual differences and pupils' achievements]. Warszawa: Wydawnictwa Szkolne i Pedagogiczne.

Matczak, A., Jaworowska, A., Szustrowa, T., & Ciechanowicz, A. (1995). *Bateria Testów APIS–Z(P): Podręcznik* [Battery of APIS–Z(P) Tests: Manual]. Warszawa: Pracownia Testów Psychologicznych PTP.

Nebylitsyn, V. D. (1972). *Fundamental properties of the human nervous system.* New York: Plenum.

Piotrowska, A., & Strelau, J. (1994, July). *Temperament and intellectual abilities: Persons in the twenties/thirties as compared with persons in the forties/fifties.* Paper presented at the XXIII International Congress of Applied Psychology, Madrid.

Robinson, D. L. (1985). How personality relates to intelligence test performance: Implications for a theory of intelligence, aging research and personality assessment. *Personality and Individual Differences, 6,* 203–216.

Robinson, D. L. (1993). The EEG and intelligence: An appraisal of methods and theories. *Personality and Individual Differences, 15,* 695–716.

Robinson, D. L. (1996). Intelligence differences: Neural transmission errors or cerebral arousability? *Kybernetes, 25,* 407–424.

Schönpflug, W. (1986). Effort regulation and individual differences in effort expenditure. In G. Robert, J. Hockey, A. W. K. Gaillard, & M. G. H. Coles (Eds.), *Energetics and human information processing* (pp. 271–283). Dordrecht, The Netherlands: Martinus Nijhoff Publishers.

Spearman, C. E. (1904). General intelligence objectively determined and measured. *American Journal of Psychology, 15,* 201–293.

Stankov, L., & Roberts, R. D. (1997). Mental speed is not the 'basic' process of intelligence. *Personality and Individual Differences, 22,* 69–84.

Sternberg, R. J. (1985). *Beyond IQ: A triarchic theory of human intelligence.* Cambridge, England: Cambridge University Press.

Strelau, J. (1977). Behavioral mobility versus flexibility and fluency of thinking: An empirical test of the relationship between temperament and abilities. *Polish Psychological Bulletin, 8,* 75–82.

Strelau, J. (1983). *Temperament, personality, activity.* London: Academic Press.

Strelau, J. (1992). Temperament and giftedness in children and adolescents. In F. Monks & W. Peters (Eds.), *Talent for the future: Social and personality development of gifted children* (pp. 73-86). Assen/Maastricht, The Netherlands: Van Gorcum.

Strelau, J. (1994). The concepts of arousal and arousability as used in temperament studies. In J. E. Bates & T. D. Wachs (Eds.), *Temperament: Individual differences at the interface of biology and behavior* (pp. 117–141). Washington, DC: American Psychological Association.

Strelau, J. (1995). Temperament and stress: Temperament as a moderator of stressors, emotional states, coping, and costs. In C. D. Spielberger & I. G. Sarason (Eds.), *Stress and emotion: Anxiety, anger, and curiosity* (Vol. 15, pp. 215–254). Washington, DC: Taylor & Francis.

Strelau, J. (1996). The regulative theory of temperament: Current status. *Personality and Individual Differences, 20,* 131–142.

Strelau, J. (1998). *Temperament: A psychological perspective.* New York: Plenum.

Strelau, J., & Angleitner, A. (1994). Cross-cultural studies on temperament: Theoretical considerations and empirical studies based on the Pavlovian Temperament Survey. *Personality and Individual Differences, 16,* 331–342.

Strelau, J., & Zawadzki, B. (1993). The Formal Characteristics of Behaviour–Temperament Inventory (FCB–TI): Theoretical assumptions and scale construction. *European Journal of Personality, 7,* 313–336.

Strelau, J., & Zawadzki, B. (1995). The Formal Characteristics of Behavior–Temperament Inventory (FCB–TI): Validity studies. *European Journal of Personality, 9,* 207–229.

Teplov, B. M. (1964). Problems in the study of general types of higher nervous activity in man and animals. In J. A. Gray (Ed.), *Pavlov's typology: Recent theoretical and experimental developments from the Laboratory of B. M. Teplov* (pp. 3–153). Oxford, England: Pergamon Press.

Thurstone, L. L. (1943). *Primary mental abilities.* Chicago: The University of Chicago Press.

Thurstone, L. L. (1953). *Examiner manual for the Thurstone Temperament Schedule* (2nd ed.). Chicago: Science Research Associates.

Vygotsky, L. S. (1960). *The development of higher mental functions.* Moscow: Izdatelstvo APN RSFSR.

Zuckerman, M. (1994). Behavioral expressions and biosocial bases of sensation seeking. New York: Cambridge University Press.

5

Issues in the Definition and Measurement of Abilities

David F. Lohman
The University of Iowa

Probably the greatest satisfaction I obtain from academic life is the experience of opening the door on a domain I had neglected and discovering new systems of ideas that, on reflection, help me think about more familiar ideas in new ways. In the 1970s, the door opened on information processing and then later on the broader discipline of cognitive psychology. Through the years, other doors have opened on anthropology, philosophy, history, and most recently on evolutionary biology. I make no claim, of course, to discovery. All that I have seen has been seen more clearly before. In fact, every idea I have had about human abilities is probably contained, in some form, in one of the thousands of journal articles, books, and book chapters devoted to the topic. Indeed, one lesson to this tale is that, after many months of reading and thinking about the implications of evolutionary biology for a theory of abilities, I discovered that Dick Snow had been there ahead of me. Nevertheless, it is useful—even necessary—to cross over periodically to an unfamiliar domain in order to gain perspective on one's own domain. This chapter, then, is the report of one journey of this sort.

More specifically, in this chapter I discuss different approaches to the definition and measurement of abilities. Following Mayr's (1982) summary of the biological sciences, I begin by distinguishing between population thinking and essentialist thinking. Variation and diversity are the stuff of population thinking; categories and typologies are the stuff of essentialist thinking. Population thinking characterized much of Darwin's work in evolutionary biology, particularly the Darwin–Wallace theory of natural selection (see Darwin, 1859; Wallace, 1858), and later Galton's (1869, 1883) studies of the inheritance of mental and physical traits. Essentialist thinking, on the other hand, has guided experimentalists in both biology and psychology. Attempts to reduce these two types of thinking to one are briefly reviewed. I conclude this section by arguing for the legitimacy of a differential psychology that cannot be reduced to (or explained by) experimental psychology. I then discuss four ways in which the concept of ability has been defined in differential psychology: (a) as a latent trait inferred from patterns of individual differences across tasks, (b) as level of performance on a particular task or class of tasks, (c) as a latent cognitive process inferred from within-subject patterns of performance across trials within a task, and (d) as an affordance—effectivity relation (i.e., a joint property of the union of person and environment). I show how both population thinking and essentialist thinking have differentially influenced advocates of each of these definitions of abilities. I conclude with recommendations about how to best conceptualize and measure human abilities.

WORLD VIEWS

Scholars trained in different disciplines conceptualize problems differently. Sometimes the differences in perspective and method are profound, as between the humanist and the radical empiricist. In other cases, the differences are more subtle, as, for example, when a psychologist steeped in developmental theory sees abrupt, stage-like transitions in the history of cognitive science (e.g., Gardner, 1985) or when a psychologist steeped in the categorical modes of thinking that dominate experimental psychology attempts to explain individual difference constructs of personality psychology (e.g., Cantor, 1990). I have come to believe that these general habits of thought, these characteristic ways of perceiving and organizing experience (or "world views," Pepper, 1942) are not just interesting epiphenomena in the grand show of science but are more like foundational elements that critically shape the sorts of theories we build—and, more importantly—cause conflict among those who adhere to different foundational assumptions within and between disciplines. Theories of human abilities are the product not only of data and argument but also of the personal proclivities and professional experiences of theorists; of their beliefs about what science is and how it should be conducted; and of the larger social, political, and religious themes that form the fabrics of the cultures in which they live (Lohman, 1997).

There is also the issue of the extent to which our methods—particularly the statistical methods we use—distort and mislead us. David Bakan (1973), Louis Guttman (1971), and many others have commented on this aspect of our enterprise. Statistical and psychometric methods both reflect and help perpetuate different modes of thinking. Indeed, I will argue that differential psychology requires a style of thinking quite unlike the style of thinking that serves us well in the physical sciences and in much of experimental psychology. At the outset, it is important to note that I am not arguing that one style of thinking is better than the other, or that individuals can be typed by the style they prefer. Indeed, most people move back and forth between these two ways of thinking. I claim, however, that the essentialist or typological way of thinking is easier, seems to conform more naturally with our cognitive architecture, and thus both developmentally and historically precedes probabilistic thinking.

ESSENTIALIST VERSUS POPULATION THINKING

In psychology—as in biology—one of the more pervasive differences in conceptual style is between essentialist or typological thinking and population or stochastic thinking. The distinction is suggested in the cognitive-style literature. Messick and Kogan (1963) discussed a style that they called *compartmentalization*, which refers to the tendency to isolate ideas and objects into discrete and relatively rigid categories. The obverse is a willingness to tolerate fuzzy concepts that they linked to ideational fluency, rather than to population or stochastic thinking as in this discussion.

Essentialism can be traced back to Plato, and surely earlier for anyone who cared to look. Objects in the world are but imperfect shadows of more perfect forms, ideas, or essences. These forms are more permanent and therefore more real than the particular objects through which we conceive and deduce them: Man is more permanent than Dave or Bob or Pat; the circle that I draw will someday fade but the form *circle* endures forever. Importantly, then, variation among category members reflects error or imperfection in manifestation of the essential form. The philosophy of essentialism has fitted well with the conceptual structure of the physical sciences. Carbon atoms are indeed alike; those that differ define new isotopes or ions (i.e., a new category). Closely linked with this type of categorical thinking is a deterministic (as opposed to probabilistic) view of causation. Essentialist thinkers typically work in worlds in which causal sequences may be described as "If A, then B."

In psychology, those trained in experimental methods seem most comfortable with essentialist modes of thought. This is particularly evident in attempts of experimentalists to explain individual differences. Most, of course, do not get beyond the notion of individual differences as error and, thus, see no need to explain them. But for those who do, there is usually (a) an attempt to impose a typology of some sort on the data (thus, there is not one type of person in the world but two types that, on closer inspection, are further subdivided, ad infinitum, as in stage-theoretic models of development) and (b) an attempt to escape from the unstable bog of relative measurement onto the seemingly firmer ground of absolute measurement. For example, in their early publication in which they advocated an information-processing approach to the study of human intelligence, Hunt, Frost, and Lunneborg (1973) claimed: "The gist of our argument is that intelligence should be determined by absolute measures of aspects of a person's information processing capacity rather than by measures of his performance relative to the performance of others in a population" (pp. 119–120). Hunt's research program (see, e.g., Hunt, 1977) then sought methods for measuring what were thought to be structural or mechanistic, information-free mental processes, typically on the absolute scale of response latency.

When confronted with questions of style or strategy, the experimentalist prefers an explanation that emphasizes qualitative rather than quantitative differences. This was clearly evident in the early work of Cooper (1982) on individual differences in visual comparison processes. Cooper identified two types of individuals: those who appeared to use a holistic strategy for comparing forms and those who appeared to use an analytic strategy. A similar preference for qualitative differences may be observed among more experimentally oriented personality theorists. Most of these typologies do not survive close inspection. In the case of Cooper's typology, it was, paradoxically, one of Hunt's graduate students who unmasked the continuum (see Agari, 1979).

Probabilistic thinking about populations takes the opposite tack. Population thinkers stress the uniqueness of each individual. There is thus no typical individual; mean values are abstractions. Rather, variation is the most interesting characteristic of natural populations. Moreover this variation is multi-dimensional. Causal sequences are less mechanistic and more stochastic: If A, then B, but with probability C. Indeed, C may be perceptible only at the population level. Essentialists find this sort of thinking particularly difficult. Who has not heard an essentialist argument against the connection between smoking and lung cancer that rests on a single, octogenarian counter example?

Differential psychology is, of course, grounded in population or probabilistic thinking. As such, it is more concerned with quantitative than qualitative differences and with relative rather than absolute scales of measurement. Because the differentialist is often criticized for a reliance on relative measurement, he sometimes looks wistfully at the absolute measurements that his experimental colleagues have at their disposal. However, I believe that this envy is misplaced; measures of the relative fit between persons and situations is what his discipline is all about. Thus, even when absolute measures (such as latency) are available, it is information about the relative standing of individuals that is his special concern. This brings me closer to the heart of the matter; that is differing conceptions of personality and ability constructs, particularly the latter.

PARTS OF SPEECH

One way to understand the source of differing conceptions of abilities is to examine how terms that denote abilities are used linguistically. This is another of those ideas I was sure that I had discovered but later found clearly presented in a text I know that I had read years ago (in this case, Butcher's [1968] classic). Perhaps I merely reconstructed a new version of these arguments from the kernel of a vaguely remembered idea. Or perhaps, as Dennett (1995) argued, it is not so much that some minds think alike as it is that we work within a design space that favors certain moves and discourages others. Any serious consideration of the term *ability* will eventually have to consider whether it is a noun, an adjective, an adverb, or even a verb. Although this is a much more limited undertaking than Sternberg's (1990) discussion of the metaphors that underpin different theories of intelligence, there are interesting points of convergence.

The essentialists among us—that is, those who more strongly identify with experimental rather than differential psychology—have sought to explain abilities in terms of the size or capacity of working memory, the speed or efficiency of information transmission within the system, or the attentional resources at the individual's disposal. In this way, intelligence is sometimes viewed as a reflection of a structural difference in information processing systems. Hunt (1983) asked, "What does intelligence do?" Although the question and the process view it entails seem to invite the use of verbs, the measurement procedures used at best invoke the adverbs and adjectives—larger working memories, faster processing, less proactive inhibition. In a similar, but more abstract vein, Cronbach (1977) claimed, "Intelligence is not a thing; it is a style of work" (p. 275). In other words, it is a way of characterizing how something is done, which inevitably involves a value judgment. To reason intelligently implies a different way of solving problems. So, for example, when a computer wins chess games by virtue of the brute force of computational algorithms, we do not rate its performance as particularly intelligent.

Those steeped in traditional differential methods, on the other hand, seem most comfortable with the view that intelligence is best viewed as an adjective that describes a person or a particular class of behaviors (Anastasi, 1986). Unlike some personality and stylistic traits, it is a marked adjective: There is clearly a positive valence associated with being intelligent and a negative valence with being unintelligent. The adjectival use of the word also conforms well to the notion that—like beauty or tallness—intelligence is a relative concept. Who is considered intelligent depends on the range of intellectual competence in the group; the behaviors that are considered as intelligent depend on the demands and affordances of the environment or, more generally, of the culture (Sternberg, 1985).

Ability theorists thus disagree on whether *intelligence* is best characterized as a noun (e.g., a structural property of the brain or a trait possessed in a certain amount), an adjective (e.g., identifying certain types of people), a verb (e.g., denoting certain varieties of cognition or action), or an adverb (e.g., describing the qualities of cognition or behavior, such as its speed or efficiency). Those who search for those cognitive processes and knowledge structures that generate behavior labeled intelligent often assume that some nouns will be needed, but they place the most emphasis on verbs and adverbs (i.e., how and how well one thinks). Those who study social and cultural variations in intelligence generally assume that an adjective is needed. Sternberg's (1985) componential and contextual subtheories nicely capture this divergence. In contrast, trait-based theories of personality characterize the domain as a collection of adjectives, and when traits are thought to inhere in the individual, as nouns. The interesting question, however, is whether personality can also be understood using verbs and adverbs. Some (e.g., Cantor, 1990) see this as the wave of the future; others (e.g., Cervone, 1991) are less sanguine about the possibility of a rapprochement between the experimental and differential approaches. If recent attempts to apply cognitive theory to ability constructs are any guide, then bridges will be more difficult to build than initially seems possible. However, careful attention to issues that were insufficiently addressed in ability-process research—particularly those issues concerning the definition and measurement of constructs—will surely improve the changes of meaningful progress.

DEFINITIONS OF ABILITY

Ability as Domain Referenced

Carroll (1993) noted that "although the term *ability* is in common usage in both everyday talk and in scientific discussions, its precise definition is seldom explicated or even considered" (p. 3). Indeed, some historians of science believe that scientific progress consists not only in the development of new concepts but also in the repeated refinement of definitions by which old concepts are articulated. "Particularly important," said Mayr (1982), "is the occasional recognition that a more or less technical term, previously believed to characterize a certain concept, was in reality used for a mixture of two or more concepts" (p. 43). I believe that such confusion attends discussions of ability, particularly intelligence.

I suspect that many of the would-be bridge builders between the separate kingdoms of personality theory and ability theory have failed because they assumed that one could build from the *terra firma* of ability theory into the less firmly grounded realm of personality theory. In brief, the problem is not that the supposedly *terra firma* of ability theory is *terra incognita* as much as it is *terrae firmae*. In plain English, the problem is that the term *ability* is used in quite different ways by many, but especially by experimental and differential psychologists. Attempts to link ability with personality will fare no better than attempts to link experimental and differential psychology unless we attend more carefully to the ways in which these terms are used and measured.

Ability as Trait

The first and by far most popular way in which ability is defined is as a latent trait inferred from consistencies in patterns of individual differences across tasks. In the limiting case of a single task, the latent variable is synonymous with the true score of classical test theory. When scores on multiple tasks are considered simultaneously, the latent trait is estimated from the covariation in individual differences across tasks[1]. Individual differences are thus central to this definition of ability. Further, the approach emphasizes transferable competencies, something often overlooked in task- and process-based definitions of ability.

---

[1] Spearman's (1904) original formulation seemed closer to this conception than later formulations in which error was treated as a purely random variable rather than as nongeneralizable individual difference variance (as in modern generalizability theory). Indeed, the notion of error as noise usually rests on an essentialist mode of thinking.

What Darwin (1859) discovered, Galton (1869) applied to humankind, and Pearson (1896) and Spearman (1904) showed how to measure, was the importance of relative standing within the group. Although the trait definition is grounded in population thinking, it does not have much to say about the environment. Indeed, context effects, if they are included at all, tend to be treated as moderator variables in such models. In other words, contextual factors merely limit the scope of generalizations about abilities that can be made—across types of stimuli (Is there more than g?) across ages (Does the structure or meaning of intelligence vary across the lifespan?), across treatments (Are there aptitude by treatment interactions?), or even cultures (Does the meaning of the construct vary across cultures?) This lopsided focus on the individual opens the door for the next definition of ability, which focuses on the task rather than on individual differences.

Ability as Task Performance

Ability is also sometimes defined in terms of performance on a particular task or class of tasks. For example, in the report of the Committee on Ability Testing of the U.S. National Research Council, Widgor and Garner (1982) defined ability as "how well a person can perform a task when trying to do his or her best" (p. 25). There are thus as many different abilities as there are tasks that can be administered and on which performance can somehow be observed and scored. Because everyone could fail to accomplish a task, or could succeed at it, individual differences are not a necessary component of this definition of ability. Some efforts to export the tasks of experimental psychology into differential psychology use task-based definitions of ability. For example, some researchers use measures of overall performance on the Shepard-Metzler (1971) rotation task as a measure of "mental rotations ability." This extreme focus on particular tasks is thus diametrically opposed to Spearman's (1927) principle of the "indifference of the indicator."

If items (or tasks) can be ordered such that performance can be described by a unidimensional scale, then *ability* can be defined more precisely—for example, as the point at which the probability of a correct response is 50% (Carroll, 1990; Thurstone, 1937), or at which the function relating probability of a correct response to response latency intersects a particular latency value (Lohman, 1989). Although such approaches sharpen the measurement of ability within a particular task, they do not address the issue of consistency in performance across tasks.

In educational measurement, criterion-referenced (or domain-referenced) tests exemplify this definition of abilities. Linn and Gronlund (1995), for example, defined a criterion-referenced test as "a test designed to provide a measure of performance that is interpretable in terms of a clearly defined and delimited domain of learning tasks" (p. 16). One can move from ability as performance on one task to ability as performance on many tasks only if the domain of tasks is clearly defined. Generalizability theory provides a particularly powerful method for doing this (see Kane, 1982). Educators are not the only ones who define abilities in this way. An employer, for example, is often more interested in whether the prospective employees can perform certain tasks at a given level rather than in their relative standing. The task-based definition is thus an attempt to escape the relativistic world of norm-referenced, trait-based interpretations of test scores. It is thus a retreat from population thinking. The focus is no longer on person variance but on the task and the behaviors exhibited by the test taker. It is no accident that this type of interpretation was advanced by a psychologist steeped in behavioral learning theory (i.e., Glaser). However, things are often what they seem to be. Scores on domain-referenced tests are rarely interpretable without at least some reference to the behavior of others on the test. These implicit norms are embedded in the ascription rules (Rorer & Widiger, 1983) that test interpreters use to make sense of even absolute measurements. Thus, as one wit put it, "Behind every criterion there lurks a norm."

Ability as Process

Whereas ability is inferred from the comparison of one individual's performance to that of other individuals (definition 1) or to an external standard (definition 2), *process* is inferred from the comparison of performance in one condition to performance in another condition. Because processes occur within individuals, the inference of process is not grounded in individual differences. Because of this, the measurement of process seemed to offer not only an insight into how abilities operate, but also an escape from the relativistic world of traditional ability testing. Although I am still persuaded by the need for process-like analyses of ability constructs, I am less sanguine about the utility of the process measures derived from such analyses.

For example, consider the much-studied mental rotation task. In this task, subjects are shown two stimuli that differ in orientation. They must determine if the two stimuli can be brought into congruence. Shepard and Metzler (1971) proposed that subjects confronted with such problems form mental images of the stimuli, rotate one of these images the required distance, compare the two images, and then respond. Shepard and Metzler tested their model by regressing angular separation between stimuli on response latency. The slope of this function estimates the rate at which stimuli are rotated. The expectation has been that the slope parameter would provide a relatively pure measure of spatial ability. However, if anything, it is the intercept parameter that shows consistent correlations with other variables; correlations for the slope vary from highly negative to moderately positive (see Lohman, 1994). Such results have dampened enthusiasm for using the estimated rate of rotation as a measure of spatial ability but have not seriously challenged the fundamental assumptions of methods that rely on this sort of task decomposition.

To understand why component scores and other process measures are not what they seem to be, imagine a simple person-by-item data matrix whose entries X_{pi} represent the scores of n_p persons on n_i items or trials. Figure 5.1 shows how the variability in scores may be partitioned into three sources: the person source, the item source, and the residual. The person source represents variability in row means, that is, in the average performance of each person on the task. This would be the score ordinarily reported on a mental test. It thus represents the ability construct we hope better to understand. The item source represents variability in column means, that is, in average differences in item (or trial) difficulty. In the rotation example, a large fraction of this variability can be attributed to the amount of rotation required. The residual is composed of the person-by-item interaction and other disturbances. In the language of reliability theory, it is the error variance. Individual differences in slope scores help

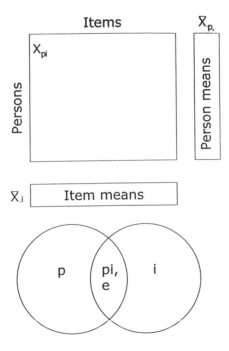

FIG. 5.1. Top panel shows a schematic of the basic person by item data matrix, with entries X_{pi}. Variation in row means ($\overline{X}_{p.}$) captures differences among individuals in overall performance, whereas variation in column means ($\overline{X}_{.i}$) captures differences in item or trial difficulties. Component or process scores capture neither of these sources of variation but instead salvage some portion of the p x i interaction, as shown in the Venn diagram in the bottom panel.

salvage variance from this residual component. However, process scores defined by within-person contrasts of any sort do not decompose and therefore cannot help explain the typically much larger person-variance component. In fact, mean scores for each person that are reflected in the person variance component will generally show high correlations with the intercept of the regression model, which is why the intercept often shows interesting and significant correlations with reference abilities, whereas component scores show inconsistent correlations with such measures (see Lohman, 1994).

The problem that confronts us is actually much more complex than this simple two-way classification suggests. Personality and style variables complicate the picture. Figure 5.2 shows a modified version of Cattell's (1966) covariation chart: persons by items (nested within tasks) by occasions (or situations). Differential psychologists typically worry about person main effects (or covariation of person main effects across several tasks). Experimental psychologists are less uniform. Those who follow an information-processing paradigm worry about variation over trials with a particular task. Situationalists, however, worry more about covariation of either task main effects (e.g., delay versus no delay of reinforcement) or person main effects across occasions. They typically emphasize the magnitude of situation effects relative to the magnitude of person effects. Developmentalists do the opposite. Then there are those who worry about interactions. The point is that any rapprochement between experimental and differential psychology has many dimensions, not just two. Person × situation is not the same as person times items within task. The bottom line is this: Just because a construct has the same name in two different literatures does not mean that it refers to the same—or even correlated—aspects

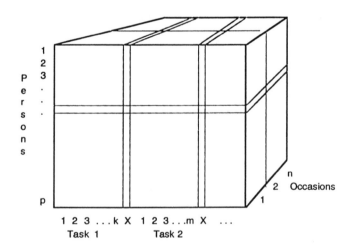

FIG. 5.2. A person by task (with items nested within tasks) by occasion data matrix.

of variation. A more systematic accounting of which aspect of variability is represented by different constructs may help us keep track of constructs and keep in line our expectations for relationships among them.

Thus, in my opinion, the attempt to define ability by individual differences in within-subject component or process scores is unlikely to succeed. As noted, process-like scores generally do not capture much of the interesting individual differences on tasks (which is not to deny that they will sometimes show interesting and replicable correlations with other variables). Furthermore, like task-based definitions of ability, the process approach emphasizes absolute rather than relative measurement. The process explanations it offers are most informative when they uncover qualitative rather than quantitative differences between individuals. Therefore, the primary contribution of an information-processing type of analysis of a task or problematic situation lies in the information such analyses provide about how subjects understood the situation or solved the task. Such analyses contribute not new scores but new methods for addressing fundamental questions about construct validity. Returning to the mental rotation example, such analyses are helpful if they can tell us if subjects are indeed mentally rotating stimuli or are instead engaging in other strategies that might compromise the interpretation of their scores as measures of the construct we call spatial ability.

Ability as Situated

The fourth and last definition of *ability* tries to bring in a vastly more relativistic definition of the stimulus environment. In other words, ability is seen not as the relative standing along some cognitive dimension of an individual within a group (definition 1), of an individual's performance relative to some well-defined domain of tasks or performances (definition 2) or even of facility in performing certain types of cognitive processes (definition 3), but rather ability is a joint property of the union of person and situation.

Snow (1994) gave the most articulate statement of this perspective. He began by borrowing Gibson's (1979) concept of affordances to describe person-situation connections:

> The affordances of a situation are what it offers the person—what it provides or furnishes, for good or ill. The term implies a complementarity of person and situation, as in an ecological niche. A niche is a place or setting that is appropriate for a person. Affordances thus reflect the invitation, demand, or opportunity structure of a situation for those persons who are tuned or prepared to receive them. (p. 28)

Thus, particular affordances invite particular actions. In Gibson's terminology, these actions are called effectivities. "Abilities," Snow concluded, "are properties of the union of person and environment that exhibit the opportunity structure of a situation and the effectivity structure of the person in taking advantage of the opportunities afforded for learning" (p. 31). There is thus a reciprocity, a dance, between person and situation. Change the demands or affordances of the situation and you change the apparent abilities of the person—which is the repeated demonstration of the Aptitude x Treatment Interaction (ATI) literature. Change the effectivity structure of the individual, and you also change the ability of the person--which is the repeated demonstration of the literature on the effects of schooling and culture on cognitive competence. But the match is always relative: Even when all are matched, some will be better matched than others; even when all are poorly matched, some will be less poorly matched than others. Indeed, as Snow (1994) noted and as Piaget (1954) demonstrated in his studies of children's errors, we can learn much about what abilities are by studying those cases where there is a clear mismatch between the inner environment of the individual and the outer environment.

Although this view of abilities seems to derive from current (see Greeno, Collins, & Resnick, 1996) and past (Gibson, 1979) theories of situated cognition, it is also fundamentally Darwinian. Long before Simon (1969) discussed the interface between inner and outer environments in terms of artifacts, Spencer (1873) concluded:

> Regarded under every variety of aspect, intelligence is found to consist in the establishment of correspondences between relations in the organism and relations in the environment; and the entire development of intelligence may be formulated in the progress of such correspondences. (p. 385)

However, Spencer saw both intelligence and environment through unidimensional glasses. Indeed, most discussions of human intelligence speak as if intelligence means superior adaptability in all environments. Those who escape this chapter of the flat earth society seem at best able to see environments as arrayed along a unidimensional scale from best to worst. A careful reading of Darwin shows greater subtlety:

> The meritocratic selector and the experimental reformer alike missed the point of Darwin's theory. The theory did not posit that *generally* superior creatures evolve. [Rather, Darwin was] concerned with fitness to survive in a *particular* ecology. To foster development of a wide variety of persons, then, one must offer a wide variety of environments. A social reform that would standardize the environment (whether to fit the average person, or the present elite, or the present proletariat) is inevitably procrustean, conservative, and self-limiting. (Cronbach & Snow, 1977, p. 11)

Although ability theorists have been guilty of ignoring situations, advocates of situated cognition have been guilty of the opposite fallacy. Indeed, some advocates wrote as if there were no consistent individual differences across situations. Transfer became "a problematic issue" for those who espoused a situated view of cognition (Greeno, Collins, & Resnick, 1996, p. 24). Because abilities may be defined as transferable knowledge and skill, an approach that finds transfer at best "problematic" seems unlikely to provide much insight into human abilities. What Snow (1994) did however, was to bring individual differences back into discussions of situated cognition. He did so in a way that goes considerably beyond early (and largely unsuccessful) attempts to define intelligence in terms of adaptability. Individuals perceive and create regularities across contexts that permit the application of old knowledge. Abilities thus allow "attunements to constraints and affordances that remain invariant across transformations of situations" (Greeno et al., 1996, p. 24).

THE UNIQUENESS OF DIFFERENTIAL PSYCHOLOGY

One of the more unfortunate consequences of the explosion of knowledge is that we rarely have time to step outside the narrow confines of our own domains to see what is happening in our neighbors' backyards. The same wars that have raged between experimental and differential psychology have also plagued biology. Experimentally oriented biologists (and their allies in the physical sciences) have scoffed at the observational-comparative methods of naturalists, paleontologists, and evolutionary biologists. Indeed, in philosophies of science written by physical scientists (or those who adulate their work), manipulative experiments are often referred to as the method of science. Yet, observation classification comparisons across individuals, groups, or time periods are all legitimate scientific methods:

> Observation led to the discovery of foreign faunas and floras and became the basis of biogeography; observation revealed the diversity of organic nature and led to the establishment of the Linnaean hierarchy and to the theory of common descent; observations led to the foundations of ethnology and ecology. Observation in biology has probably produced more insights than all experiments combined. (Mayr, 1982, p. 32)

The physical sciences have been eminently successful. They also rest securely in a categorical, typological mode of thinking that we humans seem to find congenial. They traffic in clear concepts with sharp boundaries that often can be easily mathematized. However, the organisms that the biological and psychological sciences attempt to understand are vastly more complex than the systems that physical scientists study. Every organism is the product of a history that dates back more than 3,000 million years. Indeed, generalizations in the biological and social sciences are almost invariably probabilistic. As one writer put it, "There is only one universal law in biology: All biological laws have exceptions." Similarly, in psychology, test-theoretic models of abilities are invariably probabilistic rather than deterministic (Lord & Novick, 1968). We never say "If A, then B," but rather "If A, then maybe B."

The Darwinian revolution in biological thought was rooted in a shift from typological to population thinking. Darwin (1859) realized that members of a species differed importantly from one another and that these individual differences were stuff on which natural selection operated. Without a doubt, the term *individual differences* or a synonym (*variation, diversity*) is the most frequently used term in chapter IV of *The Origin* wherein Darwin advances the theory of natural selection.

It was Galton, however, who first realized that such variation in human populations could be studied quantitatively. Quatelet, the Belgian astronomer and statistician whose work inspired Galton, believed that the mean of a distribution represented the ideal toward which nature was working; deviations from the mean were simply departures from this ideal.[2] Galton realized, however, that such distributions could be used to document the extent of variability of human biological and psychological characteristics on which natural selection operated. His interest, therefore, was not in the mean of the distribution but in its variance. (Galton, 1908, p. 305).

Spearman (1904) extended this sort of probabilistic thinking to the selection of tasks that served as indicators of intelligence. In doing so, he shed the categorical chains of thinking about thinking that haunted Binet to the end (see, e.g. Binet & Simon, 1916). But probabilistic thinking about populations cannot stand alone. Darwin was unable to get beyond a Lamarkian theory of inheritance of acquired characteristics because the black box of genetics had not yet been opened. After Wiseman and Fisher and most especially Watson and Crick, evolutionary biology has made great strides (Mayr, 1982). However, the new experimentally based theories of genetics have not and will not somehow supplant evolutionary biology. In much the same way, early theories of human intelligence were unable to move beyond a belief in innateness because they lacked a cognitive theory of learning and development. Experimental studies of thinking and its development thus usefully inform but do not dispense with the need for the study of human cognitive diversity. Sometimes I think we need to be reminded that differential psychology need not find justification outside itself. This does not mean that it should ignore the work of experimentalists. It means, rather, that differential psychology cannot be reduced to or explained away by experimental psychology.

PERSONALITY ABILITY CONNECTIONS

Thus far, I have tried to argue that the differences between experimental and differential psychology are real. The two are not only grounded in different world views, but also explain quite different aspects of variation. Differential psychology will be informed by—but cannot be reduced to—experimental cognitive psychology, neurology, or any other discipline. I have also tried to argue that the most profitable way to understand abilities is not to view them in as domain-referenced, as traits, or even on processes, but rather as Snow (1994)

---

[2] (see Hilts, 1973) Quatelet's conception of the mean as an ideal type endures in psychometrics as a *Platonic true score* (Lord & Novick, 1968).

suggested, as the joint property of person and context. This situated view of abilities has a number of interesting implications. For the purposes of this chapter, I note two that have direct implications for the ability–personality question that confronts us: the role of volition and the affective match between student and mentor.

One aspect of ability that was easily overlooked in trait definitions and the factor-analytic research it inspired is that all abilities are developed through extensive transactions with the physical and social environment. Indeed, the most important nonbiological factor in the development of what is called intelligence is formal schooling. The more schooling, the greater the gains in intelligence. Correspondingly, the single most important factor in predicting absolute gains in narrower ability and skill constructs is the amount of focused practice. In a recent review of expert performance, Ericsson and Charness (1994) concluded:

> Expert performance is predominantly mediated by acquired complex skills and physiological adaptations. For elite performers, supervised practice starts at very young ages and is maintained at a high level for more than a decade. The effects of extended, deliberate practice are more far-reaching than commonly believed. (p. 725)

Although Ericsson and Charness can rightly be accused of understating the influence of genetic factors, most ability theorists even more dramatically underestimate the cumulative effects of 5, 10, or even 20 years of guided practice. The important point here, however, is that one must not only be so fortunate as to have high quality instruction available throughout this long period, but one must somehow persist. And therein, I think, lies one of the chief connections between ability and personality. The central construct is volition.

Volition

Volition is an old term with a new lease on life. To do something of one's own volition means to do it "by one's own resources and sustained efforts, independent of external source or pressure" (Corno, 1993, p. 14). But early in this century, those who studied motivation claimed this was the proper purview of their discipline. Also, associations of volition with free will and other prescientific concepts from an earlier psychology led to the abandonment of this construct, at least by most U.S. psychologists.

The German psychologists Kuhl and Beckmann (1985) revived U.S. interest in volition with their theory of action control. Corno and Kanfer (1993) elaborated an educational view of this work. The basic idea is straightforward. Motivation, they say, concerns those affects and processes that initiate behavior, that move us from wishes to wants to actions. From a purely cognitive perspective, motivation is about goal setting. In Kuhl's (1994) view, it concerns the *predecisional* phase of action.

Volition, on the other hand, concerns those processes whereby one actively maintains an action, often in the face of competing action tendencies and negative affect. It is post decisional. Kuhl described several aspects of volition. Two of the most important are: (a) strategies for the protection of goals against competing goal tendencies, and (b) strategies for the management of affect, especially negative affect.

Corno and Kanfer (1993) listed a variety of volitional control strategies, many of which were designed to regenerate positive affect or to control negative affect. The development of high levels of competence requires extended, guided practice over many years. Thus, understanding how some are able to protect their goals and maintain their efforts to achieve these goals is a crucial topic for understanding the development of abilities. Many start the journey, but few finish it.

It is interesting that attempts to integrate modern work on volition into older stylistic or trait views of human performance use words like *responsibility*, *dependability*, and *conscientiousness* to describe the individuals who exhibit these characteristics in many situations. Yet these are the same trait labels that are included in definitions of intelligence that go beyond mere cognitive competence. For example, in the same 1921 symposium in which Thorndike gave the oft-cited definition of intelligence as "the power of good responses from the point of view of truth or fact" (p. 124), he also noted:

> It is probably unwise to spend much time in attempts to separate off sharply certain qualities of man, as his intelligence, from such emotional and vocational qualities as his interest in mental activity, carefulness, determination to respond effectively, persistence in his efforts to do so; or from his amount of knowledge; or from his moral or esthetic tastes. (p. 124)

The Nichols and Holland (1963) study of 10,000 National Merit Finalists in the United States showed this clearly. More than 150 measures were obtained on each participant, including personality and biographical data, and were correlated with 14 criteria of success in the first year of college. The best noncognitive predictor of first-year grades for these highly able students was a factor interpreted perseverance and motivation to succeed.

In order to learn how to persist, one must be challenged. Ultimately, then, attempts to develop transferable volition-control strategies are attempts to develop what used to be called character. But do volitional skills learned in one context transfer to other contexts? Certainly, the better-than-average performance of endurance athletes in college suggests that this might be the case. Such correlational evidence is open to multiple interpretations, however. Indeed, most modern students of transfer would agree with Thorndike and Woodworth (1901) that transfer is generally quite limited. Yet, in his 1913 text, Thorndike cautioned differently: "Some careless thinkers have rushed from the belief in totally general training to a belief that training is totally specialized" (p. 365). He then gave examples of "general" stimulus-response bonds:

Of special importance are the connections of neglect. Such bonds as "Stimuli to hunger save at meal times—neglect them"; "Sounds of boys at play save at playtime—neglect them"; "Ideas of lying down and closing one's eyes save at bed time—neglect them," and the like are the main elements of real fact meant by "power of attention," or "concentration" or "strength of will." In so far as a certain situation is bound to the response of neglect it is prevented from distracting one in general. (p. 419)

In modern jargon, Thorndike (1913) would agree with Kuhl (1994) that volitional control strategies are among the most transferable mental competencies.

The up side of volition is that it helps an individual maintain focus; the down side is that it may be hard to disengage these processes once they are firmly entrenched. There is a thin line between persistence and rigidity. Athletes ignore pain at their peril: the body can and does break down. Workers can persist at their tasks until work is all they have or until they burn out. Yet some do learn to manage the trade-off. Good athletes do learn to listen carefully to some pains while disregarding others. This higher level of adaptation is well captured in Sternberg's (1985) concept of "mental self-government."

Ericsson and Charness (1994) also noted that the attainment of high levels of competence requires more than persistent practice; it also requires the timely assistance and feedback of parents, teachers, coaches, and other mentors. Good teachers are not just good technicians. Long ago Augustine claimed that the most important thing a teacher brings to students is the example of character (Kevane, 1964). In other words, the mentoring process is greatly facilitated if the student cares for and identifies with the teacher. One cannot merely provide the external support and expect that learning will occur. There must be a match between the internal environment of the learner—that is, of the learners' abilities, needs, wishes, wants, and temperament—and the external environment—particularly of the mentoring provided. Using the ability-as-effectivity model, the outer environment offers various affordances for action that must mesh with the inner environment of the learner. And the nature of this coupling, this dance, changes over time. What works for one will not necessarily work for another. What works well at one time may be quite inappropriate later. What works over the short haul may not be best over the long run. Most importantly, the affordance-effectivity match has a large—and largely overlooked—affective component (see Snow, Corno, & Jackson, 1996).

SUMMARY

Snow (1994) argued that abilities are best understood as "properties of the union of person and environment that exhibit the opportunity structure of a situation and the effectivity structure of the person in taking advantage of the opportunities afforded for learning" (p. 31). Abilities are thus situated. Some persons succeed in learning in a given situation; they are in harmony with it.

Others do not, because they are not tuned to the opportunities the situation provides or to produce what it demands. Over the long haul, then, affect and volition are probably as important in the development of talent as are entry levels of ability and opportunities provided. The potential for great accomplishment may indeed be, in significant measure, a gift from one's ancestors. However, the attainment of domain expertise comes only after much learning and practice.

We work in Darwin's shadow—not the shadow of Wundt or Leeuwenhoek or Boaz or Ward. Although the disciplines that were given shape by these luminaries inform our efforts, in the end, the study of individual differences concerns the adaptation of individuals to the environments in which they are placed, they select, or they help mold (see Sternberg, 1985). Adaptation—or person-environment fit—occurs simultaneously and interactively along many dimensions that include not only the cognitive but also the affective and conative. Although there is nothing that prohibits the expansion of other definitions of ability to include these dimensions, only the situated definition demands—or, better, affords—their inclusion at the outset. Furthermore, a situated view of abilities brings us back to Darwin's (1859) insight that context matters. Therefore, as we go about the business of trying to forge alliances among the separate fiefdoms of what Cronbach (1957) dubbed the Holy Roman Empire of differential psychology, I suggest that we consider the advantages of defining ability in this way. I also suggest that, whatever definition we use, we be wary of the Siren call of essentialism and its cousin reductionism, even though advancing a discipline based on probabilistic thinking about populations means always sailing into the wind.

REFERENCES

Agari, T. T. (1979). *Individual differences in visual processing of nonverbal shapes.* Unpublished masters thesis. Seattle: University of Washington.

Anastasi, A. (1986). Intelligence as a quality of behavior. In R. Sternberg & D. Detterman (Eds.), *What is intelligence? Contemporary viewpoints on its nature and definition* (pp. 19–21). Norwood, NJ: Ablex.

Bakan, D. (1973). *On method.* San Francisco: Jossey-Bass.

Butcher, H. J. (1968). *Human intelligence: Its nature and assessment.* London: Methuen.

Cantor, N. (1990). From thought to behavior: "Having" and "doing" in the study of personality and cognition. *American Psychologist, 45,* 735–750.

Carroll, J. B. (1990). Estimating item and ability parameters in homogeneous tests with the person characteristic function. *Applied Psychological Measurement, 12,* 109–125.

Carroll, J. B. (1993). *Human cognitive abilities.* Cambridge, England: Cambridge University Press

Cattell, R. B. (1966). *Handbook of multivariate experimental psychology.* Chicago: Rand McNally.

Cervone, D. (1991). The two disciplines of personality psychology. [Review of *Handbook of personality: Theory and research*]. *Psychological Science, 2,* 371–377.

Cooper, L. A. (1982) Strategies for visual comparison and representation: Individual differences. In R. J. Sternberg (Ed.), *Advances in the psychology of human intelligence* (Vol. 1., pp. 77–124). Hillsdale, NJ: Lawrence Erlbaum Associates.

Corno, L. (1993). The best-laid plans: Modern conceptions of volition and educational research. *Educational Researcher, 22,* 14–22.

Corno, L., & Kanfer, R. (1993). The role of volition in learning and performance. *Review of Research in Education, 19,* 301–342.

Cronbach, L. J. (1957). The two disciplines of scientific psychology. *American Psychologist, 12,* 671–684.

Cronbach, L. J. (1977). *Educational Psychology* (3rd ed.). New York: Harcourt Brace Jovanovich.

Cronbach, L. J., & Snow, R. E. (1977). *Aptitudes and instructional methods: A handbook for research on interactions.* New York: Irvington.

Dennett, D. C. (1995). *Darwin's dangerous idea: Evolution and the meanings of life.* New York: Simon & Schuster.

Ericsson, K. A., & Charness, M. (1994). Expert performance: Its structure and acquisition. *American Psychologist, 49,* 725–747.

Gardner, H. (1985). *The mind's new science: A history of the cognitive revolution.* New York: Basic Books.

Gibson, J. J. (1979). *The ecological approach to visual perception.* Boston: Houghton Mifflin.

Greeno, J. G., Collins, A. M., & Resnick, L. (1996). Cognition and learning. In D. Berliner & R. Calfee (Eds.), *Handbook of educational psychology* (pp. 15–46). New York: Macmillan.

Guttman, L. (1971). Measurement as structural theory. *Psychometrika, 36,* 329–347.

Hunt, E. (1983). On the nature of intelligence. *Science, 219,* 141–146.

Hunt, E., Frost, N., & Lunneborg, C. (1973). Individual differences in cognition: A new approach to intelligence. In G. Bower (Ed.), *Advances in learning and motivation* (Vol. VII, pp. 87–122). New York: Academic Press.

Kane, M. T. (1982). A sampling model for validity. *Applied Psychological Measurement, 6,* 125–160.

Kuhl, J., & Beckmann, J. (Eds.). (1985). *Action control from cognition to behavior.* New York: Springer-Verlag.

Linn, R. L., & Gronlund, N. E. (1995). *Measurement and assessment in teaching* (7th ed.). Upper Saddle River, NJ: Merrill.

Lohman, D. F. (1989). Estimating individual differences in information processing using speed-accuracy models. In R. Kanfer, P. L. Ackerman, & R. Cudeck (Eds.), *Abilities, motivation, and methodology: The Minnesota symposium on learning and individual differences* (pp. 119–156). Hillsdale, NJ: Lawrence Erlbaum Associates.

Lohman, D. F. (1994). omponent scores as residual variation (or why the intercept correlates best). *Intelligence, 19,* 1–12.

Lord, F. M., & Novick, M. R. (1968). *Statistical theories of mental test scores.* Reading, MA: Addison-Wesley.

Mayr, E. (1982). *The growth of biological thought: Diversity, evolution, and inheritance.* Cambridge, MA: Harvard University Press.

Messick, S., & Kogan, N. (1963). Differentiation and compartmentalization in object-sorting measures of categorizing style. *Perceptual and Motor Skills, 16,* 47–51.

Nichols, R. C., & Holland, J. L. (1963). Prediction of the first year college performance of high aptitude students. *Psychological Monographs, 77* (no. 7), Whole Number 570.

Pepper, S. C. (1942). *World hypotheses, a study in evidence.* Berkeley: University of California Press.

Rorer, L. G., & Widiger, T. A. (1983). Personality structure and assessment. In M. Rosenzweig & L. Porter (Eds.), *Annual review of psychology* (Vol. 34, pp. 431–465). Palo Alto, CA: Annual Reviews.

Shepard, R. N., & Metzler, J. (1971). Mental rotation of three-dimensional objects. *Science, 171,* 701–703.

Snow, R. E. (1994). Abilities in academic tasks. In R. J. Sternberg & R. K. Wagner (Eds.), *Mind in context: Interactionist perspectives on human intelligence* (pp. 3–37). Cambridge, England: Cambridge University Press.

Snow, R. E., Corno, L., & Jackson, D. (1996). Individual differences in affective and conative functions. In D. Berliner & R. Calfee (Eds.), *Handbook of Educational Psychology* (pp. 243–310). New York: Macmillan.

Spearman, C. E. (1904). "General intelligence" objectively determined and measured. *American Journal of Psychology, 15,* 201–293.

Spencer, H. (1873). *The principles of psychology* (2nd ed.). New York: D. Appleton and Company.

Sternberg, R. J. (1985). *Beyond IQ: A triarchic theory of human intelligence.* Cambridge, England: Cambridge University Press.

Sternberg, R. J. (1990). *Metaphors of mind: Conceptions of the nature of intelligence.* Cambridge, England: Cambridge University Press.

Thorndike, E. L. (1913). *Educational psychology: Vol. 2. The psychology of learning.* New York: Columbia University.

Thorndike, E. L. (1921). Intelligence and its measurement: A symposium. *Journal of Educational Psychology, 12,* 124–127.

Thorndike, E. L., & Woodworth, R. S. (1901). The influence of improvement in one mental function upon the efficiency of other functions. *Psychological Review, 8,* 247–261.

Thurstone, L. L. (1937). Ability, motivation, and speed. *Psychometrika, 2,* 49–254.

Widgor, A. K., & Garner, W. R. (Eds.). (1982). *Ability testing: Uses, consequences, and controversies. Part 1. Report of the Committee.* Washington, DC: National Academy Press.

6

Issues in the Measurement of Temperament and Character

Peter Borkenau
Martin-Luther University

The story of the measurement of temperament and character can be told in many different ways. I could talk here, for instance, about issues like nomothetic and idiographic measurement, or of dimensional and categorical models of personality and personality disorders. I do not do that. Rather, I talk about issues in the measurement of personality that are a consequence of the predominant use of judgmental data to measure nonability attributes of personality. In this context, I am going to use the terms "personality," and "temperament," and "character" interchangeably.

A major difference between measures of abilities and measures of personality is that the measurement of abilities is based on samples of relevant behavior collected under maximal-performance instructions, whereas measurement of personality is mostly based on questionnaires and rating scales; that is, on judgments of one's own or other target persons' personality and typical behavior. As far as personality is measured by judgmental instruments, it is left to the respondents: (a) how to understand the items, (b) what evidence to recollect in responding to the items, (c) how to form impressions from this retrieved evidence, and (d) which impressions to convey. This makes it worthwhile to study the personality judgment process in some detail to clarify the assets and liabilities of self-reports and ratings and to identify ways of how they might be improved.

PROBLEMS WITH SELF-REPORTS

A specific problem of self-reports is that they confound perceiver variance with target variance. For example, if respondents have a high self-report Extraversion score, it is unclear to which extent this reflects their extraverted behavior or an extraversion self-schema that may have little resemblance to their actual level of Extraversion. It is known from research on intelligence that the correlation between psychometric IQ and self-reported intelligence is moderate at best–that is, about .30–and that the correlation between self- and peer ratings of intelligence is not much higher (Borkenau & Liebler, 1993). This indicates a substantial proportion of perceiver and error variance in ratings of intelligence. Whereas this phenomenon is of minor importance for research on intelligence, the case is worse for personality research because the extent of perceiver variance remains unexplored, as self-reports are compared to nothing except other self-reports. If respondents report their personality attributes consistently across items as well as across time, the reliability of their self-reports will be high, independent of their validity.

RATINGS BY ACQUAINTANCES

One way to overcome these problems is to collect ratings by acquaintances, preferably ratings by several acquaintances. Ratings by at least two acquaintances allow an estimate to the extent that the same target conveys similar impressions to different observers. The variance in the judgements may then be decomposed into perceiver variance, target variance, perceiver–target interactions, and—in case of repeated measurements—error variance (Kenny & Albright, 1987). And, according to the Spearman–Brown formula (Spearman, 1910) that predicts the relation between number of independent measurements and the reliability of the composite score, it is possible to increase the target variance by aggregating ratings across judges. Given this simple but important and well-known rule uncovered by Spearman, it is surprising how rarely aggregated peer ratings are used in personality research. Researchers like Funder (1995) and Hofstee (1994), who—for these reasons—advocate the use of peer ratings instead of self-reports, are probably still a minority.

Admittedly, sometimes outside observers lack the necessary information to form accurate impressions of a target person's trait level. This may occur if the judge does not have plenty of information on the target person's personality and if the construct under study refers to the very private, nonobservable world of the target person. Evidence shows, however, that attributes that are inaccurately judged by strangers may be much more accurately judged by close acquaintances. For example, for a sample of 100 targets, Borkenau and Liebler (1993) collected self-ratings of the Big Five, ratings by close acquaintances, and stranger ratings based on a 90-second videotaped sequence in which the targets read a standard text. We replicated the finding of previous studies that self–stranger agreement is particularly low for Emotional Stability (r =.11), probably because individual differences in that trait are difficult to observe in experimental settings. But the agreement between self-ratings and partner ratings of Emotional Stability was much higher (r = .45), although self-ratings and partner ratings had to be provided independently under the experimenter's supervision. It thus seems that with increasing acquaintance, knowledgeable informants are able to provide moderately accurate judgments even of traits that are difficult to observe.

Obviously, a correlation of r = .45 is not impressively high. If one subscribes to the view that validity correlations have to be squared, the self-rating and the partner rating would share 20% of their variance. And if one conceives of self-ratings and partner ratings as observable variables that reflect a common latent construct—that is, the target persons' trait level—45% of the variance in the ratings was accounted for by individual differences in the target persons' trait level. But even then, half of the variance would be unaccounted for. Why?

RATINGS BY STRANGERS

The sources of agreement and disagreement in ratings of personality can be profitably studied by investigating strangers' ratings of actual persons. Because for most personality attributes, self–stranger agreement is lower than the agreement between self-ratings and ratings by close acquaintances (Paunonen, 1989), ratings by strangers are not useful in any direct hunt for high validity coefficients. An attractive feature of ratings by strangers is that one can control the information that is available to the judges. One can also study the effects of extent and overlap of information on the consensus among strangers and on self–other agreement.

If the information that is available to the judges can be controlled, models of the judgment process can be tested empirically. I find two models particularly illuminating: Funder's (1995) Realistic Accuracy Model (RAM) and Kenny's (1994) Weighted Average Model (WAM). I describe these two models and summarize relevant research with a certain—indeed, quite heavy—bias in favor of my own research.

Funder's (1995) RAM is based on Brunswik's (1956) lens model. Funder suggested that personality traits should be conceived as latent attributes that are correlated with observable cues. Judges may perceive these observable cues and may use them to infer the target person's personality. According to RAM, perceivers form accurate impressions of a personality attribute if four conditions are met:

1. the attribute is observable in principle; that is, the latent personality attribute is correlated with observable cues;

2. the perceiver is exposed to the relevant diagnostic information; that is, the relevant observable cues are available to the perceiver;

3. the relevant and available cues are detected by the perceiver; that is, the perceiver is sensitive to the relevant information; and

4. in forming a personality impression of the target, the perceiver uses the detected cues in an appropriate way; that is, cue utilization matches cue validity.

Because accurate judgments can only be expected if all four prerequisites are met, Funder suggested a multiplicative rule to predict accuracy from these four process variables, that is:

accuracy = relevance x availability x detection x utilization.

I now discuss the four RAM process variables in more detail.

Relevance. The relevance of manifest cues refers to differences among personality traits in their relation to manifest behavior. Thus, it is tantamount to the observability of a personality attribute under optimal conditions. For example, Extraversion refers to directly observable behavior, whereas Agreeableness is more strongly related to the intention to meet other persons' needs. People's intentions may be inferred from their behavior but an inference requires observation of the behavior over longer time periods. Consequently, Extraversion is more observable than Agreeableness. More generally, the observability of a personality attribute is affected by: (a) the frequency with which relevant cues are emitted and (b) the number of cues that have to be observed to infer that attribute accurately.

Availability refers to the extent that the relevant observable cues are actually available to a perceiver; that is, that the perceiver is exposed to the relevant cues that indicate a personality attribute. Traits concerning the probability that relevant cues are emitted within a particular situation differ. This is probably the reason why minimal-information studies have consistently shown that self–stranger agreement is highest for Extraversion, second-highest for Conscientiousness, and considerably lower for the other personality domains.

Table 6.1 reports the agreement between ratings by self, strangers, and acquaintances that was obtained in a study by Borkenau and Liebler (1993). The first data column reports the correlations between self–reports and the averaged ratings by six independent strangers who provided their judgments on the basis of a 90-second videotaped sequence of the target person's behavior. Despite some procedural differences, other studies reported similar results. That self–stranger agreement is highest for Extraversion and second-highest for

TABLE 6.1
Correlations of Self-Reports with Ratings by Strangers and by Acquaintances

	Self–Stranger Agreement	Self–Acquaintance Agreement
Extraversion	.45	.44
Agreeableness	.08	.42
Conscientiousness	.23	.52
Emotional Stability	.16	.51
Openness to Experience	.14	.55

Conscientiousness is now a well-established finding. Note that the pattern of correlations between self-ratings and ratings by acquaintances is quite different.

This suggests that the traits under study do not differ that much in the relevance of observable cues but rather in the availability of relevant cues in a minimal-information context: Indeed, we found that self-rated, partner-rated, and stranger-rated Extraversion were significantly correlated with a self-assured facial expression and a sonorous and powerful voice, cues that are available as soon as a stranger starts to talk. Such cues that are: (a) relevant, (b) available, (c) easily detected, and (d) utilized by judges explain why even stranger ratings of personality may be accurate to some extent.

Another interesting issue is to study consensus among strangers, the extent that ratings by various strangers resemble each other. Kenny's (1994) WAM is particularly helpful to understand consensus. What makes Kenny's ideas attractive to psychometricians is that he conceived person perception to be basically accurate and that he formulated his model within an information-integration framework. According to Kenny, consensus among judges reflects the following variables:

- Acquaintance (number of observed acts of the target);

- Overlap of information among judges;

- Consistency of the target's impression-relevant behavior across situations;

- Similarity of the meaning systems of the judges;

- Weight of the physical appearance stereotype;

- Agreement about stereotypes; and

- Communication among judges.

Kenny's model gets considerably simpler if the same information is available to all judges (that is, information overlap is perfect) and no communication among them takes place. In this case, consensus is a function of the similarity of the meaning systems of the judges, of their agreement on stereotypes, and—as far as no correction for attenuation takes place—the reliability of the individual judges. Note that, if information overlap is perfect, consensus is only attenuated by factors that affect the detection and utilization of available information and that this detection and utilization of available information may vary between judges as well as within judges over time. For how much variance do the differences between judges in cue detection and cue utilization account?

Borkenau and Liebler (1992) did not make the entire information available to all judges. Rather, six judges saw the master videotape (sound-film condition), six saw the same videotape with the sound turned off (silent film condition), six saw a still picture of the targets that had been derived from the videotape (still picture condition), and another six judges only heard the targets' utterances from an audiotape (audiotape condition). We then collected independent ratings of the Big Five by all 24 judges. Table 6.2 reports the correlations between individual judges within conditions; that is, between judges who had been exposed to the same information.

Note that the available information was reduced from left to right; that is, from the sound–film to the silent film, from the silent film to the still picture, and from the sound film to the audiotape. This reduction of information did not result in any systematic reduction in consensus, indicating that if overlap is perfect, extent of information is unimportant for consensus. Exactly this is predicted by Kenny's WAM. The only factors that reduce consensus if information overlap is perfect are lack of shared meaning systems and of shared stereotypes in terms of Kenny's WAM (or individual differences in cue detection and cue utilization in terms of Funder's RAM). Consequently, the moderate size of the correlations in Table 6.2 shows that judges draw quite dissimilar conclusions from the same available information.

This lack of agreement between judges may reflect several sources. When rating personality traits of strangers, judges may either focus on categorical information like the targets' age, sex, or profession or on individuating information like the targets' appearance and behavior. As far as judges focus on individuating information, they may either focus on appearance information or on behavioral information. Moreover, judges may differ in their detection of available cues. Finally, an additional source of disagreement may be that judges infer different traits from the same behavioral information. Kenny referred to the latter phenomenon as "unshared meaning systems."

The extent of shared versus unique meaning systems may be investigated more directly by collecting prototypicality ratings of acts for traits and then checking the consensus between judges concerning their prototypicality ratings.

TABLE 6.2
Consensus on Target Persons' Trait Levels Among Strangers Who Had Been Exposed to Identical
Information

Trait	Kind of Information			
	Sound-Film	Silent Film	Still Picture	Audiotape
Extraversion	.42	.43	.37	.31
Agreeableness	.21	.25	.19	.19
Conscientiousness	.30	.36	.36	.31
Neuroticism	.24	.22	.04	.35
Openness	.24	.29	.25	.31
Column Mean	.28	.31	.24	.29

Alternatively, one may inform research participants that a fictitious Person A has performed act X and then ask the participants to which extent that Person A has Trait Y. Fortunately, both procedures yield almost identical results after a double correction for attenuation for the unreliability of the prototypicality ratings and of the trait ascriptions (Borkenau, 1990). I only report the reliability of the prototypicality ratings here.

Borkenau (1990) collected prototypicality ratings of 120 acts for 40 traits by eight independent judges. Each of the eight judges provided 4,800 prototypicality ratings. The average consensus correlation that indicated the agreement between two individual judges was .53, with a range from .31 to .70. The rater agreement concerning the prototypicality of acts for traits was far from perfect. This may either reflect lack of consensus among the judges, or unreliability of the judgments of individual judges.

Beck, McCauley, Segal, and Hershey (1988) checked this by a repeated measurement design; that is, they repeatedly collected prototypicality ratings of the same acts for the same traits by the same sample of judges. Whereas the average retest stability of judgments by the same judge was about .85, the average rater agreement was about .50. Thus about 50% of the variance in the prototypicality ratings were shared, another 35% were unique, and the remaining 15% were error. These figures show that lack of consensus in prototypicality ratings reflects unique meaning systems much more than error variance.

Admittedly, the retest reliablity of self-reports of personality tends to be lower than .85, particularly if single-item scales are used. This is reasonable because lack of stability of ratings of personality reflects error variance plus state variance; that is, that the judges' recollections of relevant behavioral evidence vary across time (Steyer, Ferring, & Schmitt, 1992). The data on the lack of consensus on the prototypicality of acts for traits indicates that unshared meaning systems are a major source of any lack of consensus that is found for ratings of personality.

Aggregating ratings across judges is therefore a more efficient procedure for increasing the validity of personality ratings than aggregating several ratings by the same judge. Aggregation across judges reduces the impact of unique meaning systems and the proportion of error variance, whereas aggregation across ratings by the same judge does not reduce the impact of unique meaning systems. The latter procedure is employed when multiitem self-report scales are used, but it probably reduces the less important source of unreliability in personality judgments. It is thus advisable to rely on aggregated peer ratings instead of self-reports to measure personality traits.

INFERRING TRAITS FROM BEHAVIOR

What about using online behavior counts to measure individual differences in personality? This approach is rarely used to assess individual differences in adult personality. There are several reasons for this reluctance to measure adult personality via behavior observations: First, to collect multiple-act criteria for multiple personality traits in various situations for substantial sample sizes is extremely laborious, and second, this approach has its own shortcomings.

One problem of measuring personality attributes via online behavior records is that the decision of when an activity starts and ends is, to some extent, arbitrary. A second problem is that each observable activity tends to be influenced by more than one trait and that this attenuates the correlations between traits and behaviors (Ahadi & Diener, 1989). A related third problem is that judges infer different personality attributes from the same behavior observations. A study by Borkenau and Ostendorf (1987) illustrated the last point.

In this study, we videotaped eight leaderless group discussions, each with six participants. Altogether, 3,700 activities were identified and assigned by two independent observers to one of 16 behavior-descriptive categories, for example, agrees or contradicts. The average agreement between the two judges was $\kappa =$ .30. The problem of unshared meaning systems was not reduced by letting judges classify behavior observations instead of letting them infer traits from behavior. Obviously, agreement among judges is higher if more clearly defined behaviors such as talks versus does not talk are counted. But more objective behavior counts do not reveal everything—or even the most important things—about personality.

Furthermore, observable behavior is, to a large extent, influenced by situational factors. The cross-situational consistency of behavior is moderate at best. This is likely to reduce the correlations between traits and behaviors even further.

Currently, Angleitner, Riemann, and myself conduct an observational twin study. Three hundred sets of twin's were invited for a one-day-long investigation that takes place at the University of Bielefeld in Germany. The main goal of this study is to check whether the finding of the unimportance of the shared environment for individual differences in personality is also obtained if personality attributes are measured by behavior observations. Miles and Carey (1997) published a meta-analysis that showed that the most important variable that affects the results of behavior–genetic analyses of aggression in children is whether aggression is measured via ratings or via behavior observations. Because the present chapter is not about behavior–genetic issues but rather about measurement, the distinction between monozygotic and dizygotic twins is unimportant here.

What is relevant, however, are the correlations of self- and peer ratings of the Big Five with behavior observations. Table 6.3 reports some preliminary findings.

The correlations are either nonsignificant or statistically significant but very low. No correlation exceeds $r = .16$. Moreover, 11 of the 13 significant correlations were obtained between the behavioral measures and the self- and peer reports of Extraversion and Openness to Experience. Extraverted and open participants asked more questions, made more comments, provided more utterances, and moved their arms and legs more frequently than introverted and closed participants. These effects were very weak although the self-reports, peer reports, and some of the behavioral measures were highly reliable in terms of their internal consistency. These low correlations show that the road from acts to personality dispositions is long and winding, and that it is not always advisable to travel it.

IMPLICIT PERSONALITY THEORY

So far, I have talked about the validity of ratings of personality; that is, to what extent measures of personality reflect the trait levels of individual targets. Another issue is what Loevinger (1957) referred to as structural fidelity. This is the extent to which correlations among measures of different traits reflect the actual correlations among these traits. This is an important problem for all

TABLE 6.3
Correlations (Partialled for Target Age and Sex) Between Ratings of Personality (neo-ffi) and Behavioral Measures

Personality measures	Behavioral measures			
	Number of questions	Number of comments	Number of utterances	Actometer score
Neuroticism				
Self-report	-.03	-.02	-.03	-.02
Peer report	.04	.00	-.08	-.09
Extraversion				
Self-report	.00	.10*	.06	.14**
Peer report	.10*	.13**	.11*	.16**
Openness				
Self-report	.05	.07	.05	.12*
Peer report	.12*	.13**	.10*	.10*
Agreeableness				
Self-report	-.08	-.06	-.11*	.00
Peer report	-.03	-.09	-.06	.00
Conscientiousness				
Self-report	.07	-.05	-.05	-.13*
Peer report	-.01	-.06	-.01	-.03

Note:
N = 426.
$p < .05$;
** $p < .01$

approaches in psychology that employ correlations among ratings of personality attributes, for example, factor analyses of ratings of personality or structural equation models that employ ratings of personality.

There has been some controversy over whether such correlations among ratings of different attributes reflect the semantic relations among the attributes, whether they reflect the judges' implicit personality theories, or whether they reflect the actual correlations among the personality attributes. Shweder and D'Andrade (1979) compared the relations among three kinds of data: (a) correlations among online behavior counts, (b) correlations among retrospective ratings of the same categories of behavior, and (c) the semantic-similarity relations among the behavior-descriptive categories. Table 6.4 summarizes the structural correspondences between the kinds of data that were obtained in seven studies.

TABLE 6.4
Structural Correspondences Between Retrospective Ratings, Online Behavior Counts, and
Semantic-Similarity Relations

Study	Online codings x retrospective ratings	Online codings x semantic similarities	Retrospective ratings x semantic similarities
Borgatta et al.	.34	.03	.60
Mann			
- task condition	.14	.20	.61
- emotional condition	.12	.14	.91
Newcomb			
- Group 1	.51	.47	.83
- Group 2	.38	.48	.77
Shweder & D'Andrade	.22	.00	.75
Borkenau & Ostendorf	.28	.14	.68
Average	.28	.21	.74

Note: The correlations estimate the extent of structural correspondence and were calculated across category pairs. For more details see Borkenau (1992).

Obviously, the highest correspondence is found between retrospective ratings and the semantic similarity structure. Shweder and D'Andrade (1979) concluded from such findings that retrospective ratings reflect the semantic similarity structure of the behavior-descriptive terms instead of the actual structure of behavior. But what is the actual structure of behavior? As early as 1884, Galton noticed that "each word expressive of character has a separate shade of meaning while each shares a large part of its meaning with some of the rest." This referential overlap among behavior-descriptive terms is probably high for the global categories like agrees, supports, and so on that were used in the studies that are summarized in Table 6.4. The online judges, however, were instructed to assign each observed activity to only one category. Thus, it might have been that the retrospective judges double counted observed activities because they believed that these activities were relevant for more than one category of behavior. This kind of referential overlap may be highly related to the semantic similarities of the behavior-descriptive terms.

To pursue this hypothesis, Borkenau and Ostendorf (1987) let judges assign 3,700 activities to 16 behavior-descriptive categories using two coding schemes. Two judges used a forced-choice, online coding scheme: They assigned each observed activity to exactly one category. Two other judges used a multiple prototypicality coding scheme. They indicated how good an example each activity was for each of the 16 categories. Act frequencies were then derived from both coding schemes, the correlations among the act frequencies were computed, and these correlations were compared to the correlations among the retrospective frequency ratings and to semantic similarity estimates of the behavior-descriptive terms. Figure 6.1 shows that the two coding schemes yielded quite different results.

The structural correspondence between online behavior records and retrospective frequency ratings was low ($r = .28$) if a forced-choice coding scheme was applied. But it rose to .65 if a multiple prototypicality coding scheme was used. Thus, only if the online judges were allowed to double count their behavior observations, was the structure of online counts and retrospective ratings quite similar.

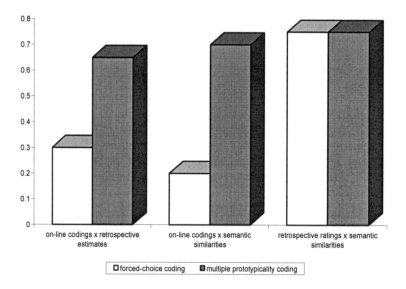

FIG. 6.1. Structural correspondences (correlations across category pairs) between online behavior counts, retrospective act frequency ratings, and semantic similarities between the behavior-descriptive terms, separately for two on-line coding schemes.

This referential overlap is important because correlations among judgments of different personality attributes play a major role in personality research. For example, the Big Five model of personality was established by factor analyses of personality ratings. And because correlations among ratings of different traits reflect the referential overlap relations among the trait terms to some extent, the Big Five reflect dimensions that judges apply to classify actual individual differences in personality. It may well be, as Hogan (1983) and Buss (1991) argued, that these dimensions reflect the adaptive landscape of our evolutionary relevant ancestors; that to attend to these individual differences was particularly important for individual survival and reproduction in the important evolutionary past of humankind.

However this may be, judgmental measures of personality have various shortcomings, and I suggest that personality researchers should seriously consider developing alternative approaches to measure individual differences in personality.

REFERENCES

Ahadi, S., & Diener, E. (1989). Multiple determinants and effect size. *Journal of Personality and Social Psychology, 56,* 398–406.

Beck, L., McCauley, C., Segal, M., & Hershey, L. (1988). Individual differences in prototypicality judgments about trait categories. *Journal of Personality and Social Psychology, 55,* 286–292.

Borgatta, E. F., Cottrell, L. S., & Mann, J. H. (1958). The spectrum of individual interaction characteristics: An inter-dimensional analysis. *Psychological Reports, 4,* 279-319.

Borkenau, P. (1990). Traits as ideal-based and goal-derived social categories. *Journal of Personality and Social Psychology, 58,* 381–396.

Borkenau, P. (1992). Implicit personality theory and the five-factor model. *Journal of Personality, 60,* 295–329.

Borkenau, P., & Liebler, A. (1992). Trait inferences: Sources of validity at zero acquaintance. *Journal of Personality and Social Psychology, 62,* 645–657.

Borkenau, P., & Liebler, A. (1993). Convergence of stranger ratings of personality and intelligence with self-ratings, partner ratings, and measured intelligence. *Journal of Personality and Social Psychology, 65,* 546–553.

Borkenau, P., & Ostendorf, F. (1987). Retrospective estimates of act frequencies: How accurately do they reflect reality? *Journal of Personality and Social Psychology, 52,* 626–638.

Brunswik, E. (1956*). Perception and the representative design of psychological experiments.* Berkeley: University of California Press.

Buss, D. M. (1991). Evolutionary Personality Psychology. *Annual Review of Psychology, 42,* 459–491.

Funder, D. C. (1995). On the accuracy of personality judgment: A realistic approach. *Psychological Review, 102,* 652–670.

Galton, F. (1884). Measurement of character. *Fortnightly Review, 36,* 179–185.

Hofstee, W. K. B. (1994). Who should own the definition of Personality? *European Journal of Personality, 8,* 149–162.

Hogan, R. (1983). A socioanalytic theory of personality. In M. Page (Ed.), *Nebraska Symposium of Motivation* (pp. 55–89). Lincoln: University of Nebraska Press.

Kenny, D. A. (1994). *Interpersonal perception: A social relations analysis.* New York: Guilford.

Kenny, D. A., & Albright, L. (1987). Accuracy in interpersonal perception: A social relations analysis. *Psychological Bulletin, 102,* 390–402.

Loevinger, J. (1957). Objective tests as instruments of psychological theory. *Psychological Reports, 3*, 635–694.

Mann, R. D. (1959). *The relation between personality characteristics and individual performance in small groups.* Unpublished doctoral dissertation. University of Michigan.

Miles, D. R., & Carey, G. (1997). Genetic and environmental architecture of human aggression. *Journal of Personality and Social Psychology, 72*, 207–217.

Newcomb, T. M. (1929). *Consistnecy of certain extravert-introvert behavior patterns in 51 problem boys.* New York: Columbia University, Teachers College, Bureau of Publications.

Paunonen, S. V. (1989). Consensus in personality judgments: Moderating effects of target-rater acquaintanceship and behavior observability. *Journal of Personality and Social Psychology, 56*, 823–833.

Shweder, R. A., & D'Andrade, R. G. (1979). Accurate reflection or systematic distortion? A reply to Block, Weiss, and Thorne. *Journal of Personality and Social Psychology, 37*, 1075–1084.

Steyer, R., Ferring, D., & Schmitt, M. J. (1992). States and traits in psychological assessment. *European Journal of Psychological Assessment, 8*, 79–98.

7

Ability and Temperament

Paul Kline
University of Exeter, Devon, UK

It is obvious from the vast range of the chapters in this book that the topic of the relationship between character, temperament, and personality is enormous. This view is reinforced by the many chapters and the colossal reference lists on this subject in the *Handbook of Personality and Intelligence* (Saklofske & Zeidner, 1995). To deal adequately with all this quickly is, fortunately, impossible. I say "fortunately" because there are two kinds of academics; those who revel in references, and their opposites. I am in the latter class.

Therefore, I intend to deal with just one aspect of the problem but one that I hope is central to many of the issues: the structure of personality and ability, or the relation between the ability and the personality spheres, in the language of Cattell (1957). Cattell has always argued that these two spheres were distinct from each other and from that of motivation. The 16PF (16 personality factors) tests contain a measure of factor B, intelligence, simply because in applied psychology a measure of intelligence is always useful, however crude.

Correlations between measures of intelligence and personality variables, such as N (Neuroticism) and E (Extroversion) are usually low, even if in large samples they are statistically significant. However, even if the tests are highly valid, it is difficult to argue that this low correlation is not, to some extent, at least, a function of the difference types of items. Intelligence test items consist of problems which are examples of the tasks thought to require intelligence for their solution. Items in personality questionnaires, on the other hand, are usually self-reports of behavior, thought, or feelings. They are not examples of the traits in question. Indeed, as Heim (1975) argued, it is embarrassing to give many personality tests to intelligent subjects: "Does your heart beat in the morning?": "Would you drink blood?" or I like to go to a show, once a week, more than one a week, less than once a week?" I remember giving that item to a farmer near Yelverton, in a study of pacemaker patients. He explained that the bus did not run on Sunday, but that even if it did, the show was not that good but it was only once a year, or so he believed.

The disparity in the items minimizes correlations and, the analyses of test-construction items, loading on both personality and intelligence factors would be rightly removed.

However, it does appear that there is some evidence that these spheres are not as isolated as might first appear. Eysenck (1995), in his studies of genius, implicated both high intelligence and factor P, psychoticism. This is not dissimilar to the work of Claridge (1985) who has linked creativity and the schizoid personality that is certainly related to Eysenck's P factor. Here, therefore, if this theorizing is near the mark, is an interaction between personality and intelligence with important real-life implications. However, a word of caution is required. If there is a set of orthogonal variables, by a small proportion of individuals will be at the extremes on all of them. This would account, in part, for the rarity of genius. Incidentally, a study of the profiles of different occupational groups on the 16PF test is interesting from this viewpoint. Professions that are easily filled have profiles in which most of the scores are around the mean. Accountants are an outstanding example, as this is a profession not known for originality or charismatic personality. Artists and writers, on the other hand, had a relatively large number of extreme scores.

Creative individuals, according to Guilford (1967), are divergent thinkers, high in fluency, a salient factor on the well-established second-order ability factor of retrieval (Carroll, 1993; Cattell, 1971). Fluency and flexibility at their negative poles are often described as rigidity. This is interesting because rigidity, in normal, nonpsychological English that is rarely heard in conferences of this sort and treated usually with contempt, is a trait of personality or character. Indeed, in the literature of personality research, rigidity is regarded as a trait involved in obsessional personality (Hazari, 1957), in dogmatism (Rokeach, 1960), the anal character (Freud, 1908) and the authoritarian personality (Adorno, Frenkel-Brunswick, Levinson, & Sandford, 1950).

It is noticeable that all these well-known syndromes of personality are absent, or so it would appear, from the current account of the structure of personality, and I now scrutinize this as briefly as possible.

THE STRUCTURE OF PERSONALITY

Convergent thinkers seem, in recent years, to have dominated the field of the structure of personality. The hideously named Big Five, promulgated relentlessly by Costa and McCrae (e. g., 1992), seem to be regarded as the best and most parsimonious set of factors accounting for the variance in personality questionnaires. These are: extraversion, anxiety, agreeableness, conscientious-ness, and openness. To summarize a huge amount of research, these factors are claimed by Costa and McCrae to account for the variance in most personality scales, even those not designed, originally, to measure such factors.

There are some points about this apparent consensus of findings that need to be made.

There is considerable evidence that the five-factor model does not represent simple structure, as Stankov, Boyle, and Cattell (1995) pointed out in a useful survey of research, which is, however, biased toward the Cattellian viewpoint. It should be pointed out that the attainment of simple structure is important because, as Cattell (1978) demonstrated, it is only from simple structure rotations that causal factors emerge. This is often forgotten in the current preference for confirmatory analyses. Here, too, it must be remembered that confirming a target matrix does not mean that other hypotheses might not be confirmed.

Any scientific account of personality structure ought to deal with variables that are biologically rooted. It is inconceivable that human personality could be profoundly different from that of the great apes with whom more than 90% of our genes are shared. It should be noted, on this account, that two of the factors in the five-factor model, anxiety and extraversion, are satisfactory from this viewpoint. These, of course, are parts of Eysenck's system.

In fact, research with the five factors of the NEO (based on Neuroticism, Extroversion, Openness) indicates clearly that O (Openness), C (Conscientiousness) and A (Agreeableness) are not independent. This was shown by Kline and Barrett, 1994, just for example. In a further study of the NEO and the Eysenck Personality Questionnaire (EPQ) (Draycott & Kline, 1995) we found that in a simple structure rotation, O and E loaded a factor as did C, A and Eysenck's P. Furthermore O loaded another factor with N. These findings run counter to the five-factor model and support, to some extent the three factor solution of Eysenck, although, as I argue next, I believe this is also too simplified. Canonical analysis of these two variable sets, the NEO and the EPQ, showed that much of the NEO variance was explicable in terms of the EPQ and that the extra variance was not coherent.

In brief, I claim that although there is good evidence for extraversion and anxiety or neuroticism, the evidence for the other three factors is weak. Psychoticism is a highly interesting factor, but it is by no means so clear cut as the first two.

McCrae (1996) published a study of openness that turned out to be crucial to the arguments of this chapter concerning the relationship between personality and intelligence. McCrae claimed that the following traits characterize openness: vivid fantasy, artistic sensitivity, depth of feeling, behavioral flexibility, intellectual curiosity, and unconventional attitudes. These descriptions are of interest for a number of reasons. First, they show what a muddle of traits this factor is. Second, they indicate that openness may well be a factor confounding personality and intelligence. Thus intellectual curiosity and behavioral flexibility are both aspects of intelligence or traits more likely to be shown by intelligent than unintelligent individuals. However, unconventional attitudes are considered by Eysenck (1995) to be aspects of high P scorers. Vivid fantasy is also probably aided by high P, as in the delusions of the full-blown psychotic. Indeed, much of the evidence adduced by McCrae (1996) as to the nature of the person high on openness fits the description "intelligent." As a striking confirmation of this argument he used as an exemplar of the trait, the philosopher Rousseau. No matter how misguided his philosophy—perhaps one must be misguided to be a philosopher at all—there can be little doubt that he would have scored extremely high on any intelligence test. Rousseau had a remarkable ability to master new materials and fields and to analyze arguments.

Thus, it is arguable that openness represents a syndrome of traits that is common in intelligent individuals, as Goldberg (1983) suggested. Of course, some of these may be originally determined by intelligence, but they can be mimicked by those who wish to appear intelligent. Hence, the popularity of impenetrable mathematical accounts of consciousness and the universe, beloved by readers of the Guardian (a British daily newspaper), whose mathematical expertise reaches its limit in the calculation of their private incomes.

However, there is more than the suggestion that openness is somehow related to intelligence. McCrae (1996) demonstrated that O is related to other constructs in the field of personality. These include dogmatism, intolerance of ambiguity, sensation-seeking, radicalism, intellectual efficiency, and flexibility.

This list of traits brings back old memories. They read much like the description of the authoritarian personality, a syndrome that seemed so important in the 1950's for obvious reasons but that for somewhat trivial psychometric reasons gradually fell into disrepute. Yet despite all the problems with yea saying and with left-wing bias, which are undeniable, there always seemed to me some sense in this construct.

Over the years, I have carried out innumerable factor analyses of personality and ability tests. I have never had the good fortune or that feeling for research to have discovered much, or frankly anything, that will be remembered. However one investigation with my colleague at Exeter, Dr. Colin Cooper, is relevant to this thesis (Kline & Cooper, 1984). We factored and rotated to simple structure a large number of measures of rigidity, authoritarianism, dogmatism, and the anal character. This was done to test my claim that in addition to extraversion and anxiety, there is another higher order factor, obsessionality, that accounts for much variance in personality questionnaires (Kline & Barrett, 1983).

The results were interesting because a factor emerged, loading on all these measures. Obsessional personality, rigidity, and authoritarian personality all loaded this clear obsessional factor. It was concluded that all these syndromes are different aspects of obsessionality: authoritarianism in the realm of social and political behavior, obsessionality in the realm of personal habits, dogmatism in the world of beliefs. It should be pointed out that P generally correlates negatively with measures of the obsessional factor (Kline & Barrett, 1983).

Yet, as was well argued by Brown (1965), authoritarianism is not independent of intelligence. Thus, again, as with openness, which would undoubtedly load on this broad factor, and together with C, Conscientiousness, we see a link between personality and intelligence.

CONCLUSIONS

I think it clear from this brief scrutiny of some topics that involve huge numbers of studies that there are some real problems in elucidating the relationship of intelligence and personality. I invoked them so that we can be aware of their existence in discussions, for they tend to be forgotten in the apparent consensus that only five factors, are required to understand personality. It is clear that the authoritarian personality, under whatever name or aspect, factor G, superego C, conscientiousness, dogmatism or obsessionality, rigidity, anal character, openness, or psychoticism, is still a worthy subject of study and is related to intelligence.

REFERENCES

Adorno, T. W., Frenkel-Brunswick, E., Levinson, D. J., & Sandford, R. N. (1950). *The authoritarian personality*. New York: Harper & Row.

Brown, R. (1965). *Social psychology*. Glencoe, IL: The Free Press.

Carroll, J. B. (1993). *Human cognitive abilities*. Cambridge, England: Cambridge University Press.

Cattell, R. B. (1957). *Personality and motivation structure and measurement*. Yonkers, NY: World Book.

Cattell, R. B. (1971). *Abilities: Their structure growth and action*. New York: Houghton Mifflin.

Cattell, R. B. (1978). *The scientific use of factor analysis in behavioral and life sciences*. New York: Plenum.

Claridge, G. S. (1986). *Origins of mental illness*. Oxford, England: Blackwell.

Costa, P. T., & McCrae, R. R. (1992). *The NEO Personality Inventory (Revised) Manual*. Odessa, FL: Psychological Assessment Resources.

Draycott, S., & Kline, P. (1995). The big three or the big five—the EPQ-R vs the NEO-PI: A research note, replication and elaboration. *Personality and Individual Differences, 18,* 801–804.

Eysenck, H. J. (1995). *Genius*. Cambridge, England: Cambridge University Press.

Freud, S. (1908). Character and anal egotism. In *The standard edition of the complete psychological works of Sigmund Freud* (Vol. 9, pp. 169–175). London, Hogarth Press and The Institute of Psychoanalysis.

Goldberg, L. R. (1983). *The magical number five, plus or minus two. Some conjectures on the dimensionality of personality descriptions*. Paper, Gerontology Research Center, Baltimore.

Guilford, J. P. (1967). *The nature of human intelligence*. New York: McGraw-Hill.

Hazari, A. (1957). *Psychological testing.* London: Oxford University Press.

Heim, A. W. (1975). *Psychological testing.* London: Oxford University Press.

Kline, P., & Barrett, P. (1994). Studies with the PPQ and the five factor model of personality. *European Review of Applied Psychology, 44,* 35–42.

Kline, P., & Barrett, P. (1983). The factors in personality questionnaires among normal subjects. *Advances in Behaviour Research and Therapy, 5,* 141–202.

Kline, P., & Cooper, C. (1984). A factorial analysis of the authoritarian character. *British Journal of Psychology, 75,* 171–176.

McCrae, R. R. (1996). Social consequences of experiential openness. *Psychological Bulletin, 120,* 333–337.

Rokeach, M. (1960). *The open and closed mind: An investigation into the nature of belief systems and personality systems.* New York: Basic Books.

Saklofske, D. H., & Zeidner, M. (Eds.). (1995). *The international handbook of personality and intelligence.* New York: Plenum.

Stankov, L., Boyle, G. J., & Cattell, R. B. (1995). Models and paradigms in personality and intelligence research. In D. H. Saklofske & M. Zeidner (Eds.), *International handbook of personality and intelligence* (pp. 15–44.) New York: Plenum.

PART II

INTELLIGENCE AND CONATION

8

Conative Individual Differences in Learning

Lyn Corno for R. E. Snow
Teachers College, Columbia University

"Conative Individual Differences in Learning" is the title Dick Snow selected for this chapter. When unforeseen illness prevented Dick's appearance at the Spearman Seminar and I was asked to stand in, I decided to retain his title and to follow the outline of his original abstract as closely as possible. Accordingly, the first section of this chapter considers a number of recent developments in theory and research on conative individual differences in learning.

Modern psychology's dominant conceptual frameworks characterize conative qualities, such as the tendency to follow through on tasks, as socially influenced and cognitively mediated. Related empirical observations indicate that environments vary in affording opportunities for conation and that the mediation of individual motivations and volition is partly developmental. When goal accomplishment requires sustained effort under suboptimal conditions, some students are inevitably better than others at planning and protecting their intentions to learn. Academic situations therefore provide a particularly fruitful backdrop for studying human diversity in conative qualities like foresight and follow-through.

The second section of this chapter touches what is known currently about learning environments that successfully prepare and support individuals in their motivation and volition. This research has taught us about how people gain perspective on the future and learn to use available resources to accomplish long-term goals. It has also provided models of productive resource management.

Goal coordination and resource management are two of the intentional systems that psychologists believe underlie the broad construct of conation. The functioning of each of these systems appears susceptible to intervention. Strategic self-management can be taught, thus allowing some learners to gain control over aspects of temperament that may be problematic, such as impulsivity or slow response to change. Individuals can also use strategic self-management to function more successfully in resource-limited academic situations or when goals involve learning that is novel or complex. Addressing the issue of educational intervention, even in a limited way, thus seems important for rounding out the personality–intelligence connection in this chapter, which begins with issues of theory.

THEORETICAL ISSUES AND CONTRIBUTIONS

At the most general level, it can be said that simple linear relations are not the rule in the conative domain; some theories even predict curvilinearity. The best of this theory looks forward to examine conation together with cognition and affection. Many conative constructs seem to mix constituent aspects of underlying conative, cognitive, and affective functions. To complicate the picture even more, some of the most promising constructs are highly contextualized and reflect different levels of referent generality. Better research avoids unnecessarily tying a construct to the particularities of any one measure, but multitrait, multimethod studies remain the exceptions. A few examples serve to illustrate each of these general observations.

The Commitment Pathway

In writings over the past few years, separately and together, Dick Snow and I tried to make the case for bringing volition into perspective with motivation in educational theory and research (see e.g., Corno, 1989, 1993; Snow, 1989; Snow, Corno, & Jackson, 1996). Emerging theory and evidence does support the role of volition in various aspects of learning and performance (see Figure 8.1).

We have been much influenced by Heckhausen and Kuhl's (1985) hypothesized "commitment pathway" connecting motivation and volition and yet maintaining the distinction between them.

According to these theorists, motivation establishes goals, whereas volition implements them. Motivation promotes goals, whereas volition protects them. Motivation involves individual thinking about goals, whereas volition involves the initiation of processes for accomplishing goals. Motivation embraces foresight, whereas volition embraces follow-through. To bring important long-term projects to completion, individuals must regulate and coordinate the many instrumental steps necessary along the way (see also Corno, 1994; Corno & Kanfer, 1993). Taken together, the two categories of motivational and volitional individual differences that mark the commitment pathway represent the theoretical construct of conation. To quote from the dictionary of psychological terms (English & English, 1958), conation is "an intrinsic unrest . . . the opposite of homeostasis a conscious tendency to strive . . . that is not a specific form of behavior, but an aspect of all behavior" (p. 104).

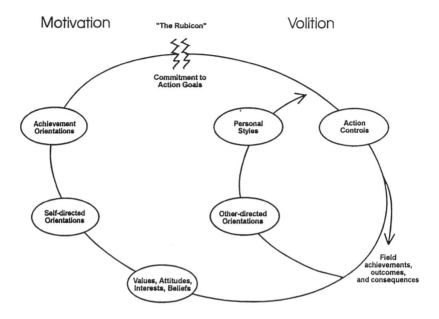

FIG. 8.1. Schematic representation of conative individual difference constructs in the motivation-volition cycle. Source: Snow, Corno, and Jackson, 1996, p. 225.

Although few theorists dispute that learning is supported by coordinating various "self-regulatory processes," Heckhausen and Kuhl's unique contributions are twofold. First, they steadfastly refused to avoid controversy surrounding use of the term, "volition." As Kuhl (personal communication, February 10, 1991), once put it, the full sense of conation just does not seem to be captured by motivation alone, and avoiding the controversy by reference to "self-regulatory processes" fails to distinguish between the constructs at hand.

The other unique contribution made by these theorists is their characterization of the process components that actually distinguish volition from motivation; namely, the increased receptivity to new information and the so-called volitional strategies that bring wishes along into action (Kuhl, 1984, 1985). In studies Heckhausen conducted with Gollwitzer and others (Gollwitzer, Heckhausen, & Ratajczak, 1990; Gollwitzer, Heckhausen, & Steller, 1990; Heckhausen & Gollwitzer, 1987), subjects were experimentally induced into pre- and postdecisional states. While in predecisional states (the arena of motivation), subjects reported having thoughts about the value of various decision alternatives. They also had greater memory span, indicating an enhanced receptivity to incoming information. In contrast, inductions of a postdecisional (or volitional) state were associated with procedural concerns or thoughts about implementing a decision into action and a decreased receptivity. Put simply, it is harder for subjects to go back and reconsider their goals once thoughts about implementation have begun to take place—hence, the metaphor of "crossing the Rubicon" (Kuhl, 1985). This result alone has important implications for intervention programs supporting student conation, to be noted later this chapter.

Despite Heckhausen and Kuhl's extensive research on the volitional processes of action control, including the development and validation of performance-based measures (see Kuhl & Kraska, 1989), the term *volition* remains a pariah in some psychological circles. Researchers have instead elected to study the volitional aspects of conation under rubrics such as self-regulated learning (Zimmerman, 1990), possible selves (Markus & Nurius, 1986), mindfulness (Salomon, 1987), or finding flow (Csikszentmihalyi, 1997). The "Big Five" personality factor of conscientiousness or will is another accepted rubric (Digman, 1990).

Referent Generality

In the arena of motivation (the left-hand side of Figure 8.1), the constructs that have been studied most extensively in relation to learning include achievement orientations, goals, interests, and various aspects of self (see Corno & Kanfer, 1993). Snow, Corno, and Jackson (1996) tried to devise some provisional lattices on which to hang hypotheses and results as research continues in the conative domain. Figure 8.2 is our attempt to represent schematically the different levels of referent generality needed for affective and conative constructs related to learning.

Some constructs in these domains appear more stable across time and situations than others. Those constructs, dubbed traits and styles in Figure 8.2, have more stability than habits and strategies, for example.

Constructs defined to apply only to particular contexts or groups of persons are even less stable. Their very definition as contextual arises from the union of persons and particular situations. Some of the contextual constructs are among the most interesting research targets in the conative domain. Consider, for example, persuasibility, as it has been updated in work by McGuire (1985, 1990). McGuire documented intelligence–persuasion relationships that are curvilinear (see also Rhodes & Wood, 1992; Snow, Corno, & Jackson, 1996, review some of this research). Another intriguing construct is Bereiter's (1990) acquired contextual module for intentional learning, which includes both cognitive and conative features. A third is Willingham's (1985) productive follow-through, one of the few conative constructs not measured by self-report. In Willingham's study, productive follow-through scores, formed from students' records of extracurricular participation in high school, added appreciably to predictive variance in college grade point average after Scholastic Aptitude Test scores were taken into account. Although these three attunements are each specialized for particular situations, they can also be manifested outside situations that define them, either overtly or covertly, and thus gain referent generality.

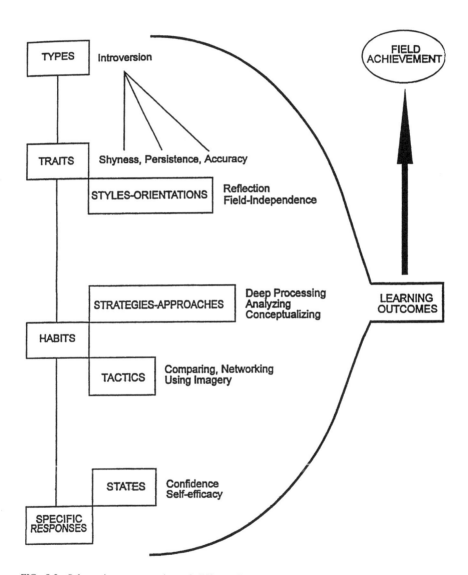

FIG. 8.2. Schematic representation of different levels of referent generality for affective and conative aptitude constructs related to learning outcomes and field achievements. Source: Snow, Corno, and Jackson, 1996, p. 251.

Future research needs to identify constituent aspects of situations along with the processes thought to underlie responses depicted by various extant measures. Too often, conative constructs are represented as psychometric scales or their derived statistical combinations. Researchers also need to become better at tracking the referent generality of different constructs. The nature of theory and research on conative constructs is necessarily complex.

Snow's Situated Aptitude Theory

Snow's (1981, 1991, 1992) own aptitude theory argues that the most useful individual difference constructs for education will be those derived from analyses of person–situation interactions using both general constructs and rich, local descriptions. This theory will be advanced by the discovery of instructional conditions in which each general or local individual difference construct does or does not serve as aptitude—as a characteristic that reliably predicts response to instruction. Although this kind of situativity theory has advanced in the area of cognitive functioning (see Greeno, Collins, & Resnick, 1996), it has been pursued far less vigorously in the conative domain. And yet, a situated and dynamic aptitude approach to the study of conation raises some issues that have been inadequately addressed to date.

For example, the study of conation as aptitude highlights the need for a better understanding of the learning characteristics of self-regulatory activities. Brown, Bransford, Ferrara, and Campione (1983) suggested that conceptualizing volitional control as a skill implies that it will become less effortful and conscious with overlearning. Although conation may begin as a conscious, strategic awareness of the need to set goals and monitor progress toward them, ultimate automation of these procedures results in efficiency, and that is adaptive. Procedures that run automatically, even when they may not need to, absorb less processing capacity. Although psychologists, such as Kuhl (1985) and Gollwitzer (1993) have data showing that strategies can be used with little deliberate effort, intervention studies in education have rarely attempted to train self–regulation to the point of overlearning. The success that Kanfer and Ackerman (1989) have had in this area with military recruits provides one model for educational research.

Another issue raised by the new aptitude theory involves the dynamic interplay between conation and other psychological determinants of action—namely, cognition and affection. Most researchers agree that learning is a joint function of these factors; and almost every teacher–practitioner will say, "Of course motivation and emotion both matter in school learning."; Yet little is understood about the way these factors interact in different educational situations.

One way to chart complex interactions was illustrated by an interesting curriculum evaluation with Dutch first-year medical students conducted by Wijnen and Snow (1975). A new curriculum was offered, which was problem-or case-based, with lots of small-group discussion among students without teachers—something novel for Dutch medical students. The researchers plotted verbal ability by achievement relations for 1-month blocks of instruction over the course of a year and then examined the scatterplots.

Results from the first block of instruction were hard to fit with a simple regression line; the data appeared curvilinear. Particularly among higher ability students, the data seemed to run in opposite directions. Rules for fitting ellipses and partitioning scatterplots into area groups were used to produce one area in which a strong ability–outcome relation was evident. Performance depended on ability in this curriculum, but only for these students. To unpack the rest of the data, Wijnen and Snow used personality scales administered at pretest to identify constructs that might distinguish students in the other groups.

The area group in which performance depended on ability comprised those middle-ability students who described themselves as more "codependent" and who valued social learning. They did particularly well in this first block of instruction. The higher ability students, with more of an independent learning style, tended to do poorly with the cooperative-interpersonal activity required. Now, this relation seems predictable from prior theory and research. If the methods these authors used were novel, surely their results were not.

But when the students were followed through successive blocks of instruction, another story was told. The higher ability, independent learners who responded poorly at course outset began to adapt to the new instruction over time. They emerged at the top of the class by the end of the fifth block! At this point in the curriculum the content became increasingly demanding and technical. In contrast, some other students who did well in the beginning of the course declined on achievement tests as the course wore on.

Wijnen and Snow concluded from these data that the combined (ability–personality) aptitude complex that accounted for performance at an early stage shifted at a later stage of instruction. That is, what were inaptitudes initially became aptitudes later on, and vice versa. This study shows the value of detailed analyses of aptitudes in relation to instruction over time. It also illustrates how cognitive, conative, and affective interactions can be understood through even local educational evaluations, and not just large-scale, factor analytic studies of individual differences.

Motivation researchers need to pay particular attention to results like these—for few of them even collect data on cognitive abilities along with their motivation measures, much less seek to examine interactions among constructs (Weiner, 1990). And yet, historically, the evidence is clear that there are interactions between ability or knowledge and skill in learning domains and various conative and affective aptitudes. Particularly in relation to instruction that is student- or socially-centered in the extreme, looking only at the motivational variables—anxiety, attributions, self-efficacy, or whatever—tells just part of the story. And many of the learning situations that are so popular among education reformers today have this quality—for example, the "learner centered principles" that the American Psychological Association has distributed widely to American schools (APA Board of Educational Affairs, 1995).

I would like to quote from a letter that Snow wrote to David Berliner and Robert Calfee in 1992, just after he read drafts of two chapters for their *Handbook of Educational Psychology* (Berliner & Calfee, 1996) that covered motivation theories and instructional applications, respectively. The points that Dick made are endlessly important, and worth repeating again:

"They (the authors of these two chapters) say that research on individual differences has contributed little and the approach has greatly declined. They add that trait approaches fail because, for example, people don't show high need achievement in all situations. They recommend that we search first for general laws rather than explore person–situation interactions; later on, individual differences can be included to refine generalizations . . . I think (the authors) confuse and misrepresent several issues. . . .They seem to think that a "trait" approach requires generalization to all situations;" they cite Mischel in support. But Mischel . . . adopts a person–situation interaction approach. Other interactionist research (e.g. by Magnusson & Engler; Cronbach & Snow) shows many such interactions involving achievement motivation, test anxiety, and related personality measures. And if any field is distinctly not in decline, it's research on test anxiety (which is the same as fear of failure, which is a central constituent of Atkinson's achievement motivation). It's fine for (the authors) to show that Atkinson's theory and Rotter's theory were discarded because they had weaknesses, but this in no way . . . invalidates either all possible trait approaches or all ATI approaches. Dweck's mastery vs. performance orientation is an individual difference construct. So is Seligman's "explanatory style" or "attributional style." So are self-efficacy beliefs and learned helplessness beliefs—if they are acquired and accumulated in some type of situation to exhibit relative stability as a predisposition when that type of situation again is faced. Other constructs . . . also have individual difference aspects. Maybe this comes from (the authors') trait misconception. (But) an individual difference variable can be important in some situations and be completely overridden by situation factors in others. The authors can say what they want to (about individual difference research being outmoded or in decline), but this hardly disposes of the issue . . ."

ADVANCES IN MOTIVATION THEORY

To be fair, there are some motivation researchers making theoretical contributions in the direction Snow favored. Some studies offer extensions to recent developments in goal theory, for example. In the goal-theoretic framework, studies of so–called task involvement, or learning-mastery orientation (see Lepper, 1988, for an integration of this work) have identified learners who report wanting to master new knowledge and skills, to value learning, and to believe that their learning-related efforts will lead to academic success. Brophy (1997) called such students motivated to learn.

These learners stand in contrast to those who worry about how they appear to others in school and who question the utility of their own efforts unless they are in direct competition with others. These students have been called "performance-oriented" (Ames, 1992; Dweck, 1988). Although goal theorists disagree about the origins of the individual differences they describe and some measures of goal orientation are even based on students' ratings of teachers and classes rather than on their own self-reports, the data are generally treated as antecedent to students' learning-related behavior and achievement. Whatever the origins of one's orientation toward learning, it apparently predicts response to instruction under different situations, at a variety of age levels (Blumenfeld, 1992; Wigfield, 1997).

What studies influenced by goal theory have not often done is include measures of investment, limited investment, and avoidance together in the same data set. Single measures of the goal-orientation construct are typical. And yet, a battery of measures including other established constructs theoretically associated with achievement goals (such as efficacy, self-regulated learning, help seeking, interest, and so on) would serve to advance more than one hypothesis at a time. The more complicated hypotheses derived from goal theory—that one might hold both learning and performance goals simultaneously, or circle back and around them like an elliptical orbit around two points (Corno, 1992)—are hard to test with standard measures of performance or mastery goals.

One study breaks this mold. Middleton and Midgly (1997) developed a scale that assessed avoidance together with approach goals and gave it to 700 sixth graders. With both sorts of goals in the same regression, these authors found that approach goals predicted efficacy, self-regulated learning, and low levels of avoiding help. The avoidance goals were negative predictors of efficacy, and positive predictors of help avoidance and test anxiety. In addition, students with lower grade point averages were more likely than students with higher grade point averages to endorse both approach and avoidance dimensions of performance goals at once. So, in this study, at least, a more complicated hypothesis of goal theory—that students might hold both approach and avoidance goals at once—was supported for an interesting portion of the sample, those students who were lower achieving. The authors suggested that lower-achieving students might be particularly concerned with how their ability compared with that of others. They would be oriented to demonstrate ability but would hide their lack of ability relative to others.

A logical observation is that both effort and avoidance appear to be mindful, volitional proclivities. This is something few researchers have acknowledged. Notably different is the work of Nuttin and Lens (1985), which actually bridges motivation and volition by explicitly connecting individual thinking about goals to the initiation of processes for accomplishing goals. The construct of "future time perspective," developed by these authors, refers to "temporally localized (goal) objects . . . that occupy (an individual's) mind in a certain situation" (p. 21). Future time perspective is thus a truly conative (read: bridging motivation and volition) factor that may be used to motivate and regulate purposive behavior.

One hypothesis is that individuals extend their viewpoints to consider desired goals in their future. Some persons construct longer, more realistic, and more accessible perspectives than others, or perspectives that are more balanced with respect to proximal and distal goals. A long, realistic, and accessible time perspective facilitates the effectiveness with which individuals can formulate and realize long-term projects. Individuals must move from plans to implementation—from motivation to volition. Another individual difference hypothesis is that learners who are unable to perceive the connection of their present studies to some far-distant career will put forth insufficient effort in school.

Nuttin and Lens showed that a forward-looking perspective on realistic goal objects facilitates the effectiveness with which learners actually realize their long-term goals. Interestingly, these differences relate to age and contextual variables, and the age–time perspective relationship appears curvilinear (Lens & Gailly, 1980). These kinds of findings cry out for case studies of individuals over time. The point is that some research on motivation makes a contribution in seeking to approach conative constructs as personal belief systems that operate in academic contexts.

SUPPORTING CONDITIONS IN ACADEMIC SITUATIONS

I would be remiss in a chapter about conative individual differences in learning if I did not highlight some conditions that support student conation in school. I have discussed this topic in more detail elsewhere (see e.g., Corno & Randi, 1999; Xu & Corno, 1998). Here there is space to discuss just three conditions in the most general sense—that is, simply exemplifying the evidence for each. These general conditions definitely recur in research-based efforts to actually develop (and not just support) student conation in academic situations. Each condition has been given recent and historical attention in empirical research; each also has a legacy in educational practice. They are environmental affordance, mediational strategy instruction, and consequence and resource management, respectively.

A long-standing cornerstone of ecological psychology, affordance (Gibson, 1979) has been spotlighted by the growing literatures of aptitude for school learning and curricular reform. Mediational and coping strategies have been the focus of much correlational and classroom intervention research in both educational and school psychology. Strategies also been imported into studies of subject matter learning since the early 1980s. How consequence management, as behaviorism's soul, plays into the more complex agenda of modern conative theory has been less widely discussed, but is important to consider. And finally, the management of personal and environmental resources is also fronted in modern conative theory.

The most general point to be made about these conditions is that, like other presumably favorable dispositional tendencies, conative strengths require opportunities to develop. The potential for motivation and volition exists in all of us but the experience of learning not to be short-sighted in life and of pressing ahead to make things work for you often appears fundamentally different depending on individual and group circumstances. Not only does current educational practice potentially disadvantage individual conation along status characteristic lines, even within status groups (at least in the United States), many students do not learn to display conative dispositions and skills along anything like a normative developmental trajectory (cf. Scarr, 1988). The development of conation has sociological as well as psychological significance for individuals and societies; as Kanfer and I reported (Corno & Kanfer, 1993), these personal qualities predict performance outcomes in the workplace as well as in school.

Environmental Affordance

This condition may well be necessary for learning personal responsibility and volitional self-control. The evidence is now textbook that forward-thinking is learned, in part, through exposure and the experience of forward-thinking—in the vicarious and enactive modeling that teaches by example and appropriation, as well as in the expressed values and expectations of people who provide support along the way.

From their extensive review of research on children of poverty, Knapp and Shields (1991) concluded that, without daily living environments conducive to initiating and sustaining forward-thinking in learning, conventional successes are hard won—in school and other effortful tasks. Particularly when children have early lives marked by family circumstances that put them at risk for academic problems, school and classroom environments need to provide multiple opportunities for volitional self-control and to encourage students to seize them.

Reform-based interventions such as those implemented in some model urban schools in the United States have successfully created smaller schools, schools that have become learning communities, in which administrators, teachers, parents, and students together build a strong commitment to a well-defined academic and social agenda. Classroom environments are conducive to learning—routines are established and expectations are clear. But teaching assumes that all students can develop the beliefs and practices for classroom success. Students and teachers work together in smaller, cooperative groups in which a melange of volitional strategies are taught directly as well as modeled. Student performance is carefully monitored and assessed using multiple methods and individual, diagnostic profiles (see e.g., Meier, 1992). In other words, there are many ways for all kinds of students to experience the pleasures involved as part of a community that values serious learning accomplishments in these reform-driven schools. Evaluation results are similar for these and other opportunity-based interventions, such as Comer's (1988) child development model; Madden and Slavin's "Success-for-All" (Madden, Slavin, Karweit, Dolan, & Wasik, 1993); and Levin's accelerated schools (1992). The good news is that many schools are adapting these models for their own circumstances. And, if the schools cannot do this, other opportunities can sometimes be found on the outside.

McLaughlin, Irvy, and Langman (1994) illustrated the possibilities inherent in both formal and informal community youth organizations. Here, so-called hopeful youth managed to break away from strong negative family and peer influences to make better lives for themselves. These researchers meticulously documented how the youth organizations and their directors (dubbed "wizards") literally created opportunities out of the interests of the youth they served so the youth could take the long view on enabling actions and events.

The wizards orchestrated performances such as film productions, art shows, and concerts—each of which had responsible self–management inherent in its creation. Through their encouragement and guidance, the wizards served as sponsors, mentors, and friends. Their involvement on a personal level helped to buffer the youth from peer pressure to return to unproductive modes of thinking and behavior.

Thus, unconventional youth organizations run by wizards for hopeful and resilient students and interdependent learning communities in schools are two complementary forms of affordance for motivational and volitional development that exists within the experiences young people encounter every day. Common sense suggests synchronizing these two different strands of research with existing work on mentoring (see e.g., Bendixon-Noe & Giebelhaus, 1997).

Mediational Strategy Training

Although affordance may be a necessary condition for fostering student conation, it is insufficient for some percentage of students who need explicit instruction in strategic self-management. By learning ways to manage resources and tasks, as well as one's own (personal) motivations and thoughts, many lower achieving students can begin to succeed in learning.

The motivation and emotion-management strategies, in particular, are abstract and covert. Most children under the age of 7 will need discussions of why it matters to set subgoals, how they can productively budget time and energy in school and on homework, how to reward themselves for accomplishments, and how to juggle competing intentions. Bereiter (1990) wrote that intentional learning in school may also require "a moral dimension . . . a code of conduct that includes an obligation to pursue truth and depth of understanding, accompanied by an aversion to superficiality and pretense of knowledge" (p. 616). Observations that my students and I have done with second graders doing homework show clearly that some parents deliberately teach volitional control strategies and serious attitudes about learning to their children (Xu & Corno, 1998). Observations of elementary classrooms show that some teachers do this as well. But this is not the norm for either parents or teachers—nor is it for coaches or school psychologists—who ought to be addressing mediational strategies and attitudes.

Researchers such as Pressley (1995), Graham and Harris (1994), Brown (1992), and Schunk (1996), have all perfected ways to teach self-regulation in the context of regular curricular activities. However, it remains important to pursue interventions with children from diverse backgrounds who might learn mediational strategies best in less conventional ways.

Work by Moll, Amanti, Neff, and Gonzalez, (1992) provides an example of the gains that can be made when previously marginalized children are given opportunities for self-regulated learning that draw upon unique features of their home environments. Working in the State of Arizona, with a Mexican-American border population, Moll and a cadre of school teachers did ethnographic fieldwork to identify the kinds of knowledge historically endemic to these communities. Their emphasis was on finding ways to teach the strategic knowledge and activities essential for both household functioning and regional productivity. So, instead of a unit on songs and artifacts from this culture, there were units on cooking candy, equipment maintenance, ranching, and masonry. Teachers used these topics to instruct students in "inquiry processes, becoming active learners, and on using their social contacts outside the classroom strategically, to access new knowledge for the development of their studies" (p. 138). The work's importance lies in the self-observation of the study's teachers that, prior to this research, their classroom instruction actually inhibited Mexican-American students from using the knowledge they already had, and, in doing so, positioned them as deviant in relation to the norms of the larger school community.

Consequence Management

To work toward foresight and follow through, children need to begin to manage their own consequences. As theorists Deci and Ryan (1994) argued, it is hard to learn to do that in conventional classrooms where consequences are managed prodigiously on the students' behalf. The same holds for overly controlling home environments. Theorists agree that self-regulation of effort involves a gradual removal of scaffolds and a press to fly solo while looking for sustaining signs of progress.

Eisenberger (1992) showed through a number of experiments that effortful behavior is experienced by most people as aversive. To get people to do things that do not come easily, the experience has to have secondary rewards. It may then be viewed as valuable, meaningful, or at least useful, if not pleasurable in some personal way. And it is now recognized that these secondary rewards often are not the usual, idiosyncratic extrinsic reinforcers. For many adolescents, secondary rewards for motivated behavior involve the very signs of sustained progress—increased adult interchange and peer support—that seem so hard to come by in their everyday environments.

One of the things that modern theory and research on volition rather uniquely emphasizes is the need to learn to find and use resources for coping. Clinical psychological research long ago established significant advantages for individuals who can cope cognitively and emotionally in the face of both real and imagined adversity. The new work on coping in volitional psychology includes the notion that education can assist individuals and communities in learning to move forward despite real obstacles.

Several "resource management strategies" have been suggested by volition theory—teaching students ways to use their own internal resources to cope with difficult situations, as well as ways to locate hard-to-find external resources for coping with challenging events. The point is that resourcefulness in finding sources of support is a talent that can be developed (Little, 1983; Smith, Lizotte, Thornberry, & Krohn, 1997). It often involves pausing to assess situations, reflecting on goals, and ruling out options. Careful monitoring and pointed effort to alter perceived stressors or to seek out sources of support is another aspect. Envisioning oneself carrying out various plans of attack and compromising have now become staple recommendations of self-help programs, as have attempts to regulate negative emotions and regain self-control (Boekaerts, 1995). Coping is necessary for both motivational stress, such as boredom, and emotional distress, such as frustration. If our teaching interventions can model and promote adaptive seeking after resources and active use of these resources in ways that will help realize individual visions, perhaps we can actually make probable in students what Markus and Nurius (1986) called visions of "possible selves."

In summary, research on the learning conditions that support student conation boils down to a combination of (a) multiple opportunities, or multiple "ways in"; (b) careful strategy and attitudinal instruction, and (c) when the time comes, being willing to push the bird out of the nest toward self-management of consequences and new sources of support. To effectively practice foresight and follow through, individuals must be accompanied toward foresight and follow through. This is both an answer and a challenge for future research on conative individual differences in learning.

CONCLUSION

This chapter has examined the nature of individual differences in conative aptitudes for learning, including the important distinction between motivation and volition. Conation is an old construct, used by Spearman (1927) and Binet (translated by Terman, 1916), as well as other pioneers (see e.g., Hilgard, 1980; Webb, 1915; also, Snow, Corno, & Jackson, 1996, provide some history). But taxonomies have been slow to develop in this domain and construct proliferation has been steady. As it has moved away from earlier research on personality variables such as achievement motivation and anxiety, theory and research on conation has progressed to a situated aptitude perspective (Stanford Aptitude Seminar, in press). Conative constructs are no longer viewed as in the heads of individuals, but rather as unions of persons and situations that necessarily cross functional boundaries between cognition, affection, and affording activities. These "aptitude complexes" (Snow, 1981), or "contextual modules" (Bereiter, 1990), in turn show important interactions with instructional treatments and also account uniquely for individual differences in learning beyond the variance attributable to cognitive ability differences alone.

ACKNOWLEDGMENT

I am honored to be representing Dick Snow's presence in this volume along with my own. He reviewed an earlier draft of the manuscript and approved of the dual author line. Various portions of this chapter are adapted from writing that Dick and I have done separately or together. Although what I have written may not be precisely what Dick would have written himself, he was present with all of us intellectually at the Second Spearman Seminar, and his work continues to influence others who do research at the interface of personality and intelligence.

REFERENCES

Ames, C. (1992). Classrooms: Goals, structures, and student motivation. *Journal of Educational Psychology, 83*, 261–271.

APA Board of Educational Affairs (1995). *Learner-centered psychological principles: A framework for school redesign and reform.* Washington, DC: American Psychological Association.

Bendixon-Noe, M., & Giebelhaus, C. (1997). Mentoring: Help or hindrance? *Mid–Western Educational Researcher, 10*(4), 20–23.

Bereiter, C. (1990). Aspects of an educational learning theory. *Review of Educational Research, 60*, 603–624.

Berliner, D. C., & Calfee, R. C. (Eds.). (1996). *Handbook of educational psychology.* New York: Macmillan.

Blumenfeld, P. C. (1992). Classroom learning and motivation: Clarifying and extending goal theory. *Journal of Educational Psychology, 84*, 272–281.

Boekaerts, M. (1995). The interface between intelligence and personality as determinants of classroom learning. In D. H. Saklofske & M. Zeidner (Eds.), *Handbook of personality and intelligence* (pp. 161–183). New York: Plenum.

Brown, A. L. (1992). Design experiments: Theoretical and methodological challenges in creating complex interventions in classroom settings. *Journal of the Learning Sciences, 2*, 141–178.

Brown, A. L., Bransford, J. D., Ferrara, R., & Campione, J. (1983). Learning, remembering, and understanding. In J. Flavell & E. Markman (Eds.), *Carmichael's manual of child psychology* (Vol. 5, pp. 77–166). New York: Wiley.

Brophy, J. (1997). *Motivating students to learn.* Boston: McGraw–Hill.

Comer, J. P. (1988). Educating poor minority children. *Scientific American, 259*, 42–48.

Corno, L. (1989). Self–regulated learning: A volitional analysis. In B. Zimmerman & D. Schunk (Eds.), *Self–regulated learning and academic achievement* (pp. 111–142). New York: Springer–Verlag.

Corno, L. (1992). Encouraging students to take responsibility for learning and performance. *Elementary School Journal, 93*, 69–83.

Corno, L. (1993). The best–laid plans: Modern conceptions of volition and educational research. *Educational Researcher, 22*(2), 14–22.

Corno, L. (1994). Student volition and education: Outcomes, influences, and practices. In D. Schunk & B. Zimmerman (Eds.), *Self–regulation of learning and performance: Issues and educational applications* (pp. 229–254). Hillsdale, NJ: Lawrence Erlbaum Associates.

Corno, L., & Kanfer, R. (1993). The role of volition in learning and performance. In L. Darling-Hammond (Ed.), *Review of research in education* (Vol. 19, pp. 3–43). Washington, DC: American Educational Research Association.

Corno, L., & Randi, J. (1999). A design theory for classroom instruction in self–regulated learning? In C. R. Reigeluth (Ed.), *Instructional design theories and models* (Vol. 2, pp. 293-318). Hillsdale, NJ: Lawrence Erlbaum Associates.

Csikszentmihalyi, M. (1997). *Finding flow.* New York: Basic Books.

Deci, E., & Ryan, R. (1994). Promoting self–determined education. *Scandinavian Journal of Educational Research, 38*, 3–14.

Digman, J. M. (1990). Personality structure: Emergence of the five–factor model. *Annual Review of Psychology, 41*, 417–440.

Dweck, C. S. (1988). Motivational processes affecting learning. *American Psychologist, 41*, 1040–1048.

Eisenberger, R. (1992). Learned industriousness. *Psychological Review, 99*, 248–267.

English, H. B., & English, A. C. (1958). *A comprehensive dictionary of psychological and psychoanalytic terms.* New York: Longman.

Gibson, J. J. (1979). *The ecological approach to visual perception.* Boston: Houghton-Mifflin.

Gollwitzer, P. M. (1993). Goal achievement: The role of intentions. In W. Stroebe & M. Hewstone (Eds.), *European review of social psychology, 4* (pp. 141–185). Chishester, England: John Wiley.

Gollwitzer, P., Heckhausen, H., & Ratajczak, H. (1990). From weighing to willing: Approaching a change decision through pre- or postdecisional mentation. *Organizational Behavior and Human Decision Processes, 45,* 41–65.

Gollwitzer, P., Heckhausen, H., & Steller, B. (1990). Deliberative and implemental mind–sets: Cognitive tuning toward congruous thoughts and information. *Journal of Personality and Social Psychology, 59,* 1119–1127.

Graham, S., & Harris, K. R. (1994). The role and development of self–regulation in the writing process. In D. H. Schunk & B. J. Zimmerman (Eds.), *Self–regulation of learning and performance: Issues and educational applications* (pp. 203–228). Hillsdale, NJ: Lawrence Erlbaum Associates.

Greeno, J. G., Collins, A. M., & Resnick, L. (1996). Cognition and learning. In D. Berliner & R. Calfee (Eds.), *Handbook of educational psychology* (pp.15–46). New York: Macmillan.

Heckhausen, H., & Gollwitzer, P. (1987). Thought contents and cognitive functioning in motivational vs. volitional states of mind. *Motivation and Emotion, 11,* 101–120.

Heckhausen, H., & Kuhl, J. (1985). From wishes to action: The dead ends and short cuts on the long way to action. In M. Frese & J. Sabine (Eds.), *Goal directed behavior: The concept of action in psychology* (pp. 134–160). Hillsdale, NJ: Lawrence Erlbaum Associates.

Hilgard, E. R. (1980). The triology of mind: Cognition, affection, and conation. *Journal of the history of behavioral sciences, 16,* 107–117.

Kanfer, R., & Ackerman, P. (1989). Motivation and cognitive abilities: An integrative/aptitude-treatment interaction approach to skill acquisition [Monograph]. *Journal of Applied Psychology, 74,* 657–690.

Knapp, M. S., & Shields, P. M. (Eds.) (1991). *Better schooling for the children of poverty: Alternatives to conventional wisdom.* Berkeley, CA: McCutchan.

Kuhl, J. (1984). Volitional aspects of achievement motivation and learned helplessness: Toward a comprehensive theory of action control. In B. A. Maher (Ed.), *Progress in experimental personality research* (Vol. 13, pp. 99–171). New York: Academic Press.

Kuhl, J. (1985). Volitional mediators of cognition–behavior consistency: Self–regulatory processes and action versus state orientation. In J. Kuhl & J. Beckmann (Eds.), *Action control: From cognition to behavior* (pp. 101–128). New York: Springer–Verlag.

Kuhl, J., & Kraska, K. (1989). Self–regulation and metamotivation: Computational mechanisms, development, and assessment. In R. Kanfer, P. Ackerman, & R. Cudeck (Eds.), *Abilities, motivation, and methodology: The Minnesota Symposium on Individual Differences* (pp. 343–374). Hillsdale, NJ: Lawrence Erlbaum Associates.

Lens, W., & Gailly, A. (1980). Extension of future time perspective in motivational goals of different age groups. *International Journal of Behavioral Development, 3*(1), 1–17.

Lepper, M. R. (1988). Motivational considerations in the study of instruction. *Cognition and Instruction, 5,* 289–310.

Levin, H. M. (1992). Accelerated visions. *Accelerated Schools, Winter,* 2–3.

Little, B. (1983). Personal projects: A rationale and methods for investigation. *Environmental Behavior, 15,* 273–309.

Madden, N. A., Slavin, R. E., Karweit, N. L., Dolan, L. J., & Wasik, B. A. (1993). Success for all: Longitudinal effects of a restructuring program for inner-city elementary schools. *American Educational Research Journal, 30,* 123–149.

Markus, H., & Nurius, P. (1986). Possible selves. *American Psychologist, 41,* 954–969.

McGuire, W. J. (1985). Attitudes and attitude change. In G. Lindzey & E. Aronson (Eds.), *Handbook of social psychology* (3rd ed., Vol. 2, pp. 233–346). New York: Random House.

McGuire, W. J. (1990). Dynamic operations of thought systems. *American Psychologist, 45,* 504–512.

McLaughlin, M., Irby, M. A., & Langman, J. (1994). *Urban sanctuaries.* San Francisco: Jossey-Bass.

Meier, D. (1992). Reinventing teaching. *Teachers College Record, 93*, 594–609.

Middleton, M. J., & Midgley, C. (1997). Avoiding the demonstration of lack of ability: An under–explored aspect of goal theory. *Journal of Educational Psychology, 89*, 710-718.

Moll, L., Amanti, C., Neff, D., & Gonzalez, N. (1992). Funds of knowledge for teaching: Using a qualitative approach to connect homes and classrooms. *Theory Into Practice, 31*, 132–141.

Nuttin, J., & Lens, W. (1985). *Future time perspective and motivation*. Hillsdale, NJ: Lawrence Erlbaum Associates.

Pressley, M. (1995). *Advanced educational psychology for educators, researchers, and policymakers*. New York: Harper Collins.

Rhodes, N., & Wood, W. (1992). Self-esteem and intelligence affect influenceability: The mediating role of message reception. *Psychological Bulletin, 111*, 156–171.

Salomon, G. (1987, September). *Beyond skill and knowledge: The role of mindfulness in learning and transfer*. Paper presented at the Second European Conference for Research on Learning and Instruction, Tubingen, Germany.

Scarr, S. (1988). Race and gender as psychological variables: Social and ethical issues. *American Psychologist, 43*, 56–59.

Schunk, D. H. (1996). Goal and self-evaluative influences during childrens' cognitive skill learning. *American Educational Research Journal, 33*, 359–382.

Smith, C. A., Lizotte, A. J., Thornberry, T. P., & Krohn, M. D. (1997). Resilience to delinquency. *The Prevention Researcher, 4*(2), 4–7.

Snow, R. E. (1981). Toward a theory of aptitude for learning: Fluid and crystallized abilities and their correlates. In M. P. Friedman, J. P. Das, & N. O'Connor (Eds.), *Intelligence and learning* (pp. 345–362). New York: Plenum.

Snow, R. E. (1989). Toward assessment of cognitive and conative structures in learning. *Educational Researcher, 18*(9), 8–14.

Snow, R. E. (1991). The concept of aptitude. In R. E. Snow & D. F. Wiley (Eds.), *Improving inquiry in social science* (pp. 249–284). Hillsdale, NJ: Lawrence Erlbaum Associates.

Snow, R. E. (1992). Aptitude theory: Yesterday, today, and tomorrow. *Educational Psychologist, 27*, 5–32.

Snow, R. E., Corno, L., & Jackson, D. N. III (1996). Individual differences in affective and conative functions. In D. Berliner & R. Calfee (Eds.), *Handbook of educational psychology* (pp. 243–310). New York: Macmillan.

Spearman, C. (1927). *The abilities of man*. New York: MacMillan.

Stanford Aptitude Seminar (in press). *Remaking the concept of aptitude: Extending the legacy of Richard E. Snow*. Mahwah, NJ: Lawrence Erlbaum Associates.

Terman, L. M. (1916). *The measurement of intelligence*. Boston: Houghton-Mifflin.

Webb, E. (1915). Character and intelligence. *British Journal of Psychology*, Monograph Supplement, Vol. I, No. III.

Weiner, B. (1990). History of motivational research in education. *Journal of Educational Psychology, 82*, 135–142.

Wigfield, A. (1997). Children's motivations for reading and reading engagement. In J. T. Guthrie & A. Wigfield (Eds.), *Reading engagement* (pp. 14–33). Newark, DE: International Reading Association.

Wijnen, W. H. F. W., & Snow, R. E. (1975). *Implementing an evaluation system for medical education* (Tech. Rep. No. 1). Maastricht, The Netherlands: Medische Faculteit Maastricht.

Willingham, W. (1985). *Success in college*. New York: The College Board.

Xu, J. & Corno, L. (1998). Case studies of third grade families doing homework. *Teachers College Record, 100, 402-436*.

Zimmerman, B. J. (1990). Self-regulated learning and academic achievement: An overview. *Educational Psychologist, 21*, 3–18.

9

How Goals and Plans Affect Action

Peter M. Gollwitzer
Bernd Schaal
Universität Konstanz, Germany

The concepts of goals and plans have not only played an important role in research on motivation and self-regulation (Ach, 1935; Carver & Scheier, 1981; Kruglanski, 1996; Lewin, 1926; Miller, Galanter, & Pribram, 1960), but goals and plans and their effects on affect, behavior, and cognition have become a very popular research topic in social psychology (Frese & Sabini, 1985; Gollwitzer & Bargh, 1996; Halisch & Kuhl, 1987; Pervin, 1989). The goal concept has also received recent attention in educational psychology (Snow & Corno, 1996). Modern goal theories can be classified in two groups: (a) goal content theories, and (b) self-regulation theories of goal striving. How these goal theories contribute to theorizing about educational implications of goal setting and goal striving is discussed in this chapter.

THE HISTORY OF THE CONCEPT OF GOALS

From the behaviorist perspective, goal-directed behavior is defined by a number of observable features. Central to this definition is the persistence of behavior until the desired end-state is attained (Tolman, 1925). Besides persistence, later researchers (Bindra, 1959) pointed to the appropriateness of goal-directed behavior in the sense that the goal-directed organism adopts an effective course of action in response to barriers on the way to the goal, which subscribes to a powerful incentive (e.g., food). If, for instance, one way of goal attainment is blocked, another course of action to the same goal is taken. Likewise, when the goal changes location, the goal-directed organism readily adapts to these changes by following the goal. Finally, besides persistence and appropriateness, hyperactivity and restlessness is observed in goal-striving organisms when exposed to stimuli that are associated with a previously pursued goal. This restlessness is commonly referred to as searching for the goal.

The observable features of goal-directed behavior compiled by behaviorist researchers (i.e., persistence, appropriateness, and searching) describe the phenomenology of goal-directed behavior from an external perspective. The behaviorist perspective falls short of what qualifies, for the individual, as an actual goal. The reference point of modern goal theories is, in contrast to the behaviorist view, exactly the internal subjective goal. Goal-directed behavior is studied in relation to goals held by the individual (e.g., a person's goal to quit smoking serves as a reference point for his or her efforts to achieve this goal). Research questions focus on whether and how setting personal goals affects a person's behaviors. This theoretical orientation has its own historical precursors that reach back far beyond the heydays of behaviorism. James' (1890) included a chapter on will in which he discussed the following question: How is it possible that a behavior that a person intends to perform (i.e., has been set as a goal by this person) fails to be executed? James referred to such problems as issues of the obstructed will, but he also raised questions related to what he called issues of the explosive will (i.e., how is it possible that an undesired behavior is performed even though a person has set the goal to suppress it?).

James' theorizing rests on the assumption that behavior can potentially be regulated by a person's resolutions (or intentions or subjective goals) even though in certain situations and at certain times it may be difficult for such resolutions to come true. In any case, the individual's subjective goal is the reference point for the goal-directed action and not a powerful incentive focused on by an outside observer (or scientist). The question raised by James is whether people meet their goals in their actions, not whether their actions toward an incentive carry features of persistence, appropriateness, and searching.

A further prominent historical figure in theorizing about subjective goals and their effects on behavior is McDougall. He explicitly saw the reference point for goal-directed behavior as being in a person's subjective purpose or goal (McDougall, 1908). He postulated that subjective goals guide a person's behavior. This guidance is thought to be achieved through cognitive activity pertaining to the analysis of the present situational context and the envisioned event or goal state to be realized. Furthermore, progress toward and attainment of the goal are seen as pleasurable experiences, whereas thwarting and failure are seen as painful or disagreeable. With respect to the observable features of goal-directed activity, however, McDougall referred to the same aspects as the behaviorists (e.g., persistence and appropriateness).

In the history of German psychology, the issue of goal-directedness of behavior played a particularly prominent role and resulted in an intensive exchange of opinions. This controversy began at the beginning of the century and lasted up to the 1930s. The main protagonists were Ach (for a summary see Ach, 1935) and Lewin (1926). In an attempt to establish a scientific analysis of the phenomenon of volitional action or willing (*Willenspsychologie*), Ach used a very simple paradigm. Subjects were trained to respond repeatedly and consistently to specific stimuli (e.g., numbers or meaningless syllables) with certain responses (e.g., to add or to rhyme, respectively). When these responses had become habitual, subjects were instructed to employ their will and execute antagonistic responses (e.g., to subtract or read, respectively). Ach discovered that forming the intention to respond to the critical stimuli with an antagonistic response helps "to get one's will." The theorizing on how an intention achieves the reliable execution of the intended action was based on the concept of determination. Ach assumed that linking, in one's mind, an anticipated situation to a concrete intended behavior creates what he called a determination and this determination would in turn urge the person to execute the intended action once the specified situational stimulus is encountered. The strength of the determination should depend on how concretely people specify the intended action and the respective situation; concreteness was thought to intensify determination. Moreover, the intensity of the act of intending (willing) should also increase determination because intensive willing induces a heightened commitment ("I really will do it!"). Determination was expected to elicit directly the intended behavior without a person's conscious intent to get started. Ach speculated that determination may affect perceptual and attentional processes so that the specified situation is cognized in a way that favors the initiation of the intended action.

Lewin (1926), in contrast, proposed a need theory of goal striving. Intentions, like needs, assign a valence (in German: *Aufforderungscharakter*) to objects and events in people's social and nonsocial surroundings. For a person who intends to mail a letter, a mailbox entices (or at least calls or reminds) him or her to deposit the letter, very much like food entices a hungry person to eat. Because needs can be satisfied by various types of behaviors that may all substitute for each other in terms of reducing need tension (e.g., eating fruit, vegetables, bread, and so forth), many different intention-related behaviors qualify for satisfying the quasi-need associated with an intention. The amount of the tension associated with the quasi-need was assumed to directly relate to the intensity of a person's goal strivings. The exact amount of tension may vary. First, it is affected by the degree of quasi-need fulfillment (i.e., tension comes to a final rest when the goal is achieved), but it is also thought to depend on the strength of the relevant real needs (i.e., superordinate drives and general life goals) and how strongly these are related to the quasi-need. It is assumed that people commonly see more than just one route to goal achievement (e.g., contacting a friend) and that all these routes may substitute for each other (e.g., phone, fax, e-mail, letter). In other words, an intention can be realized in many different ways and the blocking of one of them should readily lead to attempts to realize the intention through alternative routes (Lissner, 1933; Mahler, 1933; Ovsiankina, 1928).

The major difference between Ach's and Lewin's accounts of how intentions affect behavior is that Lewin employed classic motivational variables such as needs and incentives (valences) and attempted to predict the effects of intentions on the basis of these variables. Ach, however, focused on how people form intentions and attempted to predict the effects of intentions by the intensity of the act of intention formation and the framing of the intention. He postulated that these volitional (willing) variables function independently of the motivational basis of an intention.

MODERN GOAL THEORIES

Many of the ideas on goal-directed behaviors, as presented by James (1890), McDougall (1908), the German psychology of will, and, to a lesser degree, the behaviorists, have been adopted by modern goal theories. Today, there are no big theoretical controversies and we rarely observe experiments that critically compare different theories, but there is a wealth of different theories and ideas on goals and goal-directed behavior. In order to arrive at a comprehensive presentation of the many different theories, we have grouped them according to aspects of similarity. This has led to two major categories:

1. Content theories of goal striving, which attempt to explain differences in goal-directed behaviors and their consequences in terms of what is specified as the goal by the individual. Differences in goal content are expected to drastically affect a person's behaviors.

2. Self-regulation theories of goal striving, which attempt to explain the volitional processes that mediate the effects of goals on behavior. As we explain in this chapter, there are two different types of self-regulation theories, one of a more motivational, the other of a more cognitive nature.

GOAL CONTENT THEORIES

Goal contents vary because goals may be challenging or modest, specific or vague, abstract or concrete, proximal or distal, with a negative or positive outcome focus, and so forth. But goals may also cover different themes and issues because they can be based on different needs and incentives. Moreover, the type of implicit theory the individual holds regarding the functioning of the subject matter involved further determines goal attainment. The research strategy adopted by goal content theorists compares the effects of goals varying on the dimension of interest (e.g., specific vs. vague goals, goals based on autonomy needs vs. goals based on material needs) on a relevant dependent variable (e.g., quantity or quality of performance).

Goal Specificity

The prototype of a goal content theory is the goal setting theory, put forth by Locke and Latham (1990). The basic thesis in this theory is that challenging goals that are spelled out in specific terms have a particular positive effect on behavior. In a very large number of mainly experimental studies, challenging specific goals were superior to modest specific goals, as well as to challenging vague goals (i.e., "do your best" goals). In a typical study conducted in a work setting (Latham & Yukl, 1975), woodworkers were sent out to the forest equipped with goals with different contents or no goals at all. Challenging goals (i.e., standards above what can be achieved with normal effort expenditure) led to a higher productivity as observed in the no-goal control group when goals were formulated in specific terms (e.g., number of trees to be cut). Specific non-challenging goals implying modest standards failed to increase productivity, as did challenging but vague goals, such as "do your best."

Needs as Sources of Goals

Locke and Latham, in their theorizing, focused on structural features of goal content (i.e., specifity and challenge). Deci and Ryan (1991) criticized this point of view by stating that not all goals are created equal. According to Deci and Ryan, goals affect a person's behavior differently depending on the kind of need that is the source of a person's goal setting. Based on their self-determination theory, Deci and Ryan postulated that goals in the service of autonomy, competence, and social integration needs lead to better performances in the sense of greater creativity, higher cognitive flexibility, greater depth in information processing, and more effective coping with failure. Deci and Ryan argued that the respective needs are assumed to further autonomous, self-determined, and authentical goal-striving. This positive kind of goal activity is contrasted with a less effective, negative kind, which is unreflectively controlled from outside (e.g., goal assignments by authorities) or from inside (e.g., goal setting based on feelings of obligation).

Implicit Theories as Sources of Goals

A further goal content theory is suggested by Dweck (1991; Elliot & Dweck, 1988). Dweck's theory focuses on achievement goals and postulates a distinction between learning goals and performance goals. The source of goal setting is a person's implicit theory about the nature of ability, not a person's needs, as asserted by Deci and Ryan. In an achievement situation, persons set themselves learning or performance goals depending on whether they hold an entity theory (i.e., they believe that the amount of ability is fixed and cannot easily be changed) or an incremental theory (i.e., they believe that the amount of ability can be improved by learning). Entity theorists try to find out via task performance how capable they are, thus making inferences on the amount of their respective talent. They set themselves performance goals. Incremental theorists want to know where and why they are making mistakes in order to learn how to improve—they set themselves learning goals. These distinct types of goals have important behavioral consequences, in particular when it comes to coping with failure. For individuals with performance goals, negative outcomes signal a lack of intelligence and thus result in helpless reactions (e.g., low persistence). People with learning goals, on the other hand, view setbacks as cues to focus on new behavioral strategies. Their behavior is oriented toward mastering the causes of the setback.

Further Goal Content Theories

Two other important distinctions of goal content theories need to be mentioned. The first is discussed by Bandura and Schunk (1981) and relates to the time frame of goal attainment. Proximal goals relate to what one does in the present or the near future, whereas distal goals point far into the future. Bandura and Schunk (1981) observed that proximal goals improved children's arithmetic attainment. This effect was mediated by an increase in the children's strength of self-efficacy and intrinsic interest in mathematics. Distal goals, however, are too far removed in time to guide a person's action effectively, as they fail to provide small successes that promote self-efficacy and interest.

A second important difference in the framing of goals has been introduced by Higgins, Roney, Crowe, and Hymes (1994) and pertains to the valence of one's goal pursuit. Achievement goals with a positive outcome focus (i.e., goals that focus on the presence or absence of positive outcomes) favor task performance, whereas goals with a negative outcome focus (i.e., goals that focus on the presence or absence of negative outcomes) undermine it. In addition, individuals with chronic discrepancies between their actual and ideal selves (i.e., people who fall short of their ideals) are found to prefer to set themselves positive outcome focus goals, whereas individuals with discrepancies between their actual and ought selves (i.e., people who fall short of their duties) prefer negative outcome focus goals.

SELF-REGULATION THEORIES OF GOAL STRIVING

As experience tells us, there is often a long way from goal setting to goal attainment. Having formed a goal is often just a first step toward goal attainment and requires that a host of subsequent implementational problems are solved successfully. These problems are manifold, as they pertain to initiating goal-directed actions and bringing them to a successful ending. To solve problems effectively, people step up efforts in the face of difficulties, bypass barriers, compensate for failures and shortcomings, and negotiate conflicts between goals. Self-regulation theories analyze how the individual effectively solves these problems of goal implementation. Often, these theories focus on one of these problems in particular and ignore the others. All of the self-regulation theories, however, attempt to propose general principles that apply to the problems of implementation of all goals, despite differences in content.

Regulating Competing Goal Pursuits

Kuhl (1983, 1984; Kuhl & Beckmann, 1994) focused on self-regulatory processes that contribute to goal achievement in the face of competing action tendencies. Following Atkinson and Birch's (1970) theorizing on the dynamics of action, it is assumed that at any given point, many different action tendencies, both waxing and waning in strength, coexist. For an ordered action sequence to occur, Kuhl assumed that a current guiding goal had to be shielded from competing goal intentions. He termed this shielding mechanism "action control" and differentiated a number of control strategies, such as attention control, emotion control, motivation control, and environment control. Kuhl further assumed that whether and how effectively these strategies are employed depends on the current control mode of the individual. Two control modes are defined by Kuhl: (a) action orientation, which leads a person to concentrate on the planning and initiation of goal-directed action and to respond flexibly to the respective contextual demands effectively, using the listed control strategies, and (b) state orientation, which implies that a person cannot disengage from competing incomplete goals and is caught up in dysfunctional persevering thoughts, directed at past or future successes or failures.

Goal researchers are becoming increasingly aware that goals are not created in isolation. People set themselves many goals, and these goals may come into conflict with each other. When goals are short term, the process of shielding an ongoing goal pursuit from competing others seems most important. Other self-regulatory processes are needed, however, when the conflicting goals are enduring, such as self-defining goals (Wicklund & Gollwitzer, 1982), personal strivings (Emmons, 1989), or life tasks (Cantor, 1994). Emmons and King (1988) observed that conflict between and within personal strivings is associated with poor well-being. Conflict was found to relate to negative affectivity and/or physical symptomatology. Emmons (1996) argued that creative integrations of a person's strivings might reverse the negative effects of conflict.

Conflict between goals has also been discussed in the theoretical framework of life tasks (Cantor & Fleeson, 1994). Life tasks, such as doing well academically, exert specific influences on behavior, as they are interpreted differently over the life course and across situational contexts. Life tasks are often confronted with difficulties, frustrations, anxieties, and self doubts, and the individual's style of appraising these hindrances leads to a typical pattern of action goals aimed at overcoming these obstacles. For instance, college students who worry about their abilities when they experience failure (i.e., outcome-focused individuals; Harlow & Cantor, 1994) may, in a strategic effort to meet their academic life task, turn for reassurance to others who they regard as confidantes and encouragers. In this case, social goals are put in the service of academic goals.

Regulation of Goals and Reduction of Goal Discrepancies

If one considers a person's goal pursuit as an issue of discrepancy reduction, a host of further self-regulatory processes can be identified. Discrepancy-reduction theories of goal pursuit do not conceive of goals as something attractive (i.e., specifying a positive incentive corresponding to some vital need) that pulls the individual in the direction of goal attainment. The set goal only specifies a performance standard. Prototypical are Bandura's (1991) ideas on the self-regulation of action. According to Bandura, goals have no motivational consequences per se; they only specify the conditions that allow a positive or negative self-evaluation. If the set goal is attained through one's actions, a positive self-evaluation prevails, whereas staying below one's goal leads to a negative self-evaluation. Thus, the individual is pushed by the negative self-evaluation associated with the discrepancy, and pulled by the anticipated positive self-evaluation intrinsically linked to closing the gap between the status quo and the goal (i.e., performance standard).

These basic ideas imply that goals stimulate effortful acting toward goal attainment (what Bandura referred to as high performance motivation) only when people recognize a discrepancy between the status quo and the set goal. Bandura therefore proposed attaining feedback as a powerful measure to stimulate goal pursuit. Moreover, people are expected to engage in effort to reduce the experienced discrepancy only when they have acquired a strong sense of self-efficacy with respect to the required actions. Doubts about possessing the capabilities necessitated by these actions undermine a person's readiness to act on the goal.

Bandura's ideas remind one of control theory as suggested by Carver and Scheier (1981). Stimulated by Miller, Galanter, and Pribram (1960), Carver and Scheier applied a control theoretical framework to the study of goal-directed action. The central conceptual unit of their analysis is the negative feedback loop. In a negative feedback loop, a reference criterion is compared with a perceptual input in a comparator. If there is a difference between the two, a signal is generated (i.e., an error is detected). The detected error elicits behavior that reduces the discrepancy between the reference criterion and the perceptual input. Following Powers' (1974) proposal that behavior is organized hierarchically, Carver and Scheier assumed a cascading loop structure. A positive affective response as a consequence of goal attainment is not assumed, however, nor is the detection of error associated with negative affect. Rather, the speed of progress toward a goal is seen as the source of positive or negative feelings in a person's goal pursuit. The intensity of these feelings is regulated again in a feedback loop: If the speed meets a set reference criterion, positive feelings emerge, and vice versa (Carver & Scheier, 1990).

The Model of Action Phases

The Rubicon model of action phases (Gollwitzer, 1990; Heckhausen, 1991; Heckhausen & Gollwitzer, 1987) stands for an integration of motivational and volitional aspects of goal setting and goal striving within a single theoretical framework. It emphasizes that distinct tasks have to be solved in the various action phases. The model assumes that a person's motives and needs produce more wishes and desires than can possibly be realized. People therefore have to make choices on the basis of deliberating the feasibility and desirability of various wishes and desires. This consideration is reminiscent of the classic motivational variables (see Atkinson & Birch, 1970) of desirability (i.e., expected value of the goal) and feasibility (i.e., expectations on whether the goal can be realized). However, the action phases model was introduced as a critique of traditional motivational theorizing on goal-directed action in an attempt to integrate research on motivation and volition. The variables of desirability and feasibility may suffice for explaining choices of wishes and desires but they definitely fall short of explaning the implementation of a chosen goal. The model of action phases was therefore designed to explicate the differences between the motivational issue of goal choice and the volitional issue of goal implementation by taking further variables into account.

The model takes a comprehensive temporal (horizontal) view of the course of goal pursuit, which extends from the origins of a person's wishes and desires to the evaluation of the attained outcomes. The course of goal pursuit entails four different consecutive action phases. In each of these phases, a qualitatively distinct goal-attainment-related problem has to be faced in order to translate wishes into desired end-states. In the first action phase (predecisional phase), the various wishes and desires are deliberated in light of the evaluative criteria of feasibility and desirability in order to select those wishes and desires that one decides to implement. A positive decision transfers a wish or desire into a binding goal, which is accompanied by a feeling of determination or obligation and marks the transition into the subsequent phase. This second action phase (postdecisional and preactional phase) is characterized by the task of initiating goal-directed actions. Initiating goal-directed actions may be simple if action initiation is well practiced or routine. But if the goal-directed action is unfamiliar, complex, or one is still undecided about when and where to act, initiation of goal-directed behavior is problematic. However, by planning the when, where, and how of acting, this problem can be easily solved. With the initiation of goal-directed behaviors, the individual enters the third action phase (actional phase). The task associated with this phase is bringing goal-directed behaviors to a successful ending. For this purpose, it is necessary that the individual readily responds to opportunities that allow progress toward the goal and increases efforts in the face of difficulties and obstacles. In the final action phase (postactional, evaluative phase), the individual, after having achieved some kind of outcome, evaluates goal achievement by comparing what has been achieved with what has been desired. The individual looks back at the original deliberation and evaluation of wishes and desires that may trigger renewed deliberation and reevaluation of the feasibilities and desirabilities. As a consequence, standards of performance may be reduced or other wishes and desires may now appear more feasible and desirable, and decisions to act on a certain goal may be confirmed or altered.

Action Phases and Mind-Sets

The Rubicon model of action phases stimulated theoretical notions that help to understand people's functioning at the various stages of goal pursuit. The first notion is the distinction between deliberative and implemental mind sets. Based on the Würzburg school of thought's concept of mind-sets (Külpe, 1904; Watt, 1905), it is argued (Gollwitzer, 1990; Gollwitzer & Bayer, 1999) that people develop corresponding mind-sets when addressing the various tasks implied by the different action phases. These mind-sets are thought to be functional for task solution and thus effectively promote people's goal pursuits.

Studies conducted on the mind-sets associated either with deliberating about one's wishes and desires (i.e., the deliberative mind-set of the predecisional phase) or with planning the initiation of goal-directed actions (i.e., the implemental mind-set of the preactional phase) support this idea. When subjects are asked to engage in intensive deliberation of whether to turn an important personal wish or desire into a goal, a cognitive orientation (i.e., the deliberative mind-set) with the following features originates: People become more open-minded with respect to processing available information, and heeded information is processed more effectively while peripheral information is also encoded (Gollwitzer, 1991; Heckhausen, & Gollwitzer, 1987). Second, people process information that is relevant to making decisions (e.g., desirability-related information) more effectively than implementation-related information (e.g., information on the sequencing of actions; Gollwitzer, Heckhausen, & Steller, 1990). Finally, with respect to desirability-related information, the pros and cons of making a decision are analyzed in an impartial manner (Beckmann & Gollwitzer, 1987). Moreover, feasibility-related information is analyzed in a relatively objective, nonillusionary way. As compared to a control group, Gollwitzer and Kinney (1989) observed reduced illusion of control judgments with subjects in a deliberative mind-set, and Taylor and Gollwitzer (1996) obtained more modest self-perceptions (on personal attributes such as creativity, intellectual ability, social intelligence) and self-evaluations (i.e., answers on the Rosenberg Self-Esteem Scale). The various features of the cognitive orientation associated with the deliberative mind-set should facilitate the making of good (i.e., realistic) goal decisions because they prevent perceiving one's wishes (i.e., the potential goals) as more desirable or feasible than they actually are.

When people are asked to plan the implementation of a chosen goal or project, a cognitive orientation (i.e., the implemental mind-set) with quite different attributes originates: People become closed-minded in the sense that they are no longer distracted by irrelevant information (Gollwitzer, 1991). They are also very effective in processing information related on implementation-related issues (e.g., the sequencing of actions; Gollwitzer, Heckhausen, & Steller, 1990). Moreover, desirability-related information is processed in a partial manner, favoring pros over cons (Beckmann & Gollwitzer, 1987), and feasibility-related information is analyzed in a manner that favors illusionary optimism. This optimism extends to the illusion of control in the face of uncontrollable outcomes (Gollwitzer & Kinney, 1989) to a person's self-perception of important personal attributes (e.g., cheerfulness, academic ability, sensitivity to others, self-respect, drive to achieve, leadership ability), and to the perceived invulnerability to both controllable and uncontrollable risks (e.g., developing an addiction to prescription drugs or losing a partner to an early death, respectively). Finally, the implemental mind-set elevates people's mood and their self-esteem. It is important to note that the mind-set effects on self-perception and perceived vulnerability to risk are not mediated by mood or self-esteem changes (Taylor & Gollwitzer, 1996). All of the listed features of the implemental mind-set should facilitate goal achievement, as they allow the individual to effectively cope with classic problems of goal implementation, such as being distracted with irrelevant things, doubting the attractiveness of the pursued goal, or being pessimistic about its feasibility.

In summary, it appears that the stages of goal pursuit are more efficiently traversed when a person develops the appropriate mind-sets at the various phases of goal pursuit. When it comes to goal-setting, a deliberative mind-set seems most conducive. It can be created by intensively weighing the desirability and feasibility of one's wishes and desires. When it comes to the implementation of chosen goals, however, an implemental mind-set seems more appropriate. People can establish this mind-set by planning the implementation of their goals.

Implementation Intentions Versus Goal Intentions

A second theoretical notion stimulated by the action phases model is that of the distinction between goal intentions and implementation intentions (Gollwitzer, 1993, 1999). Implementation intentions relate to a particular form of planning where the individual commits him or herself to perform an intended goal-directed behavior when a particular situation is encountered. Implementation intentions are qualitatively distinct from goal intentions in four different aspects. First, there is the difference in format. Goal intentions are commonly the end result of the deliberation of one's wishes and desires in the predecisional phase and are formulated as "I want to achieve outcome X" (e.g., a slim body) or "I intend to achieve behavior X" (e.g., eat vegetables). Implementation intentions, however, are the result of deliberating different ways of goal attainment in the preactional phase. They specify a certain situation in which a highly specified behavior is intended to be executed and are formulated as "If situation Y (e.g., restaurant) arises, I will perform behavior Z" (e.g., order a vegetarian meal). Thus, implementation intentions link an anticipated future situation (opportunity) to a certain intended goal-directed behavior. Second, goal intentions and implementation intentions differ in their hierarchicality. Goal intentions are superordinate intentions defining a certain desired end-state, whereas implementation intentions are subordinate intentions defining the when, where, and how of a goal-directed behavior. Third, these two kinds of intentions differ in their purpose. Goal intentions are formulated in order to turn wishes and desires into binding goals and to create determination and commitment to the goal. Implementation intentions are formulated to promote goal pursuit (i.e., the initiation of goal-directed behaviors) toward an existing goal. The fourth difference relates to the distinct consequences of these two types of intentions. As a consequence of forming a goal intention, a commitment to achieving the desired end-state develops and the reduction of any realized goal discrepancy becomes an issue. Forming implementation intentions, on the other hand, creates a commitment to perform a certain goal-directed behavior in the presence of a critical situation.

Implementation intentions constitute a powerful strategy for overcoming problems in pursuing one's goals. Forming implementation intentions increases a person's readiness to terminate deliberation (Gollwitzer, Heckhausen, & Ratajczak, 1990) and helps to get started with goal-directed actions. Goal intentions that are furnished with implementation intentions are completed more often than mere goal intentions (Gollwitzer & Brandstätter, 1997). Implementation intentions achieve their effects by passing on the control of goal-directed behavior from the self to environmental cues, thus facilitating the initiation of goal-directed behaviors in the presence of the anticipated situation (specified good opportunity). It is assumed that the mental representation of the specified opportunity becomes highly activated, thus making it more accessible. Moreover, it is hypothesized that the initiation of the intended goal-directed behavior in the presence of the critical situation becomes automated. Several experimental studies were conducted to test these hypotheses (Gollwitzer, 1993, 1999).

One series of studies examined the question of whether forming implementation intentions leads to heightened activation of the mental representation of the critical stimuli. In a study by Steller (1992), the embedded figures test was used (Gottschaldt, 1926; Witkin, 1950). This test consists of geometrical figures (b-figures) that contain a smaller partial figure (a-figure). Using Gestalt principles, the a-figure is hidden in the b-figures and is thus difficult to detect. Still, following the idea that implementation intentions would lead to heightened accessibility and better detection of the a-figure, it was observed that participants showed an enhanced detection performance when they had formed implementation intentions that used the a-figure as the critical situational cue.

More evidence for the hypothesis of heightened activation of the mental representation of implementation intention relevant stimuli was found in a dichotic listening experiment by Mertin (1994). It was observed that critical words describing the anticipated situations specified in implementation intentions were highly disruptive to focused attention. Participants' performance of shadowing (i.e., efficient repeating of the words presented to the attended channel) was severely hampered when critical words were presented to the nonattended channel. Apparently, even when efforts are made to direct attention to the shadowing task, the critical words still managed to attract attention, as indicated by a weakened shadowing performance.

Finally, in a recall experiment by Seehausen, Bayer, and Gollwitzer (1994), participants were first asked to form implementation intentions with respect to performing two different tasks (a computer task and a handicraft task). Numerous ways of performing these tasks were offered (i.e., different means, different places, different times, and so forth). In a subsequent incidental recall test, participants had to recall all of the offered possible ways of performing these tasks. Participants recalled the ways they had specified in their implementation intentions better than the nonchosen ways. This was true even when the incidental recall test occurred 48 hours after participants had formed the implementation intentions.

Gollwitzer (1993, 1993) interpreted these findings by assuming that the mental representation of the anticipated situations specified in implementation intentions becomes highly activated and thus easily accessible. This has perceptual, attentional, and memory-related consequences. The situations specified in implementation intentions are more easily detected, more readily attended to, and more easily retrieved from memory. All of this furthers effective action initiation once the anticipated critical opportunity is encountered.

A second series of experiments dealt with the issue of the automatization of action initiation through forming implementation intentions. Implementation intentions are expected to lead to automatic initiation of the intended goal-directed behavior when the situation that was specified in an implementation intention arises. If this were true, people who have formed implementation intentions should initiate goal-directed behaviors with comparatively higher immediacy. Gollwitzer and Brandstätter (1997) exposed experimental participants to an offensive videotape in which a male made racist remarks. Participants were instructed to either form goal intentions to counterargue or goal intentions that were furnished with implementation intentions that specified good opportunities to present counterarguments. When participants were finally allowed to counterargue, implementation intention participants initiated their counterarguments more immediately when these good opportunities arose than did mere goal intention participants.

High immediacy of initiation of goal-directed behavior implies that little cognitive capacity is needed. A more direct test of the efficiency of action initiation requires a dual task experiment, however. Brandstätter (1992) performed an experiment that involved a button-pressing task embedded as the secondary task in a dual task paradigm. Participants were instructed to form the goal intention to press a button as soon as possible whenever numbers appeared on the screen but not when letters were shown. Participants in the implementation intention condition were asked to form the further intention to press the button particularly fast when the number 3 was presented. Implementation intention participants showed a substantial increase in speed (the number 3 lead to faster reactions than the other numbers) as compared to a control group. This effect was independent of whether the simultaneously demanded primary task was easy or difficult to perform. Apparently, the immediacy of responding as induced by implementation intentions is effortless in the sense that it does not put much cognitive load on limited processing resources and thus persists even when the cognitive demands of the primary task in a pair of tasks are high.

Further evidence that forming implementation intentions leads to automatization of action initiation comes from a study by Malzacher (1992). She used a retaliation paradigm (Zillmann & Cantor, 1976) in which participants were first angered by one of the two experimenters. The second experimenter, in a subsequent phase of the experiment, encouraged the participants to retaliate. One group of participants formed the mere goal intention to retaliate, whereas another group of participants also formed implementation intentions ("As soon as I see the other experimenter again, I'll tell her what an unfriendly person she is."). Then, the second experimenter performed a reading speed task with the subjects that actually used a subliminal priming procedure. Pictures of the unfriendly experimenter and of a neutral person served as primes. Targets were words describing positive and negative personal attributes. Implementation intention participants read negative target words comparatively faster and positive target words comparatively slower when subliminally primed with the picture of the unfriendly experimenter as compared to the neutral picture; no such effect was observed with goal intention participants. This finding indicates that situational cues specified in an implementation intention directly elicit cognitive processes without conscious intent; in this case, the activation of relevant knowledge and the inhibition of irrelevant knowledge, which facilitate the initiation of the intended action. That implementation intentions may lead to immediate and efficient action initiation without conscious intent is also suggested by an experiment conducted by Lengfelder (1996). Lengfelder replicated the findings of Brandstätter's (1992) dual task experiment with frontal lobe patients who are known to be deficient in the conscious control of action.

The reported series of experiments suggests that forming implementation intentions not only affects the mental representation of the critical stimuli but also the initiation of the intended action. Action initiation becomes more immediate, efficient, and no longer requires conscious intent. These are all features of the automatic initiation of action and therefore it can be concluded that forming implementation intentions is a self-regulatory strategy that transforms the conscious control of action into automatic control.

The presented experiments only speak to the control of wanted behaviors through implementation intentions. But what about the control of unwanted behaviors? Schaal (1993) conducted an experiment to test whether implementation intentions support an ongoing goal pursuit by resisting a response to unwanted distractions. Subjects in this experiment had to work on a boring but strenuous task (i.e., a series of arithmetic problems) under conditions of repeated but unexpected exposure to highly disruptive distractions (i.e., clips of award-winning commercials). Subjects were either asked to form the goal intention to not let oneself get distracted or to form additional implementation intentions regarding these distractions. Two types of implementation intentions were distinguished. One group of subjects was asked to form task-facilitating implementation intentions (i.e., to work harder as soon as the distractions arise), the other group was asked to form temptation-inhibiting implementation intentions (i.e., to ignore the distractions as soon as they arise). Schaal found that implementation intentions led to higher resistance to distractions as demonstrated by a better performance on the strenuous task. Although both implementation intention groups outperformed the goal-intention-only group, the results of the implementation intention groups differentiated. Temptation-inhibiting implementation intentions supported goal pursuit to a higher degree than task-facilitating implementation intentions. In two follow-up studies, Schaal and Gollwitzer (1997) explored the reasons for the superiority of temptation inhibiting implementation intentions over task-facilitating implementation intentions. As it turned out, task-facilitating implementation intentions produce overmotivation and thus hamper successful performance in the ongoing goal pursuit. This implies that task-facilitating implementation intentions can only be expected to show effects when the motivation to perform the ongoing goal pursuit is not very high. If this motivation is high, however, people are better off forming temptation-inhibiting implementation intentions, as this type of implementation intention guarantees effective goal pursuit independent of one's motivation to be successful.

EDUCATIONAL IMPLICATIONS OF MODERN GOAL THEORIES

The goal theories just described have educational implications, because different goal-setting and goal-striving strategies should have differential educational impacts. In what ways can educators and their students learn from these theories and the extensive research findings concerning goals? Two questions seem to be central for the application of what is known about the consequences of goal setting and goal striving in educational and instructional settings. First, there is the question of the consequences of goal setting and second, the question of how goal regulation plays its role. These two issues are discussed next on the basis of the goal content and goal regulation theories reported previously.

How Should Goals Be Framed?

As known by the work of Locke and Latham (1990), goal attainment is more likely when challenging goals are formulated in a highly specific manner. The superiority of specific goals lies in the concreteness of defining what is to be attained. In educational settings, this can be achieved by concrete definitions of what should be learned how much and until when. For example when a student tries to learn how to solve complex arithmetic problems, the learning should be more effective when learning goals are set in terms of concrete step-by-step goals and the amount of time for learning the single steps is explicitly defined. "Do-your-best" goals, however, should lead to less time spent on these problems (more breaks and earlier termination of studying). The practicing of already acquired arithmetic skills should also benefit from setting goals that concretely specify the amount of time of practicing, the amount of problems to be practiced, or both. Following Deci and Ryan (1991), however, such learning or exercise goals should always be embedded into students' autonomy and competence needs. Although solving algebraic equations, for instance, may not immediately appeal to these needs, educators will have to create such links by highlighting the long-term consequences of acquiring mathematical skills.

The educational implications of Dweck's (1991) theory on the impact of people's implicit theories on goal setting relate to teachers and students alike. It is the educator's task to evaluate their students' performance, to give feedback in a way that provides students with sufficient information about their past performance, and to give hints and advice on how to do better in the future. But the teacher's giving of feedback should depend on their implicit theories about their students' abilities and capabilities. Teachers who favor an entity theory about students' abilities and talents should differ in their feedback from teachers who favor incremental theories about abilities and talents. Teachers with entity theories should be characterized by making global judgments, having fixed opinions about the capabilities of individual students, and verification of these opinions via biased information processing. As a consequence, self-fulfilling prophecies and labeling effects should be observed on the side of the students. Teachers who favor incremental theories, on the other hand, should be characterized by giving feedback that aims at improving each individual student's abilities (i.e., feedback that focuses on possible changes and installs a mastery orientation in students). Giving such feedback requires an individuated information processing of students. Teachers' reflecting on their own implicit theories appears to be a prerequisite for promoting incremental theories in their students. Teachers who hold entity theories do not seem to be able to install incremental theories with their students, who in turn will have to learn without the volitional benefits associated with incremental theories about abilities and talents.

But the students' implicit theories about their capabilities and talents are important as well. Students holding an entity theory about their abilities differ in many ways from students who hold incremental theories. According to Dweck (1991, 1996), entity theorists (i.e., personal attributes such as intelligence are perceived as fixed and stable) make self-evaluations that focus on the amount of talent one possesses, which in turn leads to retreat and self-punishment in the case of failure experiences. Implicit entity theorists prefer to set themselves performance goals that are known to be correlated with negative outcome expectancies, low appraisal of self-efficacy, fear of failure, and inferior performance (Elliot & Church, 1997). Implicit incremental theorists, on the other hand, aim to develop their personal attributes (e.g., intelligence). They therefore prefer to set themselves learning goals, as they need to understand the dynamics of improving their standing on these attributes. Failure experiences thus lead to analyzing the conditions and processes responsible for the negative outcome. Learning goals and the associated striving for mastery are correlated with positive outcome expectancies, high self-efficacy appraisals, and hope for success and superior performance. Thus, concluding from Dweck's (1991) theorizing, educators should not only adopt incremental theories and set themselves learning goals with respect to the promotion of their students' capabilities, they should also help their students adopt such theories and set themselves learning goals.

Finally, distinguishing between positive versus negative outcome focus seems also relevant to goal-setting in educational settings. Teachers and students should avoid framing their educational goals in terms of a negative outcome focus (i.e., the focus is on the presence and absence of negative outcomes: "If I fail to attain the goal, this will be horrible" or "I simply have to avoid being a failure", respectively). Rather, setting goals that are framed with a positive outcome focus is called for (i.e., the focus is on the presence and absence of positive outcomes: "If I succeed in attaining the goal, this will be wonderful" or "Not succeeding on the goal will make me sad," respectively). Focusing on positive outcomes favors task performance and persistence in the face of difficulties, whereas a negative outcome focus undermines performance and persistence (Higgins et al., 1994). Highlighting the negative consequences of failing to meet educational goals is thus a counterproductive instructional strategy that leads to decreased effort, decreased persistence and inferior performance.

It appears then that promoting efficient learning in educational settings is not only a matter of good teaching in the sense of making it easier for students to cognitively grab the presented materials, but it is also a matter of goal setting. If educational settings induce the framing of goals that are challenging and highly specific, related to students' autonomy and competence needs, and focused on improving one's standing and on positive outcomes rather than negative outcomes, learning should be more interesting, successful, and persistent. Certainly, there should be further goal-framing dimensions other than the ones we have named so far that are relevant in educational contexts. One of these is the dimension of proximity of the goal. Proximal goals should benefit learning more than distal goals, as the latter provide fewer opportunities to receive feedback on one's progress toward the goal (Bandura & Schunk, 1981).

How Should Goals Be Regulated?

Progress toward educational goals can be blocked because they fall prey to competing goals (e.g., leisure-activity goals). In order to regulate competing goal pursuits, students may engage in a number of different control strategies such as attention control, emotion control, motivation control, and environment control. Engaging in these control strategies, the student develops an action orientation that is described by Kuhl (1983, 1984) as the counterpart of state orientation, which is associated with failing to disengage from competing incomplete goals and being caught up in persevering thoughts. Educators should therefore instruct students in the use of these control strategies, thus enabling them to shield a current, guiding goal from other competing goals. Becoming involved with the named action control strategies leads, according to Kuhl (1983, 1984), to the effective implementation of ongoing goal pursuits.

However, progress toward educational goals may become problematic when goals contradict each other (for instance, the conflict between goals of becoming an expert in some academic field versus goals related to personality development). Such conflicts between self-defining goals (Wicklund & Gollwitzer, 1982), personal strivings (Emmons, 1989), or life tasks (Cantor, 1994) were found to relate to negative affectivity and poor well-being. Encouraging the creative integration of such conflicting goals should therefore be a prominent task of educators (Emmons, 1996), because solving such conflicts allows for successful personality development across the life span.

Bandura (1991) considered a person's goal pursuit as a reduction of discrepancies between an actual situation and a to-be-attained end-state. Goals, per se, do not motivate a person to act toward a desired end-state; rather, it is the detection of a discrepancy between the actual state and the desired end-state and the anticipated reduction of this discrepancy. The detection of discrepancies thus plays a primary role. In many educational settings, goal discrepancies arise when the teacher or educator gives performance feedback. The person who gives feedback should thus ensure that the feedback is objective and reflects the discrepancy that still exists. As only high self-efficacious individuals set out to reduce discrepancies, the feedback should also inform the student on how to reduce the discrepancy. Feedback that focuses only on the existing discrepancy should be sufficient only for students who feel highly self-efficacious to begin with.

A very effective volitional strategy that educators can suggest to their students is the planning of goal-directed actions. One of the effects of planning is that it stops reflections on whether to pursue a certain goal or not (Gollwitzer, Heckhausen, & Ratajczak, 1990). Planning the implementation of a chosen goal moreover leads to an implemental mind-set that promotes biased processing of desirability-related information in the way of favoring the pros over the cons of the chosen goal. Planning also produces positive illusions about the feasibility of a chosen goal (Gollwitzer & Kinney, 1989; Taylor & Gollwitzer, 1996) that affects the perception of one's personal attributes as well as one's vulnerability to risks, resulting in an optimistic view of goal attainment. If students are taught how to generate implemental mind-sets, they will develop the illusory optimism and partiality that favors goal attainment. Illusionary optimism is needed in particular when goals are hard to achieve, take a lot of effort, and potentially are important in the long run but not that attractive to strive for at the moment.

As Gollwitzer and his colleagues (1993, 1996; Gollwitzer & Schaal, 1998) demonstrated, forming simple implementation intentions has beneficial effects on getting started with an intended goal-directed action. Implementation intentions produce a perceptual readiness for good opportunities on which a person intends to act, a disruption of focused attention, and a behavioral readiness to initiate the intended goal-directed behavior. Control over action initiation is given to an environmental stimulus that is highly accessible and when present initiates the respective goal-directed behavior automatically. Implementation intentions also support persistence in the face of distractions and temptations to give up the ongoing pursuit of a goal. They also lead to superior recall of goal-related information preventing one from forgetting of how to perform a given goal. These activation and automatization effects arise from a rather simple mental act of linking a certain anticipated situation to an intended goal-directed behavior. This kind of volitional tool is easy to use, has low costs concerning time and capacity, but still has pronounced consequences for controlling one's own behavior in order to attain certain goals. Educators should thus inform students about the existence of this tool and how it is used. In addition, educators should help their students to identify good opportunities and appropriate behaviors for goal attainment. Forming implementation intentions can be learned by guided mental simulations and it can be practiced in all kinds of contexts, such as playing games or exercising. That implementation intentions can be used successfully in educational settings has been demonstrated by Orbell, Hodgkins, and Sheeran (1997), who observed that it is much easier to lead people to perform health-maintaining behaviors when they are encouraged to form respective goal intentions that are furnished with implementation intentions.

Volitional Tools

In this chapter we have brought together various prominent goal theories that describe how people attain their goals. This theoretical work on goal attainment and volition can be analyzed in terms of the question of what kind of volitional tools can be suggested to students in order to better enable them to attain their goals, even under difficult circumstances. Students should learn to use these various instruments of volition in combination to set goals and regulate goals in a way that makes goal attainment more likely. We know that our perspective focuses only on one side of the education of willing—the use of volitional tools—and does not take into account the issue of promoting goals that focus on self-discipline and other personal attributes related to the character trait of willpower. Nevertheless, we believe that giving a volitional toolbox to students is highly important to help students to achieve responsibility, maturity, and self-reliance.

In our view, educators should aim at training their students in the use of effective goal setting and goal regulation strategies in their everyday goal pursuits. Providing tools that students can use to achieve their educational goals strikes us as being an important aspect of education and personality development. Acquiring goal setting and goal regulation strategies is not a formal training of the character trait of willpower, but an attempt to develop an arsenal of cognitive self-regulatory skills that can be used at will to attain what we have decided to strive for.

REFERENCES

Ach, N. (1935). Analyse des Willens. In W. Abderhalden (Eds.), *Handbuch der biologischen Arbeitsmethoden* (Bd. 6). Berlin: Urban & Schwarzenberg.

Atkinson, J. W., & Birch, D. (1970). *The dynamics of action*. New York: Wiley.

Bandura, A. (1991). Self-regulation of motivation through anticipatory and self-reactive mechanisms.In R. Dienstbier (Ed.), *Nebraska Symposium on Motivation: Perspectives on motivation* (pp. 69–164). Lincoln: University of Nebraska Press.

Bandura, A., & Schunk, D. H. (1981). Cultivating competence, self-efficacy, and intrinsic interest through proximal self-motivation. *Journal of Personality and Social Psychology, 41,* 586–598.

Beckmann, J., & Gollwitzer, P. M. (1987). Deliberative vs. implemental states of mind: The issue of impartiality in pre- and postdecisional information processing. *Social Cognition, 5,* 239–279.

Bindra, D. (1959). *Motivation*. New York: Ronald Press.

Brandstätter, V. (1992). *Der Einfluß von Vorsätzen auf die Handlungsinitiierung: Ein Beitrag zur willenspsychologischen Frage der Realisierung von Absichten*. Frankfurt am Main: Peter Lang.

Cantor, N. (1994). Life task problem solving: Situational affordances and personal needs. *Personality and Social Psychology Bulletin, 20,* 235–243.

Cantor, N., & Fleeson, W. (1994). Social intelligence and intelligent goal pursuit: A cognitive slice of motivation. In W. Spaulding (Ed.), *Nebraska Symposium on Motivation: Integrative views of motivation, cognition, and emotion* (Vol. 41, pp. 125–179). Lincoln: University of Nebraska Press.

Carver, C. S., & Scheier, M. F. (1981). Control theory: A useful conceptual framework for personality, social, clinical, and health psychology. *Psychological Bulletin, 92,* 111–135.

Carver, C. S., & Scheier, M. F. (1990). Origins and functions of positive and negative affect: A control process view. *Psychological Review, 97,* 19–35.

Deci, E. L., & Ryan, R. M. (1991). A motivational approach to self: Integration in personality. In R. Dienstbier (Ed.), *Nebraska Symposium on Motivation: Perspectives on motivation* (pp. 237–288). Lincoln: University of Nebraska Press.

Dweck, C. S. (1991). Self-theories and goals: Their role in motivation, personality, and development. In R. Dienstbier (Ed.), *Nebraska Symposium on Motivation: Perspectives on motivation* (pp. 199–255). Lincoln: University of Nebraska Press.

Dweck, C. S. (1996). Implicit theories as organizers of goals and behavior. In P. M. Gollwitzer & J. A. Bargh (Eds.), *The psychology of action: Linking cognition and motivation to behavior* (pp. 69–90). New York: Guilford.

Elliot, A. J., & Church, M. A. (1997) A hierarchical model of approach and avoidance achievement motivation. *Journal of Personality and Social Psychology, 72,* 218–232.

Elliott, E. S., & Dweck C. S. (1988). Goals: An approach to motivation and achievement. *Journal of Personality and Social Psychology, 54,* 5–12.

Emmons, R. A. (1989). The personal strivings approach to personality. In L. A. Pervin (Ed.), *Goal concepts in personality and social psychology* (pp. 87–126). Hillsdale, NJ: Lawrence Erlbaum Associates.

Emmons, R. A. (1996) Striving and feeling: Personal goals and subjective well-being. In P. M. Gollwitzer & J. A. Bargh (Eds.), *The psychology of action* (pp. 313–337). New York: Guilford.

Emmons, R. A., & King, L. A. (1988). Conflict among personal strivings: Immediate and long-term implications for psychological and physical well-being. *Journal of Personality and Social Psychology, 54*, 1040–1048.

Frese, M., & Sabini, J. (Eds.). (1985). *Goal-directed behavior: The concept of action in psychology.* Hillsdale, NJ: Lawrence Erlbaum Associates.

Gollwitzer, P. M. (1990). Action phases and mind-sets. In E. T. Higgins & R. M. Sorrentino (Eds.), *Handbook of motivation and cognition* (Vol. 2, pp. 53–92). New York: Guilford.

Gollwitzer, P. M. (1991). *Abwägen und Planen.* Göttingen: Hogrefe.

Gollwitzer, P. M. (1993). Goal achievement: The role of intentions. In *European Review of Social Psychology, 4*, 141-185.

Golwitzer, P. M. (1999). Implementation intentions. Strong effects of simple plans. *American Psychologist, 54*, 493–503.

Gollwitzer, P. M., & Bayer, U. (1999). Deliberative and implemental mindsets in the control of action. In S. Chaiken & Y. Trope (Eds.), *Dual process theories in social psychology* (pp. 403-422). New York: Guilford.

Gollwitzer, P. M., & Bargh, J. A. (Eds.). (1996). *The psychology of action: Linking cognition and motivation to behavior.* New York: Guilford Press.

Gollwitzer, P. M., & Brandstätter, V. (1997). Implementatin intentions and effective goal pursuit. *Journal of Personality and Social Psychology, 73*(1), 186-199.

Gollwitzer, P. M., & Kinney, R. A. (1989). Effects of deliberative and implemental mind-sets on the illusion of control. *Journal of Personality and Social Psychology, 56*, 531–542.

Gollwitzer, P. M., Heckhausen, H., & Ratajczak, H. (1990). From weighting to willing: Approaching a change decision through pre- or postdecisional mentation. *Organizational Behavior and Human Decision Processes, 45*, 41–65.

Gollwitzer, P. M., Heckhausen, H., & Steller, B. (1990). Deliberative and implemental mind-sets: Cognitive tuning toward congruous thoughts and information. *Journal of Personality and Social Psychology, 56*, 531–542.

Gollwitzer, P. M., & Schaal, B. (1998). Metacognition in action: The importance of implementation intentions. *Personality and Social Psychology Review, 2*, 124–136.

Gottschaldt, K. (1926). Über den Einfluß der Erfahrung auf die Wahrnehmung von Figuren. I. Über den Einfluß gehäufter Einprägung von Figuren auf ihre Sichtbarkeit in umfassenden Konfigurationen. *Psychologische Forschung, 8*, 261–317.

Halisch, F., & Kuhl, J. (1987). *Motivation, intention, and action.* Berlin: Springer-Verlag

Harlow, R. E., & Cantor, N. (1994). The social pursuit of academics: side-effects and 'spillover' of strategic reassurance seeking. *Journal of Personality and Social Psychology, 66*, 386–397.

Heckhausen, H. (1991). *Motivation and action.* New York: Springer Verlag.

Heckhausen, H., & Gollwitzer, P. M. (1987). Thought contents and cognitive functioning in motivational versus volitional states of mind. *Motivation and Emotion, 11*, 101–120.

Higgins, E. T. (1996). Ideals, oughts, and regulatory focus: Affect and motivation from distinct pains and pleasures. In P. M. Gollwitzer & J. A. Bargh (Eds.), *The psychology of action: Linking cognition and motivation to behavior* (pp. 91-114). New York: Guilford.

Higgins, T. E., Roney, C. J. R., Crowe, E., & Hymes, C. (1994). Ideal versus ought predilections for approach and avoidance: Distinct self-regulatory systems. *Journal of Personality and Social Psychology, 66*, 276–286.

James, W. (1890). *Principles of psychology.* New York: Holt.

Kruglanski, A. W. (1996). Goals as knowledge structures. In P. M. Gollwitzer & J. A. Bargh (Eds.), *The psychology of action: Linking cognition and motivation to behavior* (pp. 599–618). New York: Guilford.

Kuhl, J. (1983). *Motivation, Konflikt und Handlungskontrolle.* Berlin: Springer-Verlag.

Kuhl, J., & Beckmann, J. (Eds.). (1994). *Volition and personality: Action versus state orientation.* Göttingen, Germany: Hogrefe & Huber.

Kuhl, J. (1984). Volitional aspects of achievement motivation and learned helplessness: Toward a comprehensive theory of action control. In B. A. Maher & W. B. Maher (Eds.), *Progress in experimental personality research* (pp. 99–171). New York: Academic Press.

Külpe, O. (1904). Versuche über Abstraktion. *Bericht über den Kongress für experimentelle Psychologie, 1*, 56–68.

Latham, G. P., & Yukl, G. A. (1975). Assigned versus participative goal setting with educated and uneducated wood workers. *Journal of Applied Psychology, 60*, 299–302.

Lengfelder, A. (1996). Die Bedeutung des Frontalhirns beim Abwägen und Planen. Frankfurt am Main: Peter Lang.

Lewin, K. (1926). Vorsatz, Wille und Bedürfnis. *Psychologische Forschung, 7*, 330–385.

Lissner, K. (1933). Die Entspannung von Bedürfnissen durch Ersatzhandlungen. *Psychologische Forschung, 18*, 218–250.

Locke, E. A., & Latham G. P. (1990). *A theory of goal setting and task performance.* Englewood Cliffs, NJ: Prentice-Hall.

Mahler, W. (1933). Ersatzhandlungen verschiedenen Realitätsgrades. *Psychologische Forschung, 18*, 27–89.

Malzacher, J. T. (1992). *Erleichtern Vorsätze die Handlungsinitiierung? Zur Aktivierung der Vornahmehandlung.* Unpublished doctoral dissertation, Ludwig-Maximilians-Universität, München.

McDougall, W. (1908). *Introduction to social psychology..* London: Methuen.

Mertin, M. (1994). Aufmerksamkeitszuwendung bei vorgenommenen Gelegenheiten. Unpublished diploma thesis, Heinrich-Heine-Universität, Düsseldorf.

Miller, G. A., Galanter, E., & Pribram, D. H. (1960). *Plans and the structure of behavior.* New York: Harper.

Orbell, S., Hodgkins, S., & Sheeran, P. (1997). Implementation intentions and the theory of planned behavior. *Personality and Social Psychology Bulletin, 33*, 209–217.

Ovsiankina, M. (1928). Die Wiederaufnahme unterbrochener Handlungen. *Psychologische Forschung, 11*, 302–379.

Pervin, L. A. (Ed.). (1989). *Goal concepts in personality and social psychology.* Hillsdale, NJ: Lawrence Erlbaum Associates.

Powers, W. T. (1974). *Behavior: The control of perception.* London: Wildwood.

Schaal, B. (1993). *Impulskontrolle: Wie Vorsätze beherrschtes Handeln erleichtern.* Unpublished master's thesis, Ludwig-Maximilians-Universität München.

Schaal, B., & Gollwitzer, P. M. (1997, March). *Impulskontrolle: Intentionseffekte bei der Handlungssteuerung.* Paper presented at the 39. Tagung experimentell arbeitender Psychologen, Humboldt-Universität zu Berlin.

Seehausen, R., Bayer, U., & Gollwitzer, P. M. (1994, September). *Experimentelle Arbeiten zur vorsätzlichen Handlungsregulation.* Paper presented at the 39. Kongreß der Deutschen Gesellschaft für Psychologie, Hamburg.

Snow, R. E., & Corno, L. (1996). Individual differences in affective and conative functions. In D. C. Berliner & R. C. Calfee (Eds.), *Handbook of educational psychology* (pp. 243–310). New York: Prentice Hall.

Steller, B. (1992). *Vorsätze und die Wahrnehmung günstiger Gelegenheiten.* München: tuduv Verlagsgesellschaft.

Taylor, S. E., & Gollwitzer, P. M. (1996). The effects of mind-sets on positive illusions. *Journal of Personality and Social Psychology, 69*, 213–226.

Tolman, E. C. (1925). Purpose and cognition: The determinants of animal learning. *Psychological Review, 32*, 285–297.

Watt, H. (1905), Experimentelle Beiträge zu einer Theorie des Denkens. *Archiv für die gesamte Psychologie, 4*, 289–436.

Wicklund, R. A., & Gollwitzer, P. M. (1982). *Symbolic self-completion.* Hillsdale, NJ: Lawrence Erlbaum Associates.

Witkin, H. A. (1950). Individual differences in ease of perception of embedded figures. *Journal of Personality, 19*, 1-15.

Zillmann, D., & Cantor, J. R. (1976).Effect of timing of information about mitigating circumstances on emotional responses to provocation and retaliatory behavior. *Journal of Experimental Social Psychology, 12*, 38–55.

10

The Role of Interest in Motivation and Learning

Ulrich Schiefele
University of Bielefeld

Before "motivation" became prevalent as a scientific concept in psychology, many important issues related to motivational phenomena have been dealt with under the label of *interest*. It is not surprising, therefore, that there is a long list of educational and psychological scientists who have put special emphasis on interest in their theories (e.g., Dewey, 1913; Herbart, 1806/1965; Kerschensteiner, 1922; see overviews by Krapp, Hidi, & Renninger, 1992; and Prenzel, 1988). When the term *interest* was replaced by *motivation*, not all aspects of the meaning of interest were transferred to the concept of motivation. There was only one major research area in which the term *interest* continued to be used, namely diagnostic approaches to vocational interests (cf. Walsh & Osipow, 1986). According to these theories, specific vocational interests are rooted in stable personal traits such as realistic interest, social interest, or artistic interest (Holland, 1985). A typical definition of vocational interest was provided by Todt (1978). He defined vocational interests as general and stable dispositional tendencies that are directed at relatively broad classes of activities or subject areas and include affective, cognitive, and conative components. In contrast to this approach, I do not define interests as "traits" in the traditional sense of the term. It is also noteworthy that vocational interest research mainly serves diagnostic and counseling purposes and is neither related to other motivational concepts nor to learning processes.

The revival of research and theorizing on interest beyond vocational and personality psychology has been initiated by a number of authors for various reasons (Hidi & Baird, 1986; Renninger & Wozniak, 1985; H. Schiefele, 1978; H. Schiefele, Hauber, & Schneider, 1979). H. Schiefele et al. (1979) argued that the prevailing expectancy-value theories of motivation, specifically achievement motivation, have neglected incentives attached to activities and objects or subject areas. If self-evaluation, external evaluation, and progress toward superordinate goals are the only incentives of action (Heckhausen, 1991), then it is impossible to assume that some students like their subjects and learn because they value the process of being engaged in certain fields of knowledge (see also Brophy, 1983; Dweck, 1986; Deci & Ryan, 1985).

In educational contexts, interest is used as a central motivational term for obvious reasons. Teachers and instructors wish to interest their students in the subject matter they teach. In their view, motivated students are those who seem to like the contents being taught. In addition, teachers, parents, and students often use the term "interest" when they refer to motivational phenomena. It is not surprising then, that educational scientists (e.g., Dewey, 1913) have given interest a central place in their theories of education and schooling.

INTEREST AS A MOTIVATIONAL CONSTRUCT

From Extrinsic to Intrinsic Motivation

Psychological theories of motivation usually ignore the content or object of motivated action. This is true for theories of motives as well as theories of motivation (cf. Eccles, Wigfield, & Schiefele, 1998; Graham & Weiner, 1996; Heckhausen, 1991; Weiner, 1980). In this century, research on motivation has been dominated to a large extent by the expectany-value paradigm. This research tradition was founded by Lewin (1926, 1935). In the theory of aspiration levels (Lewin, Dembo, Festinger, & Sears, 1944), the motivation to choose a specific level of task difficulty was defined as the difference between two products: (a) valence of success times probability of success and (b) valence of failure times probability of failure. This theory was later reformulated and adapted by Atkinson (1957) in his model of achievement motivation. Atkinson's model was highly influential and instigated a multitude of empirical studies and the development of similar theories (e.g., Heckhausen, 1991; Weiner, 1986). At the core of these theories is the assumption that motivation to act results from some combination of expectancy and valence cognitions that are related to the respective action and its possible consequences.

When applying these theories to the domain of learning or achievement in school or college, problems become evident (e.g., Brophy, 1983; Deci & Ryan, 1985; Maehr, 1974; H. Schiefele et al., 1979). Most notably, achievement motivation theory has neglected incentives that are inherent (or intrinsic) to an activity. It follows that learning activities are only motivated by their consequences, such as self-evaluation, external evaluation, and progress toward superordinate goals (Heckhausen, 1991).

Rheinberg (1985, 1989) criticized the extrinsic focus of expectancy-value models of motivation and suggested a new form of incentives, namely activity-related incentives (as opposed to consequence-related incentives). This type of incentive can easily be incorporated in existing expectancy-value models of motivation (Rheinberg, 1998). Activity-related incentives refer to a wide range of positive affective states that a person may experience while performing an activity. These states, however, should not be related to the expectation of external consequences (e.g., anticipated joy). For example, sports activities may be accompanied by enjoyable physical states and by feelings of control, competence, excitement, or challenge. If a person's behavior is motivated by positive activity-related incentives, then "intrinsic motivation" is the proper term for the behavior. This is in line with Deci and Ryan (1985), who maintained that intrinsically motivated behavior is rewarded by feelings of competence and autonomy. According to Csikszentmihalyi (1975), the experience of flow is a major incentive of intrinsically motivated behavior. Flow is characterized by high levels of focused attention, merging of action and consciousness, and feelings of control.

Rheinberg (1985, 1996a) conducted a number of studies that explored the structure of activity-related incentives of various leisure activities (e.g., playing music, painting, skiing, motorcycling, surfing) and was able to show that these activities were motivated by a large variety of (activity-related) incentives beyond feelings of flow, autonomy, and competence (e.g., intense experience of nature, enjoying being alone, relaxation, expression of one's self).

It is important to note, however, that Rheinberg's (1989, 1996a) conception of activity-related incentives does not cover all possible forms of intrinsic motivation. Rheinberg's model suggests that a person is intrinsically motivated to learn because the learning activity is associated with positive experiential qualities. This view, however, does not take into account the object of the activity. In fact, most of the activities investigated by Rheinberg (e.g., motorcycling) do not involve an object in the same way as do reading or learning. It is quite likely that a person is motivated to engage in a learning activity because he or she values the subject area towards which the learning activity is directed. In this case, it is possible that incentives related to the learning activity are not very important for being motivated to learn. The role of objects or knowledge domains in motivation is most explicitly adressed by *interest theory* (e.g., Krapp, 1992; Prenzel, 1988; Renninger, Hidi, & Krapp, 1992; H. Schiefele, 1978; H. Schiefele et al., 1979; U. Schiefele, 1991b, 1996a). From the viewpoint of interest theory, a learner is intrinsically motivated when his or her main incentive for learning is related to qualities of the respective knowledge domain.

Personal interest is usually distinguished from situational interest (Hidi, 1990; Krapp et al., 1992; Renninger, 1989, 1990; U. Schiefele, 1991b). Personal interest is conceived of as a relatively stable evaluative orientation toward certain domains, whereas situational interest is a temporary emotional state aroused by specific features of an activity or task (e.g., personal relevance or novelty; see Hidi & Baird, 1986, 1988). More specifically, situational interest is characterized by "focused, prolonged, relatively effortless attention, all of which are accompanied by feelings of pleasure and concentration" (Krapp et al., 1992, p. 7). In the following, I only refer to personal interest. Before I go into more detail, it is necessary to define those terms that are basic to an understanding of personal interest and its integration into a broader motivational framework.

Motivationally Relevant Cognitions and Beliefs

First of all, it is useful to distinguish between motivation as an actual state and as a more stable motivational characteristic of a person. Two general forms of stable personality characteristics are to be distinguished (cf. Pekrun, 1988, 1993): Dispositional and habitual forms of mental processes or behavior. Dispositional characteristics refer to identifiable cognitive structures. The distinction between dispositional and habitual characteristics is important because the former ones have greater explanatory power. Habitual characteristics refer to the frequency of specific behaviors or mental processes and do not allow conclusions about factors that underlie these behaviors or processes. Dispositional characteristics, on the other hand, are conceptualized as relatively stable cognitive representations that are stored in long-term memory. And as such, they can be used to explain behavior and mental processes.

According to this distinction, motivational characteristics may either refer to relatively stable beliefs (e.g., valences, expectancies) or to the fact that a person repeatedly exhibits the same kind of actual motivation (cf. Figure 10.1). Pekrun (1988, 1993) used the term "habitual motivational characteristic" to describe individual differences with respect to the frequency of specific forms of (actual) motivation. For example, we may observe that a student is frequently motivated to learn because he or she wants to be praised by the teacher. In this case, we would diagnose a high level of habitual extrinsic motivation. It is interesting to note that many motivation questionnaires assess motivational orientations as habitual characteristics, sometimes in contrast to theoretical definitions (e.g., Gottfried, 1986; Nicholls, 1989; see overview by U. Schiefele, 1996a).

Stable beliefs qualify as motivationally relevant beliefs only if they are important antecedents of actual, motivationally relevant cognitions and resulting intentions to act (Heckhausen, 1991; Pekrun, 1988, 1993). These beliefs are called *dispositional motivational characteristics*. Among the various concepts that may fall into this category (see Pekrun, 1993), self-efficacy beliefs are seen as primary antecedents of motivated action by a number of authors (cf. Schunk, 1989, 1995). Self-efficacy beliefs express the expectancy to be able to perform a specific behavior or a group of behaviors in order to reach a desired outcome or goal. However, there is a number of other relevant concepts such as valence beliefs referring to particular action consequences (e.g., external evaluation), attributional beliefs, and self-concepts.

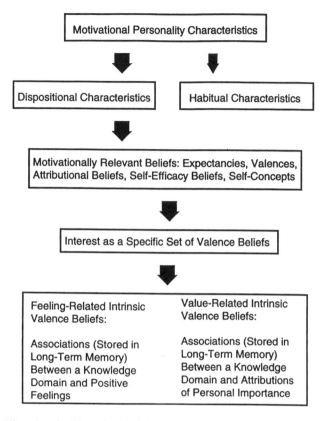

FIG. 10.1. Hierarchy of stable motivational characteristics (see text for details).

Enduring valence or expectancy beliefs, such as self-efficacy beliefs, may also take the form of actual, situation-specific cognitions. In fact, it is assumed by expectancy-value models of motivation (cf. Pekrun, 1988, 1993) that enduring beliefs exert direct influence on situation-specific expectancy and value cognitions that are the most immediate antecedents of actual motivation (i.e., specific intentions, see later this chapter).

Motivation as an actual state is defined as the intention to perform a specific activity (e.g., Rheinberg, 1989; U. Schiefele, 1996a). According to Heckhausen and Kuhl (1985; see also Gollwitzer, 1991; Kuhl, 1983), the process of motivation starts with wishes or desires and ends with the formation of specific intentions. Wishes may be characterized as cognitions of valued goals or end states of behavior. During the predecisional phase, people are deliberating their wishes (Gollwitzer, 1991, 1993). The predecisional phase ends with forming an intention to realize a specific wish ("I intend to pursue x!"). This type of intention is called a "goal intention" (Gollwitzer, 1993). For example, goal-setting theory (Locke & Latham, 1990) identified different features of goal intentions (e.g., difficulty, specificity) that have important implications for task performance.

Goal intentions are to be distinguished from "implementation intentions" that specify when, where, and how goal-directed behavior is to be initiated (Gollwitzer, 1993). After a goal intention has been formed, the postdecisional phase starts. It ends with the initiation of a specific action. The initiation of action is a volitional problem. Therefore, the postdecisional phase is characterized by volitional processes and strategies, such as encoding, emotional, motivational, and environmental control (e.g., Corno & Kanfer, 1993; Heckhausen, 1991; Kuhl, 1987, 1994). For example, emotional control strategies consist of managing emotional states that might inhibit goal-directed action, whereas motivational control strategies help to strengthen the motivational basis of intentions (e.g., by envisioning the value of desired consequences of action).

The definition of motivation to act that was given previously does not determine the reasons for which a person is engaging in an activity. For example, the intention to learn may be the result of external forces (e.g., anticipated punishment) or interest in a specific subject matter. Reasons for acting may refer to any meaningful aspect of an activity. Each of these reasons constitutes a separate form of motivation. Usually, a distinction is made between intrinsic and extrinsic forms of motivation (e.g., Deci & Ryan, 1985; Pekrun, 1988, 1993). Intrinsic motivation to learn is defined as the intention to engage in a specific learning activity because the activity itself is interesting, enjoyable, or otherwise satisfying (e.g., Deci & Ryan, 1985). In this case, the reason for learning lies within the activity itself and does not refer to events that are external to the activity (e.g., parental praise).

Defining Interest

It is my intent to define personal interest by intrinsic feeling-related and value-related valences (U. Schiefele, 1991b, 1996a). This definition is based on Pekrun's (1988) taxonomy of motivational concepts. According to Pekrun, valences are a specific form of cognitively represented relations. These relations are characterized by associations between an object (knowledge domain, activity, or event) and evaluative attributes. There are two forms of evaluative attributes: feeling-related and value-related attributes. Feeling-related attributes refer to feelings that are elicited by an object. Value-related attributes refer to the personal significance of an object, independent of its feeling-arousing qualities. Because personal interest is conceived of as a relatively stable characteristic, feeling-related and value-related valences are to be specified as object-attribute relations represented as part of the enduring cognitive system of the person. The enduring form of a valence is called "valence belief," whereas the temporary, actual form of a valence is given the label "valence cognition."

In my view, the concept of personal interest should only refer to knowledge domains and not to activities or events. Instead of assuming a personal interest in activities (e.g., interest in skiing), the existence of generalized preferences for specific activity-related incentives is suggested (e.g., a preference for experiencing the pleasure of moving fast or for experiencing moderate forms of risk). These preferences may be conceptualized as valence beliefs that refer to certain classes of activity-related incentives, not to domains of knowledge. Another possibility for making a terminological distinction would be to contrast object-related with activity-related interests.

An essential feature of feeling-related and value-related valence beliefs is their intrinsic nature. This is to say that both types of beliefs are directly related to a certain knowledge domain and are not based on the relation of this domain to other domains or events. For example, if a student associates mathematics with high personal significance because mathematics helps him or her to get a prestigious job, then we would not speak of interest. In this case, the respective value beliefs are extrinsic in nature (cf. Pekrun, 1988).

Feeling-related and value-related valence beliefs are often highly correlated (U. Schiefele, 1996a). Despite this fact, we prefer to differentiate between the two components. It seems reasonable to expect that some personal interests are based, in large part, on the experience of feelings, whereas other interests are more strongly based on the attribution of personal significance (see also Wigfield & Eccles, 1992).

To summarize, personal interest consists of intrinsic feeling-related and value-related valence beliefs (cf. Figure 10.1). Feeling-related valence beliefs refer to the feelings that are associated with a knowledge domain. Feelings of involvement, stimulation, or enjoyment are seen as most typical of interest. Value-related valences refer to the attribution of personal significance to a knowledge domain. Theoretically, there are as many feeling-related valences as there are feelings that are possibly related to a knowledge domain. To contrast, the personal importance of a domain is probably a more or less unitary concept. However, it may be possible (but has not been examined yet) to distinguish between different value-related valence beliefs, depending on the underlying reasons for the personal importance of a domain (e.g., self-realization, development of one's personality, correspondence with one's world view). It is possible to think of interest as a specific part of the network of knowledge stored in long-term memory. The basic idea is that the representation of the interest domain, which itself may constitute a complex network, is related to a number of feeling-related or value-related attributes (see Figure 10.2).

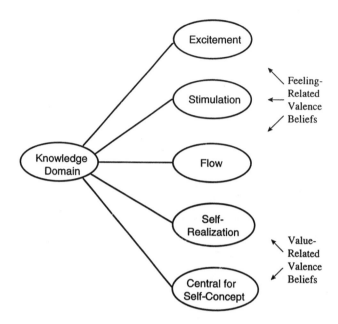

FIG. 10.2. A cognitive view of interest: Representations of relations between a knowledge domain and various feeling- and value-related attributes.

Because interest has been defined as a personal characteristic, it is possible to make a number of distinctions that are to some degree also typical for other personal characteristics (cf. Pekrun, 1988). These distinctions refer to the dimensions of intensity, specificity, stability, experience, universality, and modality. Accordingly, interests may be more or less intense, specific, stable, based on direct experience, or universal. Finally, interests that are mainly based on feeling-related vs. we may distinguish between value-related valences (modality).

Most approaches to the measurement of interests are rather simple. Usually, people are presented with a number of statements that refer to a specific interest domain. For example, in the Study Interest Questionnaire (SIQ; Schiefele, Krapp, Wild, & Winteler, 1993), the respondents have to rate statements like the following: "Being involved with the subject matter of my major affects my mood positively"; "It is of great personal importance to me to be able to study this particular subject," or "I chose my major primarily because of the interesting subject matter involved."

Instead of referring to large knowledge domains, such as one's major, it is also possible to assess more specific interests. Hoffmann and Lehrke (1985, 1986), for example, measured interest in physics by differentiating between eight domains (e.g., optics, acoustics, electronics). For each domain, the respondents have to rate their interest. Although this procedure is more differentiated than the

SIQ with respect to the number of aspects of the interest domain, it is less differentiated with respect to the meaning of interest. The SIQ uses 18 items referring to different intrinsic feeling-related and value-related valences in order to measure interest in a specific domain. The choice for a specific assessment method should depend on the nature of the domain to be investigated and the purpose of the respective study. It would be also possible, of course, to combine the two methods.

Interest and Motivation

In the preceding section, I defined interest as a dispositional motivational characteristic. Besides personal interest, there are additional constructs that are located at the same theoretical level and that may have a significant impact on actual motivation. Among these constructs, the following are most noteworthy: self-concept of ability, expectancy of success, control beliefs, attributional beliefs, task value beliefs, and goal-orientation beliefs (see Eccles et al., 1998; Pekrun, 1993; Pekrun & Schiefele, 1996; Pintrich & Schunk, 1996; Weiner, 1986). As is true for personal interest, these variables are antecedents of situation-specific valence or expectancy cognitions that form the basis of actual intrinsic or extrinsic motivation to learn (see Figure 10.3). However, along with self-concept of ability, interest is regarded as a central precondition of intrinsic motivation to learn (i.e., the intention to learn because the learning activity is satisfying in itself). Figure 10.3, exhibits a causal model of those factors contributing to actual, situation-specific motivation (see also Pekrun, 1993).

As can be seen in Figure 10.3, actual motivation is most directly influenced by situation-specific expectancy and value cognitions. Five different forms of these cognitions are included. Of course, it is possible to think of more valences or expectancies than those depicted in Figure 10.3 (see Pekrun, 1988, 1993).

We can then assume that actual, situation-specific cognitions depend on more stable and enduring cognitive structures such as self-concept of ability, attributional beliefs, and interest. The list here is not complete, of course. In addition, it is likely that basic needs influence valence or expectancy beliefs (Feather, 1995). Interest, which consists of intrinsic feeling-related and value-related valence beliefs, does have an impact on object-related valence cognitions in a specific situation. These valence cognitions exert influence on the strength of intrinsic motivation to act.

I would like to highlight two conclusions. First, interest and motivation are two different psychological phenomena. Interest is not a specific type of motivation. In contrast, it is a relatively stable set of valence beliefs stored in long-term memory, whereas motivation is understood as a specific mental state,

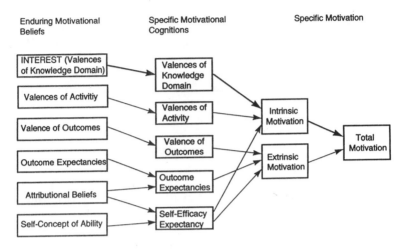

FIG. 10.3. Integrating personal interest into a model of motivation.

namely the actual wish or intention to do something. Second, interest is an important condition for intrinsic motivation. And if it is agreed that the content of learning is the major source of being intrinsically motivated to learn, then it follows that interest is the central condition of intrinsic motivation to learn.

THE IMPORTANCE OF INTEREST FOR LEARNING AND THE DEVELOPMENT OF COMPETENCE

Intrinsic Motivation and the Need for Competence

From an evolutionary perspective (e.g., Scarr, 1992, 1994; Schneider, 1996; Schneider & Schmalt, 1994), it is reasonable to analyze the role of intrinsic motivation and interest for the successful adaptation of human beings to their environment. Interestingly, the history of intrinsic motivation research is mainly a history of answers to the fundamental question of why human beings are intrinsically motivated for particular activities. In contrast to research on extrinsic motivation within the expectancy-value paradigm, intrinsic motivation theory was in search of basic explanatory models (cf. Deci & Ryan, 1985). Schneider and Schmalt (1994) proposed a theory or system of motives in which they sought to identify the biological or evolutionary basis of a number of different motives (e.g., power, achievement). In their system, however, interests do not have a role. Therefore, I try to apply their arguments to the concept of interest.

The analysis of intrinsic motivation started during the behaviorist era, when it became obvious that some behaviors in both animals and men—especially exploratory activities—could not be explained by classical or operant conditioning or by drive theories. As a consequence, two different types of theories were proposed to explain intrinsically motivated behavior. On the one hand, Hebb (1955), Hunt (1965), and Berlyne (1960, 1967) suggested that humans are motivated to maintain an optimal level of stimulation. On the other hand, White (1959) and deCharms (1968) postulated the basic, or innate, needs for competence (White) and personal causation or self-determination (deCharms) that are responsible for intrinsically motivated behavior. Deci and Ryan (1985) integrated these approaches into their theory of self-determination. According to these authors, the basic need for competence is the major reason why people seek out optimal stimulation. It is only by mastering moderate challenges that the individual is able to improve his or her competence. However, in order to be really intrinsically motivated, the individual needs to feel self-determined and free of any external pressures.

Deci and Ryan's self-determination theory centers around the assumption of the basic human needs for competence and self-determination. The major empirical support for their theory comes from studies on the debilitating effects of various kinds of extrinsic incentives or pressures on the motivation to perform inherently interesting activities (see reviews by Morgan, 1984; Deci & Ryan, 1985; see also the controversy between Cameron & Pierce, 1994, and Ryan & Deci, 1996). These studies suggest that external conditions that reduce a person's feelings of competence or self-determination (e.g., by exerting control or by giving negative competence feedback) also reduce intrinsic motivation. In addition, a number of studies show that external conditions supporting autonomy or competence (e.g., allowing choice between alternatives, giving informational and positive competence feedback) can increase intrinsic motivation (cf. Deci & Ryan, 1985). According to Deci and Ryan (1985), these findings suggest that intrinsic motivation is based on the innate needs for competence and self-determination.

In contrast to Deci and Ryan (1985), Csikszentmihalyi (1975, 1988) sought an explanation for intrinsic motivation by looking at the immediate subjective experience of people. He assumed that intrinsically motivated acitivities are rewarded by what people feel when they are performing these activities. Extensive interviews with climbers, dancers, chess players, basketball players, and composers revealed that activities in these domains are accompanied by a specific form of experience that has been called "flow" (Csikszentmihalyi, 1975). Many of the respondents indicated that when they really enjoyed an acitivity, it felt like being carried away by a current, like being in a flow. Flow characterizes a holistic feeling of being immersed in an activity. Specifically, the following components of flow are to be distinguished: (a) merging of action and awareness, (b) focusing of attention on a limited stimulus field, (c) not being self-conscious, and (d) feeling in control of one's actions and the environment.

It has been suggested by Csikszentmihalyi (1975, 1988) that flow is only possible when a person feels that the opportunities for action in a given situation match his or her ability to master the challenges. The challenge of an activity may be something concrete or physical, like the peak of a mountain to be scaled, or it can be something abstract and symbolic, like a set of musical notes to be performed, a story to be read, or a puzzle to be solved. Similarly, the skill may refer either to a physical ability or to the mastery of manipulating symbols. More recent research has shown that balance of skill and challenge alone does not necessarily produce a flow experience. Both the challenges and skills must be relatively high (i.e., above a person's average) before a flow experience becomes possible (Massimini & Carli, 1988).

There is some evidence that flow is most readily experienced in certain kinds of activities. For example, games and play are considered to be ideal flow activities. In our view, typical flow activities provide the acting person with clear goals, well defined rules, and unambiguous performance feedback. This also explains why many rituals and other religious practices enable people to go off into trance-like states. However, the experience of flow is by no means restricted to games and play. Almost every kind of activity can be structured so as to facilitate the experience of flow.

It should be noted here that Rheinberg's (1989, 1995) theory of intrinsic motivation is similar to that of Csikszentmihalyi. As was mentioned previously, Rheinberg assumed that activities may be motivated by a number of different activity-inherent incentives beyond flow. Rheinberg (1993, 1995) investigated a number of different leisure activities, such as painting, motorcycling, and playing a musical instrument. By using interview and questionnaire techniques, Rheinberg found that these activities are motivated by various action-related incentives, for example, feelings of competence, enjoyment of perfect or harmonic movements, absorption in the activity, and feelings of self-fulfillment. From the viewpoint of Rheinberg's theory, the experience of flow is just one activity-related incentive among others.

At first glance, the theories of Deci and Ryan, Csikszentmihalyi, and Rheinberg seem to be very different. Deci and Ryan (1985) explained intrinsic motivation by assuming innate, basic needs for competence and autonomy, whereas Csikszentmihalyi suggested that the reasons for intrinsically motivated acitivities are to be found in the subjective experience while performing these activities. Interestingly enough, Csikszentmihalyi also attributed an important role to competence in his theory. Flow can only be experienced when competence and task difficulty are in balance and have at least average levels (from the view of the actor). In addition, in order to be able to experience flow in the future, the person needs to develop his or her competence because the repetitive performance of well-trained behaviors leads to an imbalance of competence and task demands. In this specific case, the result would be boredom.

The theories of Deci and Ryan (1985), Csikszentmihalyi (1975, 1988), and Rheinberg (1989, 1995) can easily be reconciled by referring to Schneider's (1996) recent discussion of the evolutionary basis of intrinsic motivation. Schneider distinguished between immediate reasons (e.g., enjoyment) and ultimate reasons of behavior (e.g., survival). Intrinsically motivated behavior can be conducive to ultimate goals even though the actor is only aware of and motivated by immediate incentives. Typical cases are exploratory and play behavior. Both types of behavior help to increase an individual's competence but are usually performed because they are exciting, pleasurable, or enjoyable (however, this is not true for all kinds of exploratory behavior; cf. Schneider, 1996). The distinction between immediate and ultimate causes of behavior helps to reconcile the differing theoretical positions. Deci and Ryan focused on ultimate reasons of behavior, whereas Csikszentmihalyi and Rheinberg were mainly concerned with immediate reasons. From this point of view, it seems plausible that flow or other activity-related states are rewards that ensure that an individual is seeking to increase his or her competence. As Csikszentmihalyi suggested, the repeated experience of flow is only possible when the individual is looking for increasingly challenging tasks and is adapting his or her competence to these challenges. Consequently, Csikszentmihalyi and Massimini (1985) hypothesized that the experience of flow is a means of human evolution to promote the developmental of competence. Therefore, it seems that the need for competence plays a central role in the explanation of intrinsically motivated behaviors. In contrast to Deci and Ryan (1985), Schneider (1996) did not distinguish between the needs for competence and autonomy. According to Schneider, the need for competence is more basic and general and does imply the need for autonomy.

Although it does not seem likely that all kinds of intrinsic incentives are in the service of the basic human need for competence, it is reasonable to assume that a wide range of intrinsic motivation is more or less related to a person's development of competence. In addition, it is important to note that the need for competence does not energize only intrinsically but also extrinsically motivated behaviors (cf. Deci & Ryan, 1985).

The Possible Evolutionary Role of Interest

In the preceding section, it was argued that intrinsic motivation may ultimately serve the basic human need to interact with one's environment in a competent and effective way (White, 1959). Basically, the same hypothesis could apply to interest (see also Rheinberg, 1998). Being focused on and involved in selected domains of knowledge is an optimal precondition for developing competence and expertise. What would happen if we were not able to develop stable orientations toward certain domains? In this case, we would rely solely on activity- or object-related incentives. Probably, if we lacked stable interests, we would quite often switch between different activities or objects because our main reason for being engaged with something would be perceived incentives. From that point of view, it seems that interests serve the need for competence because a selection process is necessary in order to develop high levels of competence. To support this argument, it is interesting to look at the development of interests from childhood to adolescence (see also Eccles et al., 1998).

Based on Piaget's (1948) theory, Travers (1978) analyzed the earliest phase of interest development. He assumed that at the beginning of the intellectual development of the child, there are only universal interests. These become manifest in the search of the infant for structure in the physical and social environment. Later, depending on the general cognitive development of the child, universal interests develop into more differentiated patterns. According to Roe and Siegelman (1964), the earliest differentiation is between children exhibiting strong interest in the world of physical objects and children being more interested in people (the social world). This early differentiation eventually leads to differently strong interests in the social versus natural sciences (Todt, 1990).

The next phase of interest development—between 3 and 8 years of age—is characterized by the formation of gender-specific interests. These processes have been described by Kohlberg (1967) in his theory of sex identity and sex-role behavior. According to Kohlberg, the acquisition of gender identity leads to gender-specific behaviors, attitudes, and interests. The child strives to behave consistently with his or her self and, thus, evaluates "male" and "female" activities or objects differently. Activities or objects that are consistent with the child's gender identity are positively evaluated, whereas other activities or objects are negatively evaluated (e.g., Thompson, 1975). As a consequence, boys and girls are not developing collective interests (i.e., shared by all boys or all girls): Boys become mainly interested in cars, machines, or other "male" toys, and in activities that involve physical power. In contrast, girls become mainly interested in dolls and in housekeeping or social activities (see also Maccoby & Jacklin, 1974). The process of developing gender-specific interests is facilitated by peers and parents.

In her theory of occupational aspirations, Gottfredson (1981) assumed that the development of interests depends on the development of one's self-concept. In this respect, the relevant dimensions of the self-concept are gender, social class, and ability. At first, the self-concept of gender is formed and, thus, interests are determined by this process (see my earlier discussion.) The next stage of interest development—covering the years between 9 and 13—is characterized by the emerging self-concepts of one's social affiliation and cognitive ability. As a consequence, the development of interests consists of preferring occupations that are consistent with one's social class and ability self-concepts. It is assumed that social evaluations of occupations precede comparisons with one's ability. As Todt (1990) put it, the development of (vocational) interests can be described as a process of continuous elimination of interests that do not fit the self-concepts of one's gender, social affiliation, and ability.

According to Gottfredson (1981), the final stage of interest development is characterized by an orientation to the internal, unique self. The young person beyond age 13 or 14 develops more internally based and abstract concepts of self (e.g., of personality). Consistent with the formation of a unique self-concept, the structure of interests, as formed during the preceding stage, becomes more differentiated and specific.

Cattell (1965) suggested that needs or motives also can determine the development of interests. However, this seems to be true only for some interests. A good example are the increasing interests in biology and psychology during puberty. The need to know oneself and to cope with rapid bodily and psychological changes seems to foster interest in biological and psychological domains of knowledge, especially for women (Todt, 1990).

This overview of theories of interest development suggests that the development of interests is a process of selection. In the course of their development, young people become more and more specific in their interests. This process of specialization seems to be an important precondition of becoming competent in a specific domain.

When we look at the interests of adults, it is sometimes hard to imagine that these interests (e.g., collecting stamps, listening to music, interest in philosophy) help the person to interact with his or her environment effectively. With respect to exploratory and play behavior, the relation to ultimate goals is evident (Rheinberg, 1998; Schneider, 1996). The intrinsic motivation of these behaviors helps organisms to create a large part of their developmental stimulation for themselves. Thus, they are able to increase their competence without continuous stimulation or guidance from socialization agents. At the same time, they receive a lot of information about their environment (Lorenz, 1943; Rheinberg, 1998). This process promotes the potential of the organism to adapt to its environment.

Later in the developmental course, we observe, for example, a lot of play behaviors (e.g., playing cards) that have lost their function of increasing competence in any general sense. Following Allport's (1937) assumption of functional autonomy of motives, it could be argued that later or adult forms of intrinsically motivated behavior have developed from earlier forms but have become functionally independent of them. The same idea can be applied to interests. Early forms of interests are more directly tied to the ultimate goal of competence than later forms. In addition, it is important to note that the development of interests is itself dependent on a number of factors, such as skills or abilities, attitudes, self-concepts, and influences from the social environment.

Even though interests of adults may not obviously serve the ultimate goal of interacting effectively with the environment, it is very clear that interests cause a person to focus his or her cognitive, affective, and motor processes on a specific subject area for an extended period of time. It is likely that the person will continuously explore that subject area and learn about it. It follows that interests facilitate the long-term and persistent engagement within a particular domain and, thus, help to develop a high level of competence.

Feeling competent is probably one of the most important incentives of activities. It seems clear that learning processes initiated by interest lead to feelings of competence. Today, a wide range of objects are found interesting by people, even when the acquired competencies are not very relevant for the general effectiveness of the person in his or her environment. This may be explained by the simple fact that today (in many but not all countries), most of the factors that could threaten our survival are largely under control. Therefore, most of the abilities we have to acquire in order to be competent members of our society are not directly related to behaviors that affect our survival (e.g., hunting, fighting).

THE ROLE OF INTEREST IN ACADEMIC LEARNING

Prior Research on the Effects of Interest on Learning

In recent years, a number of authors have reviewed research on the relation between interest and intrinsic motivation on the one hand and achievement, text learning, and use of learning strategies on the other hand (e.g., Alexander, Kulikowich, & Jetton, 1994; Deci & Ryan, 1985; Deci, Vallerand, Pelletier, & Ryan, 1991; Hidi, 1990; U. Schiefele, 1996a; U. Schiefele, Krapp, & Winteler, 1992; U. Schiefele & Schreyer, 1994; U. Schiefele & Rheinberg, 1997). The results of these reviews and meta-analyses show strong evidence for a general positive relation between interest and intrinsic motivation and various indicators of academic learning. With regard to grades and achievement tests an average correlation of 0.30 between interest and learning was found (U. Schiefele et al., 1992). Similar results were obtained for the relation between intrinsic motivation and grades or achievement tests (U. Schiefele & Schreyer, 1994).

This also holds true for the relation between interest, intrinsic motivation, and text learning. In these studies, more specific indicators of learning were used than in studies involving grades or achievement tests. Usually, before studying the text, subjects were asked to rate their level of interest in the text topic or a manipulation was introduced in order to create intrinsic versus extrinsic motivation. After reading, the subjects were presented with some kind of learning test (e.g., free recall). In a review of this type of studies (U. Schiefele, 1996a; U. Schiefele & Schreyer, 1994), an average correlation of .27 between interest and text learning was found. For the relation between intrinsic motivation and text learning, an average correlation of .33 was obtained.

These results confirm a general positive effect of interest and intrinsic motivation on learning whereby an amount of 10% of explained variance is to be expected. However, despite these positive findings, several restrictions have to be mentioned. *First*, in most of the studies, cognitive ability and the level of prior achievement or knowledge were not included as additional predictor variables. As a consequence, we do not know whether motivation predicts achievement in these studies after controlling for differences in cognitive ability or competence. *Second*, almost all of the studies were corrrelational in nature and, thus, prevent causal conclusions. Therefore, it cannot be ruled out that motivation is a result of level of achievement. The only exception we have found in our review is a study by Eisenhardt (1976). In this study, cross-lagged panel correlations were computed. The results showed that interest measured at time 1 did exert influence on achievement at time 2, but the reverse relation, the influence of achievement at time 1 on interest at time 2, was even stronger.

Third, most of the studies have not differentiated between levels of quality of learning, such as deep-level versus surface-level learning. Only two of the analyzed studies found some evidence that interest affects indicators of deep-level learning more strongly than indicators of surface-level learning (Groff, 1962; Kunz, Drewniak, Hatalak, & Schön, 1992). Fourth, prior research does not allow conclusions about mediating processes. The findings do not help us to explain the effect of interest on learning or achievement.

Later this chapter, research findings are presented that were able to shed some light on the effects of interest or intrinsic motivation on different levels of depth of learning, the role of prior knowledege or intelligence, and the nature of mediating processes.

Interest and the Depth of Learning

Several authors have claimed that interest or intrinsic motivation may have an influence on the quality of learning outcomes (e.g., Benware & Deci, 1984; Entwistle & Ramsden, 1983; Marton & Säljö, 1984; Säljö, 1981; Watkins, 1983). It was shown that intrinsically motivated students being asked to learn a given text were better able to establish relations between different parts of the text and between the text and prior knowledge. In addition, the students showed better understanding of the intentions and conclusions of the author. These results were based on interview data and qualitative analyses of free recall protocols.

Kunz et al. (1992) tested a number of different predictors of text learning: prior knowledge, factors of intelligence, achievement motive, metacognitive knowledge, and topic interest. Text learning was measured by questions involving free recall, comprehension (measured by means of multiple-choice items), and application (transfer of text content to a concrete example). The cognitive predictors were more strongly related to all text learning indicators than interest. The following significant correlation coefficients were obtained for interest and text learning: .27 (free recall), .30 (comprehension test), and .39 (application). This evidence, although not very strong, suggests that interest is more highly correlated with indicators of deep-level learning.

Because of the importance of the problem, we conducted two studies in which the attempt was made to test the possible differential effect of topic interest on text learning (U. Schiefele, 1990; U. Schiefele & Krapp, 1996). In the first study (U. Schiefele, 1990), text learning was measured by asking three different kinds of free-response questions: questions for simple facts, questions for complex facts, and deep-comprehension questions. In the second study (U. Schiefele & Krapp, 1996), different levels of text learning were assessed by creating different indicators of free recall, such as number of main ideas, elaborations, and coherence of recall. The topics of the texts to be learned were "Psychology of Emotion" in the first study and "Psychology of Communication" in the second study. Besides topic interest, we also assessed intelligence and prior knowledge as predictors of text learning.

Overall, the findings of both studies were in accordance with our expectations. Topic interest was most highly (and significantly) related to outcome measures indicating deep levels of learning, such as answers to deep-comprehension questions ($r = .44$), recall of main ideas ($r = .36$), elaborations ($r = .37$), and coherence of recall of main ideas ($r = .39$). The correlations between topic interest and other indicators of learning that do not particularly represent deep levels of learning were somewhat lower or not significant (questions for simple facts: .33; questions for complex facts: .23, ns; recall of idea units: .26; coherence of recall of idea units: .20, ns).

Although it is relatively safe to assume that indicators such as deep-comprehension questions and recall of main ideas yield higher values for learners with deep understanding of the text, the same is not necessarily true for surface-level indicators. Why should a person who has reached a deep level of learning not be able to give correct answers to surface-level questions, such as asking for simple details? Therefore, it seems desirable to develop indicators of text learning that allow differentiation more clearly between surface and deep levels.

Earlier attempts to measure levels of learning outcomes were not based on a specific theory. They were, more or less, the result of intuitive considerations. As a consequence, we referred to the text processing theory of van Dijk and Kintsch (1983; Kintsch, 1986, 1988). These authors assumed that a given text is processed and represented at different levels: the verbatim, the propositional, and the situational level. The verbatim representation contains the text's superficial structure (i.e., graphemic–visual or phonetic–auditive features). In other words, at the verbatim level, only words are represented, not meanings. The propositional representation refers to the meaning of the text. It is the result of comprehension processes and expresses the semantic content of the text. Finally, the situational component is a model of the situation described by the text (e.g., people, objects, actions). In contrast to the propositional representation, the situational representation of text may also contain analogical information. The situation model represents the deepest level of text learning.

The strength of the different types of text representation is usually determined by means of sentence recognition or sentence verification tests. A strong verbatim representation is inferred when readers are good at distinguishing between original and paraphrased sentences. Readers who clearly distinguish between paraphrased and meaning-changed (but correct) sentences are attributed a strong propositional representation. Finally, a strong situational representation is indicated by a good differentiation between meaning-changed and false sentences (Schiefele, 1996b; Schmalhofer & Glavanov, 1986).

In two studies, the relation between topic interest and the three types of representation was explored (U. Schiefele, 1991a, 1996b). In the U. Schiefele (1996b) study, the subjects had to read two different texts (Text 1: The Life of Prehistoric People; Text 2: Production of a TV Show). Both studies revealed that topic interest was negatively related to the verbatim representation ($r = -.50$, -.36, and -.29) and positively related to the propositional representation ($r = .34$, .33, and .23). No significant relations between interest and the situational representation were observed. Obviously, highly interested readers developed weaker verbatim and stronger propositional representations of the text than less interested readers. In contrast to expectations, interest could not predict the situational representation significantly. It follows that interested learners do represent the meaning of text to a greater extent than less interested learners, and less interested learners are more inclined to process and store verbatim text features than interested learners.

The failure to find significant relations between topic interest and the situational representation could be due to the method of measurement. The strength of the situational representation was based on the differential recognition of meaning-changed and false sentences referring to the text content. For each sentence, the subjects had to decide whether the sentence was presented verbatim in the original text or not. According to Schmalhofer and Glavanov (1986), recognition tests are more appropriate to assess the verbatim representation, whereas verification tests are more sensitive to differences in situational representations. For this reason, a verification task was included in both studies. The following procedure was used: If the subjects were unable to recognize a sentence, they were asked to indicate whether this sentence was true or false. For those sentences that were recognized by the subjects it was assumed that the subjects also believed that these sentences were true. The results of the analysis of verification answers replicated the findings that were based on the recognition task.

Taken together, the four studies suggest that motivational characteristics of the learner, such as topic interest, may be differently related to different indicators of text learning. We were able to observe a tendency for higher relations between interest and indicators of deep-level learning. This effect was most pronounced in those studies using the text-processing model of van Dijk and Kintsch (1983). In these studies, interest was negatively related to the representation of verbatim information and positively related to the representation of text meaning. However, interest failed to be related to the situational representation that is supposed to be the deepest level of text learning (van Dijk & Kintsch, 1983). It can be concluded that simply assuming a close relation between interest and deep-level processing of text is not appropriate. However, before drawing general conclusions, it is necessary to replicate the present results by using different or more refined methods.

Interest Versus Cognitive Predictors

Cognitive prerequisites of the learner play a central role for learning processes and outcomes. An abundance of studies found support for the significant effects of a number of cognitive factors on learning and achievement (for a recent overview see Snow, Corno, & Jackson, 1996). Therefore, it seems to be quite important to provide evidence for independent effects of motivational factors. It is not possible to give general answers to this problem because, as has been argued by Snow (1989; Snow & Jackson, 1994), the effects of cognitive, conative (i.e., motivational and volitional), and affective personality constructs mainly depend on situational demands or the nature of the specific task to be accomplished (e.g., solving mathematical problems, rehearsing vocabulary, skill learning). In addition, specific constructs may interact with each other.

In my own studies, only a small number of possibly influential aptitudes was included, namely interest, domain-specific knowledge, and psychometric intelligence. Furthermore, learning expository text was used as the learning task. Thus, the results of these studies do not allow general conclusions with regard to other task situations and other motivational or cognitive factors. All studies mentioned previously (U. Schiefele, 1990, 1991a, 1996a, 1996b; U. Schiefele & Krapp, 1996) have employed measures of domain-specific knowledge and cognitive ability. Domain-specific knowledge was either measured by means of free-response questions or by multiple-choice tests pertaining to the text content. All items were directly related to key facts of the text content. In order to measure cognitive ability, parts of a German intelligence test, based on Thurstone's factor model, were used (Jäger & Althoff, 1983). In one study (U. Schiefele, 1996b), however, the subjects had either taken the Scholastic Ability

Test or the American College Test within 3 months prior to the experiment. The verbal subtests of these tests were used as measures of verbal ability. Verbal ability includes, for example, knowledge of grammar, understanding of sentence structure, and rhetorical skills.

Theoretically, it is to be expected that topic interest and topic knowledge are at least moderately correlated (cf. Tobias, 1994; Alexander, Kulikowich, & Schulze, 1994). In summary, the present studies correlations between -.09 and .42 revealed. These results are in line with prior studies that found, only in some cases, substantial correlations between interest and knowledge (cf. Tobias, 1994). The relations between interest and verbal or general intelligence were all nonsignificant or slightly negative. In one study, however, the correlations between interest and verbal ability were significantly negative (-.26 and -.27, $p <$ .05). Thus, students with higher ability exhibited somewhat lower interest in the topics than students with lower ability. In two studies, nonsignificant correlations between domain-specific knowledge and general or verbal ability were found. In one study, however, knowledge and verbal ability were substantially correlated (.38 and .40; $p < .001$). As was true for the interest–knowledge relation, there are no clear a priori expectations about the ability–knowledge relation. It seems plausible that there are only some topics or some samples for which high correlations are to be expected (e.g., intellectually demanding topics, samples with large ability differences).

In the Schiefele (1990) study, controlling for levels of intelligence and prior knowledge did not reduce any of the interest–learning relations. Mostly, the relations between intelligence, prior knowledge, and text learning were rather weak or nonsignificant (for similar findings with respect to interest and prior knowledge see Alexander, Kulikowich, & Schulze, 1994; Renninger, 1989). Cognitive ability, however, did contribute significantly to the prediction of simple questions ($r = .43$, $p < .05$) but not complex or deep comprehension questions. The results showed that after partialling out cognitive ability, the correlation between interest and simple questions was reduced to a nonsignificant level.

In the Schiefele and Krapp (1996) study, prior knowledge was significantly related to number of idea units and elaborations. Cognitive ability was not significantly related to any of the indicators of text recall. A multiple regression analysis was performed to determine the respective contributions of interest and prior knowledge to the prediction of text recall. Cognitive ability was included as a third predictor. The predictors were entered simultaneously into the regression equation. The results revealed that interest, prior knowledge, and intelligence contributed independently of one another to the prediction of text recall. No interactions among the predictors were observed.

The two studies based on van Dijk and Kintsch's model (U. Schiefele, 1991a, 1996b) produced similar results. Therefore, I only report findings from the Schiefele (1996b) study. Controlling for differences in prior knowledge and verbal ability did not change the strength of the relations between interest and text representation. Only one significant correlation between prior knowledge and the components of text representation was obtained (propositional representation, Text 2: $r = .25$, $p < .05$). Verbal ability was significantly related to the verbatim representation in Text 1 and 2 ($r = .38$, $p < .01$; $r = .33$, $p < .01$) and to the situational representation in Text 1 ($r = .28$, $p < .05$). Multiple regression analyses revealed that univariate relations between predictors and criteria did not change when all predictors were entered simultaneously into the regression equation. Again, the findings confirm that interest, prior knowledge, and verbal ability contribute independently of one another to the prediction of text learning. No interactions among the predictors were observed.

As was mentioned previously, verification tests are more appropriate than recognition tests to measure the situational representation. Therefore, alternative values for the situational representation, based on verification responses, were computed (U. Schiefele, 1996b). This analysis revealed an interesting finding with respect to verbal ability. When using verification answers to estimate the strength of the different representations, considerably stronger relations between verbal ability and the situational representation were obtained (Text 1: $r = .51$, $p < .001$; Text 2: $r = .45$, $p < .001$). This result lends support to the reasoning of Schmalhofer and Glavanov (1986), who suggested that verification tests are more sensitive to differences in situational representations. Obviously, verbal ability but not interest does have an impact on the deepest level of text learning.

Mediating Processes

In the preceding sections, I have provided evidence for a significant influence of interest on learning outcomes. I have also reported a number of studies that support the hypothesis of a differential effect of interest on different levels of learning. One of the most interesting questions that remains refers to the explanation of these effects (see Rheinberg, 1996b; U. Schiefele, 1998; U. Schiefele & Rheinberg, 1997; Wegge, 1994). What are the mediating processes of the effects of interest and other motivational variables on the outcomes of learning?

In a recently proposed framework, Rheinberg (1996b) and Vollmeyer and Rheinberg (1998) suggested that in real-life settings, motivational variables have an impact on the process and outcome of learning at three different levels. Specifically, motivation may influence (a) the duration and frequency of learning activities (e.g., time on task), (b) the mode of the executed learning activity (e.g., use of specific learning strategies), and (c) the functional state of the learner while being engaged in a learning activity (e.g., arousal, availability of processing resources).

Probably, the effectiveness of possible mediators depends highly on the nature of the task as well as on the motivational orientation of the learner. For example, a student who is highly motivated to learn because he or she wants to avoid the negative consequences of failing in an exam will be, on the one hand, strongly activated. On the other hand, he or she may exhibit a low level of cognitive control because irrelevant worry cognitions frequently interfere with task-related cognitive processes (e.g., Liebert & Morris, 1967; Schneider Wegge, & Konradt, 1993). In the case of simply structured tasks or tasks without time pressure, the interference between irrelevant and task-related cognitions will be less detrimental to the learning outcome than when dealing with more complex tasks (e.g., Eysenck & Calvo, 1992).

The second and third groups of mediators are most relevant (cf. U. Schiefele & Rheinberg, 1997). The studies described in the preceding section were also designed to explore the role of a number of variables as mediators of the relation between interest and text learning. For affective mediators, we assessed arousal, happiness, and flow. The cognitive mediators were specific learning strategies (elaboration, underlining, note-taking), and attention or concentration. All mediating variables, with the exception of learning strategies, refer to the functional state of the learner. Although significant relations between topic interest and all potential mediators were obtained, not all relations between mediators and text learning became significant. Furthermore, it was only for arousal that a significant mediating effect was revealed.

A number of authors have asserted that arousal plays a crucial role in learning (Eysenck, 1982). Humphreys and Revelle (1984) presented evidence that arousal increases the availability of information processing resources. In our studies (U. Schiefele, 1990, 1991a, 1996b; U. Schiefele & Krapp, 1996), arousal was assessed immediately after the text reading phase by means of a short version of Thayer's (1986) Activation-Deactivation Adjective Check List. Correlations between interest and arousal varied between .24 and .57. However, arousal was significantly related to text learning only in one study (U. Schiefele & Krapp, 1996). Testing for the mediating effect of arousal revealed that arousal could, in fact, mediate at least parts of the effect of interest on recall of main ideas and coherence of main idea recall.

Overall, the search for mediators of the relation between topic interest and text learning was not very successful. It is noteworthy, however, that many significant relations between interest and potential mediators and between these mediators and learning outcome measures were found. These positive relations suggest—although almost no significant mediating effects were revealed—that interest may exert indirect influence on learning outcomes in addition to its direct effects (see also Pokay & Blumenfeld, 1990; Reynolds & Walberg, 1991).

DISCUSSION

In sum, the present studies suggest that topic interest contributes significantly to the prediction of a wide variety of indicators of text learning, even when individual differences in domain-specific knowledge and cognitive ability were taken into account. No interactions between interest, prior knowledge, and ability were found. In addition, there was evidence that topic interest facilitates deep-level learning to a greater extent than surface-level learning. These findings are in accordance with a number of studies that have investigated the effects of interest or intrinsic motivation on text learning (e.g., Alexander, Kulikowich, & Schulze, 1994; Asher, 1979; Benware & Deci, 1984; Entin & Klare, 1985; Grolnick & Ryan, 1987; Renninger, 1989). The most interesting results were probably found in those studies based on van Dijk and Kintsch's text comprehension theory (U. Schiefele, 1991a, 1996b). In these studies, a clear-cut differential effect of interest on levels of learning was obtained: Interest affected negatively the verbatim representation and positively the propositional representation of text.

In contrast to topic interest, only weak and mostly nonsignificant relations between prior knowledge and cognitive ability and text learning were found. At least two reasons for the low relations between prior knowledge and learning should be considered (see also Tobias, 1994). First, the present studies were designed to allow for a maximum effect of interest by using topics about which none of the students had expert knowledge. As a consequence, it is not surprising that prior knowledge was not strongly related to text learning. Significant effects of knowledge are to be expected when there are large differences in knowledge, as is usually the case in studies involving comparisons between experts and novices (e.g., Fincher-Kiefer, Post, Greene, & Voss, 1988; Schneider & Bjorklund, 1992). A second reason for the weak knowledge–learning relations could be the low difficulty level of the texts used in the studies. Subjective ratings of text difficulty revealed that all texts were judged as relatively easy to understand. Thus, it may have been possible to understand the text even without much prior knowledge.

Just like prior knowledge, cognitive ability did not exert a strong influence on text learning in two of the studies (U. Schiefele, 1990; U. Schiefele & Krapp, 1996). However, Schiefele (1991a, 1996b) obtained a significant and strong relation between ability and the situational representation of text. This level of learning was not associated with interest.

With regard to the importance of cognitive versus motivational predictors, it can be concluded from the present results that these predictors have different and independent effects on learning. Although the evidence is not unambiguous, I would like to suggest that ability is most strongly related to the representation of surface and situational information; that is, the most superficial and deepest levels of represention. The importance of cognitive ability for the situational representation is not surprising because the situational representation represents the deepest level of learning. The importance of cognitive ability for processing the text surface may be due to the fact that the verbatim representation is the result of basic cognitive processes such as letter or word recognition and syntactic processing. These processes are an integral part of the concept of verbal ability (e.g., Perfetti, 1988).

Topic interest seems to be most influential at an intermediate level of text learning, namely, the propositional processing of text. If this assumption is correct, then it follows that those indicators of text learning being most highly correlated with interest reflect an adequate propositional representation of text (i.e., an adequate representation of the text's meaning). The results also suggest that motivational effects on learning may have certain limits. Beyond these limits, learning depends more on ability factors than on motivation. Of course, further studies are needed to test this assumption.

The interpretation of results presented previously should not be generalized. There are a number of specific features of the present studies restricting general conclusions. Among these features, the most important ones are lack of large differences pertaining to domain-specific knowledge (e.g., novices vs. experts), lack of external pressure (the students were not given a direct instruction to learn), and use of relatively easy learning materials. For example, it is reasonable to hypothesize that prior knowledge will be a more powerful predictor of text learning when students are presented with difficult learning materials making prior knowledge more necessary (see also Alexander & Kulikowich, 1991; Körkel & Schneider, 1991; Tobias, 1994). Also, if external pressure to learn increases (as often happens in school), the importance of interest may decrease.

Despite the limitations of the present studies, it can be concluded that there are situations or domains in which learning depends on nonability factors independently of indicators of cognitive ability. In addition, the results suggest that ability and nonability factors have qualitatively different effects on different components or processes of learning. In my view, it is an interesting and promising task for future research to further explore the differential effects of cognitive and motivational factors on learning.

A number of reasons may account for the failure to find powerful mediators (cf. U. Schiefele & Rheinberg, 1997). For example, most of the significant correlations between mediators and learning outcomes were found for measures of free recall. Therefore, it may be of interest to examine whether the occurrence of mediator effects depends on the kind of test used for measuring text learning. Another reason may refer to the use of short-term learning situations with limited possibilities to act. Under these circumstances, the chance of finding effective mediators is likely to be restricted. In naturalistic learning situations, the learner is able to reread the text, to look for additional literature, or to make extensive notes. Consequently, it is more probable that we observe higher levels of interindividual variance in learning behavior and, thus, higher correlations between learning behavior and text learning.

REFERENCES

Alexander, P. A., & Kulikowich, J. M. (1991). Domain knowledge and analogic reasoning ability as predictors of expository text. *Journal of Reading Behavior, 23,* 165–190.

Alexander, P. A., Kulikowich, J. M., & Schulze, S. K. (1994). The influence of topic knowledge, domain knowledge, and interest on the comprehension of scientific exposition. *Learning and Individual Differences, 6,* 379–397.

Alexander, P. A., Kulikowich, J. M., & Jetton, T. L. (1994). The role of subject-matter knowledge and interest in the processing of linear and non-linear texts. *Review of Educational Research, 64,* 201–252.

Allport, G. W. (1937). *Personality: A psychological interpretation.* New York: Holt.

Asher, S. R. (1979). Influence of topic interest on black children's and white children's reading comprehension. *Child Development, 50,* 686–690.

Atkinson, J. W. (1957). Motivational determinants of risk-taking behavior. *Psychological Review, 64,* 359–372.

Benware, C. A., & Deci, E. L. (1984). Quality of learning with an active versus passive motivational set. *American Educational Research Journal, 21,* 755–765.

Berlyne, D. E. (1960). *Conflict, arousal, and curiosity.* New York: McGraw-Hill.

Berlyne, D. E. (1967). Arousal and reinforcement. In D. Levine (Ed.), *Nebraska symposium on motivation* (pp. 1–110). Lincoln: University of Nebraska Press.

Brophy, J. (1983). Conceptualizing student motivation. *Educational Psychologist, 18,* 200–215.

Cameron, J., & Pierce, W. D. (1994). Reinforcement, reward, and intrinsic motivation: A meta-analysis. *Review of Educational Research, 64,* 363–423.

Cattell, R.B. (1965). *The scientific analysis of personality.* Harmondsworth, England: Penguin.

Corno, L., & Kanfer, R. (1993). The role of volition in learning and performance. In L. Darling-Hammond (Ed.), *Review of research in education* (Vol. 19, pp. 301–341). Washington, DC: American Educational Research Association.

Csikszentmihalyi, M. (1975). *Beyond boredom and anxiety.* San Francisco: Jossey-Bass.

Csikszentmihalyi, M. (1988). Motivation and creativity: Towards a synthesis of structural and energistic approaches to cognition. *New Ideas in Psychology, 6,* 159–176.

Csikszentmihalyi, M., & Massimini, F. (1985). On the psychological selection of bio-cultural information. *New Ideas in Psycholgy, 3,* 115–138.

deCharms, R. (1968). *Personal causation: The internal affective determinants of behavior.* New York: Academic Press.

Deci, E. L., & Ryan, R. M. (1985). *Intrinsic motivation and self-determination in human behavior.* New York: Plenum.

Deci, E. L., Vallerand, R. J., Pelletier, L. G., & Ryan, R. M. (1991). Motivation and education: The self-determination perspective. *Educational Psychologist, 26,* 325–346.

Dewey, J. (1913). *Interest and effort in education.* Boston: Riverside.

Dweck, C. S. (1986). Motivational processes affecting learning. *American Psychologist, 41,* 1040–1048.

Eccles, J., Wigfield, A., & Schiefele, U. (1998). Motivation to succeed. In N. Eisenberg (Ed.), *Handbook of child psychology. Vol. 3: Social, emotional, and personality development* (pp. 1017–1095). New York: Wiley.

Eisenhardt, W. B. (1976). *A search for the predominant causal sequence in the interrelationship of interest in academic subjects and academic achievement. A cross-lagged panel correlation study.* Unpublished doctoral dissertation, Duke University, Durham, NC.

Entin, E. B., & Klare, G. R. (1985). Relationships of measures of interest, prior knowledge, and readability to comprehension of expository passages. *Advances in Reading/Language Research, 3,* 9–38.

Entwistle, N. J., & Ramsden, P. (1983). *Understanding student learning.* London: Croom Helm.

Eysenck, M. W. (1982). *Attention and arousal.* Berlin: Springer.

Eysenck, M. W., & Calvo, M. G. (1992). Anxiety and performance: The processing efficiency theory. *Cognition and Emotion, 6,* 409–434.

Feather, N. T. (1995). Values, valences, and choice: The influence of values on the perceived attractiveness and choice of alternatives. *Journal of Personality and Social Psychology, 68,* 1135–1151.

Fincher-Kiefer, R., Post, T. A., Greene, T. R., & Voss, J. F. (1988). On the role of prior knowledge and task demands in the processing of text. *Journal of Memory and Language, 27,* 416–428.

Gollwitzer, P. M. (1991). *Abwägen and Planen.* Göttingen: Hogrefe.

Gollwitzer, P. M. (1993). Goal achievement: The role of intentions. In W. Stroebe & M. Hewstone (Eds.), *European Review of Social Psychology* (Vol. 4, pp. 141–185). London: Wiley.

Gottfredson, L. S. (1981). Circumscription and compromise: A developmental theory of occupational aspirations. *Journal of Counseling Psychology Monograph, 28,* 545–579.

Gottfried, A. E. (1986). Intrinsic motivational aspects of play experiences and materials. In A. W. Gottfried & C. Brown (Eds.), *Play interactions* (pp. 81–99). Lexington, MA: Lexington.

Graham, S., & Weiner, B. (1996). Theories and principles of motivation. In D. C. Berliner & R. C. Calfee (Eds.), *Handbook of educational psychology* (pp. 63–84). New York: Simon & Schuster MacMillan.

Groff, P. J. (1962). Children's attitudes toward reading and their critical reading abilities in four content-type materials. *Journal of Educational Research, 55,* 313–317.

Grolnick, W. S., & Ryan, R. M. (1987). Autonomy in children's learning: An experimental and individual difference investigation. *Journal of Personality and Social Psychology, 52,* 890–898.

Hebb, D. O. (1955). Drives and the C. N. S. (Conceptual Nervous System). *Psychological Review, 62,* 243–254.

Heckhausen, H. (1991). *Motivation and action.* Berlin: Springer.

Heckhausen, H., & Kuhl, J. (1985). From wishes to actions: The dead ends and short cuts on the long way to action. In M. Frese & J. Sabini (Eds.), *Goal-directed behavior. The concept of action in psychology* (pp. 134–159). Hillsdale, NJ: Lawrence Erlbaum Associates.

Herbart, J. F. (1965). Allgemeine Pädagogik, aus dem Zweck der Erziehung abgeleitet. In J. F. Herbart (Ed.), *Pädagogische Schriften* (Vol. 2, pp. 9–155). Düsseldorf: Küpper. (Original work published 1806).

Hidi, S. (1990). Interest and its contribution as a mental resource for learning. *Review of Educational Research, 60,* 549–571.

Hidi, S., & Baird, W. (1986). Interestingness—A neglected variable in discourse processing. *Cognitive Science, 10,* 179–194.

Hidi, S., & Baird, W. (1988). Strategies for increasing text-based interest and students' recall of expository texts. *Reading Research Quarterly, 23,* 465–483.

Hoffmann, L., & Lehrke, M. (1985). *Eine Zusammenstellung erster Ergebnisse aus der Querschnitterhebung 1984 über Schülerinteressen an Physik und Technik vom 5. bis 10. Schuljahr.* (unveröffentlichtes Manuskript). Kiel: Universität, Institut für die Pädagogik der Naturwissenschaften.

Hoffmann, L., & Lehrke, M. (1986). Eine Untersuchung über Schülerinteressen an Physik und Technik. *Zeitschrift für Pädagogik, 32,* 189–204.

Holland, J. L. (1985). *Making vocational choices: A theory of vocational personalities and work environments.* Englewood Cliffs, NJ: Prentice-Hall.

Humphreys, M. S., & Revelle, W. (1984). Personality, motivation, and performance: A theory of the relationship between individual differences and information processes. *Psychological Review, 91,* 153–184.

Hunt, J. McV. (1965). Intrinsic motivation and its role in psychological development. In D. Levine (Ed.), *Nebraska symposium on motivation* (Vol. 13, pp. 189–282). Lincoln: Nebraska University Press.

Jäger, A. O., & Althoff, K. (1983). *Der Wilde-Intelligenz-Test (WIT)*. Göttingen: Hogrefe.

Kerschensteiner, G. (1922). *Theorie der Bildung*. Leipzig: Teubner.

Kintsch, W. (1986). Learning from text. *Cognition and Instruction, 3*, 87–108.

Kintsch, W. (1988). The role of knowledge in discourse comprehension: A construction-integration model. *Psychological Review, 95*, 163–182.

Körkel, J., & Schneider, W. (1991). Domain-specific versus metacognitive knowledge effects on text recall and comprehension. In M. Carretero, M. Pope, P. R. J. Simons, & J. I. Pozo (Eds.), *Learning and instruction: European research in an international context* (Vol. 3, pp. 311–325). Oxford: Pergamon.

Kohlberg, L. (1967). A cognitive-developmental analysis of children's sex-role concepts and attitudes. In E. E. Maccoby (Ed.), *The development of sex differences* (pp. 82–173). Stanford: Tavistock.

Krapp, A. (1992). Das Interessenkonstrukt–Bestimmungsmerkmale der Interessenhandlung und des individuellen Interesses aus der Sicht einer Person-Gegenstands-Konzeption. In A. Krapp & M. Prenzel (Eds.), *Interesse, Lernen, Leistung* (pp. 297–329). Münster: Aschendorff.

Krapp, A., Hidi, S., & Renninger, K. A. (1992). Interest, learning, and development. In K. A. Renninger, S. Hidi, & A. Krapp (Eds.), *The role of interest in learning and development* (pp. 3–25). Hillsdale, NJ: Lawrence Erlbaum Associates.

Kuhl, J. (1983). *Motivation, Konflikt und Handlungskontrolle*. Berlin: Springer.

Kuhl, J. (1987). Action control: The maintenance of motivational states. In F. Halisch & J. Kuhl (Eds.), *Motivation, intention, and volition* (pp. 279–291). Berlin: Springer.

Kuhl, J. (1994). Motivation and volition. In G. d'Ydewalle, P. Eelen, & P. Bertelson (Eds.), *International perspective on psychological science* (Vol. 2, pp. 311–340). Hillsdale, NJ: Lawrence Erlbaum Associates.

Kunz, G. C., Drewniak, U., Hatalak, A., & Schön, A. (1992). Zur differentiellen Bedeutung kognitiver, metakognitiver und motivationaler Variablen für das effektive Lernen mit Instruktionstexten und Bildern. In H. Mandl & H. F. Friedrich (Eds.), *Lern- und Denkstrategien* (pp. 213–229). Göttingen: Hogrefe.

Lewin, K. (1926). Untersuchungen zur Handlungs- und Affekt-Psychologie II: Vorsatz, Wille und Bedürfnis. *Psychologische Forschung, 7*, 330–385.

Lewin, K. (1935). *A dynamic theory of personality: Selected papers*. New York: McGraw-Hill.

Lewin, K., Dembo, T., Festinger, L., & Sears, P. S. (1944). Level of aspiration. In J. McHunt (Ed.), *Personality and the behavior disorders* (Vol. 1, pp. 333–378). New York: Ronald Press.

Liebert, R. M., & Morris, L. W. (1967). Cognitive and emotional components of test anxiety: A distinction and some initial data. *Psychological Reports, 20*, 975–978.

Locke, E. A., & Latham, G. P. (1990). *A theory of goal setting and task performance*. Englewood Cliffs, NJ: Prentice-Hall.

Lorenz, K. (1943). Die angeborenen Formen möglicher Erfahrung. *Zeitschrift für Tierpsychologie, 5*, 235–499.

Maccoby, E. E., & Jacklin, C. N. (1974). *The psychology of sex differences*. Stanford, CA: Stanford University Press.

Maehr, M. L. (1974). Culture and achievement motivation. *American Psychologist, 29*, 887–896.

Marton, F., & Säljö, R. (1984). Approaches to learning. In F. Marton, D. J. Hounsell, & N. J. Entwistle (Eds.), *The experience of learning* (pp. 36–55). Edinburgh, Scotland: Scottish Academic Press.

Massimini, F., & Carli, M. (1988). The systematic assessment of flow in daily experience. In M. Csikszentmihalyi & I. S. Csikszentmihalyi (Eds.), *Optimal experience: Psychological studies of flow in consciousness* (pp. 266–287). Cambridge, MA: Cambridge University Press.

Morgan, M. (1984). Reward-induced decrements and increments in intrinsic motivation. *Review of Educational Research, 54*, 5–30.

Nicholls, J. G. (1989). *The competitive ethos and democratic education.* Cambridge, MA: Harvard University Press.

Pekrun, R. (1988). *Emotion, Motivation und Persönlichkeit.* München/Weinheim: Psychologie Verlags Union.

Pekrun, R. (1993). Facets of adolescents' academic motivation: A longitudinal expectancy-value approach. In M. Maehr & P. Pintrich (Eds.), *Advances in motivation and achievement* (Vol. 8, pp. 139–189). Greenwich, CT: JAI.

Pekrun, R., & Schiefele, U. (1996). Emotions- und motivationspsychologische Bedingungen der Lernleistung. In F. E. Weinert (Ed.), *Psychologie des Lernens und der Instruktion* (Enzyklopädie der Psychologie, D, Serie Pädagogische Psychologie, Bd. 2; pp. 151–177). Göttingen: Hogrefe.

Perfetti, C. A. (1988). Verbal efficiency in reading ability. In M. Daneman, G. E. MacKinnon, & T. G. Waller (Eds.), *Reading research: Advances in theory and practice* (Vol. 6, pp. 109–143). San Diego: Academic Press.

Piaget, J. (1948). *Psychologie der Intelligenz.* Zürich: Rascher.

Pintrich, P. R., & Schunk, D. H. (1996). *Motivation in education.* Englewood Cliffs, NJ: Prentice Hall.

Pokay, P., & Blumenfeld, P. C. (1990). Predicting achievement early and late in the semester: The role of motivation and use of learning strategies. *Journal of Eucational Psychology, 82,* 41–50.

Prenzel, M. (1988). *Die Wirkungsweise von Interesse.* Opladen: Westdeutscher Verlag.

Renninger, K. A. (1989, March). *Interests and noninterests as context in reading.* Paper presented at the annual meeting of the American Educational Research Association, San Francisco.

Renninger, K. A. (1990). Children's play interests, representation, and activity. In R. Fivush & J. Hudson (Eds.), *Knowing and remembering in young children* (pp. 127–165). Cambridge, MA: Cambridge University Press.

Renninger, K. A., Hidi, S., & Krapp, A. (Eds.). (1992). *The role of interest in learning and development.* Hillsdale, NJ: Lawrence Erlbaum Associates.

Renninger, K. A. & Wozniak, R. H. (1985). Effect of interest on attentional shift, recognition, and recall in young children. *Developmental Psychology, 21,* 624–632.

Reynolds, A. J., & Walberg, H. J. (1991). A structural model of science achievement. *Journal of Educational Psychology, 83,* 97–107.

Rheinberg, F. (1985). Motivationsanalysen zur Interaktion mit Computern. In H. Mandl & P. M. Fischer (Eds.), *Lernen im Dialog mit dem Computer* (pp. 83–105). München: Urban & Schwarzenberg.

Rheinberg, F. (1989). *Zweck und Tätigkeit.* Göttingen: Hogrefe.

Rheinberg, F. (1993, September). *Anreize engagiert betriebener Freizeitaktivitäten—ein Systematisierungsversuch.* Vortrag auf der 4. Tagung der Fachgruppe Pädagogische Psychologie, Mannheim.

Rheinberg, F. (1995). *Motivation.* Stuttgart: Kohlhammer.

Rheinberg, F. (1996a). Flow-Erleben, Freude an riskantem Sport und andere "unvernünftige" Motivationen. In J. Kuhl & H. Heckhausen (Eds.), *Motivation, Volition und Handlung* (Enzyklopädie der Psychologie, C, Serie Motivation und Emotion, Bd. 4; pp. 101–118). Göttingen: Hogrefe.

Rheinberg, F. (1996b). Von der Lernmotivation zur Lernleistung: Was liegt dazwischen? In J. Möller & O. Köller (Eds.), *Emotionen, Kognitionen und Schulleistung* (pp. 23–50). Weinheim: Psychologie Verlags Union.

Rheinberg, F. (1998). Theory of interest and research on motivation to learn. In L. Hoffmann, A. Krapp, K. A. Renninger, & J. Baumert (Eds.), *Proceedings of the International Invitational Conference on Interest and Gender in Seeon 1996* (pp.126–145). Kiel: Institut für die Pädagogik der Naturwissenschaften.

Roe, A., & Siegelman, M. (1964). *The origin of interests.* Washington, DC: American Personnel and Guidance Association.

Ryan, R. M., & Deci, E. L. (1996). When paradigms clash: Comments on Cameron and Peirce's claims that rewards do not undermine intrinsic motivation. *Review of Educational Research, 66*, 33–38.

Saljo, R. (1981). Learning approach and outcome: Some empirical observations. *Instructional Science, 10*, 47–65.

Scarr, S. (1992). Developmental theories for the 1990s: Developmental and individual differences. *Child Development, 63*, 1–19.

Scarr, S. (1994). Why developmental research needs evolutionary theory: To ask interesting questions. In P. Bertelson, P. Eelen, & G. d'Ydewalle (Eds.), *International perspectives on psychological science* (Vol. 1, pp. 159–179). Hillsdale, NJ: Lawrence Erlbaum Associates.

Schiefele, H. (1978). *Lernmotivation und Motivlernen*. München: Ehrenwirth.

Schiefele, H., Hauber, K., & Schneider, G. (1979). "Interesse" als Ziel und Weg der Erziehung. Überlegungen zu einem vernachläßigten pädagogischen Konzept. *Zeitschrift für Pädagogik, 25*, 1–20.

Schiefele, U. (1990). The influence of topic interest, prior knowledge, and cognitive capabilities on text comprehension. In J. M. Pieters, K. Breuer, & P. R. J. Simons (Eds.), *Learning environments* (pp. 323–338). Berlin: Springer.

Schiefele, U. (1991a). Interesse und Textrepräsentation. *Zeitschrift für Pädagogische Psychologie, 5*, 245–259.

Schiefele, U. (1991b). Interest, learning, and motivation. *Educational Psychologist, 26*, 299–323.

Schiefele, U. (1996a). *Motivation und Lernen mit Texten*. Göttingen: Hogrefe.

Schiefele, U. (1996b). Topic interest, text representation, and quality of experience. *Contemporary Educational Psychology, 21*, 3–18.

Schiefele, U. (1998). Individual interest and learning - what we know and what we don't know. In L. Hoffmann, A. Krapp, K. A. Renninger, & J. Baumert (Eds.), *Proceedings of the International Invitational Conference on Interest and Gender in Seeon 1996* (pp. 91–104). Kiel: Institut für die Pädagogik der Naturwissenschaften.

Schiefele, U., & Krapp, A. (1996). Topic interest and free recall of expository text. *Learning and Individual Differences, 8*, 141–160.

Schiefele, U., Krapp, A., Wild, K.-P., & Winteler, A. (1993). Der "Fragebogen zum Studieninteresse" (FSI). *Diagnostica, 39*, 335–351.

Schiefele, U., Krapp, A., & Winteler, A. (1992). Interest as a predictor of academic achievement: A meta-analysis of research. In K. A. Renninger, S. Hidi, & A. Krapp (Eds.), *The role of interest in learning and development* (pp. 183–212). Hillsdale, NJ: Lawrence Erlbaum Associates.

Schiefele, U., & Rheinberg, F. (1997). Motivation and knowledge acquisition: Searching for mediating processes. In M. L. Maehr & P. R. Pintrich (Eds.), *Advances in motivation and achievement* (Vol. 10, pp. 251–301). Greenwich, CT: JAI.

Schiefele, U., & Schreyer, I. (1994). Intrinsische Lernmotivation und Lernen. *Zeitschrift für Pädagogische Psychologie, 8*, 1–13.

Schmalhofer, F., & Glavanov, D. (1986). Three components of understanding a programmer's manual: Verbatim, propositional, and situational representations. *Journal of Memory and Language, 25*, 279–294.

Schneider, K. (1996). Intrinsisch (autotelisch) motiviertes Verhalten—dargestellt an den Beispielen des Neugierverhaltens sowie verwandter Verhaltenssysteme (Spielen und leistungsmotiviertes Handeln). In J. Kuhl & H. Heckhausen (Eds.), *Motivation, Volition, Handlung* (Enzyklopädie der Psychologie, C, Serie Motivation und Emotion, Bd. 4; pp. 119–152). Göttingen: Hogrefe.

Schneider, K., & Schmalt, H.-D. (1994). *Motivation*. (2nd ed.). Stuttgart: Kohlhammer.

Schneider, K., Wegge, J., & Konradt, U. (1993). Motivation und Leistung. In J. Beckmann, H. Strang, & E. Hahn (Eds.), *Aufmerksamkeit und Energetisierung* (pp. 101–131). Göttingen: Hogrefe.

Schneider, W., & Bjorklund, D. F. (1992, April). *Interest and domain-specific knowledge*. Paper presented at the annual meeting of the American Educational Research Association, San Francisco.

Schunk, D. H. (1989). Self-efficacy and achievement behaviors. *Educational Psychology Review, 1*, 173–208.

Schunk, D. H. (1995). Self-efficacy and education and instruction. In J. E. Maddux (Ed.), *Self-efficacy, adaptation, and adjustment* (pp. 281–303). New York: Plenum.

Snow, R. E. (1989). Cognitive–conative aptitude interactions in learning. In R. Kanfer, P. L. Ackerman, & R. Cudeck (Eds.), *Abilities, motivation, and methodology* (pp. 435–474). Hillsdale, NJ: Lawrence Erlbaum Associates.

Snow, R. E., Corno, L., & Jackson, D. N. (1996). Individual differences in affective and conative functions. In D. C. Berliner & R. C. Calfee (Eds.), *Handbook of educational psychology* (pp. 243–310). New York: Simon & Schuster MacMillan.

Snow, R. E., & Jackson, D. N. (1994). Individual differences in conation: Selected constructs and measures. In H. F. O'Neil & M. Drillings (Eds.) *Motivation: Theory and research* (pp. 71–99). Hillsdale, NJ: Lawrence Erlbaum Associates.

Thayer, R. E. (1986). Activation–Deactivation Adjective Check List: Current overview and structural analysis. *Psychological Reports, 58*, 606–614.

Thompson, S. U. (1975). Gender labels and early sex role development. *Child Development, 46*, 339–347.

Tobias, S. (1994). Interest, prior knowledge, and learning. *Review of Educational Research, 64*, 37–54.

Todt, E. (1978). *Das Interesse.* Bern: Huber.

Todt, E. (1990). Entwicklung des Interesses. In H. Hetzer (Ed.), *Angewandte Entwicklungspsychologie des Kindes- und Jugendalters* (pp. 213–264). Wiesbaden: Quelle & Meyer.

Travers, R. M. W. (1978). *Children's interests.* (unpublished manuscript). Kalamazoo: Western Michigan University.

van Dijk, T. A., & Kintsch, W. (1983). *Strategies of discourse comprehension.* Orlando, FL: Academic Press.

Vollmeyer, R., & Rheinberg, F. (1998). Motivationale Einflüsse auf Erwerb und Anwendung von Wissen in einem computersimulierten System. *Zeitschrift für Pädagogische Psychologie, 12,* 11–23.

Walsh, W. B., & Osipow, S. H. (Eds.). (1986). *Advances in vocational psychology. Vol. 1: The assessment of interests.* Hillsdale, NJ: Lawrence Erlbaum Associates.

Watkins, D. (1983). Depth of processing and the quality of learning outcomes. *Instructional Science, 12*, 49–58.

Wegge, J. (1994). *Motivation, Informationsverarbeitung und Leistung.* Unveröffentlichte Dissertation, Universität Dortmund.

Weiner, B. (1980). *Human motivation.* New York: Holt, Reinhart & Winston.

Weiner, B. (1986). *An attributional theory of motivation and emotion.* New York: Springer.

White, R. W. (1959). Motivation reconsidered: The concept of competence. *Psychological Review, 66*, 297–333.

Wigfield, A., & Eccles, J. (1992). The development of achievement task values: A theoretical analysis. *Developmental Review, 12*, 265–310.

11

Challenges and Directions for Intelligence and Conation: Integration

Moshe Zeidner
University of Haifa

For more than a century now, psychologists have explored the avenues linking human intelligence to a wide array of personality and conative constructs in an effort to develop comprehensive and scientifically tenable models of human behavior. Thus, researchers have longed to unravel the theoretical and practical interface between personality, motivation, and intelligence, hoping to shed light on how these constructs impact one another (and other variables) in the course of development, day-to-day behavior, and adaptive functioning. By and large, however, the tendency has been to examine the many variables described within each of these broad and sweeping areas more or less separately. Thus, intelligence theory has largely been aimed at assessing a person's ability to process information, to solve problems and cognitive tasks, and to determine one's cognitive potential to optimally adapt to the environment, whereas personality and motivational theory have been largely aimed at developing a comprehensive description of the person's traits, affective reactions, desires, goals, action tendencies, and the like. The distinction between cognitive and conative facets of personality, is, of course, artificial and a convenient means of dividing the scientific problems of psychology into simpler, more manageable chunks. Despite admonitions to the contrary, in much of the earlier work, the message received by subsequent generations of psychological scientists seems to be that the person, as well as the researcher, can be similarly divided (Snow, 1980). However, it is now readily apparent that any theoretical account of adaptive behavior in the real world requires a synthesis of cognitive, affective, and conative facets—what Hilgard (1980) aptly called the "trilogy of the mind."

This chapter sets out to address and systematically evaluate the nature of the conceptual and empirical links between conation and intelligence, two grand constructs of scientific psychology. The interest in this issue reflects the state-of-the-art research in individual differences (see Saklofske & Zeidner, 1995) and the recent upsurge of interest in the integration of the motivation–intelligence domains. I think it might be more instructive to survey contemporary and potential future directions in research on the intelligence–conation interface. I begin by presenting the historical backdrop and rationale for examining the intelligence–conation interface and highlight a number of conceptual and empirical links between these grand constructs. I then move on to present several overarching problems and issues that would appear to be relevant to future efforts in integrating the two domains.

CONTEMPORARY DIRECTIONS: CONCEPTUAL AND EMPIRICAL LINKS BETWEEN CONATION AND INTELLIGENCE.

The constructs of intelligence and conation would be expected to show important conceptual and empirical links on a number of counts. First, the two constructs are linked by virtue of being key sources of individual differences in behavior. Intelligence has been construed as constituting the cognitive part of the personality construct, whereas conation and affect are viewed as constituting, in part, the nonintellective facet of personality (Eysenck & Eysenck, 1985); these constructs are, in effect, mutually intertwined. Second, conative variables (e.g., self-control and regulation, action-control, interest, volition, etc.) may impact both the development of specific abilities as well as the actual manifestations of abilities in a variety of social situations (Cattell, 1971). Third, in the practical measurement of intelligence, a variety of conative variables (e.g., self-efficacy, test anxiety, need for achievement, self-regulation) have been shown to influence performance, thus affecting the conclusions and inferences that may be drawn about intelligence behavior (cf. Corno, 1997; Sattler, 1988; Zeidner, Matthews, & Saklofske, 1998). Furthermore, there has been an overlap in the techniques used to assess conative and intellectual variables. This is evidenced in the use of a variety of projective tests to estimate ability and diagnostic uses of IQ tests to assess certain personality and conative processes. Therefore, a variety of considerations really makes it impossible to discuss the topic of human intelligence without taking motivational factors into account.

Earlier writings by influential figures in the field of differential psychology (e.g., Binet, Terman, Wechsler, Anastasi) recognized the inextricable web of interrelationships between intelligence and nonintellective constructs such as conation. In fact, the distinction between intelligence and nonintellective factors is frequently blurred in the writings of a number of the key figures of differential psychology, such as Thorndike (1921) and Terman (1935), who believed that intelligence could not be considered separately from noncognitive factors. Wechsler's (1950) view is particularly important in this regard: He argued that conative factors (interest, volition, etc.) are integral components of the construct of intelligence and function in concert with intelligence in determining cognitive performance on tests and, in particular, social contexts. It is unfortunate that these views were lost in the flurry of psychometric activity to follow. The weight given to nonintellectual factors in the interpretation of intelligence first declined with the introduction of group tests and factorial methods for analyzing correlational data.

Current trends in scientific psychological research also stress the independence of cognitive, conative, and affective systems in shaping behavior. Contemporary thinking views salient constructs such as self-regulation or self-efficacy as mediating between intentional activity and the individual's cognitive and emotional states and behaviors. One popular hypothesized link between intelligence and conation is in the way the individual organizes and integrates both internal and environmental behavior and expresses this in behavior (Kuhl & Kraska, 1989). Whereas intellectual processes mediate incoming stimuli and change these environmental stimuli into information by assigning them meaning, conative processes mediate incoming stimuli and alter them by assigning them emotion or direction. Consequently, these processes have been predicted to interact in a reciprocal fashion.

Curiously, given the general consensus among researchers on the importance of taking both intellective, conative, and affective factors into consideration in modeling human behavior, it is truly remarkable that the conative facet of personality faded from modern psychology's consciousness for many years, and it is only in the past decade or so that attempts have been made to revive the construct of conation and incorporate it in models of intelligence and adaptive behavior. Snow (1980) argued that although an elaborate view of human adaptation implies the central need for a concept of purposeful striving and action, most models of intelligence and adaptive behavior have given only short shrift to the conative domain. Thus, prevailing models of intelligence tend to consider only those programs, plans, schemata, algorithms, heuristics, and procedures that are carried out to most optimally reach a particular goal, solve a given problem, or attain a particular standard while paying minimal attention to the very goals, intentions, and interests for which particular programs and plans are subservient. Although a person's motives, wants, desires, goals, interests, expectations, and intentions are often taken as given in current models of intelligence, in real-life situations people typically rearrange their priorities and formulate, modify, or even abort goals and intentions, thus impacting on the particular plans or problem-solving processes designed to attain these goals. Hence, it would seem to be imperative to consider the person's purposeful striving towards personally meaningful goals in the real world as relevant to intelligence research.

A recent review of the literature on intelligence, personality, and conation in the context of human adjustment by Zeidner, Matthews, and Saklofske (1998) points to a complex pattern of reciprocal relationships between intelligence and conation, with the two variables impacting each other in the course of development and day-to-day behavior. On one hand, a body of research suggests that conative variables and general motivational dispositions influence intellectual functioning (conation $\Rightarrow$ intelligence). In this respect, it is important to distinguish the effects that conative variables (such as test anxiety, self-regulation, impulse control) may have on intellectual performance, in the short term, and from effects on competence in the longer term. There is solid empirical evidence for various negative emotional and conative states tending to impair intellectual performance to a moderate degree, especially when the task is demanding of attention or working memory. For example, students low in self-efficacy may neither feel capable nor care enough to generate appropriate cognitive strategies at the point of application. Furthermore, conative variables such as self-efficacy and personal control may affect both the development and expression of human intelligence. Thus, certain motivational and conative processes such as low self-efficacy and inefficient self-regulation may act over extended periods of time to depress intellectual functioning by reducing a person's motivation to acquire and develop specific intellectual skills. For example, a person with poor impulse control or inadequate self-regulated learning skills may not be able to acquire the intellectual skills necessary to perform well in school or on an intelligence exam. Conversely, a person who is highly motivated to achieve, intellectually absorbed and interested in a particular academic domain, and who effectively employs self-regulation and metacognitive learning skills and strategies would also be expected to develop and use those intellectual abilities more effectively over the years. Some of these effects may be context-dependent, in that some kinds of conative processes may influence certain types of practical intelligence more strongly than others. It is less clear whether negative motivational and affective processes impact basic competence in addition to the person's performance on specific occasions.

On the other hand, there is a body of research reviewed by Zeidner & Matthews (2000) showing that intelligence may shape the growth and expression of certain motivational constructs (intelligence $\Rightarrow$ conation). Thus, a person with low ability may not be able to acquire the necessary self-regulated learning skills necessary to perform well in school or on an intelligence exam. Furthermore, intelligence may impact motivation and affective states through encouraging more positive cognitions of personal competence. Thus, individuals who are talented in a particular domain would be expected to apply and develop their crystallized abilities in that domain and have more favorable performance expectancies, lower evaluative anxiety, and high academic self-concept and self-efficacy with respect to that domain. Indeed, as I pointed out (Zeidner & Schleyer, 1999), the literature suggests that high-ability individuals frequently tend to evidence greater perceived control over their environment, less anxiety, more efficient self-regulation, and greater impulse control. High intelligence can aid a student in learning the realities of general and school culture and the physical world, as part of an integrated learning process, and help the person acquire more socially desirable traits. Furthermore, individuals high in intellectual functioning are frequently shown to be better adjusted, both socially and emotionally, than their less-intelligent counterparts. Reduced motivation and negative emotions may frequently be generated by more or less veridical appraisals that negative outcomes are likely, due to low ability, and negative affects and reduced effort and interest in a particular domain may result if low intelligence leads to a succession of performance failures. Students who cannot apply cognitive strategies in a particular domain may not be able to attain valued goals despite motivational beliefs. Thus, depressed motivation as well as negative affect may be a marker for poor intellectual aptitude and past achievement, and a factor that directly affects intellectual performance.

A number of studies demonstrate important empirical and conceptual links between intelligence and conative constructs. Snow (1980) reported an intriguing pattern of relationship between ability and three conative aptitudes: volition, achievement motivation, and interest in different school subjects. Data cited by Snow suggest that the optimum performance on cognitive tests comes from students with middle position on both the need for achievement and evaluative anxiety continuum and trails off as students display increases or decreases on either anxiety or achievement motivation. Also, a recent integrative review by Ackerman and Heggestad (1997) suggests that the development of both intelligence and conative dispositions proceeds along mutually causal lines, with abilities, interests, and personality developing in tandem. Accordingly, ability level (and certain personality dispositions) determine the probability of success in a particular task domain and interests determine the motivation to invest energy and attempt particular tasks and become adept at them over time.

DIRECTION FOR FUTURE RESEARCH

The rapprochement and integration of research and assessment in the ability, personality, and motivational domains is an important goal for individual differences research in the 21st century. In order to achieve this goal, I wish to point out several overarching issues that need to be addressed in any future integrative efforts in this area.

More Refined Conceptualization and Taxonomies of Constructs

One important goal for future research is developing a tractable conceptual foundation for linking individual differences in abilities and conation. As pointed out by Snow (1980), "The history of differential psychology does not provide a well-organized correlational map of individual difference constructs in the conative and affective domain of personality and their relation to cognitive abilities" (p. 436). Thus, more thought needs to be given to the conceptualization of the content and preview of each domain, and additional work is needed in a systematic mapping out of the two domains of discourse. Clearly, the construction of such a map is critical in the advancement of research and in guiding the needed analytic research. At present, with respect to certain conative constructs, such as self-regulation, it is unclear whether we are talking about two necessarily differential concepts, two intersecting categories, or superordinate–subordinate hierarchically related concepts, with one (e.g., conation) a subset of the other (e.g., intelligence).

Some of the difficulties involved in sorting out the conceptual interface between the domains of conation and intelligence as a whole may be exemplified by considering the problematic in determining the nature of the conceptual relationship between intelligence and self-regulation—a key contemporary conative construct (Boekaerts, Pintrich, & Zeidner, 2000). Cognitive self-regulatory strategies involve cognitive processes and behaviors geared toward accomplishing self-set or adopted goals. It is commonly agreed that certain self-regulatory skills, for example, forming a clear mental representation of a designated goal, the capacity to devise a plan of action and extend or revise it, and the ability to monitor and actualize plan are important conditions for learning and cognitive performance. Intelligence and self-regulatory mechanisms are part and parcel of a multifaceted view of human intelligence, with metacognitive or executive processes utilized in planning, monitoring, and decision making during cognitive performance (Sternberg, 1985). Although existing tests of ability do not measure self-regulatory skills implicitly, some skills (eg., metacognition) have been said to underlie all of intellectual activity (e.g., Sternberg, 1985). Intelligence and self-regulatory mechanisms are part and parcel of a multifaceted view of human intelligence, with metacognitive or executive processes utilized in planning, monitoring, and decision making during cognitive performance (Sternberg, 1985). Although existing tests of ability do not measure self-regulatory skills implicitly, some skills (e.g., metacognition) have been said to underlie all of intellectual activity (Sternberg, 1985). Kuhl and Kraska (1989) have gone so far as to suggest that self-regulation may be little else than an ability or component of general intelligence, so that this major conative variable would be a proper subset of the ability domain. Furthermore, although highly intelligent individuals do show benefits in strategy regulation (Borkowski & Peck, 1986), it is unclear to what extent self-regulation shapes intelligence or whether high intelligence is merely manifested in efficient self-regulatory processes.

The fragmentation and disparate, but overlapping, lines of research within both the ability and conative domain has made any attempt at integration an arduous task. Indeed, a useful summary of conation and intelligence relations has been virtually impossible for many years because little coherence existed among theory and measures of both conation and ability constructs (cf. Ackerman & Heggestad, 1997). The recent attention to the interface between conation and ability processes comes at a time when there has also been a flurry of new research activity in the field of motivational psychology (Kanfer, 1989). However, consensus has yet to be reached about the constructs that comprise the nomological network for the conative domain, and, to a lesser extent, the same holds for the ability domain. Thus, in attempting the integration, it is presently unclear which basic constructs, factors, or facets, are to be used within each domain.

A major goal for the future integration of conation and intelligence is the development of a taxonomy of individual difference constructs, akin to the periodic table of elements in chemistry. Even quite loose, provisional classification structures might help guide exploration and provide a useful framework to which to pin individual data as they accumulate. Furthermore, yet another overarching goal in mapping out the nature of the intelligence—conation interface is seeking out specific areas of the individual difference domain in which coverage is incomplete. Factor analysis has traditionally been one of psychology's key taxonomy building tools in both the cognitive and affective domains. However, the findings of factor analysis need to be supported and triangulated with other methods (Snow, 1995). It is presently unclear whether or not the concepts provided by factor analysis are both molar and molecular enough to cover all the important theoretical needs. However, it is unclear to what extent the evidence based on methods other than factor analysis educes evidence that supports similar distinctions or suggests other distinctions. As pointed out with respect to the personality–intelligence interface, the small number of factors in the intelligence domains (particularly if we suffice with a general ability factor or fluid and crystallized ability) and in personality (3 to 5 dimensions) are problematic: Although representing the law of parsimony, these factors may represent only a fraction of the total number of personality and intelligence spheres. Although the principle of parsimony should be endorsed whenever applicable, the evidence often points to relative complexity rather than simplicity.

The coverage problem has been examined by casting the list of defined intelligence and conation factors into other kinds of category systems to see what may be left out. In a recent paper by Snow, Corno, and Jackson (1996), the individual difference domain was mapped out by taking the Aristotelian categories of cognition, affect, and conation as basic constructs for the analyses. Affect was divided into temperament and emotion, conation into motivation and volition, and cognition into declarative knowledge and procedural skills, yielding a six-column array. As pointed out by Snow (1995), this mapping of known intellectual and nonintellective factors into this array suggests at least one empty space—volition. Whereas nonintellective factors seem to represent much of temperament, characteristic emotional moods, and sources of motivation and interest, and ability factors much of cognitive knowledge and skills, the column representing volition (will) was poorly covered. This construct, appearing to variables such as action control, self-regulation, metacognitive knowledge, social intelligence and beliefs about one's knowledge and style, is not well represented in the factor structures typically used.

Fortunately, more recent advances in the taxonomy of conative aptitudes (cf. Corno, 1997) and the growing consensus about the multidimensional nature of the ability domain (Carroll, 1993) provides more solid grounds for establishing conation–intelligence relations using well-established facets of each of these domains. Indeed, there is a coalescence of evidence favoring a hierarchical structure of ability (and a 5-factor model of personality). Thus, future investigations of the pattern of relations between well-established facets of both the conative and ability domains may provide for a substantially improved understanding of the nature of individual differences in each of these traditionally separated domains.

It is noted that ability researchers have traditionally viewed motivation as a unitary construct, and motivation researchers often see ability as a unitary construct. The recent research attests to the multiplicity of conative and ability constructs and processes. Thus, future research requires that each conative construct by separately related to ability or to various types of ability. Moreover, rather than deal with relationships between conation and global IQ, one might want to consider the experimental separation of global IQ into separate abilities and factors of mental speed, accuracy, persistence, and so forth look at the separate correlations of these with difference aspects of conation. To that end, it might be useful to employ a facet-analytic approach to the investigation of the conation–intelligence interface by constructing a matrix with ability constructs (j) represented by rows and motivational constructs (k) represented by columns, and the entire two-dimensional matrix (j x k), or Cartesian space, representing the domain of discourse for any future integrative attempt. A third facet, area of application (school, occupation, military, etc.) may be added to form a three-faceted cubic model for examining the much-needed integration. Indeed, tentative mapping of the domains of conation and intelligence suggest that entire areas are uncovered by present research; these lacunae need to be identified and systematically researched. In addition, Multidimensional Scaling or Smallest Space Analysis may be used profitably to create a rough map of the terrain of the ability–conation interface and may indicate where new measurement development and further research is most needed.

One major concern in any future integration among the two domains is how to integrate variables defined in qualitatively different grain sizes into a coherent behavioral and molecular level of description. It is, at present, unclear whether the concepts provided by prevalent analytic techniques (e.g., factor analysis) are both molar and molecular enough to cover all the important theoretical needs at present. Above the superfactors, there might also be the need for compound constructs at the level of types, and it is becoming clearer by the day that both broad, sweeping, higher-order constructs (e.g., self-regulation, etc.) as well as narrow, lower order constructs (e.g. metacognitive strategies, monitoring) need to be represented in research. A principal advantage of lower-order concepts is that they often have clearer psychological referents; the psychological clarity of individual-differences dimensions often seem to vary inversely with the breadth of the dimension. Lower-order categories often carry specialized and situational meanings (sports or test anxiety) not captured in the higher-order factors (Anxiety or Neuroticism). Furthermore, researchers would do well to consider other kinds of units of analysis, ranging from schemes and strategies to styles and behavioral episodes. A major task for future research is to determine the optimal grain size for conducting this integration and also to determine how to best integrate variables defined in quite different grain sizes into a coherent model of human behavior.

As pointed out by Eysenck (1994) with respect to research on the personality–intelligence interface, we need to elaborate more general theories that predict the relationship between intelligence and conation. Thus, simple attempts to correlate any old IQ that comes to mind with any old motivational measure that happens to be available are doomed to failure and are a waste of time and energy. Such studies attempt to make use of material that happens to be readily available, disregard obvious statistical warnings and come to conclusions having no scientific meaning or social usefulness. This way of doing research can only undermine the credibility of work in the field of individual differences. The optimal approach is to look at well-established theories concerning performance data, arrange experimental conditions to test deductions from these theories, and interpret results cautiously in the light of the theories in question.

Clearer Specification of the Meaning and Nature of the Interaction Between Intelligence and Conation

A casual glance at the literature (e.g., Saklofske & Zeidner, 1995) shows that authors have often urged exploring the interactions between intelligence and both affective and conative variables in a wide variety of domains. However, researchers need to be a bit clearer about the exact nature of the interactions they have in mind. Conation–intelligence interactions may take many forms and may reflect different hypotheses about particular types of interactive effects and mechanisms presumed to be operative. Also, we need to shed light on the causal mechanisms underlying observed interactions. We now briefly point out some different forms of interaction that might be considered:

Summative Effects. One possible model is an *additive coaction* (summative effects) model. In this model, both conative and intelligence variables are operative in impacting a third variable (leadership ability, creativity, health outcomes, or grade point average), but they summate in additive rather than synergistic fashion. In effect, this does not constitute interaction but rather two main effects. Thus, we surely need to entertain the possibility that the true nature of the relationship is actually additive or summative, in which conation and intelligence each contribute independently, but not interactively, to some criterion outcome, such as scholastic performance.

Synergistic Effects. If what interests us is how conation and intelligence interact to impact a third variable, we may need to consider synergistic interactions; that is, where the presence of one variable (say motivation) potentiates the effects of the other (say IQ) on some criterion performance (e.g., leadership). In this form of interaction, the effects of both factors on the third variable are greater than the sum of each. Eysenck (1995) showed how attention to specific modes of synergistic interactions between cognitive and noncognitive factors may prove useful in the production of socially important effects. Eysenck provided evidence showing that creativity may best be accounted for by the synergistic interaction between intelligence and the personality factor of psychoticism. Neither factor alone determines creativity.

Ordinal–Disordinal Interactions. These interactions refer to the interplay between different independent variables in terms of their effects on criterial outcome variables. Some conative characteristics, such as test anxiety, have differential effects on the performance of individuals of differing levels of intelligence (Zeidner, 1998). Thus, a particular level of state anxiety may be debilitating for students of low intelligence and may facilitate the performance of high ability students, as it enhances motivation (because the task is viewed more as a challenge than a threat). It is noted that these different types of interactions are distinct and should not be pooled under any umbrella category.

Dynamic Interactions. If we are mainly interested in dynamic interactions between conative and ability constructs, we need to look at the reciprocal effects of conative and intellectual variables in the course of development and day-to-day manifestations. Thus, low IQ may evoke high test anxiety in students aware of deficiencies in their cognitive abilities, which, in turn, further constrains a person's capacity to develop intellectual ability on account of high arousal and avoidance behavior, which, in turn, escalates test anxiety.

Improving Research Design, Measurement, and Analysis

One important goal for future research in this area is modeling relations through more complex measurement models and analyses. Although the scientific analysis of the conative and intelligence domains now predominates over the earlier more subjective, philosophical, and literary speculations, bivariate correlations and experimental design have been unduly emphasized at the expense of more appropriate multivariate and longitudinal designs. Also, as pointed out by Snow (1995), there are few concrete examples of research capitalizing on the power of multitrait multimethod paradigms and complimentaries of different research methods (behavioral, qualitative, experimental research, etc.) in this area.

Research would also benefit from using modern scaling techniques, such as univariate or multivariate Item Response Theory (IRT) models in constructing conative or affective assessment instruments. As pointed out by Most and Zeidner (1995), although IRT technology has been available for some time now, few individual difference researchers have taken advantage of modern test theory in constructing unidimensional scales. Furthermore, given that the measurement of the conative domain is quite tricky and problematic, it is unfortunate that there have been only a handful of attempts in recent years to find new methods of assessing conative variables for research purposes. Clearly, projective techniques have their problems, and the shortcomings of questionnaire measures are well known.

Furthermore, the bulk of the data relating intelligence to key motivational traits is of a correlational nature so that the direction of causality in the intelligence–conation association is indeterminate. The nature of the causal flow of direction in the observed relationships between intelligence and motivational constructs has been conceptualized and interpreted in a variety of different ways. Perhaps the most productive form of association is that of reciprocal determinism, with intelligence and conation showing a bidirectional relationship. Thus, for example, in the observed relationship between interests and achievement, people with specific interests would be expected to develop their abilities in their areas of interest, and conversely, people with a specific ability profile would be expected to develop interests in areas congenial to their ability.

Although, as mentioned, the relationship between conative and intelligence variables has generally been conceptualized and investigated as a linear one, there is a good possibility of a nonlinear relation between intelligence and certain motivational aptitudes. Whenever a zero-order correlation between a measure of conation and intelligence is calculated, an implicit assumption is made about the form of the function connecting these variables. It is assumed that the function can be graphed as a straight line in Cartesian coordinates. The correlation coefficient can seriously underestimate the relationship between conative and intelligence measures whenever the actual function departs from the linear (e.g., Inverted-U shaped) curve. In this situation the correlation might be null even if there is some substantial correlation. Because the bulk of research on the empirical links between conation and intelligence has relied on linear associations, the literature may have, in some cases, seriously underestimated the magnitude of the relation, which, in fact, may be curvilinear. Thus, current research has generally been insensitive to any nonlinear relations that might exist between trait families. Snow (1989) reported that in a sample of Stanford students, the correlations of Wechsler IQ scores with Holland's Realistic theme scores are $r = .06$ and $r = .05$, but the respective Etas are .41 and .65!

In addition, we need to look at multiplicative functions introducing both linear and quadratic functions of intelligence and motivational predictors of criterion performance. If leadership behavior, for example, is a curvilinear function of IQ (Simonton, 1995), then IQ should be accompanied by the same variable squared in any regression equation predicting leadership. It is important to note that if, in an applied setting, conative and intelligence predictors participate primarily in interaction rather than as noncontingent effects, we cannot expect the validity of the regression coefficient to be very good in the absence of appropriate product terms between the vectors representing conative and intellectual variables.

Furthermore, more research on the dynamic relations between a wide array of conative and intelligence variables over time is urgently needed to gauge reciprocal interactions and effects. Thus, more longitudinal research is needed that models the dynamic transactions between conative and intellectual variables over time via such procedures as structural equation modeling. Thus, employing structural equation modeling in describing the conative–intelligence relationships should greatly elucidate the dynamic interactive roles of these concepts. It would also be interesting to explore to what extent the pattern of relations between ability and conative variables vary with age. We also need to study variables that integrate intelligence and conative facets over development and individualization in a wide variety of specialized situations (learning, social contexts, sports, occupational, military settings, etc.).

In addition, more adequate sampling of both subjects and variables from both the ability and the conative domain is urgently needed. Only by strategically selecting variables can we expect to thoroughly cover both domains and facets of units, observations, and settings. Furthermore, as pointed out by Boyle, Stankov, and Cattell (1985), many studies in the individual differences domain employing factor analytic techniques have used less than the needed number of cases and are consequently flawed. The nature of the ability–conation relationship needs to be considered in both pathological and nonpathological samples. For example, Goff and Ackerman (1992) undertook several factor analyses based on the intercorrelations of combined intelligence and nonintellectual measures using a sample of 138 subjects (Boyle et al, 1985). Based on simulated data, MacCullum (1985) demonstrated that only about one half of the exploratory searches located the true model in sample of 300 and success rates in smaller samples approached 0.

One interesting question in need of further research is whether or not the structure of intelligence and relations among ability factors would emerge if these factors were extruded from populations differing in various conative parameters (e.g., self-regulation, anxiety, achievement motivation). Eysenck (1994) summarized a number of studies suggesting that factorial studies of personality may not give invariant results under changes of ability level. Thus, children high and low in Neuroticism differ in the way their mental abilities are structured (Eysenck, 1994). Very little is known about the extent to which there are reliable differences in factor structure of intelligence for groups differing in motivational parameters.

Identifying Key Bridging Concepts

A variety of stylistic concepts (e.g., mindfulness, self-absorption, cognitive flexibility) may provide a useful key by which to conceptualize the intersection and crossroads between personality, conation, and intelligence domains. The application of inappropriate measurement models to assess cognitive styles is one of the reasons why this line of research has not fared well in the past. Most measures of style have inappropriately followed the ability factor model and have yielded scores that are unipolar and value-directed rather than bipolar and value-differentiated. In fact, styles should be less concerned with how much, but should focus on how, and styles have been dealt with more as ability traits than stylistic variables. One of the important contributions that psychometricians can make to our field is through improved measurement of stylistic variables as a potential bridge between conation and intelligence.

Research suggests that intelligence would be most closely and organically related to nonintellectual variables that reflect typical ways of dealing with information, and it might be useful to have another careful and methodologically sounder look at both old and new stylistic variables. One potentially useful bridging concept is that of "Mindfulness" (Brown & Langer, 1990). *Mindfulness* is a particular style of perceiving and processing information in which a person is open to several ways or perspectives of viewing the situation. A mindful person remains open to seeing information as new, is sensitive to the context in which she or he is perceiving information, and eventually gives new meaning to the situation and creates new categories through which information may be understood (Brown & Langer, 1990). From a mindful perspective, one's response to a particular situation is not an attempt to make the best choice among available options or meet a particular standard, as is the case in ability, but rather to create new options. Rather than focus on a particular set of cognitive skills and focus on achievement as a desirable outcome, mindful individuals generate new hypothesies that may be tested in the particularity of the individual's experience.

In-Depth Research in Practical and Clinical Settings

Conative and intelligence factors are often used jointly for decision making purposes in various practical domains. There is little doubt of the importance of both constructs in influencing performance in a wide array of applied areas (school and academic performance, occupational behavior, leadership, etc.). It is at the applied or clinical level that the greatest amount of integration of cognitive and affective variables takes place by necessity. For example, the clinical or school psychologist may assess a child's poor school achievement by gathering data on the child's intelligence, learning style, motivation, anxiety, self-regulated learning skills, and self-concepts (as well as social behavior, physical and health status, and home environment) in order to arrive at a diagnosis and prescription of the most appropriate intervention program. Thus, the psychological practitioners' task is to develop a comprehensive and integrated description of the person by employing precise measurement strategies and continuously referencing the theory and research that describes the interrelationships among the various intellective and conative factors examined. Given that such an integration is not always explicit from theory or from the available research literature, clinicians may be required to make this integration on their own; that is, at an intuitive level.

Unfortunately, very little is known practitioners and clinicians conduct the integration between personality, conative, and intelligence variables in the process of psychodiagnosis and decision making. More research is needed on the considerations practitioners bring to bear in making decisions based on the integration between conative and ability constructs. For example, how does the probation officer, personnel, or school psychologist combine ability and motivational facets to make decisions that are of major importance to the individual and society as a whole? In-depth interviews, protocol analysis, and systematic observations are needed in a wide array of practical domains to shed light on this needed area.

In addition, a most worthwhile effort would be to conduct an intensive and careful analysis of individual cases, contrasting those individuals with extreme scores on one or more conative dimensions in order to identify qualitative differences between individuals. Such analysis would provide avenues for understanding what it means to be an extreme scorer and for understanding the variety of ways in which one might achieve extreme scores. In addition, cross-partitioning of individuals by intelligence and specific conative factors would help toward the development of useful typologies in various domains.

Finally, a closer partnership and correspondence is needed between theory, assessment, and practice. A case in point: Many clinicians use projective conative measures for psychodiagnostic purposes (e.g., Rorschach, Thematic Apperception Test (TAT)) although few studies have provided sufficient evidence for the structural or criterial validity aspects of these measures. Similarly, clinicians often interpret the Performance and Verbal subscales of the Wechsler Intelligence Scale for Children (WISC) or Wechsler Adult Intelligence Scale (WAIS) as though they represented two distinct factors of intelligence although little evidence is forthcoming for the factorial validity of these two scales.

CONCLUSIONS

One important goal for individual differences research in the 21st century, in my mind, is a rapprochement between the grand constructs of scientific psychology, intelligence, personality, and motivation that have developed largely along separate tracks in the past. Recent years, however, have seen an upsurge of interest in addressing important conceptual and practical links among these concepts and integrating them into a unified model of human behavior.

Current trends in individual differences research allow for the hope of an integrated understanding of the ways, that "each person is like all other people, some other people, and no other people." A truly integrative science of personality would help clear from our past pathways some of the debris of disciplinary provincialism. However, as pointed out by Lohman and Rocklin (1995), there is a difference between simple eclecticism and an integrated model that forms the basis for a unified approach and rapprochement of the domains of conation and intelligence. Such an approach would not simply look at a person from intellectual and motivational or affective perspectives but instead integrate data from these perspectives. A true integration would certainly move us a step forward in understanding both normal as well as pathological states. This appears to be a major challenge for individual differences research in the 21st century.

From a theoretical point of view, the modest and often inconsistent associations reported between intelligence and key conative aptitudes suggests that the links between these constructs may be weak. Perhaps the two constructs are really divergent and orthogonal, much as Eysenck (1994) argued for the constructs of intelligence and personality, and the research tradition of dealing with them separately has been for a good reason.

From a practical point of view, motivational variables seldom bear such a sizeable impact on intellectual performance so as to invalidate intelligence assessments or test scores as a whole. The impact of various conative factors affecting performance (e.g., anxiety, motivation), may in fact be viewed as key aspects of the individual's global intellectual capacity (Matarazzo, 1972; Wechsler, 1944). Moreover, personality factors may actually enhance rather than detract from the validity of intelligence measures. Arguably, individuals who do poorly on intelligence tests because of the debilitating effects of certain conative factors (e.g., high test anxiety, low motivation) may also do poorly on the criterion measure of performance—and for much the same reasons.

Under the assumption that both conative and intellective factors are important factors at play in any comprehensive model of human adaptation, this section of the text has been a most welcome opportunity to take another look at conation and further explore this construct in the context of individual differences research. The chapters represent some of the premier research being conducted these days in the domain of human conation, and they bear important implications for the systematic study of the intelligence–conation interface. It is high time that further research attention be directed at understanding how conative constructs are best incorporated into rapidly developing models of human intelligence and cognition. Overall, the chapters make an important contribution toward filling the gap in individual differences research so aptly pointed out by Snow (1980) some time ago, "Where in an information processing model of intelligence aspects of mental life, such as impulse, desire, volition, purposive striving and various affective states and traits fit in" (pp. 185-199).

REFERENCES

Ackerman, P. L., & Heggestad, E. D. (1997). Intelligence, personality, and interests: Evidence for overlapping traits. *Psychological Bulletin, 121,* 219–245.

Anastasi, A. (1958). *Differential psychology.* New York: Macmillan.

Boekaerts, M., Pintrich, P., & Zeidner, M. (Eds.). (2000). *Handbook of self-regulation.* San Diego: Academic Press.

Borkowski, J. G., & Peck, V. A. (1986). Causes and consequences of metamemory in gifted children. In R. Sternberg & J. Davidson (Eds.), *Conceptions of giftedness* (pp. 182–200). Cambridge, England: Cambridge University Press.

Boyle, G. J., Stankov, L., & Cattell, R. B. (1985). Measurement and Statistical Models in the study of personality and intelligence. In D. Saklofske & M. Zeidner (Eds.), *International handbook of personality and intelligence* (pp. 447–474). New York: Plenum

Brown, J., & Langer, E. (1990), Mindfulness and intelligence: A comparison. *Educational Psychologist, 25,* 305–335.

Carroll, J. B. (1993). Cognitive abilities: The state of the art. *Psychological Science, 3,* 266–270.

Cattell, R. B. (1971). *Abilities: Their structure, growth and action.* New York: Houghton Mifflin.

Corno, L. (1997, July). *Conative individual differences in learning.* Paper presented at the Second Spearman Seminar on "Intelligence and Personality." Plymouth, England, 1997.

Eysenck, H. J. (1994). Personality and intelligence: Psychometric and experimental approaches. In R. J. Sternberg & P. Ruzgis (Eds.), *Personality and intelligence* (pp. 3–31). New York: Cambridge University Press.

Eysenck, H. J., & Eysenck, M. W. (1985). *Personality and individual differences.* New York: Plenum.

Goff, M., & Ackerman, P. L. (1992). Personality–intelligence relations: Assessment of typical intellectual engagement. *Journal of Educational Psychology, 84,* 537–552.

Hilgard, E. R. (1980). The trilogy of mind: Cognition, affection, and conation. *Journal of the History of the Behavioral Sciences, 16,* 107–117.

Kanfer, R. (1989). Conative processes, dispositions, and behavior: Connecting the dots within and across paradigms. In R. Kanfer, P. L. Ackerman, & R. Cudeck (Eds.), *Abilities, motivation and methodology* (pp. 375–388). Hillsdale, NJ: Lawrence Erlbaum Associates.

Kuhl, J., & Kraska, K. (1989). Self-regulation and metamotivation: Computational mechanisms, development, and assessment. In R. Kanfer, P. L. Ackerman, & R. Cudeck (Eds.), *Abilities, motivation and methodology* (pp. 343–374). Hillsdale, NJ: Lawrence Erlbaum Associates.

Lohman, D. F., & Rocklin, T. (1995). Current and recurring issues in the assessment of intelligence and personality. In D. H. Saklofske & M. Zeidner (Eds), *International handbook of personality and intelligence* (pp. 447-474). New York: Plenum Press.

MacCullum, R. (1985, July). Some problems in the process of model modification in covariance structure modeling. Paper presented at the European Meeting of the Psychometric Society, Cambridge, England.

Matarazzo, J. D. (1972). *Wechsler's measurement and appraisal of adult intelligence* (5th ed.). Baltimore: Williams & Wilkins.

Most, B., & Zeidner, M. (1995). Constructing personality and intelligence instruments: Methods and issues. In D. Saklofske & M. Zeidner (Eds.), *International handbook of personality and intelligence* (pp. 475–503). New York: Plenum.

Sattler, J. M. (1988). *Assessment of children* (3rd ed.). San Diego: Author.

Simonton, D. K. (1995). Personality and intellectual predictors of leadership. In D. Saklofske & M. Zeidner (Eds.), *International handbook of personality and intelligence* (pp. 739–757). New York: Plenum.

Snow, R. E. (1989). Cognitive–conative aptitude interactions in learning. In R. Kanfer, P. L. Ackerman, & R. Cudeck (Eds.), *Abilities, motivation and methodology* (pp. 435–474). Hillsdale, NJ: Lawrence Erlbaum Associates.

Snow, R. E. (1980). Intelligence for the year 2001. *Intelligence, 4,* 185–199.

Snow, R. E., Corno, L., & Jackson, D. N. (1996). Individual differences in affective and conative functions. In D. C. Berliner & R. Calfee (Eds.), *Handbook of educational psychology* (pp. 243-310). New York: MacMillan.

Snow, R. E. Foreword. In D. Saklofske & M. Zeidner (Eds.), *International handbook of personality and intelligence* (pp. XI–XV). New York: Plenum.

Sternberg, R. J. (1985). *Beyond IQ: A triarchic theory of intelligence.* Cambridge, England: Cambridge University Press.

Terman, L. M. (1935) (Ed). *Mental and physical traits of a thousand gifted children* (Vol. I). Stanford, CA: Stanford University Press.

Thorndike, E. L. (1921). The Correlation between interests and abilities in college courses, *Psychological Review, 28,* 374–376.

Wechsler, D. (1944). *The measurement of adult intelligence* (3rd ed.), Baltimore: Williams & Wilkins.

Wechsler, D. (1950). Cognitive, conative, and nonintellective intelligence. *American Psychologist, 5,* 78–83.

Zeidner, M. (1998). *Test anxiety: The state of the art.* New York: Plenum Press.

Zeidner, M., Matthews, G., & Saklofske, D. H. (1998). Intelligence and mental health. In H. Friedman (Ed), *Encyclopaedia of mental health.* (Vol. 2, 521-534). New York: Academic Press.

Zeidner, M., & Matthews, G. (in press). Intelligence and personality. In R. J. Sternberg (Ed.). *Handbook of intelligence* (2nd Ed.), pp. 581–610. New York: Cambridge University Press.

Zeidner, M., & Schleyer, E. (1999). Test anxiety in intellectually gifted students. *Anxiety, Stress, and Coping, 12,* 163-189.

PART III

INTELLIGENCE AND STYLE

12

Learning Styles and Cognitive Processes in Constructing Understanding at the University

Noel Entwistle
University of Edinburgh, Scotland

This chapter describes research into student learning at the university. It suggests that the understanding of complex academic material depends on the alternation of contrasting cognitive processes that underlie distinctive learning styles. Understanding also depends on the individual's disposition toward academic understanding—a synergy between conative and cognitive processes within a particular learning context. The starting point will be the nature of intelligence and the ways in which early ideas on cognitive styles influenced the work on student learning.

Spearman argued on theoretical grounds that intelligence involved three distinct components at two levels. At the lower level, there was the *apprehension of experience,* which involved recognizing the quantitative and qualitative attributes of objects and ideas. The higher-level processes involved the *eduction* of relations and correlates—the aspects of logical analysis that came to dominate intelligence testing (Spearman, 1923). Apprehension is, however, commonly used to mean a grasp or an understanding and in that sense, the apprehension of experience—or rather the experience of apprehension—involves a much higher level ability than Spearman imagined, one that is crucially important in developing conceptual understanding at the university.

Spearman, of course, went on to justify his conviction that there was a "general intelligence" by correlating the marks that pupils had obtained in a range of school subjects. The factor extracted from this analysis indicated a form of general ability; but it cannot have been ability alone. Doing well in school depends not just on reasoning skills but also on conation and those aspects of personality that overlap cognition, namely cognitive or learning styles. Also, research on student learning has increasingly recognized the influence of all these domains on academic performance.

Much of the early work on student learning drew on existing constructs from mainstream psychology—for example, academic aptitude, personality, and motivation—all of which produced significant correlations with academic performance. The relationships, however, were not sufficiently close or direct to indicate how to improve teaching or the conditions under which students learn (Entwistle & Wilson, 1977). At this time, the general literature in social science had begun to stress the importance of ecological validity, so attempts were made to develop constructs directly related to the higher education context Entwistle, 1998). The ideas that have subsequently emerged still show recognizable links with mainstream psychological concepts and theories, but retain a separate contextualized identity.

Styles of Learning and Approaches to Studying

Although concepts drawn from mainstream psychology have proved relatively weak both in predicting academic performance and in providing practical insights into teaching and learning, they have nevertheless provided the starting point for developing more ecologically valid concepts. The idea of contrasting learning styles for education, for example, was explored by Messick (1976). He argued that:

> Cognitive styles differ from intellectual abilities in a number of ways. Ability dimensions essentially refer to the *content* of cognition or the question of *what*— what kind of information is being processed by what operation in what form? Cognitive styles, in contrast, bear on the questions of *how*—on the *manner* in which behavior occurs. Abilities, furthermore, are generally thought of as unipolar (and) value directional: having more of an ability is better than having less. Cognitive styles are (bipolar and) value differentiated: each pole has adaptive value (depending) upon the nature of the situation and upon the cognitive requirements of the task in hand. Cognitive styles (do) entail generalized habits of information processing, but they develop in congenial ways around underlying personality traits. Cognitive styles are thus intimately interwoven with affective, temperamental, and motivational structures as part of the total personality. (pp. 6–9)

The early research on student learning was also influenced by the work of Witkin and his colleagues (1977); not so much by his perceptual variable of field independence but by the more general distinction between articulated and global ways of thinking and the implications of matches and mismatches in style between teachers and students in higher education.

The link between personality and thinking styles at the university could also be seen in the work of Heath (1964). His was one of the first studies using in-depth interviews of students to explore their experiences in higher education. He described three main personality types related to studying and also found a developmental trend toward an integrated personality—the reasonable adventurer—that had echoes of Maslow's (1973) ideas on self-actualization.

Students at the apex of Heath's developmental scheme had integrated aspects not just of their personality, but also of their ways of thinking:

> In the pursuit of a problem, (the Reasonable Adventurer) appears to experience an alternation of involvement and detachment. The phase of involvement is an intensive and exciting period characterised by curiosity, a narrowing of attention towards some point of interest. This period of involvement is then followed by a period of detachment, an extensive phase, accompanied by a reduction of tension and a broadening range of perception. Here (the Reasonable Adventurer) settles back to reflect on the meaning of what was discovered during the involved stage. Meaning presumes the existence of a web of thought, a pattern of ideas to which the 'new' element can be related. We see, therefore, a combination of two mental attitudes: the curious and the critical. They do not occur simultaneously, but in alternation. (pp. 30–31)

This idea of meaning as "a web of thought, a pattern of ideas" has important significance in university education, but so too have the "two mental attitudes: the curious and the critical" that link with two of the concepts describing student learning—styles of learning and approaches to studying.

Styles of learning in higher education were investigated by Pask (1976, 1988). His concept was derived from naturalistic experiments with university students carrying out extensive and complex tasks, in which he identified the contrast between holist and serialist strategies (see Table 12.1). The holist strategy parallels the "curious" mental attitude—seeking connections between ideas in building up a personal overview of a topic—whereas the serialist strategy shows the critical attitude through the concentration on evidence and detail within a cautious logical stance. The appropriate combination of these two thinking processes indicated, to Pask, a versatile learning style that led to a more thorough understanding of the tasks. A student's ability to explain the concepts was found to depend on an alternation between an overview of the interconnections among ideas and a disciplined, logical consideration of the details. However, the existence of distinctive stylistic preferences meant that one strategy was used first and more extensively than the other.

In research on student learning, the concept of approaches to learning, introduced by Marton (see Marton & Säljö, 1976, 1997), has had a great impact, particularly in Britain and Australia. He identified marked differences between students' intentions as they tackled realistically complex academic tasks and showed how these contrasting intentions led to different learning processes and outcomes. The categories contrasted deep with surface approaches, whereas in everyday studying, an additional strategic approach was detected (Ramsden, 1979, 1997). The deep–surface dichotomy suggests opposite poles of a single

TABLE 12.1
Defining Features of Distinctive Learning Strategies (adapted from Pask, 1976)

Holist strategy	*Prefers personal organization and a broad view*
	Tries to build up own overview of topic
	Thrives on illustration, analogy, and anecdote
	Actively seeks connections between ideas
Serialist strategy	*Prefers step-by-step, tightly structured learning*
	Focuses on the topic in isolation
	Concentrates on details and evidence
	Adopts a cautious logical stance, noting objections

dimension describing learning at the university, whereas the strategic approach seems to be conceptually distinct, relating to study behavior rather than learning processes (see Table 12.2).

In psychological terms, approaches to studying can be seen as composite concepts, linking cognitive and motivational characteristics to study strategies within the university context. The three distinctive approaches are each driven by a contrasting type of motivation—*intrinsic,* interest in the course content; *anxiety,* or fear of failure; and the determination to do well or need for achievement (Biggs, 1987; Entwistle, 1988a, 1988b). Moreover, the deep approach implies an integration of the learning processes underlying serialist and holist strategies (Janssen, 1996), as well as curious and critical mental attitudes.

There are also echoes, in this description, of the components of general intelligence. In describing his triarchic theory, Sternberg (1987) illustrated the internal, experiential, and external aspects through brief vignettes of three graduate students. Alice excelled in the serialist skills of critical and analytic thinking demanded by formal assessments. Barbara's excellence derived from holistic and synthetic research skills, whereas Celia's outstanding performance was more the result of being streetsmart or strategic "in figuring out and adapting to the demands of the environment" (p. 52). These descriptions have been phrased to indicate how these aspects of intelligence can also be seen in terms of preferred learning styles (Sternberg, 1997) and contrasting approaches to studying.

TABLE 12.2
Defining Features of Approaches to Learning and Studying
(from Entwistle, 1997 p. 19)

Deep Approach *Seeking meaning*
Intention - to understand ideas for yourself **by**

Relating ideas to previous knowledge and experience
Looking for patterns and underlying principles

Checking evidence and relating it to conclusions
Examining logic and argument cautiously and critically

Becoming actively interested in the course content

Surface Approach *Reproducing*
Intention - to cope with course requirements **by**

Studying without reflecting on either purpose or strategy
Treating the course as unrelated bits of knowledge
Memorizing facts and procedures routinely

Finding difficulty in making sense of new ideas presented
Feeling undue pressure and worry about work

Strategic Approach *Organizing*
Intention - to achieve the highest possible grades **by**

Putting consistent effort into studying
Finding the right conditions and materials for studying
Managing time and effort effectively

Being alert to assessment requirements and criteria
Gearing work to the perceived preferences of lecturers

TABLE 12.3
Factor Pattern Matrix of Approaches to Studying Subscales

(N̲ = 1231) Factor	I	II	III
Approaches to Studying			
Deep Approach			
Seeking meaning	.69		
Relating ideas	.79		
Use of evidence	.74		
Interest in ideas	.65		
Strategic Approach			
Organized studying		.79	
Time management		.93	
Monitoring effectiveness	.40	.46	
Achievement motivation		.76	
Surface Apathetic Approach			
Lack of purpose			.46
Unrelated memorizing			.79
Syllabus boundness			.37
Fear of failure			.67

	Factor Intercorrelations		
	I	II	III
Factor I	1.00		
Factor II	0.44	1.00	
Factor III	-0.20	-0.22	1.00

Note: Loadings below .3 have been omitted. A maximum likelihood analysis was followed by oblique rotation to simple structure. The three factor solution was indicated by both eigen value and scree plot criteria and extracted 64.2% of the variance.

The exploration of these contrasting approaches to studying started with interviews but has since used factor analyses of self-report inventories (see, for example, Biggs, 1993; Janssen & Meyer, 1996). The three main components emerge quite clearly in Table 12.3 from an analysis of the subscales in our most recent inventory—*ASSIST* (Approaches and Study Skills Inventory for Students—Tait, Entwistle, & McCune, 1998; Entwistle, Tait, & McCune, 2000). Factor I describes the deep approach with its intention of seeking meaning, leading to contrasting learning strategies (relating ideas, holist, and use of evidence, serialist) and with its characteristic form of motivation—interest in ideas. The strategic approach is found as Factor II, with high loadings on time management and organized studying linked to achievement motivation, whereas, the final grouping brings together subscales that I correlate negatively with the others and constitute a surface, apathetic factor.

This second factor also suggests possible relationships with two other constructs in the literature on student learning–self-regulated learning (Pintrich & Garcia, 1994) through the subscales of organized studying and time management, and metacognitive awareness in studying (Vermunt, 1996) through monitoring effectiveness, loading as it does on both deep and strategic factors. Indeed, these two factors are quite closely related overall ($r = .44$).

Besides providing indications of the relative strengths of different approaches to studying, the ASSIST questionnaire has sections dealing with reasons for choosing courses, preparation for higher education, influences on studying, and preferences for different kinds of teaching. In an analysis of a sample of 604 first-year students from six departments in a technological university, poor performance was associated with non-strategic, surface apathetic approaches to studying. Table 12.4 also shows that the deep approach was not related to academic success but was associated with preferences for teaching that encouraged understanding rather than the transmission of information. This latter relationship has already been reported in a study that showed that students adopting a surface approach also preferred teaching that transmitted information (Entwistle & Tait, 1990). Other research has indicated, in more general terms that students who have a deep strategic approach are also better able to discern and utilize the aspects of a learning environment that will support their way of studying (Meyer, 1991; Meyer, Parsons, & Dunne, 1990).

From these analyses can be envisaged an even broader construct that bridges the combination of holist and serialist modes of thinking with a strategic awareness of the rules of the academic assessment game and the ability to utilize relevant aspects of the learning environment.This combination not only summarizes the characteristics of an ideally effective student—what Janssen (1996) dubbed the *studax*—but also connects with theoretical developments in educational psychology. Bereiter (1990) argued that there are coherent organizations of cognitive, conative, and affective structures that are brought into play within specific learning contexts. These cognitive structures are seen as an "entire complex of knowledge, skills, goals and feelings" that form a mutually interdependent, organic whole.

The importance of using these broader, integrated groupings in seeking to understand scholastic or academic performance has also been stressed by Snow, Corno, and Jackson (1996) in a review article on affective and conative functions in learning. Perkins (Perkins, Jay, & Tishman, 1993, 1998) among

Table 12.4
Factor Pattern Matrix For Variables Derived From ASSIST

	FACTOR		
	I	*II*	*III*
Preparation for higher education			
Choosing courses out of interest			.42
Experience in studying independently		- .25	
Having adequate prior knowledge		- .46	
Approaches to studying (excluding motives)			
Deep approach			.70
Strategic approach	.75		.27
Surface-apethetic		.53	- .39
Motives for studying			
Interest in the content			.75
Achieving high grades	.81		
Fear of failure		.78	
Influences on studying			
Social or sporting activities	- .31		
Doing paid work		.31	
Personal relationships		.39	
Difficulties with math		.38	
Teaching preferences			
Encouraging understanding			.55
Transmitting information			- .26
Academic performance			
Average first term marks	.43	- .46	

Note: Loadings below .25 have been omitted. The three factors, extracted by maximum likelihood, have been rotated to oblique simple structure to produce this pattern matrix and explain 46% of the variance. This relatively low percentage is partly explained by the presence of seven single-item variables.

others, described such groupings as disposition, which he saw as bringing together abilities, inclinations including motives, and sensitivities to context. Within this framework, the deep approach could perhaps be seen as a disposition to seek academic understanding.

The composite nature of approaches to studying is illustrated in Figure 12.1. An academic task triggers both cognitive and study processes in students who have a disposition to understand. The deep component, fueled by intrinsic interest, draws on intellectual abilities, with the balance between them reflecting distinctive stylistic preferences and their underlying personality correlates. This stylistic balance can also be seen in qualitative differences in academic performance. The strategic component, with its underlying need for achievement (nAch), makes the student alert to the implicit demands of the task in relation to the learning context as a whole. This metacognitive awareness guides the study processes toward outcomes likely to meet the target understanding of the task and, consequently, achieve high grades.

Why are these composite constructs being introduced now, when previously the main concern was to create tightly defined variables? From an educational perspective, one reason is that the broader concepts are readily recognizable to both staff and students in capturing the essence of their experiences. In psychological terms, this coalescence may imply that certain groups of variables act synergistically to produce learning outcomes, and this synergy needs to be reflected in the theory, through the use of composite constructs such as dispositions or approaches to studying.

The Nature of Academic Understanding

Figure 12.1 draws on the relationships between constructs established in empirical investigations to indicate the interplay between cognitive and study processes in carrying out an academic task. These studies have not, however, told us anything about the student's own experience of seeking conceptual understanding. Students with a deep, strategic approach actively seek to develop their own personal understandings of topics. Their success depends, however, on how well those understandings match the target understandings presented by the staff (Entwistle & Smith, 1997; Smith, 1998). Until recently, these targets were largely invisible to the students, or at least obscured by brief course outlines and vague syllabuses. Increasingly, precisely stated objectives or learning outcomes are presented to students, making the targets easier to discern, at least up to a point. But the whole target in higher education can never be fully revealed. In assessments, the adequacy of students' explanations is judged in relation to the teachers' knowledge of the discipline as a whole. Most areas of study depend on an academic discourse that students acquire only by being thoroughly immersed in the discipline, and by acquiring the skills of presenting explanations in conventional ways.

Evidence of a match between personal and target understandings, at least in traditional British universities, comes from examination answers that demand explanations or demonstrations of the understanding reached. Over the last few years, a series of hour-long interviews have been conducted with Edinburgh University students, toward the end of their final Honours year. They have been asked about their ways of preparing for final examinations, the form of their revision notes, and how they experienced their understanding of complex

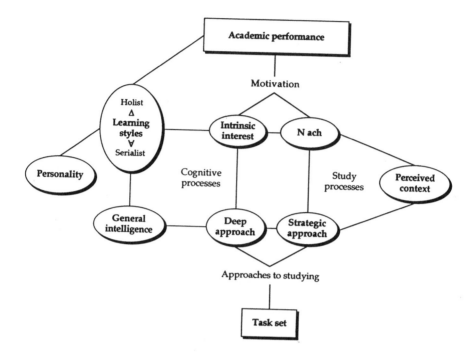

FIG. 12.1. The suggested interplay between cognitive and study processes.

academic topics (Entwistle & Entwistle, 1991, 1997; Entwistle, 1995, 1998). These interviews produced an alternative way of conceptualizing the "web of thought" or "pattern of ideas" developed by students as they relate ideas and justify their conclusions through evidence.

The interviews were analyzed to identify different experiences of understanding and then to investigate their meaning in relation to previous research findings. Although most students talked about how they were trying to understand their notes, they were actually describing very different forms of understanding. Those differences were subsequently interpreted in terms of the breadth, depth, and structure of the understanding being sought (see Table 12.5). "Breadth" describes the amount of material the student had sought to incorporate in the understanding. "Depth" indicates the amount of time and effort put into considering what the material meant, whereas five different ways of structuring the understanding could be seen in the students' responses (Entwistle & Entwistle, 1997). The five different categories are presented as a hierarchy. The

TABLE 12.5
Contrasting Forms of Understanding

Breadth of understanding
Depth or level of understanding
Structure used to organize the material being learned
1. little or no structure being imposed on the facts learned
2. relying exclusively on the lecturer's structures
3. producing prepared answers to previous years' questions
4. adapting own understanding to expected question types
5. relying on an individual conception of the topic

---

lowest category lacks any of the integration and coherence normally associated with understanding, whereas the second category describes an attempt at a highly strategic but restricted match with the perceived target understanding. The third and fourth categories move toward a more individual form of understanding, although still dominated by strategic concerns. Finally, at the top of the hierarchy is a personal understanding that matches the explicit target criteria and also shows a developed awareness of academic discourse.

Although the students differed markedly in the sophistication of the understanding they were seeking, they still tended to describe their experience of reaching understanding in rather similar terms. Repeatedly, they described understanding in terms of connectedness, coherence, and confidence in explaining, together with the feelings of satisfaction associated with them:

> (Understanding?) It's an active process; it's constructive. (It's) the interconnection of lots of disparate things—I think that's probably the best way to describe it—the way it all hangs together, the feeling that you understand how the whole thing is connected up—you can make sense of it internally. You're making lots of connections which then make sense and it's logical. It is as though one's mind has finally "locked in" to the pattern. Concepts seem to fit together in a meaningful way, when before the connections did not seem clear, or appropriate, or complete, like jigsaw pieces, you know, suddenly connect, and you can see the whole picture. It's (also) the act of being able to construct an argument from scratch. I think if you are able to reconstruct it by yourself, that shows you understood it. (adapted from extracts reported in Entwistle & Entwistle, 1992)

Several students referred specifically to how they were able to visualize their understanding "in a sort of way," through the revision notes they had prepared. They could bring to mind the pattern they had produced as a summary of each main topic, but not the words or details. The notes encapsulated students' understanding within a structure that had a mnemonic function for them. They also triggered the much more detailed knowledge associated with the nodes of that structure. This can be illustrated by comments from two students:

> I can see that virtually as a picture, and I can review it, and bring in more facts about each part. Looking at a particular part of the diagram sort of triggers off other thoughts. I find schematics, in flow diagrams and the like, very useful because a schematic acts a bit like a syllabus; it tells you what you should know, without actually telling you what it is. I think the facts are stored separately, and the schematic is like an index, I suppose.
>
> I got on to this process of constructing a kind of mental map, as a quick way of putting down the basics and making sure I don't leave anything out. Then (in the exam) I would just image it again, and as I wrote it, (add) my own thoughts on what I had picked up from other reading. That's why I have it, because (it holds things together) whilst you're writing, adding in whatever you're thinking and extra detail. (Entwistle & Entwistle, 1991, pp. 219, 220)

> The first of these comments came from one of the pilot interviews and drew attention to the use of visualization, becoming an important focus for the interviews which followed. As a result, particular interest was taken in the way mind maps were used as mnemonics for understanding. (Entwistle & Napuk, 1997)

A subsequent reanalysis of the data in collaboration with Marton (Entwistle & Marton, 1994) concentrated on how students had experienced their understandings. They repeatedly described a feeling that the material being revised had become so tightly integrated that it was experienced as a recognizable and surveyable entity with a perceived form and structure. Only its general outline could actually be produced as a mental image, but additional associated knowledge was felt to be available, whenever needed. It was this recurring experience among the students that came to be described as a knowledge object. Its defining features involve an awareness of a tightly integrated body of knowledge, visualization of structure in a 'quasi-sensory' way, an awareness of unfocused aspects of knowledge (Entwistle & Marton, 1994), and a recognition of how the structure can be used to control explanations during examinations (Entwistle, 1995). This form of awareness, with its controlling function, can be seen in the following extract—in which the knowledge object seems to be personalised almost as a guide or mentor.

> Following that logic through, it pulls in pictures and facts as it needs them. Each time I describe (a particular topic), it's likely to be different. Well, you start with evolution, say, and suddenly you know where you're going next. Then, you might have a choice to go in that direction or that direction and follow it through various options it's offering. Hopefully, you'll make the right choice, and so this goes to this, goes to this—and you've explained it to the level you've got to.

Then, **it** says "Okay, you can go on to talk about further criticisms in the time you've got left." (Entwistle, 1995, p. 50)

This extract also draws attention to the idea that the explanation, guided by the knowledge object, will differ to some extent from occasion to occasion. Other comments suggest that the structure of the knowledge object offer a generic shape to the explanation, but that the particular answer given will depend on the question set and on the dynamics of the evolving explanation. Some students were also very aware of how the examination affected the type of explanation they could provide and kept in mind the expectations of the audience for whom they were writing:

> When you're revising you're trying to convince yourself that you can convince the examiner. You can't use all the information for a particular line of argument, and you don't need to. You only need to use what you think is going to convince the examiner. The more I have done exams, the more I'd liken them to a performance—like being on a stage; . . having not so much to present the fact that you know a vast amount, but having to perform well with what you do know. Sort of, playing to the gallery. I was very conscious of being outside what I was writing. (Entwistle & Entwistle, 1991, pp. 220, 221)

In tackling an examination question, the best prepared students sought to relate the specific wording of a question to a pre-existing knowledge object, which was then used to guide the emerging logic of the answer and to pull in evidence and examples as required. These students were monitoring the evolving answer in relation to the wording of the question and to a sense of what might persuade the examiners that a deep level of understanding of the topic had been achieved. Again, there is a deep, strategic approach that is linked to a contextual awareness of both assessment demands and disciplinary imperatives.

CONCLUSION

These inevitably impressionistic descriptions of understanding gain more force when viewed alongside the factor analyses reported earlier and the increasing recognition that learning is best understood in terms of an integration of cognitive, conative, and affective components acting together to produce a learning outcome. This research also indicates that the most effective combination of these variables will depend on the specific demands being made within that learning context.

Although the factor analyses provide firm evidence of the way groups of variables co-vary, they still provide few direct indications of how students actually go about studying. It is the interviews that show the dynamics of the interrelationships and indicate why composite concepts provide more recognizable descriptions of the everyday experience of students. Comments made in the interviews have enabled us to explore the nature and the experience of understanding. They have additionally shown how specific learning contexts affect the forms of understanding that students seek to demonstrate in assessments.

The alternation of curious and critical modes of thinking, or of relating ideas and using detailed evidence, develops more effective understanding. The same holds true in research on student learning, where the alternation between introspections on experience and analysis of patterns of multivariate relationships allows a more complete picture of learning in higher education to be presented. From such complimentary descriptions of study strategies, it is much easier to draw conclusions that which are seen as plausible and justifiable by both staff and students.

REFERENCES

Bereiter, C. (1990). Aspects of an educational learning theory. *Review of Educational Research, 60*, 603–624.

Biggs, J. B. (1987). *Student approaches to learning and studying.* Hawthorn, Victoria: Australian Council for Educational Research.

Biggs, J. B. (1993). What do inventories of students' learning processes really measure? A theoretical review and clarification. *British Journal of Educational Psychology, 63*, 3–19.

Entwistle, A. C., & Entwistle, N. J. (1992). Experiences of understanding in revising for degree examinations. *Learning & Instruction, 2*, 1–22.

Entwistle, N. J. (1988a). Motivational factors in students' approaches to learning. In R. R. Schmeck (Ed.), *Learning strategies and learning styles* (pp. 21–52). New York: Plenum.

Entwistle, N. J. (1988b). *Styles of learning and understanding.* London: Fulton. (Original work published 1981.)

Entwistle, N. J. (1995). Frameworks for understanding as experienced in essay writing and in preparing for examinations. *Educational Psychologist, 30*, 47–54.

Entwistle, N. J. (1997). Contrasting perspectives on learning. In F. Marton, D. J. Hounsell, & N. J. Entwistle (Eds.), *The experience of learning* (2nd ed., pp. 3–22). Edinburgh: Scottish Academic Press.

Entwistle, N. J. (1998a). Approaches to learning and forms of understanding. In B. Dart & G. Boulton-Lewis (Eds.), *Teaching and learning in higher education: From theory to practice* (pp.72–101). Melbourne: Australian Council for Educational Research.

Entwistle, N. J. (1998b). Motivation and approaches to studying: Motivating and conceptions of teaching. In S. Brown, S. Armstrong, & A Thompson (Eds.), *Motivating students* (pp. 15–24). London: Kogan Page.

Entwistle, N. J. (1998c). Understanding academic performance at university: a research retrospective. In D. Shorrocks-Taylor, & V. Varma (Eds.), *Directions in educational psychology* (pp. 106–127). London: Whurr.

Entwistle, N. J., & Entwistle, A. C. (1991). Contrasting forms of understanding for degree examinations: The student experience and its implications. *Higher Education, 22*, 205–227.

Entwistle, N. J., & Entwistle, A. C. (1997). Revision and the experience of understanding. In F. Marton, D. J. Hounsell, & N. J. Entwistle (Eds.), *The experience of learning* (2nd ed., pp. 145–158). Edinburgh: Scottish Academic Press.

Entwistle, N. J., & Marton, F. (1994). Knowledge objects: understandings constituted through intensive academic study. *British Journal of Educational Psychology, 64,* 161–178.

Entwistle, N. J., & Napuk, S. (1997). *Mind maps and knowledge objects. Organising and explaining understanding in essays and examinations.* Research Report. University of Edinburgh, Scotland: Department of Higher Education.

Entwistle, N. J., & Smith, C. A. (2000). Manuscript submitted for publication.

Entwistle, N. J., & Tait, H. (1990). Approaches to learning, evaluations of teaching, and preferences for contrasting academic environments. *Higher Education, 19,* 169–194.

Entwistle, N. J., Tait, H., & McCune, V. (2000). Patterns of response to an approaches to studying inventory across contrasting groups and contexts. *European Journal of the Psychology of Education, 15,* 33–48.

Entwistle, N. J., & Wilson, J. D. (1977). *Degrees of excellence: The academic achievement game.* London: Hodder & Stoughton.

Heath, R. (1964). *The reasonable adventurer.* Pittsburgh, PA: University of Pittsburgh Press.

Janssen, P. J. (1996). Studaxology: The expertise students need to be effective in higher education. *Higher Education, 31,* 117–141.

Janssen, P. J., & Meyer, J. H. F. (Eds.). (1996). Individual diversity in effective studying. *Higher Education, 31*(whole issue).

Lave, J., & Wenger, E. (1991). *Situated learning: Legitimate peripheral participation.* Cambridge. England: Cambridge University Press.

Marton, F., & Säljö, R. (1976). On qualitative differences in learning. I. Outcome and process. *British Journal of Educational Psychology, 46,* 4–11.

Marton, F., & Säljö, R. (1997). Approaches to learning. In F. Marton, D. J. Hounsell, & N. J. Entwistle (Eds.), *The experience of learning* (2nd ed., pp. 39–58). Edinburgh: Scottish Academic Press.

Maslow, A. H. (1973). *The farther reaches of human nature.* Harmondsworth: Penguin.

Messick, S., & Associates (1976). *Individuality in learning.* San Francisco: Jossey-Bass.

Meyer, J. H. F., Parsons, P., & Dunne, T. T. (1990). Individual study orchestrations and their association with learning outcome. *Higher Education, 20,* 67–89.

Meyer, J. H. F. (1991). Study orchestration: The manifestation, interpretation and consequences of contextualised approaches to learning. *Higher Education, 22,* 297–316.

Pask, G. (1976). Styles and strategies of learning. *British Journal of Educational Psychology, 46,* 128–148.

Pask, G. (1988). Learning strategies, teaching strategies and conceptual or learning style. In R. R. Schmeck (Ed.), *Learning strategies and learning styles* (pp. 83–100). New York: Plenum.

Perkins, D. N. (1998). What is understanding? In M. S. Wiske (Ed.), *Teaching for Understanding. Linking research with practice* (pp. 39–58). San Francisco: Jossey-Bass.

Perkins, D. N., Jay, E., & Tishman, S. (1993). Beyond abilities: A dispositional theory of thinking. *Merrill-Palmer Quarterly, 39,* 1–21.

Pintrich, P. R., & Garcia, T. (1994). Self-regulated learning in college students: knowledge, strategies, and motivation. In P. R. Pintrich, D. R. Brown, & C-E. Weinstein (Eds.), *Student motivation, cognition, and learning* (pp. 113–134). Hillsdale, NJ: Lawrence Erlbaum Associates.

Ramsden, P. (1979). Student learning and perceptions of the academic environment. *Higher Education, 8,* 411–427.

Ramsden, P. (1997). The context of learning in academic departments. In F. Marton, D. J. Hounsell, & N. J. Entwistle (Eds.), *The experience of learning* (2nd ed., pp. 198–217). Edinburgh: Scottish Academic Press.

Smith, C. A. (1998). *Personal understanding and target understanding: Their relationships through individual variations and curricular influences.* Doctoral thesis, University of Edinburgh, Scotland.

Snow, R., Corno, L., & Jackson, D. (1996). Individual differences in affective and conative functions. In D. Berliner & R. Calfree (Eds.), *Handbook of educational psychology* (pp. 243–310). New York: Macmillan.

Spearman, C. (1923). *The nature of intelligence and the principles of cognition.* London: MacMillan.

Sternberg, R. J. (1987). The triarchic theory of human intelligence. In J. T. E. Richardson, M. W. Eysenck, & D. Warren-Piper (Eds.), *Student learning: Research in education and cognitive psychology* (pp. 49–65). Milton Keynes: SRHE and Open University Press.

Sternberg, R. J. (1997). *Thinking styles.* Cambridge, England: Cambridge University Press.

Tait, H., & Entwistle, N. J. (1996). Identifying students at risk through ineffective study strategies. *Higher Education, 31,* 97–116.

Tait, H., Entwistle, N. J., & McCune, V. (1998). *ASSIST:* A reconceptualisation of the *Approaches to Studying Inventory.* In C. Rust & G. Gibbs (Eds.), *Improving student learning: Improving students as learners.* Oxford Brookes University Oxford, England: The Oxford Centre for Staff and Learning Development.

Vermunt, J. D. (1996). Metacognitive, cognitive and affective aspects of learning styles and strategies: A phenomenographic analysis. *Higher Education, 31,* 25–50.

Witkin, H. A., Moore, C. A., Goodenough, D. R., & Cox, P. W. (1977). Field-dependent and field-independent cognitive styles and their educational implications. *Review of Educational Research, 47,* 1–64.

13

Dispositional Aspects of Intelligence

David N. Perkins
Shari Tishman
Harvard Graduate School of Education

Student lawyers are among the most intelligence of students in the psychometric sense. They are able dedicated learners who have passed the hurdles of earlier education with excellent records. Moreover, good reasoning in terms of claims and evidence is central to their enterprise. Lawyers—student or professional—need to consider not only the side of the case they are committed to defending but the other side of the case, if only to anticipate the arguments of the opposition. One would suppose, then, that student lawyers would tend to reason well about everyday public issues, certainly considering both sides of the case with some care.

However, this does not seem to be the case. A number of years ago, we conducted a series of studies examining people's everyday reasoning about a range of issues, including questions such as "Would a nuclear disarmament treaty reduce the likelihood of world war?" and "Would a bottle deposit law in the state of Massachusetts reduce litter?" As a strong trend, people's reasoning on these issues proved very one-sided (Perkins, 1985; Perkins, Allen, & Hafner, 1983). Most people would adopt one or the other stance and say hardly anything about what reasoning might apply on the other side. One sample consisted of student lawyers from a well-known university. The student lawyers paid no more attention to the other side of the case than other participants. Moreover, the series of studies revealed a provocative pattern in the relationship between IQ, which was also measured, and attention to the other side of the case. The correlation between the two was zero. People with higher IQs were no more likely to attend to the other side of the case than people with lower IQs, although people with higher IQs did tend to offer more elaborate justifications of their preferred side of the case (Perkins, Farady, & Bushey, 1991).

Thinking about the other side of the case is a perfect example of a good reasoning practice. It is a move one would ordinarily count as part of intelligent behavior. Why, then, do student lawyers with high IQs and training in reasoning that includes anticipating the arguments of the opposition prove to be as subject to confirmation bias or myside bias, as it has been called, than anyone else? To ask such a question is to raise fundamental issues about conceptions of intelligence, classic and modern.

Note that, although the students were asked to think about the issue, they were not asked specifically to think about the other side of the case. Any of them surely could have, as later studies affirmed (Perkins, 1989; Perkins, Farady, & Bushey, 1991). Most did not. Their behavior in this situation reflected not only what they were able to do, but what occurred to them to do and what they felt inclined to do. The point can be generalized: Intelligent behavior in realistic contexts is not just a matter of what a person is asked to do, nor even a matter of strong and clear situational demands. It is a matter of people's sensitivity to what the occasion invites, and of people's inclination to follow through. In sum, it is a matter of what are sometimes called thinking dispositions. This leads to the proposal that thinking dispositions need to take their place alongside abilities as fundamental to any defensible conception of intelligence.

This article aims to define and clarify the concept of thinking dispositions, sketch its historical background, and introduce some empirical studies that make a case for the importance of dispositions in any account of the mechanisms of intelligent behavior. We take up these themes by addressing six questions in turn, as follows:

1. What are thinking dispositions?
2. Why are thinking dispositions important in modeling intelligent behavior?
3. Can thinking dispositions be measured and how?
4. How much do thinking dispositions contribute to intelligent behavior?
5. How do thinking dispositions relate to thinking abilities?
6. What kinds of thinking dispositions are there?

Inevitably, such an inquiry confronts the issue of what intelligence, as a technical concept, should mean. The last section addresses this question directly and attempts to place the notion of dispositions within a broad conception of intelligence.

What Are Thinking Dispositions?

The general idea of thinking dispositions is that people behave more or less intelligently governed not only by abilities but by predilections or tendencies. Everyday vocabulary includes a number of terms that testify to our readiness to characterize people's intellectual conduct in terms of tendencies as well as abilities. We speak of people as more or less open-minded, reasonable, thoughtful, skeptical, curious, and so on. Such attributions seem to address what people are inclined to do within the range of their ability. Closed-minded people could be open-minded in the sense that it is within their mental capacity. People who lack curiosity could be more inquiring.

The term "thinking dispositions" borrows from the lay use of the term disposition to refer to a predilection to exhibit a behavior under certain conditions, but a predilection is neither necessary nor sufficient for the behavior. Accordingly, George may tend to be surly in the morning, but this neither means that George is always surly in the morning nor that other people without such a disposition are never surly in the morning. Another more philosophical source for the concept of dispositions concerns what are called dispositional properties (Ryle, 1949). A dispositional property manifests itself only when certain preconditions are met. Brittleness, for example, is a tendency to shatter when struck. This contrasts with properties like color that become apparent upon observation without acting on the object.

Contemporary attention to dispositions in analyses of intelligence and thinking began with a key paper by philosopher Robert Ennis (1986). Ennis proposed that an analysis of good thinking in terms of abilities simply did not suffice and offered a taxonomy of a number of thinking abilities alongside a number of dispositions. Ennis's list of dispositions is discussed in a later section.

Since Ennis's seminal contribution, several scholars have included attention to dispositions in their analyses of thinking and intelligence. For example, dispositions play a central role in Baron's (1985) model of rationality. Baron distinguishes between dispositions and cognitive capacities. Capacity factors like short-term memory determine what in principle a person can do. Dispositional factors, in contrast, determine what a person does do within capacity limits. In particular, Baron analyzes good thinking in terms of broad search processes such as searches for possibilities and searches for evidence that one may be more or less well-equipped to carry out (capacities) and more or less inclined to carry out (dispositions).

Relatedly, Cacioppo and Petty (1982) introduced the dispositional trait *need for cognition*. This refers to people's readiness to invest in cognitively demanding activities and enjoyment in such activities. Need for cognition has proven to be a stable individual trait largely independent of psychometric intelligence and showing significant positive correlations with school performance, thoughtful examination of arguments, and related matters (Cacioppo, Petty, Feinstein, & Jarvis, 1996). Further treatments that advance the case for the importance of dispositions—sometimes under that name and sometimes with other labels—include Dewey (1930) (Good habits of mind), Facione, Sanchez, Facione, and Gainen (1994), Perkins, Tishman, and Jay (1993), Langer (1980, 1989), (mindfulness), Passmore (1967), Paul (1990), Siegel (1988), (critical spirit), and Stanovich (1994), (dispositions toward rationality).

Most authors treat dispositions simply as tendencies, for example the tendency to think about the other side of the case. However, Perkins, Tishman and Jay (1993) introduce a further ramification. They argue that a full account of intellectual behavior requires three logically distinct and separable components: *sensitivity, inclination,* and *ability.* Sensitivity concerns awareness of occasion; inclination concerns motivation or leaning; ability concerns capability to follow through appropriately. Recall, for example, the challenge of myside bias. To attend seriously to the other side of the case in naturalistic circumstances, a person would need to be sensitive to the occasion to seek otherside reasons, inclined to invest mental effort in examining the other side of the case, and of course have the basic ability to do so. Sensitivity, inclination, and ability constitute a triad of necessary and sufficient conditions for the target behavior.

Sensitivity and inclination make up the dispositional side of this story, the side that most authors have merged together into a general tendency. But logically, sensitivity and inclination are quite different from one another. It is perfectly possible to detect a certain kind of situation (sensitivity) but not care to invest oneself in doing something about it (inclination). It is also perfectly possible for occasions to pass one by (sensitivity) even though in fact one cares quite a bit (inclination). Accordingly, an investigation of the dispositional side of good thinking needs to take into account both sensitivities and inclinations as somewhat separable contributing factors.

With this general perspective articulated, it is important to recognize three features of accounts of intelligent behavior that include dispositions. First of all, thinking dispositions are not necessarily positive, although cultivating positive thinking dispositions certainly is the educational interest. For example, closed-mindedness is a negative thinking disposition as much as open-mindedness is a positive one. Perkins (1995) identifies four broad negative thinking dispositions that mark all too much human thinking; the dispositions to be hasty, narrow, fuzzy, and sprawling in one's thinking. He argues that these can be attributed to the tendency for behavior, including thinking behavior, to automatize, as well as to other mechanisms such as ego defense and limited short-term memory capacity.

Second, while a number of scholars advance dispositions as a fundamental analytical construct, none view a disposition as monolithic in character. Open-mindedness, for instance, is not construed as one thing but a compound of beliefs, attitudes, sensitivities, and so on. No one advances a particular disposition as an "atomic" constituent of mind.

Third, it is important to distinguish the notion of dispositions from that of emotional intelligence, popularized in the recent book by Goleman (1995). Certainly dispositions bear a relation to emotional intelligence. They characteristically involve a commitment to a particular stance, as in concern for open-mindedness or fairness or evidence. However, emotional intelligence as defined by Goleman addresses skills and understandings that specifically concern the handling of emotions—the management of one's own as well as sensitive response to others. The scope of the concept of dispositions certainly includes this but extends much more widely. It includes the motivational and cognitive roles emotions play in thinking, such as when thinking is driven by curiosity or a passion for truth. Moreover, dispositions have many non-emotional aspects. A disposition can reflect a habit or policy rather than a felt commitment.

Why Are Thinking Dispositions Important for Modeling Intelligent Behavior?

Thinking dispositions have emerged over the past several years as an important construct in accounting for more and less intelligence behavior. What motivates attention to this construct? Two factors appear to be important. First of all, the notion of thinking dispositions honors the recognition in our everyday language and behavior of patterns of thinking of a dispositional character-open-mindedness, skepticism, and so on, as already noted. Of course, the presence in folk psychology of such notions does not demonstrate their psychological reality. Nonetheless, it recommends attention to them.

Secondly, an account of more and less intelligent behavior in terms of abilities alone leaves a logical gap. An ability to perform in a certain way—for instance to solve verbal analogy problems or to think about the other side of the case—does not in itself guarantee that the person will marshal such abilities on appropriate occasions. To do so, the person has to detect these occasions and follow through with the appropriate effort. Our opening anecdote of the student lawyers speaks to this point. Clearly capable of reasoning carefully about the other side of the case, the lawyers (and other subjects) by and large did not do so. In general, the notion of dispositions is an explanatory construct that addresses the gap between ability and performance by hypothesizing broad characterological traits that dispose some people more than others to marshal their abilities.

Attention to dispositions is further motivated by the ability-centric character of most efforts to account for why some people fairly consistently exhibit more intelligent behavior and some less over a range of test-like and real-world situations. The predominant view of intelligence for three-quarters of a century has been IQ or g theory, as articulated originally by Spearman (1904), plainly a theory that foregrounds ability. While g theory treats general intelligence as unitary in character, numerous challenges have been mounted against such a posture. For example, Horn and Cattell (1966) proposed the distinction between fluid and crystallized intelligence, the former reflecting performance on novel tasks demanding complex reasoning, the latter reflecting consolidated skills and knowledge such as vocabulary. Guilford (1980; Guilford & Hoepfner, 1971) introduced 150 factors involved in intelligence, generated by the cells created by three dimensions: 5 operations x 5 kinds of content x 6 kinds of products.

Gardner (1983) proposed at least seven distinct intelligences, including linguistic intelligence (dealing with words), musical intelligence, logical-mathematical intelligence, spatial intelligence (as in art, architecture), bodily-kinesthetic intelligence (as in dance, sports), interpersonal intelligence (dealing with others), and intrapersonal intelligence (awareness and handling of self). Sternberg (1985), in his triarchic theory of intelligence, argued for three interacting aspects of intelligence: Practical intelligence, concerned with adapting to, reshaping, and selecting particular environments; experiential or creative intelligence, concerned with orienting to and automatizing novelty; and componential intelligence, concerned with effective information processing and metacognition. While other challenges to the hegemony of g could be mentioned as well, most such counterproposals share an important characteristic with g theory: They are ability-centric accounts of human intelligence. They deal with what people *can* do on demand if motivated, but do not so much deal with what people actually do within the range of their capabilities.

Binet, the other principal figure with Spearman in the development of intelligence had a broader perspective. He viewed intelligence as a polymorphous attribute, a grab-bag of diverse intellectual skills and attitudes (Binet & Simon, 1911). An intelligence test was simply a crude measure of how much was in the bag. Indeed, the authors of the other theories of intelligence cited above surely are aware that more than ability shapes intellectual behavior. However, the tradition of theories of intelligence as it has developed apparently says that such theories are supposed to be theories of ability, so ability-centric theories are put forward.

The notion of dispositions is more akin to that of personality than ability. Indeed, broad personality attributes relate to intellectual behavior, for example the *conscientiousness* and the *openness* (sometimes other names are used) "superfactors" in the well-known five-factor model of personality (e.g. Cacioppo, et al., 1996; Digman, 1990). Personality traits of course influence performance within the range of a person's capability. Conventional intelligence testing tends to suppress their influence, because it creates a high-demand highly-cued situation. People know that they are supposed to perform well and generally strive to do so. Also, people know what tasks they are supposed to attempt—for example, solving verbal analogy problems or completing number series. They do not have to detect embedded and implicit occasions for thinking more carefully or deeply, as is the case in more realistic situations. Likewise, conventional intelligence tests tend to suppress the hypothesized influence of thinking dispositions. Recalling the analysis of dispositions in terms of inclination and sensitivity outlined earlier, intelligence tests create highly motivating conditions so that a person's general inclination to invest in thinking is less relevant; and create highly cued conditions so that a person's general sensitivity to occasion is less relevant.

Such circumstances are of course quite artificial. Thinking dispositions, like as personality traits, come into their own in more natural circumstances of moderate to low demand and of embedded rather than highly salient cues. Thinking dispositions contrast with personality traits largely in their focus on thinking behavior specifically. Personality traits are a construct aimed at accounting for a wide range of people's conduct, not just their conduct in handling intellectual tasks.

While these factors motivate attention to thinking dispositions, they do not of course validate the construct. As with personality traits, basic questions have to be asked: Can one measure thinking dispositions? Are thinking dispositions stable attributes of a person? The study of thinking dispositions is a relatively new field and we only have the beginnings of answers to such questions. Nonetheless, even the beginnings are informative.

Can Thinking Dispositions Be Measured and How?

At least two approaches to measuring dispositions have appeared over the past several years: a self-rating approach and a behavioral approach. One case of the former is the measure of *need for cognition* mentioned earlier. The developers used a 5-point self-rating system for a battery of questions such as *I would prefer complex to simple problems* and *I feel relief rather than satisfaction after completing a task that required a lot of mental effort* (Cacioppo et al., 1996). While these researchers did not focus on thinking dispositions by name, Peter and Noreen Facione (1992; Facione, Sanchez, Facione, & Gainen, 1994) have conducted investigations of thinking dispositions and developed a taxonomy of thinking dispositions by having students rate themselves on a long list of traits such as: *We can never really learn the truth about most things,* and *The best argument for an idea is how you feel about it at the moment.* The Faciones conducted a factor analysis of these ratings and interpreted the results in terms of 7 subdispositions (They prefer to speak of one overarching disposition to critical thinking ramified into subdispositions): open-mindedness, inquisitiveness, systematicity, analyticity, truth-seeking, critical thinking self-confidence, and maturity. This lead to the design of the *California Critical Thinking Dispositions Inventory,* Facione & Facione, 1992), a 75-item survey, to which subjects respond item by item using a six-point Likert scale ranging from "strongly agree" to "strongly disagree".

The second and behavioral approach looks not to self-ratings but to actual conduct in situations that invite thinking. The design of a methodology requires careful attention to two points. First of all, the testing must avoid the high-demand, highly cued character of typical testing of intellectual performance, because the test-taker must have the elbow room to detect or not detect and to invest or not invest in the kinds of thinking afforded. Second, if the measurement aims to distinguish between the contribution of ability and disposition to intellectual performance, the testing must include a way to determine ability, in order to compare it to subjects' non-cued, or open-ended, performance. Often this involves a two or three pass testing paradigm, in which subject receive non-cued then more cued versions of a task.

More than one such methodology has been developed. Perkins et al. (1991) studying myside bias, asked subjects to reason about everyday issues aloud, and then scaffolded by asking for more reasons on both sides of the case. This study will be discussed later. Norris (1994), in an effort to distinguish between the contribution of disposition and ability on critical thinking test performance, provided some test-takers with "surrogate dispositions"—guidelines identifying the kind of critical thinking called for on the test, such as "seek alternative explanations"—and compared their test scores to examinees who did not receive the surrogates. His rationale was that the surrogate dispositions could only be enacted if the subject already had the abilities needed to support them.

Ennis (1994), in a theoretical analysis of different approaches to measuring dispositions, argued for a guided, open-ended approach that is designed to elicit full dispositional behavior without separating out the contribution of ability. One such procedure he has found promising asks subjects to take a multiple-choice critical thinking test, and then provide written justification for their answers.

Stanovich and West (1997), in an effort to explore the separability of cognitive skills and thinking dispositions as predictors of reasoning performance, has developed a methodology that makes novel use of a two-task sequence. The methodology first measures subjects' prior beliefs about a controversial topic. Then, on an instrument administered later, subjects are asked to evaluate the quality of arguments related to the controversial topic. Results indicate that even after controlling for cognitive capacities, individual differences can be predicted by thinking dispositions—revealed in the first instrument—such as dogmatism and absolutism, and open-mindedness.

We describe in somewhat more detail a methodology we designed not only to contrast dispositions with abilities but to discriminate sensitivity, inclination, and ability. The research paradigm consists in a sequence of three related tasks, each of which corresponds to an element of triad. The sequence works as follows.

First, subjects read a very short story (about a paragraph long). Embedded in the story is a thinking shortfall. For example, in one story, a woman Mrs. Perez faces a decision about what to do when the company she works for relocates. The shortcoming in Mrs. Perez's thinking is that she fails to look for options other than the obvious ones, even though the situation warrants a broader search. In this first task, subjects are asked to underline any portion of the story they think reflects poor thinking, and to make a note in the margin explaining what's wrong with the thinking and how it might be made better. In Mrs. Perez story, the target portion of the text occurs when Mrs. Perez says she will relocate with the company, even though neither she nor her daughter particularly want to move. "I have no other choice," said Mrs. Perez. "There's no other decision I can think of in this situation." Task one reveals sensitivity, because it asks the subject to detect an occasion for a certain kind of thinking and indicate a direction for improvement.

In the second task, subjects are presented with the now-disembedded shortcoming and asked whether they think the shortcoming is problematic, and, if so, what should be done about it. For example, in the Perez story, the second task states: "Some of Mrs. Perez's friends think she should have tried more options. Other friends believe she tried hard enough to find options. Suppose you were in Mrs. Perez's place. What would your thinking be like?" In this second task, the disembedded shortcoming "stands in" for sensitivity, and effectively says to the subject: "Here's a potential problem; how are you inclined to think it through?"

In the third and final task, the task-design stands in for both sensitivity and inclination, so that all that remains is an ability task. For example, in the Perez story, subjects are straightforwardly asked to list several other options for Mrs. Perez, thus revealing their ability to generate alternative options, independently of their sensitivity or inclination to do so.

How Much Do Thinking Dispositions Contribute to Intelligent Behavior?

Such a methodology and others like it have the potential of identifying stable sensitivities and inclinations in individuals. In this developing field, validating measures with respect of test–retest reliability and other considerations is a substantial undertaking on which we have made only limited progress. Much of our work has focussed not on whether dispositions are stable traits of individuals but whether, indeed, the dispositional side of thinking makes an important contribution at all to intelligent behavior. If not, then how stable the dispositional side of thinking may be is a moot point, since it would explain little in any case. We have conducted four studies to date that address this issue and further studies are underway.

Study 1. This study includes the group of student lawyers mentioned at the outset. Undertaken a number of years ago, it predates, and indeed motivated, much of theory outlined here and does not reflect the full methodology described earlier. The principal investigation involved 320 subjects ranging from freshman in high school through college students and graduate students to people who had been out of school a number of years. As noted earlier, issues current at the time were posed to subjects. They were asked to think about them for a while, arrive at a position if they felt comfortable doing so, and then explain their reasoning. Pretesting of the issues permitted selecting issues that were genuinely vexed (some people preferred one side, some the other) and complex (a number of reasons could be advanced on both sides).

While a number of findings have interest, here we will focus on the pattern of results around myside bias, which speaks most directly to the theme of this article. Across all ages, and in follow-up studies, subjects showed a strong tendency to elaborate reasons on their preferred side of the case while neglecting the other side. On average, subjects offered about one third as many considerations on the other side of the case as on their preferred side, including possible objections immediately dismissed.

This pattern of findings raised the natural question whether subjects could do better if prompted. Perhaps their thinking was trapped in particular mental models of the problem situation that allowed little latitude for more flexible reasoning. Follow-up studies were conducted with secondary-school subjects using the same methodology for administering the issues and collecting subjects' initial reasoning. At that point, the experimenter intervened, pressing subjects to elaborate the arguments they had already offered. Could they list more reasons on their own side of the case? Could they raise objections to their own arguments? Could they list reasons on the other side of the case? It turned out that subjects could easily do all of these things. The most dramatic extension of their previous reasoning occurred with the otherside arguments, where subjects increased their counts by an impressive 700% on the average. These results suggested what we have come to call the "disposition effect:" People's ability substantially outstripped their performance. For one reason or another, they were not disposed to think nearly as well as they could. Research by others in a somewhat similar style as corroborated such shortfalls (Baron, Granato, Spranca, & Teuval, 1993).

Study 2. The aim of this study was to discover whether the three elements of the triad—sensitivity, inclination, and ability were indeed psychologically separable. The experiment followed closely the full paradigm described earlier, with 64 eighth graders addressing four stories, each with two thinking shortfalls embedded in them, in a 3-step process that stretched over two separate 1-hour periods. The study investigated two thinking dispositions: the disposition to seek alternative options or ideas, and the disposition to seek reasons on both sides of a case. Each of these was examined in two contexts or "problem types," decision making and problem solving. There were four disposition/problem type combinations, each one repeated twice. The Perez story just described is an example of the first combination, the disposition to seek alternative options in the context of decision making.

Performance was scored by counting a subject's hit rate across the three tasks. A hit consisted in the subject underlining the target in Task 1, and in all three tasks displaying the thinking called for. For example, a subject doing Task

1 might underline Mrs. Perez's "I have no other choice" statement and write either that Mrs. Perez should search for other options (scored as a hit) or actually suggest other options (also scored as a hit) Final scores were cumulative: Task 2 scores were Task 1 scores plus new hits on Task 2. Task 3 scores were Task 1 and 2 scores plus new hits on Task 3.

If performance on this task were principally a matter of ability in the sense of being able to generate options or reasons on both sides of a case, then subjects would not add many hits from Task 1 to Task 2 to Task 3. If, in contrast, detecting targets and investing in following through on them were bottlenecks in performance, subjects would add considering to their Task 1 hits on Task 2, and again on Task 3. This is in fact what happened. Figure 13.1 displays the cumulative hit counts for Tasks 1, 2 and 3, for both options and pros and cons.

Another way of representing the data looks at the rations Task 1 score / Task 2 cumulative score, and Task 2 cumulative score / Task 3 cumulative score. These rations can be interpreted as probabilities of detecting a hit at Task 1 and Task 2 respectively. Thus, the first ratio represents the detection probability, or sensitivity. The second ratio represents the follow-through probability assuming detection, or inclination. Figures for this experiment are presented in Figure 13.2. It is important to note the very low sensitivity figure. In most of the writings on dispositions, the dispositional side of thinking is framed largely as a matter of inclination: the person does not care enough about the matter at hand to invest in careful thinking about it. However, these results suggest that the principal dispositional bottleneck is in fact sensitivity: people do not detect potential shortfalls in the first place.

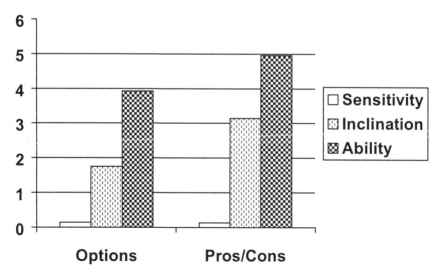

FIG. 13.1. Number of responses at Sensitivity, Inclination, and Ability Stages.

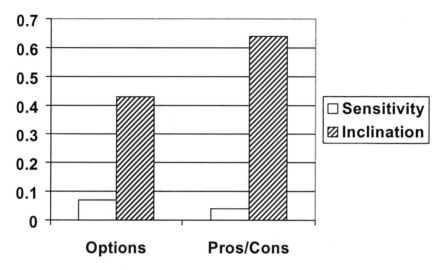

FIG. 13.2. Study #2: Probability of target detection at Sensitivity and Inclination stages

Study 3. The three-task paradigm in the study just described yielded an instrument that served well for proof-of-concept work, but that was lengthy to administer and time-consuming to score. The aim of study 3 was to test a streamlined version of the instrument, potentially practicable in classroom settings, that would be easier to administer and score, and also yield more data.

The experiment consisted of a two-task sequence that focused on sensitivity and ability, and omitted the middle "inclination" probe. The justification for omitting the inclination probe was the finding, described about, that the "disposition effect"—the gap between what people *can* do and what they *do* do—is attributable more to shortcomings in sensitivity than in inclination.

In addition to omitting the inclination step, the instrument also used shorter stories. This revised instrument allowed for the sampling of a greater number of disposition instances. With an N of 105, the experiment looked at the same two dispositions as the earlier study—the disposition to seek alternative options or ideas, and the disposition to seek balanced reasons. It examined these dispositions in three contexts, or "problem types"—decision making, problem solving, and causal explanation. In total, subjects did 18 two-task sequences, yielding 18 samples of subjects' dispositional behavior—three times for each disposition-problem type combination.

Performance was scored by using a Likert scale for each task that rated the quality of the performances 1 to 6. The same Likert scale was used for both tasks. Low-rating performances were characterized by sparse, unelaborated responses, premature cognitive commitment, biased thinking, and other factors generally taken to be signs of poor thinking. High-rating performances were characterized by richly elaborated responses, a breadth of ideas, open-mindedness, and so on. Scorers' judgments were made intuitively, with the assistance of heuristic scoring rubrics. After several cycles of refinement in the rubrics and the scoring conventions, high interrater reliability was achieved. However, scoring turned out to be more lengthy and complicated than anticipated (interestingly, non-intuitive scoring yielded substantially lower interracter reliability than intuitive scoring). Although the instrument was not as easy to score as the experimenters had hoped, the results from the experiment were quite striking.

To measure the disposition effect, results were calculated by creating composite scores for both the sensitivity task and the ability task and comparing their means. However, before simply summing subjects' scores at task one and task two to create composites, correlations between all of the sensitivity task scores on each scenario and all of the ability task scores were computed to determine if in fact the scenarios seem to be tapping into a common construct, either sensitivity or ability. Additionally, internal consistency was assessed and factor analysis was performed.

For the most part, scores on the sensitivity task were moderately correlated and significant, falling in the range of .40 to .60. The same pattern was evident in the scores on the ability task. Reliability coefficients (internal consistency) were high for both task one (Cronbach's alpha A.92) and task two (Cronbach's alpha A.89). Factor analysis confirmed that there was only one underlying factor in the data for the sensitivity task, and one for the ability task.

Recall that if performance was principally a matter of ability - if detection of potential shortfalls and investment of mental effort in characterizing them could be taken for granted—the mean for task one (sensitivity) should be close to the mean for task two (ability). A comparison of the means of the composites showed that there *was* a significant difference (F-ratio = 348.288, p < .0001) between the means of task one (mean = 31.8, SD = 8.36) and task two (mean = 44.68, SD = 9.95). The difference in the means of the two groups (approximately 13 points) was almost one and one half standard deviation, a substantial spread.

To compare the sensitivity and ability performances in terms of hits, as in previous studies, we established a threshold on the ratings scales for an adequate performance. Figure 13.3 shows the results organized by type of shortfall—alternatives and reasons. Figure 13.4 shows the results organized by the problem type within which the shortfalls were embedded—decision making, problem solving, or explanation. Both graphs reveal essentially the same pattern: Low sensitivity but reasonably high ability.

Study 4. The goal of this study was to probe more deeply the nature of sensitivity and the ways in which it constitutes bottleneck to thinking. When subjects failed to detect a thinking shortfall, what went wrong? At least three possibilities came to mind:

1. Perhaps the subject lacked the knowledge or judgement needed to make such discriminations.
2. Perhaps the subjects had sufficient knowledge and judgement, but did not approach such situations alert to likely shortfalls.
3. Or perhaps shortfalls were difficult to detect regardless of appropriate knowledge and alertness.

The experiment we designed to examine these alternatives followed the general approach of the first step of the paradigm described in the two previous experiments. That is, it aimed to measure sensitivity by asking subjects to read several short stories and detect shortfalls in thinking embedded in the texts. In this experiment, however, there were no follow-up steps to measure inclination or ability. Rather, two manipulations were introduced, crossed over four conditions. The manipulations were as follows.

Saliency. In two of the four conditions, the stories included underlined text that made the thinking shortfalls visually salient. If detection was the major bottleneck, making the shortfalls salient should allow subjects to explain them well.

Priming. This was an effort to inform and alert subjects to what they should be looking for. In two of the four conditions, a "crib page" of 5 prompts called "thinking handles" was given to subjects at the outset of the test. The instructions urged subjects to adopt a critical mindset to help them identify and discriminate the thinking shortfalls. The thinking handles consisted of sentences like: "this is a place where it is important to look for an alternative explanation" or "this is a place where it is important to make a plan," and so on. In effect, they were efforts to induce heightened sensitivity to particular kinds of shortfalls.

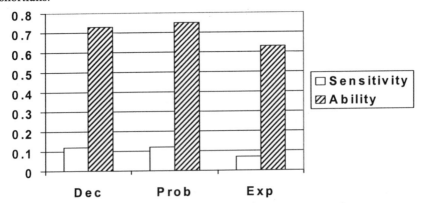

FIG. 13.3. Study #3: Hit rate at Sensitivity and Ability Stages by problem types Decision Making, Problem Solving, and Explanation.

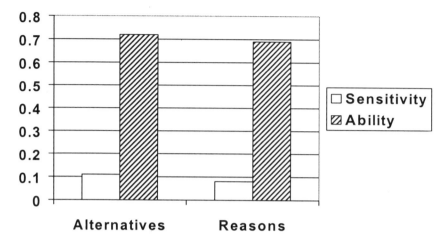

FIG. 13.4. Study #3: Hit Rate at Sensitivity and Ability Stages by dispositions Seeking Alternatives and Seeking Reasons

The subjects, 105 eighth graders from a middle and working class setting, were divided into four approximately equal and gender-balanced groups, corresponding to the four conditions. Subjects read and responded to eight one-page stories, across which were distributed 30 thinking shortfalls, evenly divided among the five handles and corresponding dispositions.

Performance was scored in two ways: *detection* and *discrimination.* Detection indicated whether or not subjects detected and underlined a thinking shortfall, regardless of how they explained it thereafter. Of course, detection was only scored in the nonsalient conditions. Discrimination rated whether a response to a thinking shortfall (underlined or detected without underlining) offered a reasonable explanation—one either matching the intended one of the five handles or bringing forward another relevant consideration. The results appear in Table 13.1.

The figures yield an interesting comparison of detection and discrimination rates. Detection rate was much lower than discrimination rate for shortfalls detected or made salient. The figures also offer a clear reading of the influence of priming and saliency. Priming yielded hardly any differences in the nonsalient condition and a modest improvement in the salient condition, significant at the .05 level. In contrast, saliency, by disembedding thinking shortfalls for subjects, enabled them to achieve a much higher discrimination rate.

The findings suggest that the challenge of sensitivity lies in detecting potential thinking shortfalls in an ongoing stimulus stream and disembedding them for consideration, even when one is capable of making the relevant discriminations though. The findings resemble that of a test conducted by Norris (1994), referred to earlier, in which subjects were given "surrogate dispositions." Surrogate dispositions were Norris's name for lists of critical thinking guidelines that are given to subjects prior to taking a critical thinking test. The guidelines were in effect an attempt to induce a critical mindset. Norris found that there was not a significant difference in test performance between subjects who received surrogate dispositions and subjects who did not.

How Do Dispositions Relate to Abilities?

The findings summarized above make a case that sensitivity and inclination constitute significant components of intellectual behavior, at least outside of high-demand high-task-saliency circumstances. This does not, of course, mean that sensitivity and inclination are unrelated to ability. It might be that they are simply other faces of ability. The data gathered over several studies permits examining this question in two ways: How do sensitivity and inclination correlate with ability measures in these studies? And how do sensitivity, inclination, and ability as gauged in these studies correlate with IQ or academic aptitude? Low correlations between sensitivity and inclination on the one hand, and ability in the studies, or IQ, or other measures of academic aptitude on the other, would suggest that the dispositional side of intelligent behavior is somewhat independent of the ability side of intelligent behavior. High correlations, of the order one expects in subtests of an IQ test for example, would allow that sensitivity and inclination might represent the same underlying causal factor as ability, although of course correlations are not proof of causation.

During Study 1, the study of everyday reasoning, the experimenters also administered a vocabulary-based short form IQ test. The correlations between scores on reasoning on one's preferred side of the case and IQ ranged around .4 or .5. In contrast, the correlations between reasoning scores on the other side of

Table 13.1 Mean Rate of Detection and Discrimination of Thinking Shortfalls in Study #4		
	Unprimed condition	Primed condition
Nonsalient condition		
Shortfalls detected	40%	37%
Shortfalls detected and discriminated	35%	31%
Discrimination rate for shortfalls detected	88%	84%
Salient condition		
Discrimination rate for shortfalls made salient	67%	85%

the case and IQ were essentially zero. This suggests the possibility that the disposition to look at the other side of the case is independent of psychometric intelligence, although of course such a result should be corroborated by other studies.

Study 2 included a short-form vocabulary-based IQ test. Unfortunately, the correlations among sensitivity, inclination, ability, and IQ were generally low and unpatterned, revealing nothing about the current issue. The experimenters concluded that, although the data showed strong aggregate patterns as discussed earlier, the instrument did not include sufficiently many items per subject to acquire a good profile of individual performance.

For Study 3, the experimenters could not obtain permission to administer a short-form IQ test. However, grade point averages were obtained and used as a gauge of academic aptitude. Sensitivity correlated with ability measures at .72. Sensitivity correlated with academic standing at .36. Ability correlated with academic standing at .61. It will be recalled that this study did not collect inclination scores. None of this varied greatly when the two dispositions or the two problem types involved in the study were separated. These data present an ambiguous pattern on the issue at hand, a high correlation between sensitivity and ability as measured, but a lower correlation between sensitivity and academic standing than between ability and academic standing.

In Study 4, the same short-form vocabulary test was used as in Study 2. The nonsalient conditions of course best represented sensitivity, since the thinking shortfalls were not underlined for subjects. The correlations between discrimination scores in these conditions and vocabulary scores were .32 for the unprimed condition and .26 for the primed condition, neither significant at the .05 level. The correlations between discrimination scores and vocabulary scores for the salient conditions were .45 for the unprimed condition and .44 for the primed condition, both significant at the .05 level. Although the contrast between the correlations in the nonsalient and salient conditions is hardly dramatic, it continues the pattern of lower correlations with IQ and related indices for sensitivity measures than for ability measures in these tasks.

Looking beyond our own studies, another dispositional construct noted earlier that has received considerable attention is *need for cognition* (Cacioppo & Petty, 1982; Cacioppo et al., 1996). This measure has been shown to gauge people's inclination to seek out and enjoy complex cognition. Correlations with measures of intelligence have proved to be quite low, ranging from -.03 to .32 in the review by Cacioppo et al. (1996). *Need for cognition* does not distinguish between sensitivity and inclination, although, involving self-assessment of people's conduct as the measure does, it plausibly reflects inclination more than sensitivity.

In summary, there is some evidence that the dispositional side of thinking may be more than just another face of ability in general and psychometric intelligence in particular. However, the evidence is certainly limited and partial.

What Kinds of Thinking Dispositions Are There?

Taxonomic questions lie at the heart of any analysis of intelligence. Spearman (1904) established a case for a single general factor g that remains in some ways persuasive even today. Others in the psychometric tradition have proposed multiple factors (e.g., Guilford, 1967, Guilford & Hoepfner, 1971) or significant subfactors (e.g., Carroll, 1993; Horn, 1989; Horn & Cattell, 1966). Within the psychometric tradition, versions of factor analysis have provided the principal techniques for determining components of intelligence. However, other contemporary theories of intelligence adopt more conceptual and interpretive foundations. Gardner (1983) acknowledged that the justification for the component intelligences of his theory of multiple intelligences include considerations of the professions and activities prominent in our culture. Sternberg's (1985) triarchic theory of intelligence appears to be a conceptual construct reflecting several important aspects of intelligent behavior.

Even though this article examines a dispositional perspective rather than an abilities perspective on intelligence, the taxonomic question still applies: What dispositions are there? Although it was noted earlier that thinking dispositions can be negative (close-mindedness) as well as positive (open-mindedness), proposed taxonomies of dispositions are usually formulated in terms of positive dispositions. As in ability-centered theories, in principal one might look toward factor analytic answers and toward answers more conceptually driven.

We know of only three attempts to achieve the former. The first is the *need for cognition* construct mentioned earlier. A number of actor analyses of *need for cognition* have generally yielded a single factor. A few have yielded multiple factors but not with consistency from analysis to analysis (Cacioppo et al., 1996). The second is the taxonomy of thinking dispositions based on self-ratings developed by the Faciones, discussed earlier, with its seven subdispositions of open-mindedness, inquisitiveness, systematicity, analyticity, truth-seeking, critical thinking self-confidence, and maturity (Facione, Sanchez, Facione, & Gainen, 1994).

The third effort occurred in the course of our own research. The sensitivity data from Study 3 were factor analyzed. The data might have disclosed factors representing the two dispositions involved in Study 3 or the two problem types, or some unexpected structure. However, only a single factor emerged. The contrast between Faciones' and these findings may appear anomalous, but the fundamentally different methodologies should be recalled. The Faciones worked with self-ratings, whereas the studies reported here involved actual thinking performances. We conjecture that the self-ratings yielded a factor structure reflecting cultural attitudes about various aspects of thinking, as elaborated below. In actual performance, attention to one of those aspects may in fact covary with the others, yielding a single performance factor. However, certainly not enough work of this sort has been done to make this more than a speculation.

Most of the proposed taxonomies of dispositions represent reflective analyses of plausible dispositions rather than empirical methods. Given the emphasis on statistical approaches in the classic work on intelligence, this may seem odd. However, in our view, dispositions have a rather different character than the factors sought in the psychometric approach, which presumably represent neural architecture at some level of analysis. In our view, the dispositions people display are in large part a cultural phenomenon. They are not hardwired into the brain, and taxonomies of thinking dispositions should not be construed as aiming to classify natural classes of neurobiological phenomena. Dispositions emerge from our interactions with the beliefs, values, and norms in our environment, as well as the contextual demands of specific intellectual challenges. For example, the disposition to be open-minded is a *value*, not a natural neurobiological tendency, one connected to a Western, reason-based conception of mind.

At the same time, of course, hardware does impose some broad constraints. For instance, consider open-mindedness, which is emphasized either explicitly or implicitly in all of the taxonomies described in this article. Open-mindedness often manifests itself as a willingness to resist generalizations and consider multiple interpretations or possibilities. While this intellectual value is often underserved, from a computational point of view—whether the computing mechanism is a neurobiological system or a microchip—it would be paralyzingly inefficient to entertain all possibilities all of the time. If we did, we would never get beyond the manifold ways of simply getting out of bed in the morning!

With these points in mind, a further broad distinction among taxonomies concerns grain size. Some scholars claim there is one overarching thinking disposition, while others have put forth taxonomies that include several high-level thinking dispositions. This distinction does not run deep—those who argue for one overarching thinking disposition readily task about subdispositions—but it is a useful way to enter the territory.

The view that high-level thinking is characterized by a single overarching thinking dispositions is perhaps most fully worked out by psychologist Ellen Langer (1980, 1989). Although Langer does not herself use the term thinking dispositions, she advances the view that good thinkers have the tendency towards *mindfulness*. Mindful thinkers tend to create new categories, or simply pay attention to given contexts: they tend to be open to new information; and they tend to cultivate an awareness of more than one. Educational psychologist Gavriel Salomon also recognizes mindfulness as an overarching thinking disposition. However, Salomon offers his own list of key characterological components of mindfulness. These include a positive attitude toward ambiguous and complex situations, a preference for novelty and incongruity, and an intention to seek out such situations, or even shape situations in a way that makes them fit the preference (Salomon, 1994).

The philosopher Richard Paul argues that the "strong sense" critical thinker is characterized by the overarching disposition towards fair-mindedness (Paul, 1990). According to Paul, this disposition includes several traits of mind, such as intellectual humility, intellectual courage, intellectual perseverance, intellectual integrity, and confidence in reason. Philosopher of education Harvey Siegel talks about the "critical-spiritedness" required to engage in reason assessment. This tendency, he argued, is composed of objectivity, intellectual honesty, impartiality, a willingness to confirm judgment and action to principle, and a commitment to seek and evaluate reasons (Siegel, 1988).

Although the above scholars often mention multiple characteristics of their overarching dispositions, they do not intend these specifically as subdispositions. Another group of scholars have advanced taxonomies of high-level thinking dispositions that include numerous dispositions. For example, Robert Ennis currently recognizes not one, but fourteen separate critical thinking dispositions (Ennis, 1994). According to Ennis, critical thinkers have a tendency to:

- be clear about the intended meaning of what is said, written, or otherwise communicated
- determine and maintain focus on, the conclusion or question
- take the total situation into account
- seek and offer reasons
- try to be well-informed
- look for alternatives
- seek as much precision as the situation requires
- try to be reflectively aware of one's own basic beliefs
- be open-minded: seriously consider other points of view and be willing to consider changing one's own position
- withhold judgement when the evidence and reasons are sufficient to do so
- use one's critical thinking abilities
- be careful
- take into account the feelings and thoughts of other people

Educator, Arthur Costa, does not use the term thinking dispositions but instead refers to passions of mind (Costa, 1991). He identified 5 key passions that characterise the good thinker: efficacy, flexibility, craftsmanship, consciousness, and interdependence.

In our own work, we have advanced a view of seven key critical thinking dispositions (Perkins, Jay, & Tishman, 1993), on which the research we described earlier is based. Although the list represents many of the trends in intellectual behavior included in others' list, we acknowledge the taxonomy as unabashedly normative. The claim is that in our culture, these seven dispositions provide the best leverage on the kinds of thinking and learning challenges young people in our society face (Tishman, 1994). They are:

- The disposition to be broad and adventurous
- The disposition toward wondering, problem finding, and investigating
- The disposition to build explanations and understandings
- The disposition to make plans and be strategic
- The disposition to be intellectually careful
- The disposition to seek and evaluate reasons
- The disposition to be metacognitive

Perhaps the most striking difference among the various taxonomies is the grain size at the top level of organization: As noted earlier, some scholars emphasize one overarching disposition with several characteristics or subdispositions, while others emphasize a set of dispositions all at the same level. Other differences concern varying degrees of emphasis on the attitudinal and ethical dimensions of dispositions. Paul, for instance, used value-laden terms like "integrity," "courage," and "humility" to describe dispositions. Langer places special emphasis on the attitudinal features of mindfulness.

But there are no truly unbreachable differences among the taxonomies. They have considerably more points of agreement than disagreement. They all represent a normative conception of high-level thinking that emphasizes reasonableness and reflection, but not to the exclusion of imagination and creativity. All of them identify several different aspects of high-level thinking, either as characteristics or subdispositions. Most of the taxonomies emphasize a humane concern for others, in the form of thoughtfulness and respect for other viewpoints. And all of the taxonomies emphasize attitude and awareness in addition to ability to perform cognitive tasks.

Perhaps their most striking similarity is that they all share an intellectual ethos that values critical thinking, creative inquiry, and independent thought. This is a Western-based ethos that has been around since before Socrates. It is normative in the sense that it prescribes the type of intellectual behaviors that are most likely to lead to positive knowledge and scientific achievement as defined by out culture. Clearly, other cultural orientations have different conceptions of how best to gain knowledge. For example, some cultures emphasize attentive obedience to authority. Some cultures emphasize spiritual practices that alter consciousness. Some culture emphasize gaining knowledge by cultivating an intuitive understanding of nature. While the ethos shared by the taxonomies reviewed here is not intended to represent the only or even the best conception of normative intellectual performance, it is decidedly not arbitrary. The taxonomies describe the intellectual behaviors that scholars believe are most likely to yield effective, humane products of thought, within the parameters of the shared culture inhabited by the taxonomies' authors.

A Dispositional View of Intelligence

Theories start with the identification of a problem. This chapter began by pointing out a problem with traditional ability-centered theories of intelligence: they account for what people are able to do, but not account for what people often *do* do in everyday circumstances. The concept of thinking dispositions has been advanced as an explanatory construct that addresses the gap between ability and performance by identifying characterological traits, beyond or in addition to basic intellectual capacity, that are needed to mobilize ability.

The view presented here identifies three distinct and separable components of dispositions: *sensitivity,* which involves detection of occasion, *inclination,* which involves motivation or leaning, and *ability,* which concerns the capability to follow through with appropriate kinds of thinking. Sensitivity and inclination are the dispositional side of the story. A full account of intelligent behavior requires the three aforementioned logically distinct and separable components. The presence of these components constitutes necessary and sufficient conditions for intelligent behavior to be enacted. This triadic analysis of intelligence behavior has yielded a research paradigm that has thus far proven to be fruitful.

Thinking dispositions provide a good explanatory story for everyday intelligent behavior, illuminating cases such as that of the student lawyers, where people are not disposed to use intellectual abilities they clearly possess. But if a good story is to be more than a fairy tale, in the company of intelligence theorists at any rate, it has to have empirical legs to stand on. The research reviewed in this paper shows that thinking dispositions indeed do have a measurable psychological reality, whether they are treated as the other side of abilities (Norris, 1994; Stanovich & West, 1997) or through a triadic analysis into sensitivities, inclinations, and abilities, as we have described in this paper.

There is relative convergence among researchers working in this area on the types of dispositions or subdispositions that characterize intelligence, although the specific lists that are advanced vary somewhat. Broadly, these lists emphasize critical thinking, creative inquiry, reflectiveness and open-mindedness. This normative view of the "right stuff" of thinking dispositions is without question culturally influenced. But no more culturally influenced than the lists of abilities in classic theories of intelligence. All intelligence theorists, whether they emphasize the dispositional side of thinking or not, are working with a culturally influenced conception of rationality—a conception, that is, of what the goals of intelligence behavior should be, and which abilities and tendencies best serve them.

New theories, if they are to have any shelf life at all, need to do more than simply explain gaps in previous theories. They also must suggest new and fruitful avenues of research. In the case of thinking dispositions, this means research that can shed further light on the mysteries of human intellectual behavior. Several such avenues seem to be suggested by the work reviewed here. For one, there is some evidence that thinking dispositions can predict intellectual behavior in cases where cognitive abilities do not. Stanovich, for example, has shown that dispositions such as dogmatism, absolutism, and open-mindedness can better predict performance on reasoning tasks than ability measures (Stanovich & West, 1997). Research on *need for cognition* has demonstrated that people with high need for cognition look more analytically at arguments and information sources, although not necessarily without bias (Cacioppo et al., 1996). Our own work in the area of sensitivity suggests that sensitivity may explain intellectual performance on everyday reasoning tasks in ways complementary to ability, including IQ. More research is needed that explores the predictive power of sensitivity and inclination across a variety of thinking dispositions and in a range of everyday contexts.

Another promising area of research concerns manipulations that boost thinking dispositions, and in particular, manipulations that boost sensitivity. The research reported in Study 4, and Norris's research concerning surrogate dispositions in test-taking situations (Norris, 1994) suggest somewhat surprisingly that inducing a critical mindset is not an especially effective way to increase intellectual performance. It may not help subjects much to disembed from noisy context matters that require thoughtful attention. This raises questions about the mechanisms of sensitivity and what might enhance them— for instance affectively-oriented manipulations or manipulations that boost mindfulness.

Yet another fruitful strand of research would address the stability of dispositional traits. Such findings are available for *need for cognition* (Cacioppo et al., 1996). Reliability has been reported for the Faciones' Critical Thinking Disposition measure. And our own work has begun to address the issue of test–retest reliability, with initially promising results. However, more research is needed here, particularly research that looks at a variety of types of thinking dispositions.

Finally, there is the issue of empirically grounding the conceptual work concerning the ontology of thinking dispositions. Several scholars have proposed conceptual schemes that identify different thinking dispositions and subdispositions. These schemes tend to be normatively grounded and logically justified, but empirically undertested. Indeed, a challenge in this area concerns when and how empirical methods should be applied to these schemes. Simply because a disposition is unabashedly labeled a cultural norm does not mean that it is therefore exempt from empirical examination. For example, consider the disposition toward open-mindedness. Empirical methods can be used to examine whether it is an isolatable psychological tendency, regardless of whether or not it is valued by the culture or not.

This chapter has raised the question of whether the concept of thinking dispositions is an illuminating addition to models of intelligent behavior. We have argued that the answer is yes, and tried to show how the concept has both explanatory power and also the capacity to generate fruitful investigations. The research agendas suggested by the work thus far are rich in possibility. The reward—a deeper understanding of the mechanism of human intelligent behavior and as a result more effective methodologies for cultivating it—is an alluring one, and surely one worth striving for.

REFERENCES

Baron, J. (1985). *Rationality and intelligence.* New York: Cambridge University Press.

Baron, J. (1991). Beliefs about thinking. In J.F. Voss, D.N. Perkins, & J.W. Segal (Eds.), *Informal reasoning and education* (pp. 169-186). Hillsdale, NJ: Lawrence Erlbaum Associates.

Baron, J., Granato, L., Spranca, M., & Teuval, E. (1993). Decision-making biases in children and early adolescents: Exploratory studies. *Merrill-Palmer Quarterly, 39*(1), 22-46.

Binet, A., & Simon, Th. (1911). *A method of measuring the development of the intelligence of young children.* Lincoln, IL: Courier Company.

Cacioppo, J. T., Petty, R. E., Feinstein, J. A., & Jarvis, W. B. G. (1996). Dispositional differences in cognitive motivation: The life and times of individuals varying in need for cognition. *Psychological Bulletin, 119,* 197-253.

Carroll, J. B. (1993). *Human cognitive abilities: A survey of factor-analytic studies.* New York: Cambridge University Press.

Costa, A. L. (1991). *The school as a home for the mind.* Palatine, IL: Skylight Publishing.

Digman, J. M. (1990). Personality structure: Emergence of the five-factor model. *Annual Review of Psychology, 41,* 417-440.

Ennis, R. H. (1986). A taxonomy of critical thinking dispositions and abilities. In J. B. Baron, & R. S. Sternberg (Eds.). *Teaching thinking skills: Theory and practice* (pp. 9-26). New York: W.H. Freeman.

Ennis, R. H. *Assessing critical thinking dispositions: Theoretical considerations.* Paper presented at Annual Meeting of the American Education Research Association (1994, April). New Orleans, LA.

Facione, P. A., & Facione, N. C. (1992). *The California critical thinking dispositions inventory.* Millbrae, CA: The California Academic Press.

Facione, P. A., Sanchez, C. A., Facione, N. C., & Gainen, J. (1994). The disposition toward critical thinking. *Journal of General Education, 44*(1), 1-25.

Gardner, H. (1983). *Frames of mind.* New York: Basic Books.

Goleman, D. (1993). *Emotional intelligence: Why it can matter more than IQ.* New York: Bantam Books.

Guilford, J. P. (1967). *The nature of human intelligence.* New York: McGraw-Hill.

Guilford, J. P., & Hoepfner, R. (1971). *The analysis of intelligence.* New York: McGraw-Hill.

Horn, J. (1989). Models of intelligence. In R. Linn (Ed.), *Intelligence: Measurement, theory, and public policy* (pp. 29-73). Chicago: University of Illinois Press.

Horn, J. L., & Cattell, R.B. (1966). Refinement and test of the theory of fluid and crystallized intelligence. *Journal of Educational Psychology, 57,* 253-270.

Langer, E. (1980). Rethinking the role of thought in social interaction. In J. Harvey, W. Ickes, & R. Kidd (Eds.), *New directions in attribution research* (vol. 2). Hillsdale, NJ: Lawrence Erlbaum Associates.

Langer, E. (1989). *Mindfulness.* Reading, MA: Addison-Wesley.

Means, M. L., & Voss, J. F. (1996). Who reasons well? Two studies of informal reasoning among children of different grade, ability and knowledge levels. *Cognition & Instruction, 14*(2), pp. 139-178.

Norris, S. P. (1994). The meaning of critical thinking test performance: The effects of abilities and dispositions on scores. In D. Fasko (Ed.), *Critical thinking: Current research, theory, and practice.* Dordrecht, The Netherlands: Kluwer.

Paul, R. W. (1990). *Critical thinking: What every person needs to survive in a rapidly changing world.* Rohnert Park, CA: Center for Critical Thinking and Moral Critique, Sonoma State University.

Perkins, D. N. (1985). Postprimary education has little impact on informal reasoning. *Journal of Educational Psychology, 77*(5), 562-571.

Perkins, D. N. (1989). Reasoning as it is and could be. In D. Topping, D. Crowell, & V. Kobayashi (Eds.), *Thinking: The third international conference* (pp. 175-194). Hillsdale, NJ: Lawrence Erlbaum Associates.

Perkins, D. N. (1995). *Outsmarting IQ: The emerging science of learnable intelligence.* New York: The Free Press.

Perkins, D. N., Allen, R., & Hafner, J. (1983). Difficulties in everyday reasoning. In W. Maxwell (Ed.), *Thinking: The frontier expands* (pp. 177-189). Hillsdale, NJ: Lawrence Erlbaum Associates.

Perkins, D. N., Faraday, M., & Bushey, B. (1991). Everyday reasoning and the roots of intelligence. In J. Voss, D.N. Perkins, & J. Segal (Eds.), *Informal reasoning* (pp. 83-105). Hillsdale, NJ: Lawrence Erlbaum Associates.

Perkins, D. N., Jay, E., & Tishman, S. (1993). Beyond abilities: A dispositional theory of thinking. *The Merrill-Palmer Quarterly, 39*(1), 1-21.

Ryle, G. (1949). *The concept of mind.* London: Hutchinson House.

Salomon, G. (1994, April). *To be or not to be (mindful).* Paper presented at the Annual Meeting of the American Educational Research Association, New Orleans, LA.

Siegel, H. (1988). *Educating reason: Rationality, critical thinking, and education.* New York: Routledge.

Spearman, C. (1904). General intelligence, objectively defined and measured. *American Journal of Psychology, 15,* 201-293.

Stanovich, K. E. (1994). Reconceptualizing intelligence: Dysrationalia as an intuition pump. *Educational Researcher, 23*(4), 11-12.

Stanovich, K. E., & West, R. F. (1997). Reasoning independently of prior belief and individual differences in actively open-minded thinking. *Journal of Educational Psychology, 89*(2).

Sternberg, R. J. (1985). *Beyond IQ: A triarchic theory of human intelligence.* New York: Cambridge University Press.

Tishman, S. (1994). What makes a good thinker: A look at thinking dispositions. *Harvard Graduate School of Education Alumni Bulletin, Vol. 39,* 1.

14

Style in the Organization and Defense of Cognition

Samuel Messick
Educational Testing Service

The concept of style refers to stable individual differences in the manner or form of psychological functioning. This is distinct from the level of functioning or what it might contain. Because personal styles are consistent patterns in the way psychological substance is processed they may entail mechanisms for the organization and control of processes that cut across substantive areas (Messick, 1987). To the extent that personal styles display generality in the organization and control of attention, thought, feelings, and motives, they constitute important cross-cutting variables. They bridge the cognitive, conative, and affective modes. These self-consistent regularities in the manner or form of human activity imply that, styles may be both integrative and pervasive. Several kinds of styles have been distinguished empirically, including expressive styles, response styles, cognitive styles, learning styles, and defensive styles (Furnham, 1995; Grigorenko & Sternberg, 1995; Messick, 1994).

The main goal of this chapter is to integrate the cognitive styles of attentional scanning, with defensive styles. In particular, two cognitive styles of attentional scanning are examined in relation to four prominent defensive styles associated with obsessive–compulsive, paranoid, hysterical, and impulsive neurotic pathologies (Shapiro, 1965). In this account the pre-existence and the causal nature of the two cognitive styles are held to contribute to the development of the defensive styles.

Two general cognitive styles of attentional scanning are the focus of the first part of the chapter. One style is known as *sharp-focus versus broad-focus scanning*; and the other as *serial scanning for signal detection versus parallel-process scanning* that apprehends incidental information. However, the second part of the chapter concentrates on *cognitive styles and defensive styles* (obsessive–compulsive, paranoid, hysterical, and impulsive) as well as their potential interrelationships. Because these four defensive styles are distinguished one from another in part by their distinctive ways of apprehending and dealing with information, the question naturally arises as to how they relate, if at all, to the two scanning styles.

To pursue this integrative effort, the two scanning styles are next described in more detail, followed by a more comprehensive description of the four defensive styles. These two accounts form the groundwork for examining their likely interrelationships.

COGNITIVE STYLES AND DEFENSIVE STYLES

Cognitive styles are usually conceptualized as characteristic modes of perception, memory, thought, and judgment. They derive from information-processing regularities that develop in congenial ways around underlying personality trends (Messick, 1984). Styles of behavior are inferred from consistent individual differences in ways of organizing and processing information and experience. They appear to serve as higher-order regulating systems derived from learning based on past experiences. These systems, or heuristics, control more specific strategies, propensities, and abilities: And these systems organize them into behavioral patterns characteristic of the individual.

Defensive styles, on the other hand, organize and control intrusive affects and impulses in cognition and behavior (Shapiro, 1965). They represent consistent modes of accommodating anxiety and conflict. At the same time defensive styles maintain reasonably adaptive cognitive functioning. They are by no means limited to pathology, but are also visible distinctively characteristic trends within the normal range of personality. For example one can be characterized as being somewhat impulsive, or obsessive or paranoid while being well adjusted to adult life. To illustrate from real life: One perhaps would prefer otherwise normal human beings who were also tax inspectors to be mildly obsessive (concentrating on getting the details right). This tendency would be preferable to their being somewhat paranoid (ignoring details that would allay their fears and suspicions about a tax return) while they went about their business!

Clues from Scanning Styles, Eye Movements and Defense Mechanisms. These two scanning styles represent different preferences for serial as opposed to parallel information processing and different modes of narrow versus broad-band search in the external and internal worlds. However, traditional measures of attentional scanning based on eye movements (Gardner, 1970) confounded these two styles, so that correlates of the confounded scores need to be reappraised in light of more refined measures of the separate styles.

As an instance, among the correlates of eye-movement measures of scanning are Rorschach indices of *both* isolation *and* projection. *Isolation* is the preferred defense mechanism of *obsessives* and projection the preferred defense of *paranoids* (Gardner & Long, 1962a, 1962b). These findings suggested that eye movement measures were confounded; and that distinct types of scanning might exist (Messick, 1976). They motivated the quest for a search for separate scanning styles and potential relationships with defensive styles. Of special interest for psychopathology are the ways in which unrelated ideas become interconnected, whether by broad bandwidth scanning or by the failure of inhibition in parallel processing. A phenomenon that Eysenck (1993) called the "widening of the associative horizons" (see also Stavridou & Furnham, 1996).

Cognitive Styles of Attentional Scanning

When the results of tests are processed, individual consistencies in attentional processes in perception and memory underlie stylistic dimensions of attentional scanning at the first-order factor level. Bipolar patterns of these dimensions yield higher order factors of scanning cognitive style (Messick, 1989). In particular, two second-order bipolar factors have been identified that contrast *sharp-focus versus broad-focus* and *signal versus information scanning*. These factors operate in memory as well as perception and they are related to personality in quite different ways. Moreover, these two second-order style dimensions appear to be comparable in the two sexes. Because the patterns of results are not the same in males and females they nevertheless suggest underlying dynamics that are gender specific. These gender differences are important contributions to our understanding of styles.

Scanning Tasks. To give some sense of the nature of these more pervasive second-order scanning styles common in men and women, I briefly describe the kinds of tasks from which they were derived and summarize the structure of the intertask correlations. Although the detailed findings are presented in an earlier publication (Messick, 1989), here is a very brief summary. In addition to markers for verbal and quantitative abilities, there were tests of perceptual speed and closure, breadth of categorizing, inkblot perception, and scores on a variety of personality scales. Many of the tests were scored not only for the number of correct responses but also for the number of wrong and omitted responses.

Measures were included for detecting stimuli or stimulus classes in *unorganized* or randomly structured fields. Typical tasks were to find four-letter words in arrays of letters; to detect misspelled words; and to identify words containing the letter "a" in long lists of words. Tasks of scanning in *organized* fields demanded the discovery of a simple pattern embedded in a complex figure; or finding faces camouflaged in the background of pictures.

Scanning takes place not only in perception, but also in memory retrieval. The type of scanning dictates how internal fields of memory, meaning, and knowledge are surveyed. Because of this, measures were also included for remoteness of word association as well as for fluency in the production of class instances. For example, asking people how many instances of round things or blue things they could think of.

Distinguishing Serial From Parallel-Process Scanning. In deciding what tests to use, we tried very hard to differentiate between two possible modes of attention; namely, serial scanning for signal detection and parallel-process scanning that notices not only the signal, but incidental information in the background.

Accordingly, we used search tasks where one had to find stimuli or signals embedded in meaningfully organized visual fields. The example I used was finding faces camouflaged or embedded within in picture backgrounds. At the end of the search task, the respondents were then asked specific questions about the overall content of the pictures, although the pictures were no longer in front of them. People who take in incidental or background information in the process of scanning could thus be differentiated from those whose attention is limited in detecting the hidden signals—or in the case of the example, the faces.

Measures such as the *Stroop Color-Word Test* (MacLeod, 1991) were also included, wherein parallel-processing of irrelevant stimuli interferes with task requirements and must be actively suppressed for effective task performance. Let me explain why the Stroop test is a key to our understanding of these processes. The Stroop task consists of color names printed in different colored inks. For example the word *green* might be printed in *blue* ink. Subjects must name the ink *colors* as quickly as possible and not name the *words*. Because the meaning of the word contrasts with the perception of the colour, semantic interference with color perception can be expected. As a consequence, this is by no means an easy task and it requires sustained attention.

Resistance to color–word interference is thought to be a function of two processes. One is selective deployment of attention successively to the appropriate aspects of the stimulus and the response, namely, to the color of the ink and its corresponding color name. The other process is flexible control of both suppressing wrong and producing correct responses in dealing with successive color–word stimuli. That is, active inhibition of the printed color name and simultaneous (or successive) production of the name of the contrasting colored ink in which it is printed (Gardner, Holzman, Klein, Linton, & Spence, 1959; Klein, 1964; Rand, Wapner, Werner, & McFarland, 1963). There are consistent individual differences in each process as well as in the relative balance with which they occur together.

In extreme cases, some individuals may rely on only one or the other. Individuals who rely relatively more on the first process of selective attention on color in the Stroop test would be expected to deploy selective attention serially as a strategy (or perhaps a style) of signal detection. In contrast, those tending toward parallel processing would be expected to develop automatically multiple encodings of incidental information. Some of these automatic encodings (such as the meaning of the word in a different color on the Stroop test) interfere with task performance and need to be actively inhibited. Parallel processors are identified because they rely relatively more on the second Stroop process of response inhibition and flexible control.

Serial Versus Parallel Processing Styles. Of the two bipolar scanning styles identified, one pole or end of the spectrum was signal scanning for both unique targets (such as the letter "a") and class instances (such as round things). The other end of the pole showed information scanning of a type identified by loadings for measures of incidental knowledge.

This dimension of attention to discrete signals as opposed to a more diffuse attention band picking up background information is reminiscent of Pask's (1976) distinction between operation learning and comprehension learning, with its associated serialist versus holist cognitive styles. More fundamentally, this cognitive style of signal versus information scanning appears to be anchored by processes involved in serial versus parallel processing (Messick, 1996). In this interpretation, it resembles the distinction between successive and simultaneous cognitive systems studied by Das and his colleagues (Das, Kirby, & Jarman, 1979; Das, Naglieri, & Kirby, 1994) and of Luria's (1973) theory of brain functioning on which those studies are based.

Gender Contrasts in Scanning Operations. In serial scanning, intrusive objects are treated passively, solely through the removal of attentional resources. That is, attention is selectively deployed to move intrusive objects from the periphery to regions of nonfocus. In contrast, in parallel-process scanning, according to Shiffrin (1988), "objects presented in regions of nonfocus will be processed automatically and hence will generate encodings that must be inhibited in order to carry out the requirements of the main task" (p. 785). In males, the second-order factor of serial versus parallel-process scanning identified one extreme as serial selective attention for signal detection and the other as information apprehension combined with active inhibition of intrusive or unwanted details. In females, the comparable dimension contrasted serial selective attention with information apprehension combined with low inhibition.

Indeed, two of the first-order factors in the scanning study (Messick, 1989) were consistent with this view. For males, one factor involved signal scanning for both unique targets via perceptual search and class instances via memory search. The other factor involved information scanning, with loadings for incidental knowledge of the pictorial scenes as well as other tasks facilitated by multiple encodings. Furthermore, the Stroop interference score loaded substantially on both factors, consistent with the view that signal scanning implicates one of the two Stroop processes (serial selective attention) and information scanning implicates the other (active inhibition of the intrusive effects of parallel processing). These two first-order factors were negatively correlated and, along with some other first-order factors, generated the bipolar second-order dimension of signal versus information scanning that is reflective, as we have seen, of serial scanning versus a combination of parallel processing with active inhibition.

In the female sample, the corresponding bipolar second-order factor is quite comparable, with similar tests loading it in a hierarchical analysis, but the contributing first-order factors were somewhat different. In particular, the Stroop interference score loads only the signal-scanning factor in the female sample, suggesting that females depend primarily on selective attention in Stroop test performance with little reliance on inhibitory processes. As a consequence, the corresponding second-order scanning dimension in females appears to pit serial scanning against an amalgam of parallel processing and low inhibition.

Consistent with this interpretation is a number of ancillary factor loadings indicating *overinclusiveness*. An example is a measure of remoteness of word association. One would expect inhibitory processes to screen out associations that are psychologically distant in favor of responses that are close to the stimulus word. In contrast, the absence or "failure of inhibitory processes produces overinclusiveness" (Eysenck, 1995, p. 240). Given that active inhibition was associated with parallel processing in the male sample, remoteness of word association loaded in the serial scanning direction—that is, closeness of association was associated with active inhibition. In females, on the other hand, because parallel processing (with its multiple encodings of information) was combined with low inhibition, remoteness of association instead loaded in the parallel processing direction.

Sharp-Versus Broad-Focus Scanning in Males and Females. The other bipolar scanning style is interpretable as sharp-focus versus broad-focus scanning in both male and female samples. In males, the broad bandwidth appears to involve attenuated processing because several wrong and omit scores on closure tests load in this direction, as do measures of rigidity and authoritarianism. One of the contributing first-order factors loading in the broad-focus direction involves quick closure via broad estimation, which helps where approximations are adaptive but, in other instances where approximations are not sufficient, also carries the maladaptive baggage of premature closure. Premature closure, a form of intolerance of ambiguity, is consistent with the finding that broad bandwidth scanning in males correlates with rigidity and authoritarianism (Frenkel-Brunswik, 1949). Hence, this cognitive style is better characterized for males as sharp-versus loose-focus scanning or focused versus unfocused scanning (Messick, 1989). The major contrast here is one of high fidelity versus attenuated search, or critical and refined attention as opposed to approximate and coarse attention.

In contrast, the broad bandwidth pole in females may be more integrative: It is negatively correlated with rigidity and authoritarianism and positively correlated with self-sufficiency and measures of affective as opposed to effective interests. Furthermore, broad-bandwidth processing was not associated with wrong or omit scores for females. These correlates suggest that this factor might be better characterized for females by something like tight- versus open-focus scanning. Another difference between males and females is that all but one first-order factor for females cut across both perception and memory, whereas for males, separate factors emerged for scanning external perceptual fields and internal memory fields, mediated by the isolation of affect (Messick, 1989).

Moreover, in the female sample, a separate factor emerged at the first-order level representing preference for complexity as opposed to simplicity. This factor exhibited a number of personality correlates, suggesting that preference for complexity is affectively based in females. In the male sample, on the other hand, preference for complexity was associated with both sharp-focus scanning and parallel-process scanning in the periphery, suggesting that males are comfortable processing complexity as a function of sharply focused perusal combined with parallel processing in regions of nonfocus. Incidentally, as I show this stylistic combination turns out to be characteristic of the paranoid defensive style.

The Attentional Core of Defensive Styles

A key feature of defensive styles is their characteristic mode of deploying attention in dealing with intrapsychic conflict, ego threat, and intrusive affects and impulses. To underscore an earlier point: Although identified clinically in psychopathology as obsessive–compulsive, paranoid, hysterical, and impulsive neurotic styles, they represent less extreme characteristic trends having consequences for cognition *within the normal range* of personality (Shapiro, 1965). Specifically, obsessive–compulsive style is associated with rigid cognition, paranoid style with suspicious cognition, hysterical style with impressionistic cognition, and impulsive style with unintegrated cognition (Messick, 1987; Shapiro, 1965). We next examine each defensive style in turn with special emphasis on their distinctive attentional features.

Obsessive-Compulsive Style and Rigid Cognition. The obsessive–compulsive style derives from strong tendencies to repress disturbing affects; to treat everything, even aesthetic and affective experiences, in ideational terms; and to favor abstract reasoning approaches to problem solving (Smokler & Shevrin, 1979). Persons with this style rely on the isolation of affect and ideas as a preferred defense mechanism, frequently using intellectualization and rationalization as ways of avoiding affects and impulses (Shapiro, 1965).

Obsessive–compulsive style is also characterized by extensive serial scanning of stimulus fields using a narrow, high-fidelity attentional bandwidth. By means of such scanning, obsessive–compulsives are intellectually active, even driven, and are careful to compile an extensive collection of facts before acting or making decisions. In a sense, then, the extensive scanning of obsessive –compulsives serves to offset persistent uncertainty and indecisiveness. The massive detail that obsessives gather in this sequential manner consists of sharply focused and discrete but unrelated perceptions and ideas. The concern is over small technical details viewed one at a time, with little attention given to relationships among them (Wachtel, 1967).

A hallmark of obsessive–compulsive style is rigid cognition. This characteristic is associated with a tendency to be preoccupied with particular ideas or aims. There is a narrow focus on relevant information. Anything surprising or unexpected, being potentially distracting and disruptive, is apprehended only peripherally. This style has a quality of what has been called "active inattention" to external influences and new ideas, the very essence of rigidity and dogmatism (Rokeach, 1960; Shapiro, 1965). Indeed, dogma compensates defensively for the excessive doubt and uncertainty that are symptomatic of this style. Yet the same narrow focus on technical details that makes for rigidity in some circumstances also endows the obsessive–compulsive person in other contexts with technical facility and an adaptive capacity to concentrate on technical problems. Pace, our efficient and benign tax inspector.

Paranoid Style and Suspicious Cognition. The hallmark of the paranoid style is suspicious cognition, which is characterized both by preoccupation with certain ideas and by unwarranted beliefs such as a continual expectation of trickery (Shapiro, 1965). Thus, suspicious cognition is highly compartmentalized by fixed and preemptive predictions of what the world will turn out to be like. Although the world is repeatedly searched, it is mainly for confirmation of these expectations.

Prominent in paranoid style is an extensive scanning of stimulus fields by means of a sharply-focused attentional beam combined with parallel processing in regions of nonfocus. Parallel processing promotes the incidental apprehension of multiple sources of information. At the same time, the sharp focus helps to screen out to the periphery unwanted or inconsistent findings. Parallel-process scanning permits individuals exhibiting this style to collect and maintain extensive evidence in support of their fixed ideas. They also remain alert to anticipated dangers that might be lurking anywhere—indeed, suspicious people are both hypersensitive and hyperalert. But by attending selectively to what is considered pertinent and consistent, all other aspects of the perceptual field are ignored or inhibited, thereby assuring that the evidence fits (Wachtel, 1967). Such a style in the inspector must be every taxpayer's nightmare.

The contrast between the obsessive–compulsive's discrete attention to a succession of unrelated facts and the paranoid's idiosyncratic screening of the multiple encodings of parallel processing may represent the dark side of Pask's

(1976) serialist versus holist cognitive styles. Indeed, Pask anticipated this by identifying *improvidence* (the ignoring of important connections) as a pathology of serialist thinking; and *globetrotting* (the making of inappropriate connections) as a pathology of holist thinking. Globetrotting—as exemplified by inconsistent scores on the Remote Associate Test—were also found to be associated with schizotypy (Zanes, Ross, Hatfield, Houtler, & Whitman, 1998).

Hysterical Style and Impressionistic Cognition. The hysterical style derives from strong tendencies to repress disturbing ideas, to be subject to emotional liability, and to favor concrete stimulus-bound approaches to problem solving (Smokler & Shevrin, 1979). A hallmark of hysterical style is impressionistic cognition, which is global, relatively immediate but diffuse, and lacking in sharpness and detail. This type of cognitive experience is marked not by sharply observed facts and carefully developed judgments but by quick hunches and impressions (Shapiro, 1965).

Consistent with this complex of hysterical symptoms is a preferred mode of attention. Parallel processing in the periphery combines with a broad, unfocused attentional beam. This attentional mode responds only to the striking and obvious features of the environment. Parallel processing helps one to take in multiple sources of input, but the broad, unfocused bandwidth makes this information vague and poorly connected. Consequently, the hysterical style does not provide a foundation for carefully considered judgments. One must then rely, at best, on impressionistic hunches.

There also seems to be hysterical incapacity for persistent or intense intellectual concentration. As a result, individuals exhibiting this style are distractible, impressionable, and remarkably deficient in knowledge. They generally live in a nonfactual world. Their thinking and problem solving is characterized not by concentration on facts, articulated principles, and steps toward solution but, rather, is dominated by hunches and vagueness. This mode of impressionistic cognition is especially conducive to forgetting of a particular kind. The loss from consciousness is not of affect (feelings and emotions) but of ideas and information. Thus, the naiveté and, in the extreme, the anti-intellectualism of hysterical individuals combine to provide a defensive way of avoiding disturbing or threatening ideas (Shapiro, 1965).

Impulsive Style and Unintegrated Cognition. The impulsive mode of cognition reveals a lack of active integrative processes. In general, purposeful concentration, the capacity for abstraction and generalization, as well as reflectiveness all seem to be impaired. Thinking and planning appear to be short-circuited by the immediate translation of whims and urges into hasty action. Impulsive behavior is speedy, abrupt or discontinuous, and unplanned.

Attentional style consonant with these impulsive symptoms involves rapid serial scanning of stimulus fields with a broad, unfocused bandwidth. The rapid serial scanning leads to quick (often superficial) connections between items or events. Moreover, the broad, unfocused attentional beam leads to poorly realized representations. This combination of rapid scanning and unfocused attention is a prescription not just for quick decisions but for premature and rash ones as well.

In the impulsive style, qualities associated with judgment and planning are especially deficient. Both judgment and planning involve a deliberate consideration of alternative possibilities and a critical examination of first impressions. They require reflective processes that are quite uncharacteristic of the impulsive style. Unintegrated cognition associated with impulsivity is not conducive to a planning, abstracting, and reflective intelligence: But it would be a mistake to think of impulsive style as necessarily immobilized or disorganized. Indeed, individuals with an impulsive style at times reveal practical intelligence consistent with and supporting speedy action. They are sometimes quick in sizing up situations in terms of their personal interests and can be relatively competent in the execution of short-range immediate aims.

The lack of a sense of intention and deliberateness also colors their experience of affect and impulse. Without a field of consciousness that is aware of intent and purpose, a defensive basis for the disavowal of personal responsibility is ensured. That is, tension discharge with no intention is not seen as blameworthy. The lack of premeditation thereby effectively serves as a defense against guilt (Shapiro, 1965). To paraphrase a current commercial for legal aid, without a claim, there can be no allocation of blame.

COGNITIVE STYLES AS ORGANIZERS OF DEFENSIVE STYLES

The four prominent defensive styles, as has been seen, are distinguished from each other in terms of their salient attentional orientations and the associated dominant modes of cognition. Because the two cognitive styles of attentional scanning represent similar attentional contrasts, the question naturally arises as to how the scanning styles and the defensive styles are related, if at all. To help the reader understand this inquiry, the salient features of the defensive styles and their relation to attentional modes and cognitive consequences are summarized in Table 14.1.

Because one of the scanning styles contrasts serial scanning with parallel process scanning and the other pits a sharply focused attentional beam against a broad unfocused attentional beam, the basis for relating the scanning and defensive styles is already implicit in Table 14.1. The table is recast into a dimensional framework by crossing the two scanning styles to generate four quadrants, as in Figure 14.1.

Defense Styles as a Cross Product of Scanning Styles

Figure 14.1 represents the two scanning styles as systematic organizers of the four defensive styles. Consistent with Table 14.1, the obsessive style reflects serial scanning with a sharply focused attentional beam, the paranoid style combines parallel processing in the periphery and a sharply focused attentional beam, the hysterical style combines peripheral parallel processing and a broad, unfocused attentional beam, and the impulsive style reflects serial scanning with a broad, unfocused attentional beam.

The obsessive style involves serial scanning of stimulus fields with a high-fidelity attentional beam to accommodate technical details and discrete facts to offset uncertainty in decision making. The paranoid style, as intimated earlier, selectively deploys sharply focused attention, often along with inhibitory processes, to process the complexity afforded by parallel processing, albeit typically in biased and idiosyncratic ways.

In contrast, the hysterical style addresses the multiple encodings of parallel processing with a broad, unfocused attentional beam, yielding a vague and impressionistic view of the world. Finally, the impulsive style involves rapid serial scanning of stimulus fields with a broad unfocussed attentional beam, yielding impoverished representations and superficial connections evocative of premature closure.

Female Caveats. The representation portrayed in Figure 14.1 is most consistent with the results of the male sample in the scanning study (Messick, 1989) and may need to be elaborated or modified to accommodate the findings of the female sample. For example, there was some indication that the broad

TABLE 14.1
Attentional and Cognitive Features of Defensive Styles

Obsessive–Compulsive Style	Paranoid Style
- serial scanning with a sharply focussed attentional beam - rigid cognition	- parallel processing in the periphery combined with a sharply focussed attentional beam - suspicious cognition
Impulsive Style	Hysterical Style
- serial scanning with a broad, unfocused attentional beam - unintegrated cognition	- parallel processing in the periphery combined with a broad, unfocused attentional beam - impressionistic cognition

attentional beam for females was not so much unfocused as it was integrative of multiple items of information encompassed by the broad bandwidth. However, because parallel processing in females was combined with low inhibition in their version of the hysterical style, any integrative tendencies would still likely be overwhelmed by the uninhibited multiple encodings of parallel processing. Nonetheless, to the extent that integrative effects are exhibited, the vague hunches symptomatic of the hysteric might be better characterized not as impressionistic but rather as intuitive or insightful.

Similarly, rapid serial scanning with a broad integrative attentional beam might lead impulsives, as already indicated, to exhibit quick closure and effective speedy action.

The representation portrayed in Figure 14.1 implies that the two cognitive styles of attentional scanning serve as rule-governed organizers of the defensive styles. That is, preferences for both sharp-focus versus broad-focus scanning *and* serial versus parallel-process scanning predispose people to a particular defensive style when confronted with intrapsychic conflict, ego threat, or intrusive affects and impulses.

Perhaps the direction of causality is instead in the opposite direction; that neurotic symptoms determine the development of attentional scanning styles specialized to cope with the pathology. However, this possibility seems unlikely because the cognitive styles of attentional scanning are more general than any defensive functions they might serve. The scanning styles operate prior to as well as outside of these defensive functions, being applicable to a large variety of attentional phenomena in the broad range of normal personality functioning.

It thus appears that cognitive styles serve as organizers of defensive styles, thereby answering a small part of Shapiro's (1965) searching question as to what

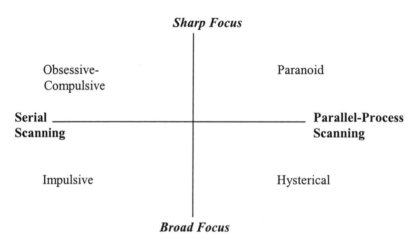

FIG. 14.1. Defense Styles as a Cross Product of Scanning Styles.

are the form-giving structures in personality that give rise to stylistic consistencies in behavior. Cognitive styles appear to be the form-giving structures underlying defensive styles. But there still remains an even more fundamental aspect of Shapiro's quest: What are the form-giving structures of personality that underlie cognitive styles?

ACKNOWLEDGMENTS

This chapter was presented as a paper at the Second Spearman Seminar, University of Plymouth, England, July, 1997. Acknowledgments are gratefully extended to Walter Emmerich, Ann Jungeblut, Richard Snow, and Lawrence Stricker for their helpful comments on the manuscript.

REFERENCES

Das, J. P., Kirby, J. R., & Jarman, R. F. (1979). *Simultaneous and successive cognitive processes.* New York: Academic Press.

Das, J. P., Naglieri, J. A., & Kirby, J. R. (1994). *Assessment of cognitive processes: The PASS theory of intelligence.* Boston: Allyn & Bacon.

Eysenck, H. J. (1993). Creativity and personality: A theoretical perspective. *Psychological Inquiry, 4,* 147-246.

Eysenck, H. J. (1995). Creativity as a product of intelligence and personality. In D. H. Saklofske & M. Zeidner (Eds.), *International handbook of personality and intelligence* (pp. 231–247). New York: Plenum.

Frenkel-Brunswik, E. (1949). Intolerance of ambiguity as an emotional and perceptual personality variable. *Journal of Personality, 18,* 108–143.

Furnham, A. (1995). The relationship of personality and intelligence to cognitive learning style and achievement. In D. H. Saklofske & M. Zeidner (Eds.), *International handbook of personality and intelligence* (pp. 397–413). New York: Plenum.

Gardner, R. W. (1970). Scores for the cognitive control of extensiveness of scanning. *Perceptual and Motor Skills, 31,* 330.

Gardner, R. W., Holzman, P. S., Klein, G. S., Linton, H. B., & Spence, D. (1959). Cognitive control: A study of individual consistencies in cognitive behavior. *Psychological Issues, 1, Monograph 4.*

Gardner, R., W., & Long, R. I. (1962a). Cognitive controls of attention and inhibition: A study of individual consistencies. *British Journal of Psychology, 53,* 381–388.

Gardner, R. W., & Long, R. I. (1962b). Control, defense and centration effect: A study of scanning behavior. *British Journal of Psychology, 53,* 129–140.

Grigorenko, E. L., & Sternberg, R. J. (1995). Thinking styles. In D. H. Saklofske & M. Zeidner (Eds.), *International handbook of personality and intelligence* (pp. 205–284). New York: Plenum.

Klein, G. S. (1964). Semantic power measured through the interference of words with color-naming. *American Journal of Psychology, 77,* 576–588.

Luria, A. R. (1973). *The working brain.* London: Penguin.

MacLeod, C. M. (1991). Half a century of research on the Stroop effect: An integrative review. *Psychological Bulletin, 109,* 163–203.

Messick, S. (1976). Personality consistencies in cognition and creativity. In S. Messick (Ed.), *Individuality in learning: Implications of cognitive styles and creativity for human development.* San Francisco: Jossey-Bass.

Messick, S. (1984). The nature of cognitive styles: Problems and promise in educational practice. *Educational Psychologist, 19,* 59–74.

Messick, S. (1987). Structural relationships across cognition, personality, and style. In R. E. Snow & M. J. Farr (Eds.), *Aptitude, learning, and instruction. (Vol. III): Conative and affective process analyses.* Hillsdale, NJ: Lawrence Erlbaum Associates.

Messick, S. (1989). *Cognitive style and personality: Attentional scanning and orientation toward affect* (ETS RR 89–16). Princeton, NJ: Educational Testing Service.

Messick, S. (1994). The matter of style: Manifestations of personality in cognition, learning, and teaching. *Educational Psychologist, 21,* 121–136.

Messick, S. (1996). Bridging cognition and personality in education: The role of style in performance and development. *European Journal of Personality, 10,* 353–376.

Pask, G. (1976). Styles and strategies of learning. *British Journal of Educational Psychology, 46,* 128–148.

Rand, G., Wapner, S., Werner, H., & McFarland, J. H. (1963). Age differences in performance on the Stroop Color-Word Test. *Journal of Personality, 31,* 534–558.

Rokeach, M. (1960). *The open and closed mind.* New York: Basic Books.

Shapiro, D. (1965). *Neurotic styles.* New York: Basic Books.

Shiffrin, R. M. (1988). Attention. In R. C. Atkinson, R. J. Herrnstein, G. Lindzey, & R. D. Luce (Eds.), *Stevens' handbook of experimental psychology (2nd ed., Vol. 2): Learning and cognition.* New York: Wiley.

Smokler, I. A., & Shevrin, H. (1979). Cerebral lateralization and personality style. *Archives of General Psychiatry, 36,* 949–954.

Stavridou, A., & Furnham, A. (1996). The relationship between psychoticism, trait-creativity and the attentional mechanism of cognitive inhibition. *Personality and Individual Differences, 21,* 142–153.

Wachtel, P. L. (1967). Conceptions of broad and narrow attention. *Psychological Bulletin, 68,* 417–429.

Zane, J., Ross, S., Hatfield, R., Houtler, B., & Whitman, D. (1998). The relationship between creativity and psychosis-proneness. *Personality & Individual Differences, 24*(6), 879–881.

15

Self-Concept and Status as Determinants of Cognitive Style

Sidney H. Irvine
University of Plymouth, England

There are substantive issues yet to be resolved in the meaning and measurement of style. Spearman (1927, p. 52) isolated its most important, and perhaps most neglected, assumption, the tendency for mental processes to persist in activity long after the cessation of the conditions to which they were originally due. This encapsulation of the common ground among proponents of types of personality is the beginning to Spearman's cognitively based critiques of Stern, Gross, Heymans, Jung, and others. His critique could just as easily be extended to modern proponents of style. The purpose of this contribution is not to embark on such an extension but to provide by eclectic empiricism some keys to the understanding of Spearman's fundamental postulate, that mental processes persist long after the original means of bringing them about have stopped. Even the largest of large-scale g studies reveal, however, that *g* is not everything, nor even the only thing, in learning new skills (Ree, Earles, & Teachout, 1995). Moreover, Messick (1996) hinted that the constructs of style may require more than one mode of measurement to deliver them from the self-imposed bonds of means and the products of moments, legacies of Spearman's correlational model of measurement. To that end, there are four different formal sets of data: one cross-cultural, which derives from work completed almost 40 years ago; one classroom-based, completed 20 years ago; another occupational, completed 5 years ago; and one completed only last year. Together, they demonstrate the diverse roles of cognitive consistency in compliance with and in resistance to environmental press in other cultures, in classrooms, at work, and in training. They also show that the measurement of style requires the systematic application of a taxonomy of measurement procedures, including normative and ipsative measures.

THE MEANING AND MEASUREMENT OF STYLE

Messick (1996) probably defined the issues in making style a more coherent and functional field of individual differences more precisely than anyone might ever aspire to. To review the field in order to find keys to its understanding, one need only consult this particular source. After examining Messick's work, the enforced conclusion one may have to accept with reluctance is that the means of pursuing, in operational form, the elusive pimpernel of an acceptable measurement protocol for style is not available.

Even more disconcerting than this is the knowledge that nonpsychologists are well ahead in the race to capture styles in recognizable form. It has been pointed out (Irvine, 1988) that the notion of style is so intuitively certain in ordinary people untrammelled by psychologists' preoccupations with measurement, that professional entertainers make a very good living by mimicking styles among the great, the good, the bad, and the ugly. If style is so easy to capture and to imitate, why is it so difficult to measure?

Part of the answer to this question lies in the operational bricolage (Berry & Irvine, 1986) employed by psychologists in their day by day moulding and cobbling together of constructs with what materials are available. Dissatisfaction with much of what passes for empiricism in the measurement of individual differences is not new; and this is also a recurring and reassuring undertone in Messick's publication on style. In fact, he recommended a qualified departure from normative measurement in pursuit of procedures described as "contrasted measurement." For example, it has been established that the cognitive style of field dependence-independence is characterised by differential group test measurements in the figural and verbal domains. The question remains as to whether these differences are intra-individual. Given the inherent unreliability of norm-based difference scores, this may be an unaskable question.[1] Field independent groups of subjects have relatively higher scores than field dependent subjects where the stimuli are figural and the task is one of disembedding or else of object reconstruction in working memory. Verbal group measures as often as not show that field dependent subjects perform more accurately and quickly than field independent subjects. It is but a short step from this to observe that "male" could be substituted for field independent and "female" for field dependent and it almost always has been, at least in North America. To extend the analogy, right-brain and left-brain could, and have been offered: or testosterone and progesterone. Even more all-embracing and high-inference (Irvine, 1981) quasi-independent variables such as familial and or societal characteristics are large parts of the stylistic repertoire. Then, categories such as family autonomy and dependence, hunter-gatherers and agriculturists, or nomadic and sedentary become labels to attach to the opposite

---

[1] When the reliability of any two test scores approaches their intercorrelation, so the reliability of difference scores derived from these test scores approaches zero.

poles and so on down the panoply of all possible associations with, and implied causal effects of, style. So far, the number of binary divisions mentioned are sex, hemispheres, hormone levels, family and societal mobility and food accumulation. This produces 64 categories or treatments if Cartesian sets were to be constructed in order to trace possible influences on style by analysis of variance. Perhaps this is not a *reductio ad absurdum*, but one hopes it may begin to convey all the self-deceptive characteristics of an infinite regression. One has to begin somewhere. In short, stylistic theory may be constructed with greater impact when inferences from variables are shortened considerably.

THE ANTECEDENTS OF STYLES

One might advance from this standpoint, not by questioning one of the fundamental tenets of cognitive style, that females tend to carry out more field dependent roles than males but by examining its operational corollary: that this is empirically demonstrated by a universal measurement contrast: high verbal, low figural score differentiation among women, and the opposite for men. Berry (1976) for example, showed that the size of the bi-serial correlation between maleness and better performance on figural tests increases as the cultural background of the subjects becomes socially more complex in structure (Westernized). From this, he asserted that the score pattern itself is a variable closely associated with cultural differences. The elegant, remarkable, and virtually ignored meta-analysis of sex difference studies in African, Asian, and Western groups by Born, Bleichrodt, and van der Flier (1987) provides much wider confirmation of their instability, and by implication, of Berry's empirical insights.

Logically, as was demonstrated, to stop infinite regressions in all kinds of dispositional, social, and cultural categories, some finite endpoint has to be assumed. It is possible that some quite straightforward endpoint has been overlooked in Berry's catalogue of cultures. The common antecedent to style is how males and females are encouraged or discouraged in learning verbal and figural manipulation skills from the days that they begin to attend schools. For those of us whose experience extends beyond the classrooms of America and Britain, this has always seemed to be a low-inference end point because of important measurement outcomes in classrooms themselves. Classrooms of 30 plus or minus 5 children taught by a single adult are the universal learning context of childhood (Jackson, 1968, p. 5). Even when these conditions diversify after specialist teachers arrive with transfer to secondary schools, stylistic habits formed in classrooms may be expected to persist. Status accorded in classrooms, mediated by rewards and punishments in controls antecedent to learning, has to be related to differential functioning.

The data presented now are a retrospective of the doubts about the operational use of variables to account for style that have been entertained by applied psychologists for some decades. They do form a cohesive construct around what Messick (1996, p. 13) termed the concept of contrasted measurement. What evolves now are a number of contrasts, each of which has a place in the measurement of style but no one that constitutes an adequate sample of all the evidence that can be produced for it, or must indeed eventually be produced.

The contrasts begin across schools within African cultures (Drenth, van der Flier, & Omari, 1979; Irvine, 1969, 1979; MacArthur, Irvine, & Brimble, 1964; Omari, Drenth, & van der Flier, 1983). They continue within classrooms across cultures (Davis, 1977; Owen, 1987; Scanlan, 1984). They end with an examination of the factors influencing individual differences in style in work contexts, contrasting both normative and ipsative data (Irvine, 1996; Irvine, Mettam, & Syrad, 1994). All of these studies address the issue of what makes styles possible, taking as a premise Spearman's (1927, p. 52) view that styles or psychological types derive from that tendency for mental processes to persist in activity long after the cessation of the conditions to which they were originally due. Styles are learned and it follows that the conditions that make them persist have to be delineated and measured wherever possible.

STYLE OUT OF AFRICA

Since the 1980's, however, there has been much evidence from Africa to support the view that the field independent-dependent cognitive style is not well represented by the conventional North American belief that it consists primarily in a higher disembedding-spatial and lower verbal contrast. In fact, the cadre of evidence from Africa underlines that the field independent style is quite different, being high verbal and lower disembedding, and that the male–female difference is most pronounced in the verbal domain (Bakare, 1972; Born, Bleichrodt, & van der Flier, 1987; Bowden, 1969; Drenth, van der Flier, & Omari, 1979; Fourie, 1967; Hendrix, 1975; Hoare, 1983; Irvine, 1966, 1969, 1979; Klingelhofer, 1967; MacArthur, Irvine, & Brimble, 1964; Munroe & Munroe, 1971; Omari, Drenth, & van der Flier, 1983; Swanepoel, 1975). In spite of the breadth and consistency of this evidence, it has seldom if ever even been granted a footnote in any major review of cognitive style.

In all of these African contexts, the conventional wisdom is that males are more active in exploring the environment, more dominant, more intellectually curious, more independent, and less compliant because of their need to work outside the subsistence economy than females. Moreover, African schooling in the several countries of origin, from Nigeria to South Africa via Kenya, Tanzania, Zambia, and Zimbabwe, follows a pattern that is recognizably formal and modelled on an American or European grade system designed to transmit cognitive skills of literacy and numeracy. Conventional wisdom[2] of male roles being adaptive is not only justified by observation and data from psychologists and sociologists (Irvine, 1988), it is reinforced through one crucial difference from the original school systems inherited by African nations. *The teachers at the time that the data were collected were almost invariably males, except in the very rare circumstance of all-female boarding schools.* Moreover, in every classroom except where sex segregation was practised as a matter of religious policy, females were an obvious minority, sometimes being outnumbered by as many as ten to one in isolated rural schools. In such contexts, the field-independent style has to find its habitual expression in learning by males, rewarded by male teacher approval.

Figure 15.1 shows a pattern of results comparing males and females in a national survey in Zimbabwe. The results are reported in stanine values by sex within school types, and show that males always outperform females within school type. There are significant effect sizes for sex differences and for schools. These are smallest (typically .15 to .20) in the professionally administered tests with figural content, but larger in English Language subjects (.3 to .4), and largest of all in Geography and Nature Study and in History and Current Affairs (.6 to .7), which are also assessed in English. Within the sexes, female groups do not always show comparatively higher verbal than figural means, whereas males certainly do.

In Zimbabwe schools at that time, roles were well defined and structurally tight. Teachers were male; female students quiet; and compliant minorities usually seated at the teacher's right-hand front corner of the class in an enclave; and males vocal, dominant, and independent. This particular empirical pattern is repeated many times in the cited literature. There can be only one conclusion: The outcome of cognitive skill acquisitions, and the habits of mind associated with them—style by any other name—is not a universal fixed pattern, it is a cultural variable whose antecedents lie in what is learned in school.

---

[2] See *Tsumo-Shumo; Shona proverbial lore and wisdom*, Edited by M.A. Hamutyeni and A. B Plangger, Mambo Press, Harare, Zimbabwe for many proverbs confirming this view. One in particular, Kuzvara ndume/kuzvara hadzi translates "To beget a male is to beget a female." When a girl marries she is subordinate in the family of her husband (p. 242). In fact, a proverb Mwanasikana ndimapfumise "A daughter enriches her family" is often quoted to *console* parents who have not produced a male child (p. 237).

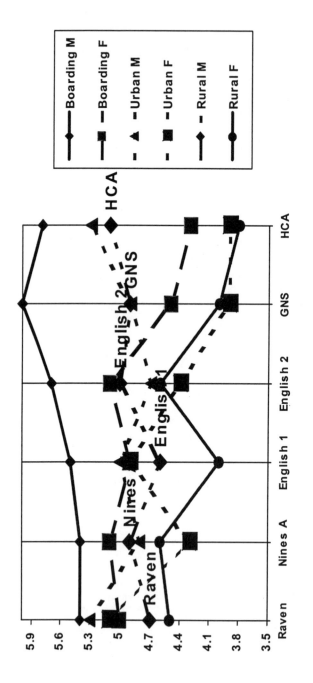

FIG. 15.1. Figural and Verbal Test contrasts by Gender and School Type.

THE SPECIAL RELATIONSHIP

As cultural variables, the controls exerted on learning by teachers have to be *antecedent* to individual differences in its forms of expression. Knowledge of what differentiates individuals in North American and European classrooms is certain and has a long history in the literature, again notably absent from discussions on style. The landmark references are given here. The enduring legacy of both individual and behavioural psychology is the principle that the distribution of rewards and punishments is critical in motivation to learn. This principle has been well established for primary school classroom enclosures for almost 50 years, with no sign that it has changed (de Groat & Thompson, 1949, Meyer & Thompson, 1956); and by extension, to the selection by students in them of what to learn and how to learn it. Moreover, individual rewards and punishments are known to be unequally distributed between sexes within classrooms (Becker, Madsen, Arnold, & Thomas, 1967, Meyer & Thompson, 1956); and among children from lower and middle-class backgrounds (Hoehn, 1954). Finally, individual 'summary executions' of teacher approval and disapproval are publicly witnessed and perceived from an early age (Davidson & Lang, 1960; Davis & Slobodian, 1967) by about thirty plus or minus five other members of the class. This publicity creates status within the group: and in some cases beyond its immediate boundaries.

A contrast is presented as before. First, it is possible to summarize findings in six different Grade 5 classrooms, two in Canada and four in England. Versions of the original de Groat and Thompson (1949) questionnaire were used to ask children in each class to guess which pupils were most closely represented by a short description. Thereafter the questions were divided into praise and blame questions and the nominations are summed for each child, who was assigned a peer Perceived Approval and a Perceived Disapproval score. Teachers for each class were also asked to provide an estimate of their own perceived approval and disapproval ratings based on a Likert scale of 10 equal intervals. Standardized attainment and IQ test scores were also provided from current school records.

Table 15.1 shows the correlations between school achievements and teacher control behavior as perceived by pupils in each class, using the Guess Who inventory already described. Six classes at the end of primary school are represented. The studies for four Plymouth classes were carried out by Scanlan

(1984) and Owen (1987); and for the two Canada classes by Davis (1977).[3] As is to be expected, some within class variation is apparent because not all the correlations are of the same order.   But the general outcome is substantial positive correlation between individual achievement and the amount of approval that the class members report is given to individuals; and somewhat less negative correlation between antecedent disapproval directed by teachers at individuals and their subsequent achievements in numeracy and literacy.

Having established the pattern, it is possible now to examine data more closely, and the results of the scrutiny are evident in Table 15.2. The Canadian classrooms are the focus of the detailed analysis here because all relevant dataare available, including the sex of the pupils. Moreover, the same students were taught language and math by different teachers in the same classes. There are some important serendipitous consequences of this organizational variable. Because the Plymouth classrooms were single-teacher contexts, variations in praise and blame within each subject grouping can not readily be observed.

By assigning ranks to the Guess Who scores within classes, it was possible to analyze the distribution of praise and blame status by sex of pupil and with IQ as a package variable, as a covariate. Although IQ is taken here as an intellective measure, it is also recognized as a proxy for socio-economic status. The results are shown in Table 15.2. In the lower half of the table, achievement grades in English language and Mathematics were analyzed with sex as the main factor, and three covariates the two perceived praise ranks (one for each subject teacher) and IQ.

TABLE 15.1
School Achievement and Teacher Control Correlations

School	Pupil Perceived Approval				Pupil Perceived Disapproval			
	IQ	Lang	Math	Read	IQ	Lang	Math	Read
Plymouth 1	48	51	74	58	-13	-15	-16	-19
Plymouth 2	25	37	55	13	-35	-48	-40	-30
Plymouth 3	-	12	-13	-03	-	41	23	54
Plymouth 4	-	32	31	-20	-	-45	-45	-12
Canada 1LT	42	57	55		-32	-45	-55	
Canada 1MT	31	32	65		-35	-45	-56	
Canada2 LT	52	75	45		-54	-55	-36	
Canada2 MT	57	78	43		-54	-67	-38	
Notes: LT=Language Teacher MT=Math Teacher								

[3] The correlations ($N = 21$ in each class) from the Plymouth schools are as reported in Scanlan (1984) and Owen (1987). The original records from Canadian schools, provided by Davis, have been put into a new SPSS database and all calculations (within classes $N = 21$ across classes $N = 42$) reworked by the author, who wishes to acknowledge with gratitude the special contributions made by these students to this synthesis.

TABLE 15.2
Sex, Approval, and IQ: Status Determinants of Style

Distributions of Approval by Sex and Regressions				Grades in Language and Math and Regressions			
Approval	M_Rank	r_{sex}	R_{sex+IQ}	Language	Gr_(adj)	r_{sex}	$R_{sex+IQ+App}$
Females	14.0	.51	.52	Females	76 (72)	.38	.84
Males	8.0	(26%)	(38%)	Males	66 (69)	(15%)	(71%)
Disapproval	M_Rank	r_{sex}	R_{sex+IQ}	Mathematics	Gr_(adj)	r_{sex}	$R_{sex+IQ+App}$
Females	7.0	.63	.69	Females	82 (78)	.29	.70
Males	14.6	(40%)	(47%)	Males	73 (77)	(9%)	(49%)

Praise and blame are perceived by pupils as being delivered in unequal amounts to boys and girls. Girls are seen as receiving most praise, or status enhancing controls, and boys as receiving disapproval, or status diminishing controls. The lower half of the table shows what is the result of adjusting group differences in achievement for approval by the language teacher *and* math teacher, regardless of outcome grade. In both analyses, the difference between groups showed dramatic reductions in effect size to the point of parity. IQ was a consistent effect. The approval variable that was significant, however, was the approval given *in that subject*. The other approval variable added no more to the equation. With the N in the equation no more than 42, this is not all together unexpected. Nevertheless, it would have been counterintuitive if the pattern of significance had been different, reversed or inconsistent.

It is perhaps not possible nowadays to claim a universal for one case study, like Freud and the Viennese woman, but the results have the added weight of confirming cross-nationally the trends of the last 50 years. Unlike the summary of contrived aptitude–treatment interaction studies reported by Davis (1991) there is little in the way of equivocation. Status is conferred by teachers within a subject area, and differential performance is a function of that status. The verbal superiority of girls in England and America is a function of life in classrooms largely controlled by female teachers in primary schools. In these, males are a minority group for approval, and a majority group for disapproval. With so much emphasis on the acquisition of language in the early years of schooling, it is hardly surprising that rewards for girls will result in more than transient cognitive skills for processing verbal information. Where conditions favouring males exist, as in Africa, the opposite outcome is the result.

Field independence is not, then, operationalized by a universal verbal–figural contrast. Its operational outcome in the cognitive domain is conferred by status. The delineation of the mechanism follows, of course, from what Irvine and Berry (1988, p. 4) designate as the law of cultural differentiation, or Ferguson's Law (Ferguson, 1956). This states that cultures determine what shall be learned at what age; and that different cultural environments lead to different patterns of ability. This kind of contrasted measurement seems to be one that should be added to Messick's plea for ipsative measures of individuals.

IPSATIVENESS, THE CORRELATIONAL PARIAH IN INDIVIDUAL DIFFERENCES

It is appropriate now to turn to the second issue raised by Messick, the future of ipsative, that is self-referent measures in the delineation of style. Much has been written, not all of it coherent, about the use of self-referent vs. normative measurement. Attention has been given recently to ipsative measures of personal qualities of motivation and style, as if their use constituted a special case

(Johnson, Wood, & Blinkhorn, 1988). In fact, the distinction between the two types of measure in appraisal of personal qualities is, as Horst (1965, Ch. 13) points out, and as Johnson et al. fail to observe, not an easy one to justify. Horst, in a short and incisive discussion, argues that even scales based on norms can be self-referent. Individuals may have an internal mean by which all items in a scale are compared in a relative manner—a self-ipsatising procedure in which each person who completes the scale has a point of origin unknown to the scale constructor. Given this as a premise, it is arguable that the comparison of normative scale scores between any two candidates may be illogical.

Johnson, Wood, and Blinkhorn (1988) raise another question about the use of self-report measures that are ipsative in another sense. Much heat is directed at users who may be unaware of that when the sum of a number of measures is constant for each person, correlations among these measures carry with them systematic autocorrelation that constrains their interpretation. None of their concerns is new, and for light one might refer to Burnham and Crawford, 1935; Roberts, 1959, 1963; Guilford, 1964, pp. 277, 508; Edwards, 1970, p. 203. The one truly illuminating source that offers technical solutions, for those seeking to understand the range of correlational problems that the use of ipsative measures may portend, resides in Horst (1965, Ch. 13, pp. 286-314). Forced-choice formats and constant-sum totals of inventories are only two examples of the problems of ipsativeness described by Horst. Others include the summation of beta-weights in regression to unity, and so on. Although these may be points of academic contention, Horst lists several other psychological assumptions and their attendant mathematical difficulties, associated with what he collectively defines as "problems of origin", or fixed reference points for calculating differences from the mean that are the stuff of variance and covariance.

VALID OR VALIDER?

Debates over how to intercorrelate ipsative measures are commonplace. Debates over the predictive validity of ipsative and normative measures are singularly lacking. There have been very few attempts to validate self-referent measures with hard criteria. By this is meant external and unequivocal data against which to relate ipsative data (Irvine, Mettam, & Syrad, 1994). In the adult domain, where styles of behavior are assumed to be both causal and permanent, the ideal context is a well-practiced, constrained, unsupervised at the point of operation, occupational role and a criterion of effectiveness. If styles vary within the role and, by varying, affect work performance, different styles should be associated with success and failure. The data relate to a severely constrained and almost invariably unsupervised role, and the criterion is utterly reliable, objective, and external. Here are reported the ipsative self-reports of a complete group of 50 London bus drivers from within a single garage and all operating the same routes. The profiles are charted by Accident Rate Quartiles.

The raw accident rates for each quartile are 0.55, 2.18, 2.30, and 6.6 respectively. When these are converted into an average per year of completed service, they are 0.04, 0.15, 0.45, and 1.57 respectively. Accident rate rank correlates .44 with the D (Dominance) scale, -.47 with the C (Compliance Scale). Those drivers who report that they are more Steady and Compliant than Influential and Dominant have the lowest accident rates. Those who report that they are more Influential, Steady, and Dominant than Compliant have the worst accident rates. 'Blind' profile reports generated from the DiSC system reveal substantive differences in the predicted work style behavior of the two ideal profiles, one for Low Accidents and the other for High Accidents. While both profiles show personal affability, the low accident profile emphasizes pleasure in routines, persistence, and dependability. The high accident profile predicts more directness, less patience, and tendency to stress.

With initial screening validities of this size, one would not be either reasonably surprised or disapproving if all airline pilot selection were by public demand to be given over to ipsative measures, regardless of their correlational properties. But, like Mrs. Beeton, we must first catch our hare of validity. What might be the limits of ipsative measures as far as styles are concerned?

The undeniable value of ipsative measures lies in the reduction of social desirability responses by forcing choices among valid scales. Nevertheless, do they predict normative standings with any degree of success?

SELF-CONCEPTUAL STYLES IN ADULTS

An attempt was made by Irvine (1996) to answer in part, these and related questions. In that work he synthesized positions by Stephenson (1939), Eysenck (1953), Vernon (1964), and Irvine, Mettam, and Syrad (1994). He described how a number of inventories were presented to purposive samples of 70 UK Managerial, Sales, and Support employees, and 200 USA Air Force inductees at Lackland Air Force Base.[4] An ipsative frame (PINR) for responses consisted of 100 trait-like adjectives with short phrase definitions. They were constructed around 20 facets each of five words, and they were designed to define four working styles, Proactive, Interactive, Nurturant, and Reactive. The words were presented in 25 blocks of four, and each word had to be assigned a single rank from 1 to 4, where 4 represented "most like me" and 1 represented "least like me." The four scales had internal consistency reliabilities from .86 to .91. In

[4] The contributions of Dr. Patrick Kyllonen, Janice Hereford, and Richard Walker, of the U.S. Air Force Armstrong Laboratory, Brooks Air Force Base, San Antonio, Texas, in making subjects available, are gratefully acknowledged.

addition, a True-Self Inventory Report (TS_IR) was administered. This consisted of 90 Likert-scale items based on six defining constructs; Proactive, Interactive, Nurturant, Reactive, Equable, and Cognitive Interests. The reliabilities of these scales were all close to .90, with .87 as the modal value.

Finally, the standard DiSC (Irvine, 1988b) inventory was included. In all 202 items were administered. All scores were put into ranks, ratings or Z-scores with similar variances.

The data matrix was transposed to enable the correlation of persons. The matrix was factored and three factors emerged. The first defined a Proactive work style. The occupations of those with the highest identification with the style were company director, sales consultant, chief executive and a personal aide to a company chairman. The interactive factor had the word "co-ordinator" in three of the five job titles with highest loadings. The third factor was one of technical support, with high loadings on the reactive factor. Typical jobs included engineering consultants, head of care service and an interior decorator, self-employed. The three factors emerging from the correlations of persons are given ipsative representation on the DiSC profile by averaging the scale scores for the five persons with the highest loadings on the factors. Three quite distinct profile shapes appear. The Proactive work style is represented by persons who say that they are more Dominant by far, than Influential, and more Influential than they are Steady and Compliant. Interactive roles are more Influential than Steady, and least of all Compliant and Dominant.

Reactive workers report they are more Steady and Compliant than Outgoing and Dominant. Blind scrutiny of these generic profiles in the DiSC report system produced the following trait-like adjectives.

- Proactive: *Direct, forceful, demanding, shrewd, mobile, alert, inquisitive, competitive, impatient, energetic.*
- Interactive: *Friendly, persuasive, relaxed, independent, strong-willed, accommodating, communicative, sympathetic, sincere, articulate.*
- Reactive: *Precise, steady, secure, patient, thorough, supportive, dependable, loyal, optimistic, stubborn, kind.*

They overlap very little, if at all, confirming analyses of variance that revealed significant scale mean differences for those identified on the three profiles. They are undoubtedly work styles. Whether they indicate personal cognitive styles is an interesting question. There are however some data that speak to it. The ipsative items (100 in the PINR Scale) can be regressed on the normative TS_IR scale scores. The multiple R range for the scales is .77 to .95. This degree of correlation allows reasonably accurate decile placement on the TS_IR norms for any single ipsatised scale score. Because the TS_IR scale is based on

Big Five Theory plus a Proactive dimension, it is at worst modish and at best indicative of well-defined individual differences in ways of adapting to circumstances. Far more significant, perhaps, is the realization that ipsative data need not prevent one from making normative inferences, quite contrary to much of traditional psychometric wisdom.

CONCLUSIONS

This chapter began with two quite different aims. The first was to try to dispel the systematically misleading assertion that cognitive style score patterns were universal phenomena. To this end, data from Zimbabwe showed that field-independence was manifest in higher verbal than figural performance. Microanalysis of data from Canadian and English primary schools showed that differential achievements were functions of control mechanisms in classrooms, revealing that females were high verbal achievers because of differential status accorded to them by teachers, and publicly observed by class members. By analogy, it is argued that cultural differences ensure that African male pupils enjoy the same degrees of approval from male teachers as female pupils in American and English schools do from women teachers.

The second aim of the chapter was to show how self-concepts at work are functions of successful role performance. These work habits reinforce broad styles of manifestly successful coping behavior, of which three are well defined by ipsative and by normative measures. The validity of self-report ipsative scales was demonstrated conclusively by the retrospective accident records of 50 London bus drivers from a single garage working in a severely constrained pattern of work.

If the notion of status and self-concept as determinants of style is not wholly proven here, then a prima facie case has been made for more direct and contextually sensitive operational measures to produce adequate useable and recognizable style profiles. If mimics can do it and raise much laughter, perhaps psychologists can do it and avoid ridicule.

REFERENCES

Bakare, C. G. M. (1972). Social-class differences in the performance of Nigerian children on the Draw-a-Man test. In L. J. Cronbach, P. J. D. Drenth, (Eds.) *Mental tests and cultural adaptation* (pp. 363-366). The Hague: Mouton.

Becker, W. C., Madsen, C. H., Arnold, C. R., & Thomas, D. R. (1967). The contingent use of teacher attention and praise in reducing classroom behaviour problems, *Journal of Special education, 1,* 287-307.

Berry, J. W. (1976). *Human ecology and cognitive style* (pp. 167-169). New York: Sage

Berry, J. W., & Irvine, S. H. (1986). Bricolage: Savages do it daily. In R. J. Sternberg & R.K. Wagner, (Eds.), *Practical intelligence.* New York: Cambridge University Press.

Bowden, E. A. F. (1969). Perceptual abilities of African and European children educated together. *Journal of Social Psychology, 79*, 149-154.

Born, M. P., Bleichrodt, N., & van der Flier, H. (1987). Cross-cultural comparison of sex-related differences on intelligence tests. *Journal of Cross-Cultural Psychology, 18*, 283-314.

Burnham, P. S., & Crawford, A. B. (1935). The vocational interests of a pair of dice. *Journal of Educational Psychology, 26*, 508-512.

Davidson, H. H., & Lang, G. (1960). Children's perceptions of their teachers' feelings towards them related to self-perception, school achievement and behaviour. *Journal of Experimental Education, 29*, 107-118.

Davis, D. A. (1977). *A study of the effects of manifest teacher approval and disapproval on academic achievement in a fifth grade class.* Unpublished Master's Thesis, Brock University, St Catherines, Ontario, Canada.

Davis, J. K. (1991). Educational implications of field-dependence—independence. In S. Wapner & J. Demick (Eds.), *Cognitive style across the life-span* (pp. 149-176). Hillsdale, NJ: Lawrence Erlbaum Associates.

Davis, O. L., & Slobodian, J. J. (1967). Teacher behaviour towards boys and girls during first grade reading instruction. *American Educational Research Journal, 4*, 261-269.

de Groat, A. A., & Thompson, G. (1949). Study of the distribution of teacher approval and disapproval among sixth-grade pupils. *Journal of Experimental Education, 18*, 57-75.

Drenth, P. J. D., van der Flier, H., & Omari, I. M. (1979). The use of classroom tests, examinations and aptitude tests in a developing country. In L.H. Eckensberger, W. J. Lonner, & Y. H. Poortinga, (Eds.) *Cross-cultural contributions to psychology.* Lisse, Netherlands: Swets and Zeitlinger.

Edwards, A. L. (1970). *The measurement of personality traits by scales and inventories.* New York: Holt.

Eysenck, H. J. (1953). *The structure of human personality.* London: Methuen.

Ferguson, G. A. (1956). On transfer and the abilities of man. *Canadian Journal of Psychology, 10*, 121-131.

Fourie, A. B. (1967). *A study of the implications of standardised tests for standard six Bantu pupils* (Original in Afrikaans). Unpublished Doctoral Dissertation. University of Pretoria, South Africa.

Guilford, J. P. (1964). *Fundamental statistics in psychology and education.* New York: McGraw-Hill.

Hamutyeni, M. A., & Plangger, A. B. (1974). *Tsumo-Shumo: Shona proverbial love and wisdom.* Gwelo, Zimbabwe: Mambo Press.

Hendrix, E. A. (1975). Spatial reasoning and mathematical and scientific competence: A cross-cultural study. In J. W. Berry & W. J. Lonner (Eds.), *Applied cross-cultural psychology* (pp. 219-223). Lisse, Netherlands: Swets & Zeitlinger.

Hoare, R. M. N. (1983). The assessment of aptitude in black school beginners. *Humanitas-RSA, 9*, 175-180.

Hoehn, A. J. (1954). A study of social status differentiation in the classroom behaviour of nineteen third grade teachers. *Journal of Social Psychology, 39*, 269-292.

Horst, P. (1965). *The factor analysis of data matrices* (pp. 291-295). New York: Wiley.

Irvine, S. H. (1966). Towards a rationale for testing abilities and attainments in Africa. *British Journal of Educational Psychology, 36*, 24-32.

Irvine, S. H. (1969). The factor analysis of African abilities and attainments. *Psychological Bulletin, 71*, 20-32.

Irvine, S. H. (1979). The place of factor analysis in cross-cultural methodology and its contribution to cognitive theory. In L. H. Eckensberger, W. J. Lonner, & Y. H. Poortinga (Eds.), *Cross-cultural contributions to psychology.* Lisse, Netherlands: Swets & Zeitlinger.

Irvine, S. H. (1981). Culture, cognitive tests and cognitive models: pursuing cognitive universals by testing across cultures. In M. Friedman, J. P. Das, & N. O'Connor (Eds.), *Intelligence and learning*. New York: Plenum.

Irvine, S. H. (1988) Constructing the intellect of the Shona: A taxonomic approach. In J. W. Berry, S. H. Irvine & E. B. Hunt (Eds.), *Indigenous cognition* (pp.157-176). Dordrecht, Netherlands: Nijhoff.

Irvine, S. H. (1996, November). *Parametric measurement of persons: A very plausible alternative.* Paper presented at the International Military Testing Association Conference, San Antonio, Texas.

Irvine, S. H. (1998b). Personal profile analysis: technical handbook. Ormskirk, England, Thomas Lyster.

Irvine S. H., & Berry J.W. (1988). The abilities of mankind. In S. H. Irvine, & J. W. Berry (Eds.), *Human abilities in cultural context*. New York: Cambridge, University Press.

Irvine, S. H., Mettam, D., & Syrad, T. (1994). Valid and more valid? Keys to understanding personal appraisal processes at work. *Current Psychology, 13*, 27-59.

Jackson, P. (1968). *Life in classrooms*. New York: Holt, Rinehart & Winston.

Johnson, C. E., Wood, R., & Blinkhorn, S. F. (1988). Spirouser and Spiriouser: the use of ipsative personality tests. *Journal of Occupational Psychology, 61*, 153-162.

Klingelhofer, E. L. (1967). Performance of Tanzanian secondary school pupils on Raven's Standard Progressive Matrices. *Journal of Social Psychology, 72*, 205-215.

MacArthur, R. S., Irvine, S. H., & Brimble, A. R. (1964). *The Northern Rhodesia Mental Ability Survey*, Lusaka: Institute of Social Research, University of Zambia.

Messick, S. J. (1996). Bridging cognition and personality in education: The Role of style in performance and development. *Research Bulletin (RB_96_22)*, Educational Testing Service, Princeton, NJ.

Meyer, W. J., & Thompson, G. G. (1956). Sex differences in the distribution of teacher approval and disapproval among sixth grade children. *Journal of Educational Psychology, 47*, 385-397.

Munroe, R. L., & Munroe, R. H. (1971). Effect of environmental experience on spatial ability in an East African society. *Journal of Social Psychology, 83*, 15-22.

Omari, I. M., Drenth, P. J. D., & van der Flier, H. H. (1983). A Longitudinal study in predicting school performances in Tanzania. In S. H. Irvine & J.W. Berry (Eds.), *Human assessment and cultural factors* (pp. 635-649). New York: Plenum.

Owen, A. J. (1987). *An empirical investigation of the relationship between self-concept, perceived status and pupil academic achievement*. B.Sc. Honours Thesis, University of Plymouth, UK.

Ree, M. J. et al. (1995). Role of ability and prior knowledge in complex training performance. *Journal of Applied Psychology, 80*, 721-730.

Roberts, A. O. H. (1959). "Artifactor"–analysis: Some theoretical background and practical demonstrations. *Journal of the National Institute for Personnel Research , 7*, 168-188.

Roberts, A. O. H. (1963). Simple methods of deriving means, standard deviations and composite scores, with applications. *Psychologia Africana, 10*, 159-164.

Scanlan, M. R. (1984). *An investigation of the relationship between perceived approval and disapproval and pupil academic achievement*. B.Sc. Honours Thesis, University of Plymouth, England.

Spearman, C. (1927). *The abilities of man*. London: MacMillan.

Stephenson, W. (1939). Two contributions to the theory of mental testing. *British Journal of Psychology, 30*, 19-35 (Part 1: A new performance test for measuring abilities as correlation coefficients); and 230-247 (Part 2: A statistical regard of performance).

Swanepoel, H. F. (1975). *A psychometric investigation of the validity and use of the Guidance Test for Bantu pupils in form 3*. Unpublished doctoral dissertation Potchefstroom University, RSA.

Vernon, P. E. (1964). *Personality assessment*. London: Methuen.

16

Test-Taking Style, Personality Traits, and Psychometric Validity

Adrian Furnham
University College, London

Any test administrator who has done a group-administered ability, intelligence, or personality test cannot help being both surprised and impressed by the differences between how testees approach their task. With non-timed tests such as attitude or personality batteries, the first person to complete the task may do so in less than half the time that the last person dutifully hands in their booklet. Equally, with timed tests, some testees appear to approach the task with intense earnestness, as if their lives, or at least their careers, depended on it, whereas others appear cavalier, even nonchalant.

Many testees seem unhappy about forced-choice answers, particularly when it comes to personality. One reason for forced-choice answers (yes, no) is that testers have found that some testees use "can't decide" as an option quite excessively. Because "can't decide" is wasted data for the tester, these are avoided. But perhaps the greatest problem the personality and style (as opposed to ability) tester faces is the problem of dissimulation—subjects not giving honest answers.

This chapter considers three aspects of test-taking style—time taken, can't decide usage, and dissimulation. It is argued that there is evidence that these behavioral styles are indeed stable over time, consistent across situations, and unobtrusive measures of traits. First, the general concept of style in psychology is briefly discussed.

THE CONCEPT OF STYLE

The concept of style in psychology can be traced back to the 1920's (Wulf, 1922). It is probably true that the concept of cognitive style preceded others. Many of the early concepts were about information processing and were laboratory tested. Learning, teaching, and personality style, as well as the later styles (attrition, coping) were more broadly based, linking cognition and affect, but tending to be focused on specific areas of social behavior. Messick (1976) listed 19 cognitive style variables alone. Messick (1994) has argued that human activity displays both substance (content-level of performance) and style (manner-form of performance).

Consider the following list:

Attribution style	(Abramson, Seligman, & Teasdale, 1978)
Brain style	(Miller, 1997)
Cognitive style	(Witkin, Dyk, Faterson, Goodenough, & Karp, 1962)
Coping style	(Carver, Scheier, & Weintraub, 1989)
Learning style	(Honey & Mumford, 1982; Kolb, 1984)
Personality style	(Bannano & Sugar, 1990)
Teaching style	(Fischer & Fischer, 1979)

Each of these styles, particularly attribution and coping style in the clinical psychology literature, and learning and teaching style in the educational psychology literature, appears to have attracted a great deal of attention.

The idea of style, as opposed to traits, is intuitively appealing. Style seems to imply choice and, therefore, change. One can choose a learning style, adopt a cognitive style, and moderate an attributional style. Unlike the concept of ability or (biologically based) traits, one can choose a style. As Sternberg and Grigorenko (1997) claimed, in academic circles, styles have been out of fashion because of commercialism and also poor validity; yet, they asserted, without evidence, they are on the return.

Many personality and cognitive theorists and psychometricians have given up on stylistic concepts and measures. The field is fragmented, idiosyncratic, and egocentric. Psychometricians have been heard at conferences to argue that the style concept helps face, but not incremental, validity and that nearly all cognitive style concepts have (very) poor predictive validity. Others argue that the principle of parsimony dictates that we should spend less time developing new stylistic taxonomies and more on validating what we have. Still others point out that the popularity of a style measure (like the MBTI) is inversely correlated with the extent to which it measures neuroticism. Cynics have even been heard to say that "style" is politically correct speak for "trait."

It has never been very clear how abilities, traits, and styles differ. Many attempts have been made to distinguish abilities, traits, and styles. Sternberg and Grigorenko (1997) distinguished between the cognitive-centered, personality-centered and activity-centered approach. It has always been easier to distinguish ability from style, compared to personality and style (Messick, 1984; Tiedemann, 1989):

1. Ability questions refer to how much and what; style questions to how. Ability refers to what kind of information is being processed, by what operation, in what form, and how efficiently. Style refers to the manner or mode of cognition.

2. Ability implies maximal performance; style implies typical propensities. Ability is measured in terms of accuracy, correctness, and speed of response, whereas style emphasises the predominant or customary processing model.

3. Abilities are unipolar; style is usually bipolar. Ability levels range from none to a great deal, whereas styles usually have two different poles with quite different implications for cognitive functioning.

4. Abilities are value directional; styles are value differentiated. Usually, having more of an ability is considered better than having less, whereas supposed stylistic extreme poles have adaptive value but in different circumstances.

5. Abilities are often domain specific; styles cut across domains. Abilities are often specific to various domains (e.g., verbal, numerical, or spatial areas), whereas styles often serve as high-level heuristics.

6. Abilities are enabling variables because they facilitate task performance; styles are organizing and controlling variables. Abilities dictate level of performance, whereas styles contribute to the selection, combination, and sequencing of both topic and process.

The difference between traits and styles is, however, much less clear. Studies in the area suggest correlations between established traits (i.e., Extraversion-Neuroticism) and well measured styles (i.e., learning styles) to be in the $r = .20$ to $r = .40$ range (Furnham, 1992, 1996). Indeed, most styles are measured and thought about in trait-like terms (Furnham & Steele, 1993). To some extent, several researchers have attempted to integrate personality trait and style theory. However, as Messick (1994) noted, these efforts do not fulfil the aspiration of style theorists, who believe styles embrace personality *and* cognition. It is, of course, a moot point to argue that trait theorists themselves do not take cognizance of cognitive variables. Indeed, one could argue that there are cognitive theories of traits (e.g., neuroticism) that are based very heavily on cognitive analyses (Martin, Ward, & Clarke, 1983). Equally, other more well-established variables, such as extraversion, are often tested by use of cognitive tasks (Furnham & Bradley, 1997).

Furnham (1995) pointed out a number of unsatisfactorily answered problems for the issue of style:

- Aetiology of a cognitive-teaching style: The question arises as to their origin: Are they biologically based, the result of early learning, neither, or both? This is a fundamental question that must be answered to avoid tautology. To a large extent, however, aetiology determines both how and how much a style may be changed.

- Variance accounted for: Even if styles exist and determine, in part, the learning (however defined and measured) that takes place in social behavior, few would argue that they are the only-or even the most important-factor that determines learning. The question then needs to be asked whether the amount of variance accounted for by this factor is so small as to be trivial, or, indeed, a major and central factor. Do styles have incremental validity?

- The nature of style as a variable: If cognitive-learning style is a moderator variable between intelligence, personality and learning between intelligence, and personality and learning, the precise nature of this relationship needs to be spelled out. Indeed, it is necessary to list all relevant variables that relate to learning and specify how they interact. Despite the centrality of this question to this research endeavor, it has very rarely been asked and never satisfactorily answered.

- The process's underlying style: So far, a great deal of the research in this field has been descriptive and taxonomic, aimed at identifying various styles and their consequences. Less work has gone into describing the mechanism or process whereby the style operates.

He concluded:

> A pessimist might argue that despite fifty years of research into cognitive/learning style, we still know precious little if the above questions have not been answered or even attempted. An optimist, though, might be impressed by the research effort that has gone into this topic, by the proliferation of ideas, and by the evidence already accumulated. Nevertheless, pessimists sound more profound than optimists, and hence most recent reviewers in the field tend to be highly critical of developments in this area. (p. 411)

Messick (1994) likewise noted: "The literature on cognitive and learning styles is peppered with unstable and inconsistent findings, whereas style theory seems either vague in glossing over inconsistencies or confused in stressing differentiated features selectively" (p. 131).

Yet Sternberg and Grigorenko (1997) remained in favor of the style concept. They argued that thinking style is a subset of cognitive style, which itself is a subset of style (a distinctive-characteristic method-manner of acting-performing). They provided three explanations for why psychologists would be interested in cognitive styles, none of which have anything to do with predictive validity or parsimonious explanations. The first is that style bridges the concept of cognition and personality traits (especially neuroticism; Furnham & Cheng, 1996). Second, cognitive style added to measures of ability improve the predictability of school behavior, yet very little evidence is brought to bear that support's this assertion. Third, cognitive styles help explain occupational choice and performance. Yet again, any reviewer of this literature may be equally impressed by the poor predictive power of cognitive styles in the workplace (Furnham, 1992, 1994).

They then set out the five criteria for the evaluation of theories of style:

1. **Theoretical specification:** the positing of a reasonably complete, well-specified, and internally consistent theory of styles that makes connection with extant psychological theory.

2. **Internal validity:** a demonstration by factor analysis or some other method of internal analysis that the underlying structure of the item or subtest data is as predicted by the theory.

3. **Convergent external validity:** a demonstration that the measures of styles correlate with other measures with which, in theory, they should correlate.

4. **Discriminant external validity:** a demonstration that the measures of styles do not correlate with other measures with which, in theory, they could not correlate.

5. **Heuristic generativity:** the extent to which the theory has spawned, and continues to spawn, psychological research and ideally, practical application (p. 703).

Notice that all important predictive and construct validity is missing. Indeed, it is on this issue that most measures of style fail, or at least do not exceed trait measure. Thus, whereas it is often pointed out that the correlation between personality traits and social behavior rarely exceeds $r = .30$, it is frequently lower with cognitive styles. However, even using the same criteria, they are fairly critical of the work in cognitive- and personality-centered approaches to style.

Suffice it to say that the concept of style in psychological theory and measurement remains problematic. Indeed, it could be argued that because style affects many forms of social behavior—particularly in applied setting's like work and leisure—certain behaviors in the testing situation may themselves be indices of style. That is, how people complete tests, be they behavioral or self-report, may be a good individual difference measure, be it trait or style. This chapter focus's on this backwater of psychological research.

Test Taking Style

In this chapter, I consider the aspects of test-taking style, two that have been greatly underresearched, and one that has attracted a great deal of research. Each has been limited to questionnaire test taking in this review. First, the speed of test completion is discussed. Second, the use of "can't decides" will be discussed. Third, the theory and much researched notion of dissimulation is discussed.

Test-Taking Speed. Sternberg and Grigorenko (1997) noted the importance of two styles related to "conceptual tempo": reflectivity (pausing to think before beginning a task or making a decision) and impulsivity (responding quickly without forethought or consideration). They stated:

> Operationally, reflectivity and impulsivity typically has been measured by patterns of response latencies and errors on relatively simple, highly speeded tasks. Impulsive individuals tend to have minimal anxiety about committing errors, an orientation toward quick success rather than avoiding failure, relatively low performance standards, low motivation to master tasks, and little attention in monitoring of stimuli. (p. 703)

However, they asserted that this style is different from the impulsivity trait.

The advent of computerized test administration provides an easy and accurate way to measure speed of test taking. Stankov, Boyle, and Cattell (1995) argued that, in general, the speed of doing easy tasks shows higher correlations ($r =$ about .30) with intelligence, whereas speed of doing difficult tasks (power tests) shows little or no correlation. However, they also speculated about the relationship between personality and test taking speed:

> Personality factors such as extraversion–introversion may play an important role, in that the more introverted individual may work more slowly, but also more carefully and thoroughly (double-checking all answers, etc.). Speed scores may represent different things, depending on the perceived difficulty of the task, maybe stylistic or perhaps related to self-esteem, confidence or introversion may come into play when the task becomes difficult. (p. 27)

A limited number of studies have examined computer scored response materials and test scores. Although the studies by Merten and Ruch (1996) and Merten and Siebert (1997) did not replicate very well, they did establish (using the 60-item EPQ-R) that subjects took more time to respond to the P(sychoticism) and less to the N(euroticism) items. They reported a "slight trend" of high P and E scorers and low L scorers to respond faster to personality related items. However, they pointed out that their sample size (less than 100) was inadequate.

Holden and Hibbs (1995) attempted to measure faking on a personality test. They found test-item response latency would discriminate significantly (over 80% correct classification) between subjects instructed to respond honestly and those requested to answer so "as to maximize the likelihood of their being hired for a job." Naturally, it was found that respondents faking good scores took relatively longer than honest respondents to endorse unfavorable responses. They noted: "response latencies have been demonstrated to possess construct validity and to show consistent predictable associations with corresponding scale scores and independently derived criteria for university students, clinically referred children and psychiatric patients" (p. 369). They argued that measuring latency data is simple, acceptable and cheap, but most of all valid. Although advocating the use of latency measures for faking, they did point out three limitations:

> What is the true base rate of faking and how does this base rate affect the classification hit rate? What are the consequences of misclassifying an honest respondent as a faker? What are the costs of designating a faker as an honest respondent? (p. 371)

Furnham, Forde and Cotter (1998a) looked at the time taken by job applicants to complete the Eysenck Personality Profiler (EPP; Eysenck, Barrett, Wilson, & Jackson, 1992). They predicted that the length of time spent doing a test would be associated with extraversion (negatively), neuroticism (positively), and psychoticism (negatively). There is extensive research literature based on the arousal hypothesis that shows that extraverts trade off speed for accuracy (Eysenck, 1967). In addition, there is evidence that the obsessionality component associated with neurosis means that neurotics would take longer to consider most items, especially those concerned with abnormal behavior.

They found the amount of total time taken to complete the EPP was significantly correlated with E and P: Introverts and those scoring low on psychoticism took longer (see Table 16.1). Two primary factors from extraversion were correlated with time taken - inhibited and submissive people took longer. Predictably, the obsessive-casual primary factor from the neuroticism superfactor correlated with time taken—the more obsessive one is, the longer one takes. Five of the seven primary factors from the psychoticism superfactor were correlated with time taken, one negatively. They showed that the more careful, controlled, responsible, unadventurous, and practical subjects were, the longer they took to complete the questionnaire. Equally, more obsessive anxious neurotics tend to ponder questions longer before answering them.

TABLE 16.1
Group 1: Correlations Between the Three Test-Taking Styles and the EPP Primary and Higher Order Factors

EPP factors and subfactors		Test-taking style		
Low	High	Dissumulation	Time taken	Can't decide
1. Active	Inactive	−0.05	0.05	0.02
2. Sociable	Unsociable	0.01	0.04	0.00
3. Expressive	Inhibited	0.21***	0.12***	0.06*
4. Assertive	Submissive	−0.01	0.12***	0.02
5. Ambitious	Unambitious	−0.20***	−0.04	0.02
6. Dogmatic	Flexible	0.00	0.05	0.02
7. Aggressive	Peaceful	0.26***	0.02	0.04
Extraversion	**Introversion**	**0.04**	**0.09**∗∗	**0.05**
1. Inferiority	Self-esteem	0.19***	−0.02	-0.04
2. Unhappy	Happy	0.15***	−0.01	−0.04
3. Anxious	Calm	0.22***	0.02	0.00
4. Dependence	Autonomy	0.10***	0.01	0.01
5. Hypochondria	Sense of health	0.11***	−0.06	−0.02
6. Guilt	Guilt freedom	0.19***	−0.01	−0.02
7. Obsessive	Casual	−0.15***	−0.13**	−0.03
Neuroticism	**Stability**	**0.16**∗∗∗	**−0.04**	**0.07**∗
1. Risk taking	Careful	0.25***	0.18***	0.07*
2. Impulsive	Control	0.17***	0.19***	0.00
3. Irresponsible	Responsible	0.57***	0.09***	0.01
4. Manipulation	Empathy	0.29***	0.04	0.04
5. Sensation seeking	Unadventurous	0.20***	0.13***	0.06*
6. Tough-minded	Tender-minded	−0.06	0.02	0.01
7. Practical	Reflective	0.02	−0.10**	0.05
High psychoticism	**Low psychoticism**	**0.37**∗∗∗	**0.15**∗∗∗	**0.06**∗

$N = 811$
*$p < 0.05$.
**$p < .01$.
***$p < 0.001$.

These results suggest that test-response latency may be a useful unobtrusive measure of personality. Further, item-by-item analysis (as carried out by Merten & Siebert, 1997) may yield even more insights into what sort of question troubles what sort of personality type. These results do suggest that time taken may be not so much related to reflexivity (introversion) as neuroticism, and may, therefore, be a good, unobtrusive measure of it. The increasing use of computer-administered tests means that research into the unobtrusive measure of style will no doubt increase.

Indecisiveness. Some personality tests offer a "can't decide" (CD) or midpoint response as an alternative response to "yes, no, agree, disagree."

According to Jackson, Furnham, and Lawty-Jones (1998), choice of a CD in a personality test is unlikely to be similar to choosing a third (midpoint) item in a multiple-choice test (Sidick, Barrett, & Doverspike, 1994), in which an approximately uniform distribution could be expected, or a middle item in a three-point scale used in a survey or questionnaire in which a near normal distribution could be expected. Goldberg (1981) classified the mid response of a personality scale as being the result of one or more of at least four processes—neutrality, uncertainty, ambiguity, and situationality. Test takers may be neutral about a question and "yes" or "no" answers seem like extreme responses or the question has little relevance. Alternatively, the respondents may simply be unable to answer "yes" or "no" because they lack sufficient insight and thus are uncertain of their response. It also seems possible that ambiguous words in items may lead a test taker to answer with the CD option. Goldberg noted that respondents will choose to use a CD option if the respondent is not consistent enough in the particular situation described by the item. It seems likely that a CD option will be chosen when faced with two alternative extreme choices that are equally attractive or unattractive depending on the amount of item neutrality, uncertainty, ambiguity, and situationality.

According to Jackson et al. (1998), for some subjects, the use of CDs may relieve the conflict experienced when subjects are unable to decide between answering such items. The answers of "yes" or "no" represent classic "Approach–Approach" or "Avoidance–Avoidance" conflict as originally described by classic learning theorists. It is also possible that each alternative will contain both an attractive and an unattractive component ("Approach–Avoidance") in which there is conflict between and within each alternative answer.

In their study, they predicted and found that a total CD score was moderately positively correlated with neuroticism ($r = .24$), but that the size of the correlation varied substantially according to the occupational group of test takers. Furnham, Forde, and Cotter (1998b) reported a few overall relationships between personality scores with the (EPP Eysenck et al., 1992) and the total number of CD scores. A number of the 21 primary and two of the three superfactor scores were significantly correlated with the total CD score in a single large sample ($N = 811$). High CD scores were associated with low Psychoticism, Neuroticism, Unadventurousness, Carefulness, and being Inhibited. They were surprised that the CD score had little relationship to personality scores despite its possible relationship with response latency.

In decisiveness may well be related to response latency and tap into similar traits. Certainly, there seems to be evidence that indecisiveness is consistent across both tasks and situations, suggesting a stable trait or style. However, relatively little psychometric work has been done in this field save the growing interest in procrastination, which is one form of indecisiveness (Ferrari, Johnson, & McGowan, 1997).

Faking, Lying, and Dissimulation. There has been considerable interest in faking in questionnaires, no doubt because it threatens their validity (Birenbaum & Montag, 1989; Furnham, 1986, 1997; Helmes & Holden, 1986). Thus, Ones, Viswesvaran, and Reiss (1996) did a meta-analysis of social desirability scales in testing for personnel selection and were able to conclude "that social desirability (a) is not a predictor in its own right, (b) does not function as a worthwhile suppressed variable, and (c) does not mediate the relationship between personality and job performance" (p. 671).

Researchers using both self-report and non-self-report measures have pointed out that social desirability appears to be a trait rather than a response set. Because there are consistent, stable individual differences in social desirability that correlate meaningfully with other measures (usually of adjustment), it could be argued that social desirability is not a situation-specific response set that invalidates other measures. Maintaining that social desirability is a trait begs the question as to the aetiology of this trait and its relationship to other traits.

More recently, Mersman and Shultz (1998) found the ability to fake on questionnaires was an independent construct, unrelated to self-presentation. By arguing that social desirability is a trait rather than a response set does not, however, mean that all questionnaires are equally responsive to this trait or that people cannot simulate it. If social desirability is a clinical trait that measure things akin to adjustment, it is not surprising that social desirability correlates with neuroticism and so forth and that clinical measures are so susceptible to deliberate faking. However, it is not clear that those researchers who have devised lie–social desirability scales had a clear idea of the trait that they were measuring.

There has been consistent criticism of the concept of, and the scales devised to measure, social desirability. For instance, Wiggins (1962) accused the scales of "hypercommunality" in the sense that many of the items are answered in the same way by a high proportion of the responses, implying that they measure well-defined and social norms. Thus, a failure to match the populous response pattern is a correlate of all pathology scales and shows excessive asocial responses.

Many have pointed out the two-dimensional nature of socially desirable responding and there have been numerous factor-analytic studies since Messick (1976) found nine rather unclear factors. For instance, Milham (1974) identified two dimensions: attribution (tendency to attribute socially desirable characteristics) and denial (tendency to deny socially undesirable characteristics). Romanaiah, Schull, and Leung (1977) found empirical support for these dimensions, but subsequently, work by Romanaiah and Martin (1980) suggested that these two scales are really measuring the same construct, and the previous results were attributed to specific method variance in the unbalanced scales caused by keying directions. Paulus (1984) has, however, made another two-dimensional distinction, partitioning socially desirable responses into those involving self-deception, where the respondent actually believes his or her positive self-reports, and impression management, where the respondent consciously dissimulates. Many others have made similar distinctions. In three studies, he demonstrated the independence of these factors and argued that these results have strong implications for the control of socially desirable self-reports. Clearly, it is the impression-management factor that requires most control, as there is little reason to believe that differences on the dimension often bear any intrinsic relation to central content dimensions. However, the self-deception component is different and may reflect underlying self-images or cognitive styles that are both invariant and unconscious.

Thus it seems that if social desirability is a trait, it is multi- rather than uni-dimensional. However, these dimensions need to be verified empirically and to be demonstrably trait-like in their manifestations. Eysenck and Eysenck (1975) noted, "Too little is known at the moment about the Lie scale to make dogmatic statements possible" (p. 15).

Furnham (1997) argued that faking studies can prove useful for a number of reasons. First, they can reveal what a respondent (in general) believes to be desirable or normal. Similarly, faking can show an employer what a prospective employee thinks are the most desirable traits for the job. Second, faking studies may provide a useful template of typical faked responses that could be used to actually detect people lying in the questionnaire. On the other hand, there is increasing evidence from studies on the consistency and stability of socially desirable responses to suggest that it may have trait-like qualities that relate to naïveté. Furnham (1986) argued that the reason mental health measures are so susceptible to faking (and correlated with measure of social desirability) is that giving socially desirable responses could be, in and of itself, an index of mental illness. Thus, it is possible that if people fake application questionnaires, they are likely to be unreliable employees because they are mentally unstable or prone to ingratiation and dissimulation to achieve some end. Yet, it should be pointed out that participants who are able to fake in psychiatric settings are typically better adjusted. It is possible that some mild forms of faking good are highly appropriate for job applicants in that the total absence of efforts at distortion may have psychological correlates.

Further, the degree to which fake bad responses may be meaningfully differentiated from the responses of psychologically disturbed job applicants (who are answering the questionnaire honestly) and the degree to which fake good response patterns may be meaningfully differentiated from the response patterns of extremely well-adjusted applicants (who are responding to questionnaire items honestly) is not always clear. One could only claim to have found a characteristic fake bad and fake good response pattern when such patterns have been differentiated.

CONCLUSION

It has been suggested that the style in which people complete psychological tests (ability, intelligence, and personality) is not only reliable (being stable over time and consistent across situations) but also that it is systematically related to personality traits. If styles uniquely embracing personality and cognition can be observed and measured by overt behavior, it would certainly be reasonable to expect that test taking behavior would be systematically related to what is being measured.

More important, if personality and cognitive style are related to test-taking style, there may well be a relationship between personality and intelligence test scores. As Matthews and Dorn (1995) noted:

> Neglect of the role of task demands may explain the rather patchy nature of the correlational evidence on the relationship between ability, extraversion and neuroticism. Relatively simple verbal ability tests are sensitive to interactive effects of extraversion and arousal because of their dependence on low-level verbal processing, but other types of ability test may not show the effect. (p. 389)

As Furnham, Forde, and Cotter (1998a) noted, the length of an intelligence test and the extent to which a speed–accuracy trade-off is used in the scoring may be related to introversion and extraversion. It has been established many times that extraverts trade off speed for accuracy; the opposite is true for introverts. Further, introverts seem to do better on perseverance tasks. Thus, if a test is fairly brief (say 3 or 5 minutes) and speed may be rewarded more than accuracy, or at least may favor the trade off, it seems that extraverts may have an advantage. Yet if a test demands sustained attention over a fairly lengthy period and impulsive errors are significantly punished, introverts may have the advantage (Rawlings & Carnie, 1989; Rawlings & Skok, 1993).

In addition, a highly anxious (neurotic) individual may find that affect inhibits their cognitive style. This may occur both with trait and state anxiety, the latter occurring where the results of the test may be important for the individual, such as a job application. As well as neuroticism, conscientiousness (psychoticism) may be related to test-taking style and outcome. The conscientious individual is more likely to take the whole test procedure more seriously: following instructions, doing their best, and so forth, although a tough-minded individual (low agreeableness, conscientiousness, high openness to experience) may be tempted to cheat at tests and, hence, acquire dubiously high scores.

In their study, Furnham et al. (1998a) found scores on timed intelligence tests were associated with stability (rather than neuroticism), introversion (rather than extraversion), and tender (rather than tough) mindedness. Further, they found response latency and, to a lesser extent, dissimulation, were related to the test-taking score (see Table 16.2).

Thus, although it may be possible to differentiate between ability, personality, and style, the way each is measured may indeed affect the other. What is being proposed is that test-taking style is systematically related to intelligence and personality test scores. However, whereas the latter are difficult to change, it may indeed, through training, be possible to modify test-taking style, should it be judged desirable to do so.

TABLE 16.2
Partial Correlations Between Personality (EPP) and Intelligence
(Baddeley, 1968; Wonderlic, 1992; $N = 233$; partialling out sex and age)

| EPP factors and subfactors | | Baddeley Reasoning Test | | Wonderlic |
Low	High	N attempted	Total Correct	Total
1. Active	Inactive	−0.00	0.06	0.04
2. Sociable	Unsociable	−0.01	0.02	0.07
3. Expressive	Inhibited	−0.04	0.06	0.13*
4. Assertive	Submissive	−0.07	0.03	0.05
5. Ambitious	Unambitious	0.10	0.21***	0.24***
6. Dogmatic	Flexible	−0.03	0.21***	0.29***
7. Aggressive	Peaceful	0.00	0.09	0.12*
Extraversion	**Introversion**	−0.01	0.06	0.19**
1. Inferiority	Self-esteem	0.04	0.14*	0.16**
2. Unhappy	Happy	0.12*	0.17**	0.19**
3. Anxious	Calm	0.00	0.07	0.12*
4. Dependence	Autonomy	0.10	0.19***	0.24***
5. Hypochondria	Sense of health	0.12*	0.20***	0.22***
6. Guilt	Guilt freedom	0.07	0.16**	0.23***
7. Obsessive	Casual	0.11	0.19**	0.27***
Neuroticism	**Stability**	0.08	0.13*	0.39***
1. Risk taking	Careful	−0.13***	−0.02	0.00
2. Impulsive	Control	−0.04	0.13*	0.17**
3. Irresponsible	Responsible	−0.10	−0.13*	−0.13*
4. Manipulation	Empathy	−0.03	0.11	0.08
5. Sensation seeking	Unadventurous	−0.06	0.02	0.00
6. Tough-minded	Tender-minded	−0.03	−0.08	−0.03
7. Practical	Reflective	−0.04	0.00	0.04
High psychoticism	**Low psychoticism**	−0.12*	−0.03	−0.10
	Dissimulation	−0.06	−0.10	−0.18**
	Time taken	−0.35***	−0.36***	−0.18**
	Can't decide	−0.09	−0.10	−0.17**

*p < 0.05.
**p < 0.01.
***p < 0.001.

REFERENCES

Abramson, L., Seligman, M., & Teasdale, J. (1978). Learned helplessness in humans: Critique and reformulation. *Journal of Abnormal Psychology, 87,* 32–48.

Baddeley, A. (1986). A three-minute reasoning test-based on grammatical transformation. *Psychonomic Society, 10,*341-342.

Bannano, G., & Sugar, J. (1990). Repressive personality style: Theoretical and methodological implications for health and pathology. In J. Sugar (Ed.), *Repression and dissociation.* Chicago: Cambridge University Press.

Birenbaum, M., & Montag, I. (1989). Style and substance in social desirability scales. *European Journal of Personality, 3,* 47–59.

Carver, C., Scheier, M., & Weintrab, J. (1989). Assessing coping strategies: A theoretically based approach. *Journal of Personality and Social Psychology, 56,* 267-283.

Eysenck, H. J. (1967). *The biological basis of personality.* Springfield, OH: Thomas.

Eysenck, H., Barrett, P., Wilson, G., & Jackson, C. (1992). Primary trait measurement of the 21 components of the P-E-N system. *European Journal of Psychological Assessment, 8,* 109–117.

Eysenck, H., & Eysenck, S. (1975). *The Eysenck personality questionnaire.* London: Hodder & Stoughton.

Ferrari, J., Johnson, J., & McGowan, W. (1995). *Procrastination and task avoidance.* New York: Plenum.

Fischer, B., & Fischer, L. (1979). Styles in teaching and learning. *Educational Leadership, 36,* 245–254.

Furnham, A. (1986). Response bias, social desirability and dissimulation. *Personality and Individual Differences, 7,* 385–400.

Furnham, A. (1992). Personality and learning style: A study of three instruments. *Personality and Individual Differences, 13,* 429–438.

Furnham, A. (1994). *Personality at work.* London: Routledge.

Furnham, A. (1995). The relationship of personality and intelligence to cognitive learning style and achievement. In D. Saklofske & M. Zeidner (Eds.), *International handbook of personality and intelligence* (pp. 397-413.) New York: Plenum.

Furnham, A. (1996). The FIRO-B, the Learning Style Questionnaire and the Five-Factor Model. *Journal of Social Behaviour and Personality, 11,* 285–299.

Furnham, A. (1997). Knowing and faking one's personality score. *Journal of Personality Assessment, 69,* 229–243.

Furnham, A., & Bradley, A. (1997). Music while you work. *Applied Cognitive Psychology, 11,* 445–455.

Furnham, A., & Cheng, H. (1996). Psychiatric symptomatology and the recall of positive and negative personality information. *Behaviour Research and Therapy, 34,* 731–733.

Furnham, A., & Steele, H. (1993). Measuring locus of control. *British Journal of Psychology, 84,* 443–479.

Furnham, A., Forde, L., & Cotter, T. (1998a). Personality and test taking style. *Personality and Individual Differences, 24,* 19–23.

Furnham, A., Forde, L., & Cotter, T. (1998b). Personality and intelligence. *Personality and Individual Differences, 24,* 187–192.

Goldberg, L. (1981). Unconfoundedly situational attributions from uncertain, neutral and ambiguous ones. *Journal of Personality and Social Psychology, 41,* 517–552.

Helmes, E., & Holden, R. (1986). Response styles and faking on the basic personality inventory. *Journal of Consulting and Clinical Psychology, 54,* 853–859.

Holden, R., & Hibbs, N. (1995). Incremental validity of response latencies for detecting fakes on a personality test. *Journal of Research and Personality, 29,* 362–372.

Honey, P., & Mumford, A. (1982). *The manual of learning styles.* Maidenhead: Honey Press.

Jackson, C., Furnham, A., & Lawty-Jones, M. (1999). Relationship between indecisiveness and neuroticism: The moderating effect of a tough-minded culture. *Personality and Individual Differences, 27,* 789–800.

Kolb, D. (1976). *Learning style inventory*. Technical Manual. Boston: McBer.

Kolb, D. (1984). *Experimental learning*. Englewood Cliffs, NJ: Prentice-Hall.

Martin, M., Ward, K., & Clarke, D. (1983). Neuroticism and the recall of positive and negative personality information. *Behaviour Research and Therapy, 21*, 495–502.

Matthews, G., & Dorn, L. (1995). Cognitive and attentional processes in personality and intelligence. In D. Saklofske & M. Zeidner (Eds.), *International handbook of personality and intelligence* (pp. 367–396). London: Plenum.

Mersman, J., & Shultz, K. (1998). Individual differences in the ability to fake on personality measures. *Personality and Individual Differences, 24*, 217–227.

Merten, T., & Ruch, W. (1996). A comparison of computerised and conventional administration of the German version of the Eysenck Personality Questionnaire and the Carnell Rating Scale for Depression. *Personality and Individual Differences, 20*, 281–291.

Merten, T., & Siebert, K. (1997). A comparison of computerised and conventional administration of the EPQ-R and the CRS. *Personality and Individual Differences, 20*, 283–286.

Messick, S. (Ed). (1976). *Individuality and learning*. San Francisco: Jossey-Bass.

Messick, S. (1984). The nature of cognitive styles: Problems and promise in educational practice. *Educational Psychologist, 19*, 59–74.

Messick, S. (1994). The matter of style: Manifestations of personality in cognition, learning and teaching. *Educational Psychologist, 29*, 121–136.

Millham, J. (1974). Two components of need for approval score and their relationship to cheating following success and failure. *Journal of Research in Personality, 8*, 378–392.

Miller, M. (1997). *Brain styles*. New York: Simon Schuster.

Ones, D., Viswesvaran, C., & Reiss, A. (1996). Role of social desirability in personality testing for personnel selection. *Journal of Applied Psychology, 81*, 660–679.

Paulus, D. (1984). Two component model of socially desirable responding. *Journal of Personality and Social Psychology, 46*, 598–609.

Rawlings, D., & Carnie, D. (1989). The interaction of EPQ extraversion and WAIS subtest performance under timed and untimed conditions. *Personality and Individual Differences, 10*, 453–458.

Rawlings, D., & Skok, M. (1993). Extraversion, venturesomeness and intelligence in children. *Personality and Individual Differences, 15*, 389–396.

Romanaiah, N., & Martin, H. (1980). On the two-dimensional nature of the Marlowe-Crowne Social Desirability Scale. *Journal of Personality Assessment, 44*, 507–514.

Romanaiah, N., Schull, J., & Leung, L. (1997). A test of the hypothesis about the two-dimensional nature of the Marlowe-Crowne Social Desirability Scale. *Journal of Research in Personality, 11*, 251–259.

Sidick, J., Barrett, G., & Doverspike, D. (1994). Three alternative multiple choice tests: An attractive option. *Personnel Psychology, 47*, 829–835.

Stankov, L., Boyle, G., & Cattell, R. (1995). Models and paradigms in personality and intelligence research. In D. Saklofske & M. Zeidner (Eds.), *International handbook of personality and intelligence* (pp. 15–47). New York: Plenum.

Sternberg, R., & Grigorenko, E. (1997). Are cognitive styles still in style? *American Psychologist, 52*, 700–712.

Tiedemann, J. (1989). Measures of cognitive styles: A critical review. *Educational Psychologist, 24*, 261–275.

Witkin, H., Dyk, R., Faterson, H., Goodenough, D., & Karp, S. (1962). *Psychological differentiation*. New York: Wiley.

Wiggins, J. (1962). Strategic method and stylistic variance in the MMPI. *Psychological Bulletin, 69*, 224–242.

Wonderlic, E. (1992). *Wonderlick Personnel Test*. Illinois: Libertyville Press.

Wulf, F. (1922). Uber die veranderung von vorstellungen [gedachtins und gestalt]. *Psychologische Forschung, 1*, 333–373.

PART IV

INTELLIGENCE AND PERSONALITY IN CONTEXT

17

Persons in Context: Defining the Issues, Units, and Processes

Lawrence A. Pervin
Rutgers University

In this chapter, I consider a number of issues of longstanding concern to the field of personality as well as to me personally. In their broadest terms, the issues involve fundamental conceptualizations of personality. Therefore, at the outset, let me state my own definition of the field and what I see as the major task that lies ahead. Concerning definition, two definitions of the field of personality have been common, the first emphasizing individual differences and the second, the organization of the parts into a dynamically functioning whole (Pervin & John, 1997). My own view of personality is of the latter type, defining personality as the study of how the various parts of the person interact to form a dynamic system. Of course, there are individual differences and the study of such differences is recognized as an important area of inquiry. However, I am suggesting that what is distinctive about the field of personality is its emphasis on the more or less integrated functioning of a dynamic system.

In this emphasis, I am in agreement with other personality psychologists who take what has been called a holistic approach (Magnusson, 1990, 1997). From this perspective, it seems to me that the fundamental issue for the personality psychologist is an understanding of the coherence of personality; that is, an understanding of the ways in which the different parts of the personality system interact with one another and with external contexts to produce adaptive and maladaptive functioning. Thus, within this holistic perspective, there is clear recognition of the importance of situational contexts. Indeed, a major issue of concern to me is an understanding of the coherence of personality in terms of how a complex system adapts to changing circumstances while maintaining a cohesive structure. It is the person as a dynamic system that remains the focal point of interest.

THE CONTEXTUALIZATION OF PERSONALITY

An issue of historical concern to personality psychologists has been the relation between internal and external determinants of behavior (Pervin, 1978, 1990). Allport (1955) found the issue of whether behavior is governed from within or without, above all others, divided psychologists. In more recent times, it reached the peak of controversy in the unfortunate person–situation controversy, precipitated by Mischel's (1968) attack on the "traditional" personality view (i.e., psychoanalytic theory and trait theory) of broad consistencies in behavior over time and across situations. Although the controversy appears to have lessened, fundamental differences in conceptualization remain. For example, trait theorists, in the five-factor model (McCrae & Costa, 1990) reincarnation of traditional trait theory, continue to emphasize broad consistencies in behavior, whereas Mischel (1990; Mischel & Shoda, 1995) argued for the contextualization of behavior and Kagan (1996) challenged the "pleasing idea" of broad generalizations across contexts.

It is easy to fall prey to the perception of oneself as either a trait person or a contextualist. In taking a dynamic systems perspective (Pervin, 1989), I consider myself as residing in neither camp. However, for a variety of reasons, a few research projects of mine have considered the contextualization of personality functioning. This was clear in my early research on individual–environment interaction, to which I return, as well as in my interest in understanding the ways in which people are both stable and varying in relation to situational contexts. For example, in one study of consistency and variability in personality functioning, subjects selected situations in their daily lives; developed lists of situation characteristics, feelings in situations, and behaviors in situations; and then rated the relevance of the situation characteristics, feelings, and behaviors to each situation (Pervin, 1976). The research was idiographic in that all situations, situation characteristics, feelings, and behaviors were generated by the individual subject. The question addressed was: In what ways is the person stable and in what ways varying as a function of which situational characteristics? To consider the results of one subject, Jennifer reported that she *always* was sensitive, vulnerable, and insightful, and almost always friendly, warm, and accepting. However, many aspects of her functioning varied according to such situational contexts as home, school, and with friends; each associated in her mind with specific situational characteristics. Thus, for example, she described herself as caring and concerned but also confused and suppressed in volatile home situations, as determined, cool, and compulsive in school and work situations where she experienced pressure to perform, and as concerned, caring, emotional, and responsive in relaxed situations with friends.

I later engaged a group of students in comparing various approaches to personality through studying themselves as individual cases. Each student took personality tests associated with various theoretical approaches to personality and then considered relations among the theories and data in terms of his or her own personality. In one part of this research, students completed self-ratings on 24 semantic differential scales, each scale containing seven points. This constituted the General Self. Following this they described representative situations in six categories (Home, School, Work, Peers-Recreation, Self at Best, Self at Worst) and rated themselves on the same seven-point semantic differential scales for each of the situations. Not surprisingly, there was clear evidence of variability of self-ratings by context (Home, School, Work, Recreation) and between Self at Best and Self at Worst.

One might argue that such variability reflects the norms of behavior for different contexts and that there are common characteristics to functioning at one's best as opposed to one's worst. Such a point of view, however, masks the enormous differences among subjects. Whereas some subjects report relative consistency across contexts, others report great variability across contexts—what has been referred to as an important individual difference variable of intraindividual variability (Roberts & Nesselroade, 1986). And, although some subjects report relative consistency across the four contexts, they may also report wide fluctuations between their functioning at their best and at their worst.

Although there are many self at best-self at worst differences that hold true for all subjects (e.g., more relaxed, organized, and extraverted in the former and more tense, disorganized, introverted in the latter), perhaps reflecting a social desirability element in the ratings, there also were many individual differences. For example, some subjects viewed themselves as too dependent at their worst, whereas others saw themselves as too independent, some as too submissive and others as too dominant. In other words, subjects tended to differ in their pattern of best–worst functioning. Such patterns reflect the interplay between adaptive and maladaptive resources, an important component of personality functioning.

Before considering the significance of such results, it is worth noting that the ratings of the General Self had no consistent relation to the contextual ratings. That is, although in some cases the ratings of the General Self appeared to reflect some combination of ratings across the contexts, in other cases, they appeared to follow no identifiable pattern. Indeed, in some cases the ratings for General Self were more extreme (i.e., higher or lower) than the self-ratings for any specific context, a response that is understandable within the Gestalt emphasis on the whole as different from the sum of the parts but perhaps difficult to otherwise comprehend. One may ask, then, just what is being rated when subjects give an overall rating to themselves. The General Self does not appear to express what is most consistent or representative across situations, as one trait colleague suggested, nor does it necessarily express a prototypic self or family of selves, as some social cognitive theorists suggest (Cantor & Kihlstrom, 1987). In attempting to understand the meaning of these general self-ratings, I am led to the conclusion that their organization is idiosyncratic, often involving representations of feelings rather than overt behaviors, representations more relevant to the past than the present.

These data have obvious implications for personality theory. Clearly, they raise questions concerning a pure trait view of personality. Although one could argue that the data reflect unreliability of single ratings on single scales, they are consistent with Cervone's (1997) study of self-efficacy beliefs and Shoda, Mischel, and Wright's (1994) behavioral observations in the natural environment. Although some researchers report significant self-observer correlations for trait ratings (Funder, 1980; John & Robins, 1994; Kenny, 1994; McCrae & Costa, 1990) and observers in different contexts more or less know "the same person" (Funder, Kolar, & Blackman, 1995, p. 661), in fact, context clearly makes a difference in self-observer agreement in ratings. Judges of a person in the same context clearly agree more about his or her personality than do judges of the person in different contexts. Thus, it can be suggested that both trait ratings and self-observer agreement reflect the most general stability in personality functioning that can be found across individuals and contexts. This stability is important and should be recognized. However, such views also fail to recognize the evidence of considerable contextual specificity in personality functioning. People function as dynamic systems, stable in some ways and varying in other ways, with the exact nature of the stability and variability differing in terms of the individuals and contexts involved.

PERSON–ENVIRONMENT INTERACTION

Evidence of the importance of context in personality functioning has led many to take an interactionist position. My own early thinking and research was influenced by Murray's (1938) need-press model. As a graduate student in his seminar, I well remember his story of the Harvard student who experienced enormous psychological stress and poor psychological health in the college environment but who functioned extremely well as a pilot on an aircraft carrier, making the point that what was stressful for one person was not stressful for another. This is a view championed by Lazarus (1993) and other stress researchers, although some continue to take a trait point of view (Watson & Hubbard, 1996).

My first research after graduate school involved the study of student-college interaction. Originally designed to consider academic and psychological functioning in terms of student needs and the college press, it took a turn toward studying perceived self-environment similarity when I discovered that the tests then assumed to measure parallel aspects of the person and the college environment, the Activities Index and the College Characteristics Index, did not do so. In any case, this research led to the findings of very consistent relations between perceived self–college similarity and satisfaction with nonacademic aspects of college, with students with self-perceived characteristics unhappy at one environment being happy at another, and vice versa (Pervin, 1967). The data seemed overwhelmingly supportive of Cronbach's (1957) dictum that "the organism which adapts well under one condition would not survive under another. If for each environment there is a best organism, for every organism there is a best environment" (p. 679). The data also seemed to fit with considerable evidence indicating that performance and satisfaction might best be understood within an interactionist, individual–environment fit model (Pervin, 1968).

A number of interactionist models have been considered, both in terms of what the person is interacting with in the environment and in terms of the meaning of interaction (Pervin, 1978, 1989). As noted previously in relation to student–college interaction, perceived similarity is one type of relationship between individuals—and between individuals and environments—that has been found to be of some importance (Pervin, 1968). Such studies, however, depend exclusively on self-reports and do not explain why similarity should make a difference.

Another model is the ability or competence times task requirement model, what might be described as a lock and key model. This model has obvious relevance to the educational and industrial settings but it also has been applied to the personality realm, where personality is defined in terms of abilities or competencies (Goldfried & D'Zurilla, 1969; Wallace, 1966). A relevant study of my own involved analysis of academic performance in terms of the relation between cognitive style and subject matter task requirements. In this study a relation was found between concrete cognitive style and good performance in engineering, whereas an abstract style was found to be related to good performance in the social sciences and humanities (Pohl & Pervin, 1968). In other words, neither cognitive style was found to be superior in and of itself but rather, performance was best understood in terms of the interaction between cognitive style and task requirements. Witkin (1973) similarly noted a relation between cognitive style and academic performance as well as a relation between cognitive style and student–teacher relations.

Personality variables have also been suggested to be of importance in relation to career choice and occupational performance (Dawis & Lofquist, 1984; Holland, 1985, 1987). Trait theory has experienced a resurgence of popularity in terms of the five-factor model, and the suggestion has been made that "personality measures when classified within the Big Five domains, are systematically related to a variety of criteria of job performance" (Goldberg, 1993, p. 31). The Barrick and Mount (1991) study is often referenced as demonstrating such a relationship between traits and job performance, particularly in relation to the traits of conscientiousness and agreeableness. At the same time, it should be noted that the incremental validities of such personality variables over cognitive measures is moderate, they are more often related to subjective evaluations of supervisors than objective measures of performance, and the relation between them and performance varies as a function of occupation (Barrick, Mount, & Strauss, 1993; Hough, 1992; Pervin, 1994; Schmidt, Ones, & Hunter, 1992).

A third approach to individual–environment interaction has been to consider the relation between individual goals and environmental affordances, an approach that can be traced back to Murray's (1938) need-press model (Cantor, 1994; Pervin, 1983, 1987, 1989a). This approach has particular appeal to me because it is a more dynamic, process-oriented representation of individual –environment relations than many other models and because it has ties to broader goal theories in personality and social psychology (Austin & Vancouver, 1996; Gollwitzer & Bargh, 1996; Pervin, 1989b). As I have indicated elsewhere, the goals-affordances model provides for analysis of whether various goals and plans are adaptive to the environment and how restrictive the environment is in terms of what is reinforced. It also has received empirical support (Pervin, 1989a).

Although such models of individual–environment interaction have considerable appeal to me, a variety of fundamental problems remain. Many of these have been noted in the past (Pervin, 1968, 1978). As Snow (1994) noted, the task of modeling personality–environment interactions remains an overarching problem. First, there is the question of which units of the person and the environment are to be measured. Is there any theoretical basis for deciding which person and situation characteristics are generally important, or important in particular sets of circumstances, or are findings to be on a completely ad hoc basis in this regard? Some individuals favor the development of taxonomies of persons and situations (Frederiksen, 1972; Magnusson, 1971; van Heck, 1989). This is not an approach that I favor because it fails to recognize the idiosyncratic organization of situations on the part of the person and the multidimensional, dynamic nature of situational encounters. Although it is possible to factor analyze situations or situation characteristics as person characteristics are factor analyzed, I am struck with the idiosyncratic meanings of situations for people. Not only that, but the perception of situations is multidimensional and often fluid in nature. What I mean by the former is that a situation need not necessarily be business or social but can involve elements of both. What I mean by the latter is that the emphasis on business and on social can shift frequently in the course of an individual–environment engagement.

Even the very nature of the categories individuals use in relation to situations can be very fluid (Pervin, 1981). I recall here the interaction with a subject who was being asked to develop a hierarchical classification of the situations he had generated. Following the instructions, he grouped situations together into increasingly fewer, higher order categories. When he completed the task, he noted that he had a couple of choice points that gave him some trouble; that is, he could have continued with one or another categorizing scheme, either of which made sense to him. To me, this speaks to the multidimensional, fluid nature of such categories.

The broadest point to consider is why these models, which appear to make such good sense, have not been more successful. As Messick (1996) noted in relation to the educational setting, the promise of utilizing a match between cognitive style and instructional method has not been fulfilled. Although he emphasized value issues as well as technical difficulties, the latter certainly are formidable. For example, there is evidence that various congruence measures do not agree with one another and result in different conclusions concerning individual–environment relationships (Camp & Chartrand, 1992; Spokane, 1985). As was concluded, "clearly the state of the art in congruence computation and prediction needs more science" (Lent & Lopez, 1996, p. 36). Perhaps our measures need to be more complex. Thus, for example, Gustafson and Mumford (1995) advocated a profile or pattern approach to personality and environmental variables. This remains, however, a promise to be fulfilled. In the meantime, major difficulties remain.

LOOKING FOR THE PERSON IN CONTEXT

Over the years, I have become increasingly impressed with the contextualization of behavior and the idiosyncratic nature of individual perceptions of situations. I have been struck with the importance of cultural differences and taken seriously the suggestions of some that meaning is all important in human behavior but meaning is highly idiosyncratic (Shweder, 1990). At the same time, I believe that a science of personality is possible and that regularities can be found that do not regress to principles of biological functioning. Where, then, are such regularities to be found? The question may be asked as: Given the contextualization of behavior and the idiosyncratic ways in which individuals perceive situations, where should we be looking for personality regularities?

At one point this question took me to an emphasis on goals as a way of conceptualizing the stasis and flow of behavior (Pervin, 1983). This conceptualization still makes sense to me as a way of viewing the person as a dynamic system and as a way of considering individual-environment transactions. However, strangely enough, beyond this I am led to focus increasingly on aspects of the personality system itself, independent of content and context. Thus, for example, increasingly I have become interested in the question of *processes* of personality functioning, thereby emphasizing change rather than stability.[1] In addition, I have become interested in whether such characteristics as complexity of the system, degree of integration or conflict within the system, and flexibility or rigidity of system functioning might be meaningful personality variables. Of course, to understand any person, such as when I attempt to understand a patient, knowledge of the content of the system is going to be essential. However, again, such content is likely to be highly idiosyncratic and not a useful basis for a science of personality.

The closest analogy I can come up with is Kelly's (1955) personal construct theory. For Kelly, a person was his or her constructs and individuals are very idiosyncratic in their constructs as well as in the organization and application of these constructs. At the same time, Kelly (1955) suggested that certain principles of construct functioning held true for all people (e.g., everyone attempts to predict events, everyone experiences anxiety when their constructs do not apply to situations, etc.). Constructs within the person were organized to form a construct system, and individual differences could be considered not only in terms of content but also in terms of characteristics of the organization of the construct system (e.g., complex-simple) and characteristics of construct-system functioning (e.g., permeability of constructs, loosening and tightening of predictions). In other words, his view was idiographic in its emphasis on content but nomothetic in its emphasis on principles of construct system functioning. The person has a construct system, providing some stability (i.e., structure), but the system also is dynamic in that different constructs apply to different situations and become more or less important in different contexts.

---

[1]At a recent conference, John Nesselroade, in his role as discussant, similarly raised the question of the implications of emphasizing change and, further, asked about statistical models of person functioning that took change rather than stability as the norm.

In sum, context clearly is important and the person is virtually always interacting with some aspect of the environment, whether that environment is interpersonal or noninterpersonal, real or imagined. We can probably never really know the individual without knowledge of the content of that interaction, involving characteristics of the person, the environment, and the transactions between the two. However, a science of personality may need to be based on principles of person–system functioning, involving engagement with and adaptation to changing internal and external environmental contingencies, that are content and context free.

REFERENCES

Allport, G. W. (1955). *Becoming: Basic considerations for a psychology of personality.* New Haven, CT: Yale University Press.

Austin, J. T., & Vancouver, J. B. (1996). Goal constructs in psychology: Structure, process and content. *Psychological Bulletin, 120,* 338–375.

Barrick, M. R., & Mount, M. K. (1991). The Big Five personality dimensions and job performance: A meta-analysis. *Personnel Psychology, 44,* 1–26,

Barrick, M. R., Mount, M. K., & Strauss, J. P. (1993). Conscientiousness and performance of sales representatives: Test of the mediating effects of goal setting. *Journal of Applied Psychology, 76,* 715–722.

Cantor, N. (1994). Life task problem solving: Situational affordances and personal needs. *Personality and Social Psychology Bulletin, 20,* 235–243.

Cantor, N., & Kihlstrom, J. F. (1987). *Personality and social intelligence.* Englewood Cliffs, NJ: Prentice-Hall.

Camp, C. C., & Chartrand, J. M. (1992). A comparison and evaluation of interest congruence indices. *Journal of Vocational Behavior, 41,* 161–182.

Cervone, D. (1997). Social-cognitive mechanisms and personality coherence: Self-knowledge, situational beliefs, and cross-situational coherence in perceived self-efficacy. *Psychological Science, 8,* 43–50.

Cronbach, L. J. (1957). The two disciplines of scientific psychology. *American Psychologist, 12,* 671–684.

Dawis, R. V., & Lofquist, L. H. (1984). *A psychological theory of work adjustment.* Minneapolis: University of Minnesota Press.

Frederiksen, N. (1972). Toward a taxonomy of situations. *American Psychologist, 27,* 114–123.

Funder, D. C. (1980). On seeing ourselves as others see us: Self-other agreement and discrepancy in personality ratings. *Journal of Personality, 48,* 473–493.

Funder, D. C., Kolar, D. C., & Blackman, M. C. (1995). Agreement among judges of personality: Interpersonal relations, similarity, and acquaintanceship. *Journal of Personality and Social Psychology, 69,* 656–672.

Goldberg, L. R. (1993). The structure of phenotypic personality traits. *American Psychologist, 48,* 26–34.

Goldfried, M. R., & D'Zurilla, T. J. (1969). A behavioral-analytical model for assessing competence. In C. D. Spielberger (Ed.), *Current topics in clinical and community psychology* (pp.151–196). New York: Academic Press.

Gollwitzer, P. M., & Bargh, J. A. (Eds.). (1996). *The psychology of action.* New York: Guilford.

Gustafson, S. B., & Mumford, M. D. (1995). Personal style and person–environment fit: A pattern approach. *Journal of VocationalBehavior, 46,* 163–188.

Holland, J. L. (1985). *Making vocational choices: A theory of careers.* Englewood Cliffs, NJ: Prentice-Hall.

Holland, J. L. (1987). Some speculation about the investigation of person-environment transactions. *Journal of Vocational Behavior, 31,* 337–340.

Hough, L. M. (1992). The "Big Five" personality variables—Construct confusion: Description versus prediction. *Human Performance, 5,* 139–155.

John, O. P., & Robins, R. W. (1994). Accuracy and bias in self-perception: Individual differences in self-enhancement and the role of narcissism. *Journal of Personality and Social Psychology, 66,* 206-219.

Kagan, J. (1996). Three pleasing ideas. *American Psychologist, 51,* 901–908.

Kelly, G. A. (1955). *The psychology of personal constructs.* New York: Norton.

Kenny, D. A. (1994). *Interpersonal perception: A social relations analysis.* New York: Guilford.

Lazarus, R. S. (1993). From psychological stress to the emotions: A history of changing outlooks. *Annual Review of Psychology, 44,* 1–21.

Lent, E. B., & Lopez, F. G. (1996). Congruence from many angles: Relations of multiple congruence indices to job satisfaction among adult workers. *Journal of Vocational Behavior, 49,* 24–37.

Magnusson, D. (1971). An analysis of situational dimensions. *Perceptual and Motor Skills, 32,* 851–867.

Magnusson, D. (1990). Personality development from an interactional perspective. In L. A. Pervin (Ed.), *Handbook of personality: Theory and research* (pp. 193–222). New York: Guilford.

Magnusson, D. (1997). The person in developmental research. *Reports from the Department of Psychology (Stockholm University), Number 830.*

McCrae, R. R., & Costa, P. T., Jr. (1990). *Personality in adulthood.* New York: Guilford.

Messick, S. (1996). Bridging cognition and personality in education: The role of style in performance and development. *European Journal of Personality, 10,* 353–376.

Mischel, W. (1968). *Personality and assessment.* New York: Wiley.

Mischel, W. (1990). Personality dispositions revisited and revised: A view after three decades. In L. A. Pervin (Ed.), *Handbook of personality: Theory and research* (pp. 111–134). New York: Guilford.

Mischel, W., & Shoda, Y. (1995). A cognitive–affective system theory of personality: Reconceptualizing situations, dispositions, dynamics, and invariance in personality structure. *Psychological Review, 102,* 246–268.

Murray, H. A. (1938). *Explorations in personality.* New York: Oxford University Press.

Pervin, L. A. (1967). A twenty-college study of student-college interaction using TAPE (Transactional Analysis of Personality and Environment): Rationale, reliability, and validity. *Journal of Educational Psychology, 58,* 290–302.

Pervin, L. A. (1968). Performance and satisfaction as a function of individual-environment fit. *Psychological Bulletin, 69,* 56–68.

Pervin, L. A. (1976). A free-response description approach to the analysis of person-situation interaction. *Journal of Personality and Social Psychology, 34,* 465-474.

Pervin, L. A. (1978). Theoretical approaches to the analysis of individual-environment interaction. In L. A. Pervin & M. Lewis (Eds.), *Perspectives in interactional psychology* (pp. 67–85). New York: Plenum.

Pervin, L. A. (1981). The relation of situations to behavior. In D. Magnusson (Ed.), *Toward a psychology of situations* (pp. 343–360). Hillsdale, NJ: Lawrence Erlbaum Associates.

Pervin, L. A. (1983). The stasis and flow of behavior: Toward a theory of goals. In M. M. Page (Ed.), *Personality: Current theory and research* (pp. 1–53). Lincoln: University of Nebraska Press.

Pervin, L. A. (1987). Person–environment congruence in the light of the person-situation controversy. *Journal of Vocational Behavior, 31*, 222–230.

Pervin, L. A. (1989b). Psychodynamic-systems reflections on a social intelligence model of personality. *Advances in Social Cognition, 2*, 153–161.

Pervin, L. A. (1989a). Goal concepts in personality and social psychology: A historical perspective. In L. A. Pervin (Ed.), *Goal concepts in personality and social psychology* (pp. 1–17). Hillsdale, NJ: Lawrence Erlbaum Associates.

Pervin, L. A. (1990). A brief history of modern personality theory. In L. A. Pervin (Ed.), *Handbook of personality: Theory and research* (pp. 1–18). New York: Guilford.

Pervin, L. A. (1994). A critical analysis of current trait theory. *Psychological Inquiry, 5*, 103–113.

Pervin, L. A., & John, O. P. (1997). *Personality: Theory and research* (7th ed.). New York: Wiley.

Pohl, R. L., & Pervin, L. A. (1968). Academic performance as a function of task requirements and cognitive style. *Psychological Reports, 22,* 1017–1020.

Roberts, M. L., & Nesselroade, J. (1986). Intraindividual variability in perceived locus of control in adults: P-technique factor analyses of short-term change. *Journal of Research in Personality, 20,* 529–545.

Schmidt, F. L., Ones, D. S., & Hunter, J. E. (1992). Personnel selection. *Annual Review of Psychology, 43,* 627–670.

Shoda, Y., Mischel, W., & Wright, J. C. (1994). Intra-individual stability in the organization and patterning of behavior: Incorporating psychological situations into the idiographic analysis of personality. *Journal of Personality and Social Psychology, 67,* 674–687.

Shweder, R. A. (1990). Cultural psychology—What is it? In J. W. Stigler, R. A. Shweder, & G. Herdt (Eds.), *Cultural psychology: Essays in comparative human development* (pp. 1–43). Cambridge, England: Cambridge University Press.

Snow, R. E. (1994). Foreword. In D. H. Saklofske & M. Zeidner (Eds.), *International handbook of personality and intelligence* (pp. xi–xv). New York: Plenum.

Spokane, A. R. (1985). A review of research on personality–environment congruence in Holland's theory of careers. *Journal of Vocational Behavior, 26,* 306–343.

van Heck, G. L. (1989). Situation concepts: Definitions and classification. In P. J. Hettema (Ed.), *Personality and environment: Assessment of human adaptation* (pp. 53–69). Chichester: Wiley.

Wallace, J. (1966). An abilities conception of personality: Some implications for personality measurement. *American Psychologist, 21,* 132–138.

Watson, D., & Hubbard, B. (1996). Adaptational style and dispositional structure: Coping in the context of the five-factor model. *Journal of Personality, 64,* 737–774.

Witkin, H. A. (1973). The role of cognitive style in academic performance and in teacher-student relations. *Educational Testing Service Research Bulletin.* Princeton, NJ: Educational Testing Service.

18

Contextual Studies of Cognitive Adaptation

John W. Berry
Queen's University

A fundamental concern of cross-cultural psychology is to attend equally to both human behavior and the context in which it develops and takes place. It is argued that unless we understand important features of the population (including its culture and biology, its history and current economic situation) we cannot be in a position to interpret the behaviors that we observe and measure. Research studies and reports that limit their attention to population characteristics by merely naming them (e.g., "blacks") or classifying them (e.g. "lower class") simply do not provide any basis for making inferences about the possible roots of their measurements. Lacking such contextual information, there is often an implicit invitation to draw upon stereotypical (and frequently ethnocentric) "knowledge" about what features of the population may be inferred to account for the observed behavior. One aim of this chapter is to provide an example of how to approach the study of population characteristics and contexts that are theoretically relevant to the behavior domain of interest. In a sense, it deliberately errs on the side of emphasizing *context*, as a partial antidote to the more usual problem of making a full-scale psychometric assessment and paying limited (even no) attention to the population.

A second aim of this chapter is to express a concern (shared by those interested in the relationships between culture and human behavior) about our long-standing and deep suspicion about concepts and findings that are rooted solely in Western Academic Scientific Psychology (WASP). Chief among the targets of these suspicious have been global constructs such as "intelligence" and "personality," the two topics of interest to this Second Spearman Symposium. The use of such general characterizations for whole populations has a long and continuing tradition in psychology (from Kluckhohn & Murray, 1948 to Rushton, 1995), and an equally robust stream of criticism (Berry, 1972; Shweder, 1979).

Alternative ways to understand people (both individuals and groups) *in their own terms* (as prescribed by Malinowski, 1922, and by most anthropologists since then) have been sought. These include the approaches of indigenous and cross-cultural psychology (see Berry et al., 1997 and Kim & Berry, 1994 for overviews). In the first, local conceptions of human behavior are elicited, elaborated and studied empirically; in the second, this process is carried out comparatively, often starting inevitably with WASP. These approaches are viewed as complementary, ones that can jointly be employed in the study of cognition in context (Berry, 1996).

These two concerns were expressed by Ferguson (1956) in what has been termed by Irvine and Berry (1988) Ferguson's Law of Cultural Differentiation:

> Cultural factors prescribe what shall be learned, and at what age; consequently different cultural environments lead to the development of different patterns of ability. (p. 121)

That is, cognitive development and cognitive organization are to be seen as cultural products. One implication is that cognitive competence is expressed in culturally appropriate ways, rather than as a single global entity such as "intelligence." A further implication is that since cultures inculcate characteristic patterns of development and expression that are highly variable, a small number of global "personality" constructs may not be sufficient to account for them. If cross-cultural psychology has taught us anything, it is to be wary of "one concept fits all" descriptions and prescriptions about human intelligence and personality. But even if not one, is it two, five or sixteen? And how would we find out?

This paper presents some of our[1] current thinking and research on these questions. We are attempting to extend the conceptualization and empirical assessment of the culture-cognition relationship in a way that "neutralizes" the issue. This is being accomplished in two ways: First we view cognition as *adaptive* to ecological and cultural context, without any implications of superiority or inferiority of these adaptations; second, we consider mainly the *style* of processing cognitive information, rather than the amount (i.e. the "how" rather than the "how much"). The interest is in studying the characteristic preference of cognitive performances across cultures in terms of difference models rather than as deficiency attributes (Irvine & Berry, 1988).

Our work is cast within a "universalist" theoretical framework (Berry, Poortinga, Segall, & Dasen, 1992), in which basic psychological processes are taken to be species-wide features of human psychology, on which culture plays infinite variations during the course of development and daily activity. This view allows for comparisons of cognitive performance on the basis of the common underlying process, but makes comparison worthwhile using the surface variation as basic evidence.

---

[1] "our" refers to our research group, made up of JoAnne Bennett, Peter Denny, Nigel Turner, Ramesh Mishra, and Zheng Xue, as well as numerous researchers in communities around the world.

We begin with an outline of our current thinking about how people adapt culturally (as a group) to their long-standing ecological settings, and continue with a proposal about how people develop and perform cognitively (as individuals) in adaptation to their eco-cultural situation.

Ecological and Cultural Adaptation

One continuing theme in cultural anthropology is that cultural variations may be understood as adaptations to differing ecological settings or contexts (Boyd & Richerson, 1983). This line of thinking, usually known as *cultural ecology* (Vayda & Rappoport, 1968), *ecological anthropology* (Moran, 1982; Bayda & McKay, 1975), or the *ecosystem* approach (Moran, 1990) to anthropology has a long history in the discipline (see Feldman, 1975). Its roots go back to Forde's (1934) classic analysis of relationships between physical habitat and societal features in Africa, and Kroeber's (1939) early demonstration that cultural areas and natural areas co-vary in Aboriginal North America. Unlike earlier simplistic assertions by the school of "environmental determinism" (e.g., Huntington, 1945), the ecological school of thought has ranged from "possiblism" where the environment sets some constraints or limits on the range of possible cultural forms that may emerge to an emphasis on "resource utilization" where active and interactive relationships between human populations and their habitat are analyzed.

Of particular interest to psychologists was Steward's (1955) use of what was later called the *cognized environment*; this concept refers to the "selected features of the environment of greatest relevance to a population's subsistence" (p. 51). With this notion, ecological thinking moved simultaneously away from any links to earlier deterministic views, and towards the psychological idea of individuals actively perceiving, appraising and changing their environments.

These ecological approaches have tended to view cultural systems as relatively stable, even permanent *adaptations* as a state, ignoring *adaptation* as a process, or *adaptability* as a system characteristic of cultural populations (Bennett, 1976). However, it is clear that cultures evolve over time, sometimes in response to changing ecological circumstances, and sometimes due to contact with other cultures. This fact has required the addition of a more dynamic conception of ecological adaptation as a continuous, as well as an interactive process between ecological, cultural and psychological variables. It is from the most recent position that we approach the topic. It is a view that is consistent with more recent general changes in anthropology, away from a "museum" orientation to culture (collecting and organizing static artefacts) to one that emphasizes cultures as constantly changing, and being concerned with creation, metamorphosis and recreation.

Over the years ecological thinking has influenced not only anthropology, but also psychology. The fields of ecological and environmental psychology have become fully elaborated (see Werner, Brown, & Altman, 1997), with substantial theoretical and empirical foundations. In essence, individual human behavior has come to be seen in its natural setting or habitat, both in terms of its development, and its contemporary display. The parallel development of cross-cultural psychology (see Berry & Bennett, 1992; Berry et al., 1997) has also "naturalized" the study of human behavior and its development. In this field, individual behavior is accounted for to a large extent by considering the role of cultural influences on it. But, in my own approach, ecological as well as cultural influences are considered as operating in tandem, and is known as the *ecocultural* approach (Berry, 1975, 1976, 1994).

An Ecological Approach

The current version of the ecocultural framework in Figure 18.1, was presented at the First Spearman Symposium (Berry, 1996). It proposes to account for human psychological diversity (both individual and group similarities and differences) by taking into account two fundamental sources of influence (ecological, and socio-political), and a set of variables that link these influences to psychological characteristics (cultural and biological adaptation at the population level, and various "transmission variables" to individuals such as enculturation, socialization, genetics, and acculturation).[2] Overall, the ecocultural framework considers human diversity, both cultural and psychological, to be a set of collective and individual adaptations to context. Within this general perspective, it views cultures as evolving adaptations to ecological and sociopolitical influences, and views psychological characteristics in a population as adaptive to their cultural context, as well as to the broader ecological and sociopolitical influences.

Within psychology, the early ecological work of Barker (1968) and Brunswik (1957), and the findings of the burgeoning field of environmental psychology, have attempted to specify the links between ecological context and individual human development and behavior. Cross-cultural psychology has tended to view cultures (both one's own, and others one is in contact with) as differential contexts for development, and to view behavior as adaptive to these different contexts.

The ecocultural approach offers a "value neutral" framework for describing and interpreting similarities and differences in human behavior across cultures (Berry, 1994). As adaptive to context, psychological phenomena can be

---

[2] It is a conceptual framework, rather than a testable model. As such it has served to guide a number of empirical studies (see below), which have provided evidence to support many of its components and relationships.

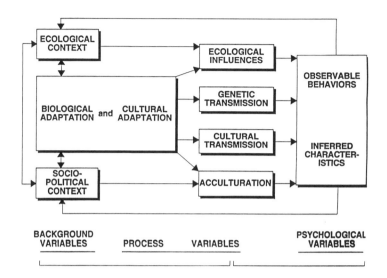

FIG. 18.1. An ecocultural framework linking ecology, cultural adaptation and behavioral outcomes (Berry et al., 1992).

understood "in their own terms," as Malinowski (Malinowski, 1922) insisted and external evaluations can usually be avoided. When two cultural contexts are involved, as in situations of culture contact and acculturation, psychological phenomena can be viewed as attempts to deal simultaneously with two sometimes inconsistent, sometimes conflicting cultural contexts, rather than pathologizing colonized or immigrant cultures and peoples.

Early Visual–Spatial Studies

Initially the link between ecology, culture and behavior was elaborated into a framework in order to predict different development of visual disembedding, analytic and spatial abilities between hunting-based and agriculture-based peoples (Berry, 1966). The first step was to propose that the "ecological demands" for survival that were placed on hunting peoples were for a high level of these visual abilities, in contrast with people employing other (particularly agricultural) subsistence strategies. Second, it was proposed that "cultural aids," such as socialization practices, linguistic differentiation of spatial information, and the use of arts and crafts would promote the development of these abilities. As predicted, empirical studies of Inuit, (then called Eskimo) in the Canadian Arctic and Temne, in Sierra Leone revealed marked differences in these abilities. Further studies were planned and carried out, and during the course of this empirical work, the ideas became further elaborated into an ecocultural framework. In each case, a consideration of ecological and cultural features of the group were taken as a basis for predicting differential psychological outcomes in a variety of domains. For example, differential degrees of reliance on hunting, and of social stratification, ranging from "loose" to "tight" (Pelto, 1968) and variations in child socialization practices, ranging from emphases on "assertion" to "compliance," were used to predict differential degrees of social conformity (Berry, 1967, 1979). Evidence revealed marked variation in conformity levels that corresponded to the sample's placement on a combined "ecocultural index."

Recent Studies of Visual–Spatial Abilities

Further work on perceptual and cognitive abilities, aligned in part to the theory of psychological differentiation and particularly the cognitive style of field dependence–field independence (Witkin & Berry, 1975) resulted in three volumes reporting results of studies in the Arctic, Africa, Australia, New Guinea, and India (Berry, 1976; Berry et al., 1986; Mishra, Sinha, & Berry, 1996).

The framework has also been used to understand sources of variation in perceptual-cognitive development (Berry, Dasen & Witkin, 1983; Dasen, 1975; Nsamenang, 1992). This focus has clear relations to an increasing interest in cross-cultural psychology in indigenous conceptions of cognitive competence and in the cognitive tasks faced by people in daily life (e.g., Berry & Bennett, 1992; Berry & Irvine, 1986; Berry, Irvine, & Hunt, 1988). In this work, it is argued that the indigenous conceptions of competence need to be uncovered; competencies are to be seen as developments nurtured by activities of daily life ("bricolage"), and as adaptive to ecological context. Understanding the indigenous conceptions, the cognitive values, the daily activities, and the contexts is an essential prerequisite for valid cognitive assessment.

Dimensions of Ecological and Cultural Variation: Unidimensional and Bidimensional conceptualizations

In order to conceptualize a number of possible human adaptations to varying habitats, a unidimensional ecocultural dimension was developed and operationalized over the range of subsistence economic activities from hunters to agriculturalists (Berry, 1966, 1976). About the same time Lomax and Berkowitz (1972) found evidence for *two independent factors* of cultural variation over the ecological range; from gatherers, through hunters to agriculturalists to urban dwellers: they called these "differentiation" and "integration." The first refers to the number and kinds of role distinctions made in the society, while the second refers to the "groupiness" or degree of cohesion among members of a society, to their solidarity, and to the social co-ordination of their day-to-day activities. Whilst there are two independent dimensions, over the *middle range* of subsistence strategies the two dimensions are *positively correlated*. It is precisely at this middle range (hunters to agriculturalists) that earlier conceptualization and operationalization took place (Berry, 1976). Thus, the unidimensional nature of my earlier ecocultural dimension was not fundamentally in error; it was just restricted in range. A more general conceptualization, able to take into account gatherers and urban societies, would need to adopt the two dimensional view of ecological and cultural variation.

In a series of papers, Boldt and colleagues (Boldt, 1976; Boldt & Roberts, 1979; Roberts, Boldt, & Guest, 1990) have pursued the possibility that there are indeed two independent dimensions (see also Gamble & Ginsberg, 1981). They argued that "structural complexity" and "structural tightness" need to be distinguished. The first refers to the number and diversity of roles in society, which "should expand the range of courses of action available to an actor, and therefore, enhance choice and individual autonomy" (Roberts et al. 1990, p. 69). The second refers to the degree to which social expectations are imposed on individuals, which should "reduce an actor's autonomy by narrowing the opportunities for negotiating a preferred course of action" (ibid, p. 69).

This "structural complexity–structural tightness" distinction corresponds to the "differentiation–integration" distinction of Lomax and Berkowitz (1972). At the same time it breaks into two components the more general sociocultural indexes such as "cultural complexity" (McNett, 1970), "tightness-looseness" (Pelto, 1968), and the ecocultural index of Berry (1976). More specifically, for the ecocultural index, it places the ecological variables of settlement pattern and mean size of local community together with the cultural variable of political stratification into one construct ("structural complexity"), but puts the other cultural variables of social stratification and socialization emphases on compliance into another construct ("structural tightness").

Although most use of the ecocultural framework has been in the study of perception and cognition, it has also been useful to explore aspects of "personality." For example, with respect to individualism and collectivism (Kim, Triandis, Kagitcibasi, Choi, & Yoon, 1993), there are some theoretical proposals that link these personal orientations to ecology and culture. In one (Berry, 1993) it is suggested that individualism may be related to the differentiation (structural complexity) dimension, with greater differentiation in a society being predictive of greater personal individualism. However, collectivism is proposed to be related more to the integration (structural tightness) dimension, with greater integration predictive of greater collectivism. It is further suggested that individualism and collectivism are usually found to be at opposite ends of one value dimension because data are usually obtained in industrial or urban societies where the two cultural dimensions, (differentiation and integration) are strongly distinguished; if data were to be collected in other types of societies (e.g., hunting or agricultural) where the two dimensions coincide, then this value opposition or incompatibility may not be observed.

In the work of Triandis (1993, 1994) the cultural antecedents to Individualism and Collectivism are identified, using the constructs of "tightness–looseness" and "complexity–simplicity."[3] In his framework they are considered to be orthogonal or independent of each other; (see Figure 1 in Triandis, 1994). His "hypothesis is that individualism will be maximal in societies in which there is both complexity and looseness; collectivism will be maximal in societies in which there is both simplicity and tightness" (p. 297).

From these theoretical considerations, it appears to be worthwhile to carry out studies of various psychological outcomes across the whole range of subsistence strategies, employing *two* dimensions of cultural variation as predictors. Most obvious would be studies of cognition and social conformity, guided by the previous work in these two areas. Although this paper concerns the area of cognition, cross-cultural studies of social conformity have recently been reviewed by Bond and Smith (1996), and provides a sound basis for further research in this area.

Empirical Developments

Given the evidence in favor of two dimensions of cultural variation across subsistence strategies, a new operationalization has been carried out. To avoid confusion with other meanings, and making value judgments, two new terms are proposed for these two dimensions: *Social Size* (cf. "Differentiation," and "structural complexity"); and *Social Conformity* (cf. "Integration," and "structural tightness").

The first, Social Size is defined and operationalized as comprising four components: settlement pattern (nomadic, semi-nomadic, semi-sedentary, sedentary); mean size of local community; political stratification; and occupational specialization. All ratings can be derived from data in Murdock, (1967). The second, Social Conformity is made up of three variables: social stratification; socialization emphases (compliance-assertion); and social obligation (degree of norm obligation, placed on individuals to conform to group standards). Ratings for stratification are from Murdock (1967), for socialization from Barry, Child, and Bacon (1959), while norm obligation can be assessed through key informants in each society. The four components of the social size dimension are positively correlated, and are combined to produce a society's placement on this dimension. Similarly, the three components of the social conformity dimension are positively correlated, and yield a placement.

---

[3] Triandis' use of these terms is similar to those of Boldt, but are operationalized slightly differently.

Schematic relationships between these two cultural dimensions and subsistence strategies are portrayed in Figure 18.2. Social Size is considered to be almost a linear function of subsistence strategy, while Social Conformity is shown to be curvilinear; relatively low in gathering and hunting societies and low in industrial societies, but higher in agricultural and irrigation societies. This portrayal has obvious similarity with that of Lomax and Berkowitz (1972). With the two ecocultural dimensions outlined, we now consider the second focus of this chapter, which is cognitive styles; a final section will attempt to link these ecocultural dimensions to variations in cognitive styles.

Cognitive Styles

Two cognitive style variables, differentiation–integration and contextualization–decontextualization have been developed recently from an earlier variable, *field-dependence-independence* put forward by Witkin. Witkin regarded the two new cognitive styles as "aspects" of field-dependence–independence (Witkin, Dyke, Faterson, Goodenough, & Karp, 1962), but as we will see, research shows that they have to be treated as separate variables (Denny, 1988).

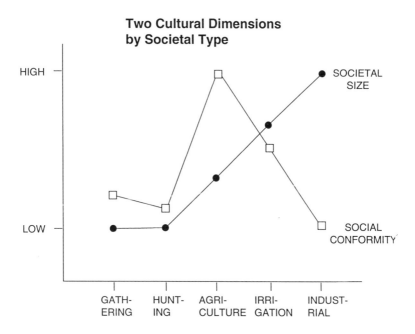

FIG. 18.2. Relationships between social size, social conformity and substistence strategies.

Differentiation–Integration

The first cognitive style variable may be introduced by a task which has frequently been used to assess it, the embedded figures test. The participant's task is to find where the smaller figure is hidden in the larger one. The thinker starts with a well-organized cognitive unit, which has no context, and is asked to differentiate out a part of it. This illustrates the essential nature of a differentiative cognitive style: fluency in separating internal aspects of cognitive units. Put another way, differentiation involves high intraunit separateness. The opposite cognitive style, integration, may be illustrated by another psychological task, which although decades old has not been much used cross-culturally. This is the closure task in which the participant is asked to complete the picture of an object when presented with only parts of it. It requires fluency in joining together parts to make up a cognitive unit; in other words, integration involves high intraunit connectedness. Differentiation and integration are opposites because they emphasize either breaking apart or putting together parts of a unit. They are one variable because both concern thought operations inside a cognitive unit. In this regard we will see that they contrast with the second cognitive style variable, contextualization.

Before going on to that, it is important to reaffirm that in addition to cognitive styles, differentiation and integration are also classes of universal cognitive processes which every human being must perform constantly. Therefore differentiative cognitive style is a learned emphasis upon certain differentiation processes so that they are better developed. The same is true of integrative thought; as a cognitive style it is a learned emphasis upon certain integration processes. Differences in cognitive style can only appear where there is some optionality in thinking. No one can afford to be less than fluent at differentiating the morphemes of their language or less than fluent at integrating them into sentences. However, even strictly structured, universal thought processes such as deductive reasoning can be performed using different cognitive styles.

Another point which our earlier examples suggest and which we will see again, is that the separate styles may be most apparent to us when the requirements for processing are particularly difficult. For example, in the embedded figures test, the larger figure is very well-integrated so that unusual differentiative skill is needed to separate out the small figure. A final basic point is that all the cognitive styles, in addition to being cross-cultural variables, are also individual difference variables and situational variables. Even though someone belongs to a highly integrative culture, one still may not have acquired the habits of integrative style which that culture tries to teach, and one may be among the least integrative members of their society. As a separate matter, any person may in some situations learn not to use the cognitive style that is most preferred in one's culture. Keeping individual and situational variation in mind, we can recognize that there is only a partial association of cognitive style with culture.

Contextualization–Decontextualization

The second cognitive style variable, contextualizing versus decontextualizing, concerns relations of a cognitive unit to information that lies outside it. It has most often been studied in psychology by using deductive reasoning tasks.

Consider the following item:

> If the weather is hot and dry, soolems will grow.
> At Reetugg the summers are cold and wet.
> Will soolems grow there?

If a reasoner requests further information before drawing a conclusion, especially about the two nonsense words, "soolems" and "Reetugg," then they are showing a contextualizing cognitive style because they are trying to link the cognitive unit, which is the deductive reasoning item itself, to other information outside that unit. The opposite cognitive style, decontextualization, is shown by thinkers who are willing to treat the cognitive unit in isolation from background information: whatever soolems are, they reason, I can conclude that they won't grow well at Reetugg, wherever that is.

Contextualizing and decontextualizing are opposite poles of one cognitive style; both are concerned with relating the cognitive unit to information outside it, but do so to different extents. Contextualization involves "extra-unit connectedness," seeking out further information with which to link the given information; in contrast, decontextualization involves "extra-unit separateness," not requiring further information in order to draw a conclusion.

The Distinction Between Styles

As the foregoing definitions and examples showed, identifying the cognitive unit is crucial to separating these two cognitive styles. In the examples given, the cognitive units can be confidently identified: the larger figure in the embedded figures test is well-integrated and no background is provided for it or elicited by it. Likewise the parts of the closure item are obviously not separate cognitive units, because they can only be identified as parts of the complete object. The deductive reasoning item is also a single cognitive unit by virtue of the special structural arrangements among the premises and the conclusion.

In contrast to these examples, there are other cases where there are ambiguities concerning the cognitive unit which may make it more difficult to separate the two variables. For example, the well-known rod-and-frame test presents such ambiguities. In this test, the participant is asked to adjust the rod to vertical, even though the rectangular frame around it is not vertical. The cognitive unit might be structured in either of two ways: the rod may be processed as a cognitive unit in relation to the frame as context, or alternatively, the rod and frame may be processed together as parts of a single cognitive unit. This ambiguity may account for some of the varying results obtained with the rod-and-frame test in comparison with the more stable results from the embedded figures test (Goodenough, Oltman, & Cox, 1987; Jahoda & Neilson, 1986). The difficulties in separating these two variables may be one reason why Witkin treated these two cognitive styles as aspects of one, field-dependence–independence variable (Witkin et al., 1962).

At this point the considerations leading to positing the two separate cognitive styles will be discussed. Observations of hunting cultures such as the Inuit lead to recognition that there must be two variables. Using the unitary notion of field-dependence-independence, Berry (1976) found that Amerindian hunting groups were as field independent as Europeans, both contrasting with the greater field dependence of African groups. Consequently, Berry was puzzled by the high acculturative stress scores shown by Amerindians (p. 190). The answer offered by separating field independence into two variables is that Amerindians are like Europeans in being differentiative, not integrative, but unlike the Europeans in being contextualizing, not decontextualizing. Therefore the decontextualized style of Western cognition is stressful to them. Differentiative and contextualizing styles are an impossible combination using just the single field-dependence–independence variable. It is possible that Witkin himself was moving in this direction, because late in his career, his research group did a study showing that embedded figures tests (and other tests that typically correlate with them) loaded on a separate factor than did tests of contextual effects (Goodenough et al., 1987).

Ecocultural Context and Cognitive Styles

To this point, we have outlined the two main conceptual components: a bidimensional ecocultural context, and two distinct cognitive styles. We now are in a position to propose a relationship between them. In Figure 18.3, the hypothesized relationships between cognitive styles and subsistence strategies is sketched. The expectation is that differentiation–integration will "track" social conformity across these strategies, and that contextualization–decontextualization will track social size. Note that for Figure 18.3, the vertical scale is inverted to emphasize the correspondence between the ecocultural and the cognitive style psychological dimensions

Empirical studies are now underway in each of the five types of societies as defined by their subsistence strategies. Cognitive style tasks assessing

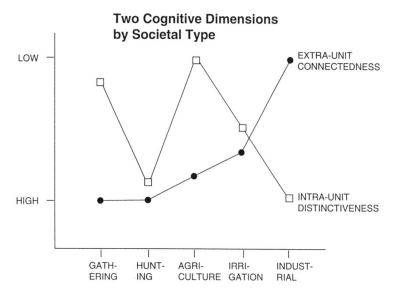

FIG. 18.3. Hypothesized relationship between subsistence strategies and two cognitive styles

differentiation-integration, and contextualization–decontextualization have been developed. Although data collection is complete, only preliminary data analyses have been accomplished so far.

CONCLUSION

This chapter has attempted to show how the analysis of culture and context can serve as a basis for understanding variations in human behavior. My goal was to provide a contrast to the usual practice of investing heavily, even totally in behavioral assessment, and then either guessing at population factors that might account for the data, or employing conventional knowledge and popular stereotypes to explain the findings. Precise psychometrics have little value, and no meaning, without an equally precise understanding of the population from which they derive.

REFERENCES

Barker, R. (1968). *Ecological Psychology*. Stanford, CA: Stanford University Press.
Barry, H., Child, I., & Bacon, M. (1959). Relations of child training to subsistence economy. *American Anthropologist, 61*, 51-63.
Bennett, J. (1976). *The ecological transition*. London: Pergamon.

Berry, J. W. (1966). Temne and Eskimo perceptual skills. *International Journal of Psychology, 1*, 207-229.

Berry, J. W. (1967). Independence and conformity in subsistence-level societies. *Journal of Personality and Social Psychology, 7*, 415-418.

Berry, J. W. (1972). Radical cultural relativism and the concept of intelligence. In L. J. Cronbach & P. J. D. Drenth (Eds.), *Mental tests and cultural adaptation* (pp. 78-88). The Hague: Mouton.

Berry, J. W. (1975). An ecological approach to cross-cultural psychology. *Nederlands Tijdschrift voor de Psychologie, 30*, 51-84.

Berry, J. W. (1976). *Human ecology and cognitive style:Comparative studies in cultural and psychological adaptation.* New York: Sage/Halsted.

Berry, J. W. (1979). A cultural ecology of social behavior. In L. Berkowitz (Ed.), *Advances in experimental social psychology, Vol. 12*, (pp. 177-206). New York: Academic Press.

Berry, J. W. (1993). Ecology of individualism and collectivism. In U. Kim, Triandis, H. C., Kagitcibasi, C., Choi, S.-C., & Yoon, G. (Eds.), *Individualism and collectivism.* Thousand Oaks, CA: Sage.

Berry, J. W. (1994). An ecological approach to cultural and ethnic psychology. In E. Trickett (Ed.), *Human diversity,* (pp. 115-141). San Francisco: Jossey-Bass.

Berry, J. W. (1996). A cultural ecology of cognition. In I. Dennis & P. Tapsfield (Eds.), *Human abilities: Their nature and measurement* (pp. 19-37). Mawah, NJ: Lawrence Erlbaum Associates.

Berry, J. W., Poortinga, Y. H., Pandey, J., Dasen, P. R., Saraswathi, T. S., Segall, M. H., & Kagitcibasi, C. (Eds.). (1997). *Handbook of cross-cultural psychology.* Vol. 1, Theory and method. Vol. 2, Basic processes and human development. Vol. 3, Social behavior and applications. Boston: Allyn & Bacon.

Berry, J. W., & Bennett, J. A. (1992). Cree conceptions of cognitive competence. *International Journal of Psychology, 27*, 73-88.

Berry, J. W., Dasen, P. R., & Witkin, H. A. (1983). Developmental theories in cross-cultural perspective. In L. Adler (Ed.), *Cross-cultural research at issue* (pp. 13-21). New York: Academic Press.

Berry, J. W., & Irvine, S. H. (1986). Bricolage: Savages do it daily. In R. Sternberg & R. Wagner (Eds.), *Practical intelligence: Nature and origins of competence in the everyday world* (pp. 271-306). New York: Cambridge University Press.

Berry, J. W., Irvine, S. H., & Hunt, E. B. (Eds.). (1987). *Indigenous cognition: functioning in cultural context.* Dordrecht: Nijhoff.

Berry, J. W., van de Koppel, J. M. H., Sénéchal, C., Annis, R. C., Bahuchet, S., Cavalli-Sforza, L. L., & Witkin, H. A. (1986). *On the edge of the forest: Cultural adaptation and cognitive development in Central Africa,* Lisse: Swets & Zeitlinger.

Berry, J. W., Poortinga, Y. H., Segall, M. H., & Dasen, P. R. (1992). *Cross-cultural psychology: Research and applications.* New York: Cambridge University Press.

Boldt, E. D. (1976). Acquiescence and conventionality in a communal society. *Journal of Cross-Cultural Psychology, 7*, 21-36.

Boldt, E. D., & Roberts, L. W. (1979). Structural tightness and social conformity. *Journal of Cross-Cultural Psychology, 10*, 221-230.

Bond, R., & Smith, P., (1996). Culture and conformity: A meta-analysis. *Psycholgical Bulletin, 199*, 111-137.

Boyd, R., & Richerson, P. (1983). Why is culture adaptive? *Quarterly Review of Biology, 58*, 209-214.

Brunswik, E. (1957). Scope and aspects of the cognition problem. In A. Gruber (Ed.), *Cognition: The Colorado Symposium.* Cambridge, MA: Harvard University Press.

Dasen, P. (1975). Concrete operational development in three cultures. *Journal of Cross-Cultural Psychology, 6*, 156-172.

Denny, J. Peter, (1988). Contextualization and differentiation in cross-cultural cognition. In John W. Berry et al. (Eds.), *Indigenous cognition: Functioning in cultural context,* (pp. 213-229). The Netherlands: Martinus Nijhoff.

Feldman, D. (1975). The history of the relationship between environment and culture in ethnological thought. *Journal of the History of the Behavioral Sciences, 110,* 67-81.

Ferguson, G. A. (1956). On transfer and the abilities of man. *Canadian Journal of Psychology, 10,* 121-131.

Forde, D. (1934). *Habitat, economy & society.* New York: Dutton.

Gamble, J. J., & Ginsberg, P. E. (1981). Differentiation, cognition and social evolution. *Journal of Cross-Cultural Psychology, 12,* 445-459.

Goodenough, D. R., Oltman, P. K., & Cox, P. W. (1987). The nature of individual differences in field dependence. *Journal of Research in Personality, 21,* 81-99.

Huntington, E. (1945). *Mainsprings of civilization.* New York: John Wiley.

Irvine, S. H. & Berry, J. W. (1988). The abilities of mankind. In S. H. Irvine & J. W. Berry (Eds.), *Human abilities in cultural context* (pp. 3-59). New York: Cambridge University Press.

Jahoda, G. (1992). *Crossroads between culture and mind.* Hemel Hempstead: Harvester Wheatsheaf.

Jahoda, G., & Neilson, I. (1986). Nyborg's analytical rod-and-frame scoring system: A comparative study in Zimbabwe. *International Journal of Psychology, 21,* 19-29.

Kim, U., & Berry, J. W. (Eds.). (1994). *Indigenous psychologies.* Thousand Oaks, CA: Sage.

Kluckhohn, C., & Murray, H. A. (Eds.). (1948). *Personality in nature, society and culture.* New York: Knopf.

Kroeber, A. (1939). *Cultural and natural areas of native North America.* Berkeley: University of California Press.

Lomax, A., & Berkowitz, W. (1972). The evolutionary taxonomy of culture. *Science, 177,* 228-239.

Malinowski, B. (1922). *Argonauts of the Western Pacific.* London: Routledge.

McNett, C. W. (1970). A settlement pattern scale of cultural complexity. In R. Naroll & R. Cohen (Eds.), *Handbook of method in cultural anthropology.* New York: Natural History Press.

Mishra, R. C., Sinha, D., & Berry, J. W. (1995). *Ecology, acculturation and psychological adaptation: A study of Advasi in Bihar.* Delhi: Sage.

Moran, E. (1982). *Human adaptability: An introduction to ecological anthropology.* Boulder: Westview press.

Moran, E. (Ed.). (1990). *The ecosystem approach in anthropology.* Ann Arbor: University of Michigan Press.

Murdock, G. P. (1967). *Ethnographic atlas.* Pittsburgh: University of Pittsburgh Press.

Nsamenang, B. (1992). *Human development in cultural context.* Newbury Park, CA: Sage.

Pelto, P. (1968). The difference between "tight" and "loose" societies. *Transaction, 5,* 37-40.

Roberts, L. W., Boldt, E. D., & Guest, A. (1990). Structural tightness and social conformity: Varying the source of external influence. *Great Plains Sociologist, 3,* 67-83.

Rushton, J. P. (1995). *Race, evolution and behavior.* New Brunswick, NJ: Transaction.

Shweder, R. (1979). Rethinking culture and personality theory. *Ethos, 7,* 255-311.

Steward, J. (1955). The concept and method of cultural ecology. *Theory of culture change.* Urbana: University of Illinois Press.

Triandis, H. C. (1993). Theoretical and methodological approaches to the study of collectivism and individualism. In U. Kim et al. (Eds.), *Individualism and ollectivism.* London: Sage.

Triandis, H. C. (1994). Major cultural syndromes and emotion. In S. Kitayama & H. Markus (Eds.), *Emotion and culture.* Washington, DC: American Psychological Association.

Vayda, A. P., & Rappoport, R. (1968). Ecology, cultural and non-cultural. In J. Clifton (Ed.), *Cultural anthropology.* Boston: Houghton Mifflin.

Vayda, A. P., & McKay, B. (1975). New directions in ecology and ecological anthropology. *Annual Review of Anthropology, 4,* 293-306.

Werner, C., Brown, B., & Altman, I. (1977). Environmental psychology. In J. W. Berry, M. H. Segall, & C. Kagitcibasi (Eds.), *Handbook of cross-Cultural psychology, Vol 3. Social behavior and applications,* (pp. 253-290). Boston: Allyn & Bacon.

Witkin, H., & Berry, J. W. (1975). Psychological differentiation in cross-cultural perspective. *Journal of Cross-Cultural Psychology, 6,* 4-87.

Witkin, H. A., Dyk, R. B., Faterson, H. F., Goodenough, D. R., & Karp, S. A. (1962). *Psychological Differentiation*. New York: Wiley.

19

Personality in Context, Control, and Intelligence

Joop Hettema
Tilburg University, The Netherlands

Personality and intelligence label two grand but heretofore distinct domains of theory and research. New research is now beginning to test this distinction, to look for relations, and to imagine integrations that might be designed for particular theoretical and practical purposes. When comparing both domains, personality seems the best starting point. Personality psychologists have always insisted that their subject should be viewed from the vantage of the entire functioning person in his or her natural habitat. Several functions like motivation, learning, and cognition have been fruitfully studied in the context of personality. Intelligence is no exception. Classical definitions conceive of intelligence as a major basis for individuals to successfully deal with their environments. Most prior definitions of intelligence emphasize adaptive cognitive functioning, or more specifically, adaptation to changing environmental circumstances in the service of perseverance toward an accepted goal (Snow, 1986).

Thus, Binet (1909) defined intelligence as "the tendency to take and maintain a definite direction; the capacity to make adaptations for the purpose of attaining a desired end; and the power of auto-criticism" (Terman, 1916, p. 45). Freeman (1955) defined intelligence as "adjustment or adaptation of the individual to his total environment, or to limited aspects thereof, and the capacity to reorganize one's behavior so as to act more effectively and more appropriately in novel situations" (pp. 60–61). Accordingly, personality in context may provide a fruitful framework.

During the past decades, few topics in personality psychology have attracted as much attention as personality in context. This approach to personality is based on the idea that the environment in which a person acts is a necessary prerequisite to understand the person's behavior. Special emphasis is put on individual adaptation, the consistency and coherence of individual behavior across different situations, person–environment relationships emphasizing transactions and the different ways in which persons exercise control, including specific modes of information processing underlying control.

CONSISTENCY

The consistency issue has received special attention during the so-called person–situation debate. Initially, the research centered around the question of whether individual behavior is primarily a function of the person or the situation. The first option implies cross-situational consistency, stressing the tendency of individuals to react with the same type of behavior in different situations. The second option looks for intrasituational consistency, emphasizing the functional relationships between situations and behaviors (Hartmann, Roper, & Bradford, 1979). To discriminate between the models, many studies have been completed, frequently molded after the person–situation experimental design. Data from studies with SR questionnaires (Endler & Edwards, 1986) were analyzed with ANOVA, sometimes followed by estimates of variance components. These studies allow for comparisons of the proportions of variance explained by each of the models. A major result of those studies is that neither the person nor the situation but the interaction between the two explains most of the variance. For instance, a review by Bowers (1973) revealed that on average, the main effect of persons accounted for 13% of the variance, whereas the main effect of situations accounted for 10%. Person x situation interactions took the lion's share at 21% of the variance.

In a subsequent review by Sarason, Smith, and Diener (1975), person effects were significant in 31%, situation effects in 66% of the cases, and person x situation interaction effects were significant in 60%. Later, Furnham, and Jaspars (1983) found that for 17 out of 24 studies person x situation interaction variance exceeded the person variance, whereas in 19 studies, it exceeded the situation variance. Those studies led to a second major conclusion: The question of whether personality consistency exists does not have a simple answer and requires knowledge of the persons acting, the situations in which actions occur, the type of responses studied, and the levels of analysis involved (Dierner & Larsen, 1983). Consistency has been studied from the perspective of the person with the so-called moderator approach, assuming that some persons are more consistent than others (e.g., Kenrick & Stringfield, 1980). However, this approach has not provided the final answer. Not only were earlier findings hard to replicate, but neither is the moderator approach embedded in a more general theoretical framework (Kenrick & Dantchik, 1983). A second approach has elaborated the idea that situations differ with respect to their power to elicit classes of acts predictably (Wright & Mischel, 1987) or to induce the same behavior in different people (Snyder & Ickes, 1985). In powerful situations persons are assumed to act more according the situationist model, whereas in weak situations, persons will act more according to a personologist model. However, the distinction between powerful versus weak situations is fraught with ambiguities (Hettema, van Heck, Appels, & van Zon, 1986).

More successful was a third approach to the consistency issue. This approach focused on different types of behavior as a major sources of (in) consistency. Least consistent across situations are social emotional behaviors, reflecting, for example, anxiety, depression, dominance, hostility, machiavellianism, affectional status behavior, conformity, and social appropriateness (cf. Furnham & Jaspars, 1983). Consistency across situations is obtained particularly with abilities, cognitive competencies, and academic achievement (Endler & Edwards, 1986; Mischel, 1973). As Spearman noted in 1927, and many studies have confirmed since, correlation matrices of intelligence tests usually reveal positive manifold, and thus there is every reason to assume intelligence to be highly consistent across situations. It is now generally agreed that an outstanding feature discriminating between intelligence on the one hand and most personality variables on the other is cross-situational consistency. To explain the difference between the two, intelligence has been labeled as a structural variable to be contrasted with other less structural personality variables (Mischel, 1973; Magnusson & Endler, 1976). However, the concept of structure remained ill-defined. A more promising approach to explain the difference may be based on an analysis of the ubiquitous transactions occurring between persons and situations.

RECIPROCAL CAUSATION AND CONTROL

Currently, person–situation interactionist perspectives have largely superseded the old person versus situation debates. It is clear that persons can behave in consistent ways in many different situations. However, there are also situations in which their behavior becomes inconsistent. A sheer consistency model is insufficient to explain the shifts. Instead, the transaction model has been proposed. Transactions are the mainstay of the interactional approach to personality (Endler & Magnusson, 1976).

According to this model, in most natural conditions, behavior assumes the shape of a continuous process of dynamic bidirectional exchange between the person and the situation. In this process, the person affects the situation as well as being affected by the situation through reciprocal causation. The major type of consistency emphasized by the transactional approach is coherence rather than cross-situational or intrasituational consistency. Coherence stresses the typical pattern of stable and changing behaviors of individuals across situations (Endler & Magnusson, 1976). Coherence can be decomposed into a consistent part and an inconsistent part. An analysis by Hettema and Kenrick (1992) suggests that behavior will remain consistent as long as persons manage to transform environments to suit their own characteristics and personal goals. However, if relevant environments resist attempts to be transformed, behavior will become inconsistent. In the latter case the person has to adapt and alter his own characteristics to keep up with environmental demands.

The finding that some types of behavior are consistent across situations although others are not suggests different systems to govern both types of behavior. A first clue to what those systems are like may be derived from a recent study by Funder and Colvin (1991). While exploring the conditions governing behavioral consistency, three authors compared personality ratings in three different laboratory conditions and in daily life. They studied psychologically meaningful behaviors as behavioral unit, classified accordingly. Analysis of the data revealed that the behaviors showed reliable and considerable differences with respect to cross-situational consistency. Behavior that is relevant for a broad range of situations appeared to be more consistent. Funder and Colvin went on to look for a more substantive interpretation of their data, emphasizing the types of behavior underlying cross-situational consistency. As a result, they found that consistency could be explained in terms of operant versus respondent behavior (Skinner, 1953). Consistent behaviors tended to have the character of operants, whereas inconsistent behaviors looked like respondents. A major difference between the two types of behavior is that respondents are correlated with specific eliciting stimuli, whereas, operants are emitted behaviors for which no such stimulus can be detected.

Respondents are unintended, elicited behaviors revealing considerable situation specificity. Operants, on the other hand, are voluntary, emitted behaviors occurring across a wide range of situations. A major function of operants is to initiate change in the environment. In the words of Skinner (1953), "We operate on the environment to generate consequences" (p. 56). Those consequences are emphasized as reinforcers in operant conditioning. From the perspective of personality in context another aspect deserves attention: control.

Control is currently recognized as a basic aspect of personality underlying physical and mental health, achievement, optimism, persistence, motivation, coping, self-esteem, personal adjustment, and success and failure in a variety of life domains (Skinner, 1996). An underlying assumption of all control theories is that humans want to produce behavior–event contingencies and thus exert control over the environment (White, 1959; Heckhausen & Schulz, 1995). To obtain, maintain, or restore control, people use two basically different modes of responding: primary and secondary control (Rothbaum, Weisz, & Snyder, 1982). *Primary control* refers to behaviors directed at the external environment and involves attempts to change the world to fit the needs and desires of the individual. *Secondary control* is targeted at internal processes and serves to minimize loss in existing levels of control. This type of control includes cognitions; for example, biased expectations, shifts in goal values, attributions of success and failure, illusions, and so forth. Secondary control is generally assumed to become active after primary control has failed. Primary versus secondary control is related to major current dichotomies like problem-oriented versus emotion-oriented coping (Folkman, Lazarus, Dunkel-Schetter, DeLongis, & Gruen, 1986), approach versus avoidance during stress (Roth & Cohen, 1986), action orientation versus state orientation (Kuhl, 1994), assimilation versus accommodation (Brandstadter & Renner, 1990), mastery versus helplessness (Dweck, 1991), and transformation of environments by persons versus transformation of persons by environments (Hettema & Kenrick, 1992). Operants versus respondents (Funder & Colvin, 1991) may reflect this dichotomy. There is reason to believe that behaviors reflecting primary control will reveal consistency across situations, whereas behaviors reflecting secondary control will be less consistent.

PRIMARY CONTROL

Recent studies have provided supporting evidence regarding primary control. Unlike most personality variables, primary control exhibits considerable consistency across situations. Thus, for instance, Buss, Gomes, Higgins, and Lauterback (1987) examined tactics of manipulation as means by which social environments are altered to correspond to the characteristics of individuals. Examples are tactics like reason, charm, regression, coercion, silent treatment, and debasement. Tactics of manipulation were studied in two major conditions. In one condition, tactics were used to get someone else to act according to one's wishes. In the other condition, tactics served to prevent someone else from acting contrary to one's wishes. The results were highly consistent across conditions, suggesting that people use the same tactics in different contexts; that is, instigation and termination of another's behavior. In this study, consistency was expressed with a median correlation of .79 for self-ratings and .74 for peer ratings.

Hettema and van Bakel (1997) examined mastery as a major condition for control. As an example they scrutinized the behavior of experienced architects during the designing process. This study was focused on the strategies architects use in situations where their intentions meet with frictions. The situations offered included a variety of situations like designing new buildings, offices, schools, hospitals, districts, renovation projects, and so forth. The strategies included examining the building location, creating a visual image or cognitive conception of the building, consulting the design program or brief, establishing a picture of the wishes of the other parties involved, and studying the architectural domain using, for example, the literature as a major source. Although the designing situations were very dissimilar, the strategies were highly consistent across 30 situations. The coefficient reflecting generalizability of strategies across situations was .72.

The Hettema and Hol (1998) study explicitly focused on primary control in interpersonal situations. Primary control was reflected in different intentions, like the intention to increase power, to increase control over resources, to increase knowledge, to reduce the distance to others, to have others behave on one's behalf, and to make preparatory efforts. Behaviors reflecting those intentions were observed in two different modes: self reports and observations of overt behavior during role playing. Both modes revealed a high degree of consistency across situations, demonstrated by a generalizability coefficient of .75. A study by Riteco (1998) corroborated this result. Using the same technique for the assessment of primary control, Riteco obtained correlations over 0.80 for cross-situational consistency. In both the Hettema–Hol study and the Riteco study, the general level of control, as well as the specific mechanisms used to gain control, appeared to be consistent. These studies suggest that primary control is a major condition for consistency across situations.

INFORMATION PROCESSING

How can these results be explained? In an attempt to answer this question, we hypothesized that different types of information processing are involved in primary control and in secondary control. In a study, we scrutinized control at the microlevel, focusing on the autonomous reactions of subjects confronted with situations that varied with respect to the amount of control present (Hettema, Leidelmeijer, & Geenen, 1998). As stimuli, we used films representing daily life situations. Subjects were placed in front of a film screen and during the films, a number of autonomous reactions were monitored continuously. Based on multivariate analyses, we identified three separate reactivity dimensions representing major attention processes proposed by Pribram and McGuinness (1975, 1992). One dimension, designated "familiarization," was connected with input elaboration. A second dimension called "readiness" reflected output preparation. A third dimension called "effort" involved activity in central executive processes. Each dimension opposed controlled serial processing with automatic parallel processing. To demonstrate relationships with control, prior to watching films, we used instructions emphasizing either primary or secondary control. In the first condition, primary control was enhanced with instructions inducing a mismatch between expectations and actual events, whereas secondary control was emphasized through instructions inducing a match between expectations and events. In the second condition, for primary control, we used instructions inducing a detached attitude toward the situation, whereas for secondary control, instructions induced maximal involvement. In the third condition, primary control was induced with instructions portraying the situation as neutral–positive, whereas secondary control was activated with instructions stressing the negative aspects of the situation. As a result, we obtained some clear differences. If our instructions enhanced primary control, we found an increase of controlled processing. With instructions stressing secondary control, we found a decrease of controlled processing, that is, increased automaticity. These outcomes were obtained in each of the three dimensions and they were consistent across films representing different situations. These findings allowed us to design an information processing model of primary and secondary control (Figure 19.1).

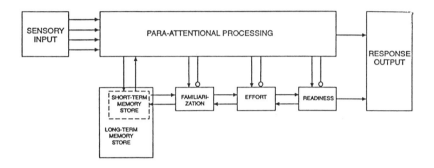

FIG. 19.1. An information processing model of primary and secondary control.

Figure 19.1 represents familiarization, effort, and readiness as serially connected subsystems. Any of the systems may be activated by para-attentional processes (downward arrows). As a consequence, the attention is directed outward. Information is processed to yield a response affecting the environment. This sequence reflects primary control. Contrary to this, the processing systems may be inhibited by para-attentional processes (downward circles). As a consequence, attention is directed inward, addressing the memory system to provide interpretations of specific events. Inward attention is generally considered to be a typical feature of secondary control (Rothbaum, Weisz, & Snyder, 1983; Heckhausen & Schulz, 1995). This model explains why primary control is concerned with actions, whereas secondary control enhances cognitive processes. The model also provides an explanation of the coherence of personality in context. As long as primary control is dominant, individual behavior will exhibit consistency across situations. However, as soon as secondary control is enhanced, the picture changes. Secondary control can interfere with primary control through inhibitory mechanisms interrupting ongoing activities. Although the activation of secondary control is a function of individual meanings, the situations in which inhibition occurs will vary from individual to individual. Consequently, secondary control will introduce inconsistencies in behavior from one situation to the other.

INTELLIGENCE AND CONTROL

Intelligence is closely related to primary control. This major thesis of this chapter may be supported with several arguments. First of all, the processes involved in intelligence include familiarizing novel situations, assuming and maintaining a definite direction, and making adaptations for the purpose of attaining a desired end. Classical definitions of intelligence like the ones mentioned in the introduction to this chapter suggest that processes of this type are crucial. There are also empirical arguments supporting this claim. Studies of autonomous reactivity during intelligence testing have provided evidence that processes of familiarization, readiness, and effort are involved in intelligence tests (Kahneman, 1973; Melis, 1997; Mulder, 1986; Pribram & McGuinness, 1975, 1992). However, the involvement of the different processes may vary as a function of the tasks offered. For example, in our laboratory, we observed subjects during psychometric tasks using autonomous measures as variables (Hettema, Vingerhoets, van der Molen, & van de Vijver, 1989). The tasks were selected to represent cognition, convergent thinking, and divergent thinking as proposed by Guilford (1967). The data were analyzed using standardized reaction patterns identified earlier during films as representing familiarization, effort, and readiness. As a result, we found some clear relationships. Reactivity patterns covaried with the type of task offered. Cognition tasks predominantly elicited familiarization, convergent = thinking tasks showed readiness, and divergent = thinking tasks elicited effort as the major type of reactivity. In this study, we also found some clear relationships between type of reactivity and task performance. A final argument may be derived from the tasks typically found in IQ tests and school settings. According to Neisser (1976), those tasks are formulated by other people, of little or no intrinsic interest, have all the necessary information and are disembedded from ordinary experience. Classical intelligence tests are unfamiliar situations, devoid of salience and value. As our film studies have shown, major conditions in which primary control is exerted are unfamiliarity, noninvolvement, and evaluative neutrality. In most intelligence tests, those conditions are implemented almost to the letter. These conditions imply that most intelligence tests emphasize primary control, whereas secondary control is prevented almost completely. Although secondary control is largely held responsible for the occurrence of person–situation interactions, this may provide a sufficient explanation for the consistency generally obtained with intelligence tests.

INTELLIGENCE IN CONTEXT

From the perspective of personality in context, intelligence may reflect persons' effectivity to obtain and maintain primary control. This is a major condition if individuals are to solve problems in a variety of conditions. An additional feature of intelligence is the consistency of intelligence across situations. This aspect has allowed researchers like Spearman to define intelligence as a general disposition, g. However, from the perspective of personality in context there are also restrictions. Classical definitions of intelligence emphasize adjustment or adaptation of persons to their total environment (Freeman, 1955). Yet, for a long time, the adaptive aspects of intelligence in real-life conditions have been put between parentheses while the study of intelligence became restricted to solving problems of an academic nature (Neisser, 1976).

Recent years reveal a new interest in the broad adaptive significance of intelligence, for example, in studies of practical and social intelligence. *Practical intelligence* is defined as "responding appropriately in terms of one's long-range and short-range goals, given the actual facts of the situation as one discovers them" (Neisser, 1976, p. 137). A practically intelligent individual is one who is able to solve the ill-defined problems that arise naturally in daily life for which there may be multiple solutions and multiple ways of obtaining them (Wagner, 1986). Emotions and feelings may accompany this kind of intellectual performance, which often satisfies motives. Practical intelligence refers to "mind in action," that is, thinking that is embedded in the large-scale, purposive activities of daily life (Scribner, 1986). In those conditions, specialized theoretical intelligence seems to be of no particular advantage. Some authors have even proposed conceiving of practical and theoretical intelligence as two completely different constructs, representing essentially different ways of thinking (Ceci & Liker, 1986; Scribner, 1986).

According to the present view, the processes are not unrelated. Rather than different systems, they reflect differences of emphasis in information processing. In practical situations as well as in test situations, the dominant type of control exerted may be primary control. However, a difference becomes manifest as soon as primary control fails to yield the outcomes intended. In test situations, failure may be of little consequence. However, in practical situations that are meaningful and salient to the person acting, failure may activate processes of secondary control.

Generally speaking, although limiting control loss, secondary control is adaptive and beneficial for the person. However, in the long run, if the search for meaning continues and the processes involved to do come to an end, they may become maladaptive while interfering with primary control. Instead of action-oriented, the person may become state-oriented (Kuhl, 1996). Kuhl's model of action orientation includes several volitional functions that serve to initiate, maintain, and complete an existing action tendency. His provisional list includes initiation of nonautomatic activity, maintenance of delayed action tendencies, inhibition of competing action tendencies, selective processing of relevant information, and readjustment of global arousal. Those functions may be disturbed by impaired facilitation of relevant processors through hesitation, volatility, or procrastination. Other disturbances may be based on excessive inhibition of irrelevant processors, like rumination, preoccupation, and superogation. As a result, action-oriented processing will be inhibited and the person will no longer be able to manifest major intentions. If intelligence is to be conceived as an integrative approach to adaptive functioning in real life conditions, the beneficial effects as well as the maladaptive effects of secondary control should be taken into account.

Modern control theory may provide a basis. For instance, Heckhausen and Schulz (1995) proposed a distinction between processes of secondary control that are functional in supporting primary control and those that are not. They listed a number of action steps to be taken if primary control fails. Examples are modifying future attempts at primary control by adjusting one's level of aspiration, restructuring one's goal hierarchy, or searching for the causes of the failure so one does not have to change the goal to maintain control.

On the other hand, strategies like self-handicapping or defensive pessimism are dysfunctional. The analysis of Heckhausen and Schulz suggests that different manifestations of secondary control may be arranged according to their capacity to restore control. This may provide a basis to design instruments measuring the functionality of secondary control used by individuals when primary control fails. Such instruments may be usefully applied in combination with classical measures of intelligence. A final question is theoretical: What is the basis for integration processes of secondary control in classical conceptions of intelligence? Binet himself gave the answer while emphasizing an aspect that has largely been overlooked in modern intelligence theories: the power of auto-criticism.

REFERENCES

Bowers, K. S. (1973). Situationism in psychology: An analysis and a critique. *Psychological Review, 80,* 307–336.

Brandstadter, J., & Renner, G. (1990). Tenacious goal pursuit and flexible goal adjustment: Explication and age-related analysis of assimilative and accommodative strategies of coping. *Psychology and Aging, 5,* 58–67.

Buss, D. M., Gomes, M., Higgins, D. J., & Lauterbach, K. (1987). Tactics of manipulation. *Journal of Personality and Social Psychology, 52,* 1219–1229.

Ceci, S. J., & Liker, J. (1986). Academic and nonacademic intelligence: An experimental separation. In R. S. Sternberg & R. K. Wagner (Eds.), *Practical intelligence: Nature and origins of competence in the everyday world* (pp. 119–142). Cambridge University Press.

Diener, E., & Larsen, R. J. (1983). Temporal stablity and cross-situational consistency of affective, behavioural, and cognitive responses. *Journal of Personality and Social Psychology, 47,* 871–883.

Dweck, C. S. (1991). Self-theories and goals: Their role in motivation, personality and development. In R. A. Dienstbier (Ed.), *Nebraska symposium on motivation* (pp. 199–235). Lincoln: University of Nebraska Press.

Endler, N. S., & Edwards, J. M. (1986). Interactionism in personality from a historical perspective. *Personality and Individual Differences, 7,* 379–384.

Endler, N. S., & Magnusson, D. (Eds.). (1976). *Interactional psychology and personality.* Washington, DC: Hemisphere.

Folkman, S., Lazarus, R. S., Dunkel-Schetter, C., DeLongis, A., & Gruen, R. (1986). The dynamics of stressful encounter: Cognitive appraisal, coping and encounter outcomes. *Journal of Personality and Social Psychology, 50,* 992–1003.

Freeman, F. S. (1955). *Theory and practice of psychological testing* (Rev. ed.). New York: Holt.

Funder, D. C., & Colvin, C. R. (1991). Exploration in behavioral consistency: Properties of persons, situations, and behavior. *Journal of Personality and Social Psychology, 60,* 773–794.

Furnham, A., & Jaspars, J. (1983). The evidence for interactionism in psychology. *Personality and Individual Differences, 4,* 627–644.

Guilford, J. P. (1967). *The nature of human intelligence.* New York: McGraw-Hill.

Hartmann, D. P., Roper, B. L., & Bradford, D. C. (1979). Some relationships between behavioral and traditional assessment. *Journal of Behavioral Assessment, 1,* 3–23.

Heckhausen, J., & Schulz, R. (1995). A life-span theory of control. *Psychological Review, 102,* 284–304.

Hettema, P. J., & Hol, D. P. (1988). Primary control and the consistency of interpersonal behavior across different situations. *European Journal of Personality.*

Hettema, P. J., & Kenrick, D. T. (1992). Models of person-situation interactions. In G. V. Caprara & G. L. van Heck (Eds.), *Modern personality psychology: Critical reviews and new directions* (pp. 393–417). New York: Harvester-Wheatsheaf.

Hettema, P. J., Leidelmeijer, C., & Geenen, R. (1999). Dimensions of information processing: Physiological reactions to motion pictures. *European Journal of Personality* (Vol. 14(1), pp. 39-63).

Hettema, P. J., & van Bakel, A. P. (1997). Cross-situational consistency in a mastery condition. *Journal of Research in Personality, 31,* 222–239.

Hettema, P. J., van Heck, G. L., Appels, M. T., & van Zon, I. (1986). The assessment of situational power. In A. Angleitner, A. Furnham, & G. L. van Heck (Eds.), *Personality psychology in Europe: Current trends and controversies* (Vol. 2, pp. 85–99). Lisse, The Netherlands: Swets & Zeitlinger.

Hettema, P. J., Vingerhoets, A. J., van der Molen, M., & van de Vijver, A. J. (1989). Construct validation of psychophysiological state patterns. In P. J. Hettema (Ed.), *Personality and environment: Assessment of human adaptation* (pp. 147–161). Chichester: Wiley.

Kahneman, D. (1973). *Attention and effort.* Englewood Cliffs, NJ: Prentice-Hall.

Kenrick, D. T., & Dantchik, A. (1983). Interactionism, idiographics and the social psychological invasion of personality. *Journal of Personality, 51,* 286–307.

Kenrick, D. T., & Stringfield, D. O. (1980). Personality traits and the eye of the beholder: Crossing some traditional boundaries in the search for consistency in all of the people. *Psychological Review, 87,* 88–104.

Kuhl, J. (1994). A theory of action and state orientation. In J. Kuhl & J. Beckman (Eds.), *Volition and personality: Action versus state orientation* (pp. 9–46). Seattle, WA: Hogrefe.

Melis, C. (1997). *Intelligence: A cognitive-energetic approach.* Unpublished doctoral dissertation. Tilburg University, The Netherlands.

Mischel, W. (1973). Toward a cognitive social learning reconceptualization of personality. *Psychological Review, 80,* 252–283.

Mulder, G. (1986). The concept and measurement of mental effort. In G. R. J. Hockey, M. G. H. Coles, & A. W. K. Gaillard (Eds.), *Energetics and human information processing* (pp. 175–198). Dordrecht, The Netherlands: Martinus Nijhoff.

Neisser, U. (1976). General, academic and artificial intelligence. In L. Resnick (Ed.), *The nature of intelligence* (pp. 135–144). Hillsdale NJ: Lawrence Erlbaum Associates.

Pribram, K. H., & McGuinness, D. (1975). Arousal, activation and effort in the control of attention. *Psychological Review, 82,* 116–149.

Pribram, K. H., & McGuinness, D. (1992). Attention and para-attentional processing: Event related brain potentials as tests of a model. In D. Friedman & G. Bruder (Eds.), *Annals of the New York Academy of Sciences* (pp. 85–92). New York: New York Academy of Sciences.

Riteco, C. R. (1998). *Job control, persoonlijkheid en qezonheid: Een exploratieve studie aan een Nederlandse universiteit.* Unpublished doctoral dissertation. Tilburg University, The Netherlands.

Roth, S., & Cohen, L. (1986). Approach, avoidance and coping with stress. *American Psychologist, 41,* 813–819.

Rothbaum, F., Weisz, J. R., & Snyder, S. S. (1982). Changing the world and changing the self: A two-process model of perceived control. *Journal of Personality and Social Psychology, 42(1),* 5-37.

Sarason, S., Smith, R. E., & Diener, E. (1975). Personality research: Components of variance attributable to the person and the situation. *Journal of Personality and Social Psychology, 32,* 199–204.

Scribner, S. (1986). Thinking in action: Some characteristics of practical thought. In R. S. Sternberg & R. K. Wagner (Eds.), *Practical intelligence: Nature and origins of competence in the everyday world* (pp. 13–30). Cambridge, England: Cambridge University Press.

Skinner, E. A. (1996). A guide to constructs of control. *Journal of Personality and Social Psychology, 71(3),* 549–570.

Skinner, B. F. (1953). *The analysis of behavior.* New York: MacMillan.

Snow, R. E. (1986). On intelligence. In R. J. Sternberg & D. K. Detterman (Eds.), *What is intelligence? Contemporary viewpoints on its nature and definition* (pp. 133–138). Norwood NJ: Ablex.

Snyder, M., & Ickes, W. (1985). Personality and social behavior. In G. Lindzey & E. Aronson (Eds.), *Handbook of social psychology* (3rd ed., Vol. 2, pp. 883–948). Reading, MA: Addison-Wesley.

Spearman, C. (1927). *The abilities of man.* London: MacMillan.

Terman, L. M. (1916). *The measurement of intelligence.* Boston: Houghton Mifflin.

Wagner, R. K. (1986). The search for intraterrestrial intelligence. In R.S. Sternberg & R. K. Wagner (Eds.), *Practical intelligence: Nature and origins of competence in the everyday world* (pp. 361–378). Cambridge, England: Cambridge University Press.

White, R. (1959). Motivation reconsidered: The concept of competence. *Psychological Review, 66,* 297–333.

Wright, J. C., & Mischel, W. (1987). A conditional approach to dispositional constructs: The local predictability of social behavior. *Journal of Personality and Social Psychology, 35,* 1159–1177.

20

Successful Intelligence: Understanding What Spearman Had Rather Than What He Studied

Robert J. Sternberg
Yale University

Charles Spearman is one of psychology's great success stories. Few theories have had the durability that his two-factor theory has had (Spearman, 1927) in influencing theory, research, and society. Although one could argue as to the continued importance of the notion of specific abilities in his theory, the notion that there is some *g,* or general intelligence, continues to permeate much thinking about intelligence, and the evidence in favor of some kind of *g*–factor for at least some aspects of intelligence is about as strong as any evidence we have for anything in psychology. I argue in this chapter, however, that *g* pertains not to all of intelligence but only to part of it, and that if societies overutilize the *g* concept, they do themselves and their members a disservice. Moreover, the bottom line is that the kind of intelligence to be described here—successful intelligence—is what Spearman had, even if it is not quite what he studied.

Societies try to identify those who have the potential to succeed to greater or lesser degree. That is why the word "intelligence" was invented in many of their languages. Of course, not all languages have quite the word. English, Spanish, and French do; Chinese, however, does not. But all of these languages have one or more terms to identify those with greater or less potential for success, especially those who potentially have the most to contribute to that society, and in many ways, may demand the least from it in terms of resources.

For this reason, societies devise a variety of ways to identify the more intelligent—whether through intelligence tests, school performance, apprenticeships, or other challenges given the young. What would happen if a society devised a means of identifying the most intelligent that identified only a small proportion of those who were really intelligent or, worse, identified the wrong people? We would then have a society that, at best, misutilized these resources to the detriment of the society, as well as to the individuals who constitute that society.

To the extent that societies rely heavily on conventional tests of intelligence in the tradition of Binet and Simon (1916), whatever particular tests they may be, I argue in this chapter that societies are committing—in the language of signal-detection theory—serious misses as well as false alarms. In other words, they are missing large proportions of their intellectual talent and are selecting individuals who are relatively undistinguished in any significant way with regard either to the goals of the society or even to the goals of these individuals. The basis of this argument is a theory of successful intelligence (Sternberg, 1996b).

Unfortunately, societies do not even have to use intelligence tests to make this mistake. If they even use for identification, the same abilities that intelligence tests measure to identify their best, they will still miss large numbers of potentially successful individuals at the same time that they generate a relatively high rate of false alarms.

In this chapter, I first describe what I see as the societal problem that needs to be solved. Then I propose a possible solution—a concept of successful intelligence. I describe what it is and why it may be important. Next, I describe the elements of successful intelligence. Finally, I discuss the interaction of these elements. In all of these discussions, I draw on empirical research to argue that conventional concepts of intelligence need to be supplemented by broader ones, whether the concept presented here, or some other.

THE SOCIETAL PROBLEM

On the island of Jamaica, many elementary schools have a very different layout than the layout to which most educators are accustomed. The school might be in one large room. Classes are arrayed around the room, each taught by a different teacher. Perhaps there are partitions separating the classes, perhaps not. When I observed classrooms, partitions sometimes appeared but other times did not. As I sat listening to lectures in various classes, I found myself wondering what kind of abilities would predict academic performance in the schools.

I did not do an empirical study, but I did come to the conclusion that two extremely important abilities would be hearing and selective attention. Because of the amount of noise in the room, it is very hard to hear the teacher, and a student with a hearing disability will be in trouble. Also, because of competition from the lectures of other teachers, it is important to filter out the irrelevant material that another teacher is teaching.

Suppose, then, a test of hearing and selective attention is devised to be given to the students. Being able to hear the instruction in class requires good hearing and selective attention. As most testing is oral (the children generally do not read well), good hearing, and selective attention are required to do well on tests of achievement as well. This setting is not so dissimilar to Alfred Binet and

Simon's (1916), where a test of certain elements may come to be viewed as an intelligence test because it predicts what it is designed to predict; namely, school performance.

Similarly, intelligence tests are designed to measure primarily memory and analytical kinds of abilities. Schools also emphasize such abilities, both in their instruction and in their assessment of achievement. The result is that intelligence tests measuring memory and analytical abilities will be valid in predicting school performance, whether or not memory and analytical abilities are none, part, or all of intelligence.

Basically, a closed loop has been created, where one set of abilities comes to be seen as very important, whether or not that set really has the importance it appears to have. Moreover, the loop extends beyond the school. If students need the identified abilities in order to be admitted to university training and thereby to be placed on a route access high-level jobs, the identified abilities will become important in predicting who gains access to those jobs. It will then be no wonder that Herrnstein and Murray (1994), among others, will discover a correlation between intelligence and job level (as well as related measures, such as SES). Without high levels of the identified abilities, access to high-level jobs will likely be denied.

The effect will obtain whether the identified abilities really matter or not. Suppose, for example, it is decided that what really matters is height. The advantage of height is that it can be more objectively measured, is more reliable in its measurement, and is harder to achieve through cheating or other means. To receive admission to a competitive university, students need to be tall. Schools like Oxford or Cambridge might require, say, that students be 7 feet tall. Schools like Dippity University might hold students to a lesser standard. Entrance to high-level graduate training would require even greater height. Of course, students who go to Oxford or Cambridge or other competitive universities get access to better jobs. Eventually, the progeny of Herrnstein and Murray will discover that height is a good predictor of job attainment, and, given the effects of self-fulfilling prophecies, height will almost certainly predict a part of job success as well.

The analogy is not silly. For many years, social class was the major contributor to job attainment. People fully believed that social class was what mattered for success; many still have this belief. They created a system wherein their prediction would come true. In medieval times, birth was all that mattered. If you were born a serf with an IQ of 200, you died a serf. If you were born a noble with an IQ of 50 (perhaps because of royal inbreeding), you nevertheless died a noble. There was no social mobility at all on the basis of intelligence. Their system seemed to work because serfs did not, in fact, achieve much, and the nobility ruled. History courses still concentrate on the contributions of the nobles, not of the serfs who were not, in fact, given the opportunity to contribute much of anything.

To people of that day, the "divine right of kings" also seemed to be a far better basis than any other for deciding who would be royal. In some countries, birth and little or nothing else still determines who gets to be king, so that royal incompetence can continue to rule.

To summarize: People often confuse person-created systems with systems that nature creates. We create the system, along with its self-fulfilling prophecies, and then assume in social–Darwinistic fashion that what we are seeing is the work of nature or what Herrnstein and Murray (1994) referred to as the invisible guiding hand of nature. The hand is perhaps invisible, but it is our own, not nature's.

We need some way of recognizing intelligence or any kind of talent that gets us out of the closed loops we create and then believe are nature's way. Successful intelligence provides one way out of these closed loops.

THE CONCEPT OF SUCCESSFUL INTELLIGENCE

What Is Successful Intelligence?

Successful intelligence is one's purposive ability to adapt to, shape, and select environments so as to accomplish one's goals and those of one's society and culture. In this view, individuals need to achieve a balance among (a) modifying themselves to suit their environment (adaptation), (b) modifying their environment to suit themselves (shaping), and (c) changing their environment when they cannot make it work for them (selection). This balance, rather mere levels of any one of the functions, is the key to successful intelligence (Sternberg, 1985a, 1996b).

Successful intelligence involves an individual's discerning his or her pattern of strengths and weaknesses and then figuring out ways to capitalize on the strengths and at the same time to compensate for or correct the weaknesses. According to this view, the traits associated with successful intelligence are partially idiographic rather than fully nomothetic. There is no one set of abilities that everyone could be measured along that would completely characterize his or her successful intelligence: People attain success, in part, in idiosyncratic ways that involve their finding how best to exploit their own patterns of strengths and weaknesses.

Intelligence Versus Successful Intelligence

Successful intelligence differs from conventional, more academic notions of intelligence in several ways. Consider some of the main differences.

Adaptation Versus Shaping and Selection as Well

Conventional definitions of intelligence stress adaptation to existing environments (see, e.g., "Intelligence and its measurement," 1921; Sternberg & Detterman, 1986). According to this view, a person is intelligent to the extent that he or she adapts to already existing environments. The problem with this definition is that it puts the individual into a relatively passive role with regard to the environmental context: The context demands; the individual responds. Although this passive role may adequately describe intelligence in many school settings and even in lower level job settings, it does not describe the role taken by people who actively set goals and meet them over the course of their lives.

For example, in current research on leadership (see, e.g. Sternberg et al, 2000), my colleagues and I are devising a model and a test of tacit knowledge for leadership—what leaders need to know in order to lead that they typically are not explicitly taught and that often is not even verbalized. Leaders are active shapers of their environment: They try to mold the environment and to convince others to follow their lead (see also Gardner, 1995). Only weak and unsuccessful leaders accept the environment totally as a given, and try to convince people to adapt to this environment, as they have as leaders. A notion of intelligence as the ability to adapt to the environment could not possibly capture what successful leaders know and do, because leaders shape rather than merely adapting to environments.

CRITERIA RELEVANT FOR ASSESSING PREDICTIVE VALIDITY

Conventional conceptions of intelligence have often been devised in relation to fairly abstract and academic kinds of tasks (e.g., Binet & Simon, 1916; Piaget, 1972). Conventional tests have stressed such tasks, and validation of these conceptions and the tests deriving from them has then often been in terms of school performance or performance on standardized achievement tests measuring scholastic performance. Successful intelligence, in contrast, cannot adequately be measured solely by abstract, academic kinds of tasks, nor could it be adequately validated by school grades.

For example, we investigated the predictive validity of a test that is commonly and almost routinely used for admission to graduate programs in the United States: the Graduate Record Examination, known as the GRE (Sternberg & Williams, 1997). This test yields four scores: verbal, quantitative, analytical, and subject matter achievement. This test is used in almost every field of graduate study and weighs heavily in many admissions decisions. But what, exactly, does the test predict?

Our review of the literature showed that the overwhelming number of research studies that had been done to validate the test had used what we considered to be relatively uninteresting criteria against which to validate the test, such as first- or second-year grades in a graduate program. But professionals are not judged by their grades. So in our study, we asked the advisors of all matriculants to the Yale University graduate program in psychology over a 12-year period to rate their advisees for (a) analytical ability, (b) creative ability, (c) practical ability, (d) teaching ability, and (e) research ability. We also asked readers of the students' doctoral dissertations (not including the main advisor) to rate the quality of the dissertations.

We found the test to be a fine predictor of first-year grades in our graduate program, especially after various corrections for restriction of range. But the test was a poor predictor of almost everything else, regardless of whether the data were corrected for restriction of range or not. None of the four subtests significantly predicted any of the ratings of women's performance. Only the analytical test significantly (but weakly) predicted ratings of men's performance. Thus, a conventional ability test that is widely used in the United States. was a good predictor of grades, but beyond that, its predictive validity was practically nonexistent. Yet the test is widely used, and users of the test simply assume that it is valid.

Life Performance. Conventional notions of intelligence seem to emphasize skills that are extremely relevant in school but that perhaps become relatively less important later on. Thus, memory and analytical skills—the kinds emphasized by traditional theories of intelligence (see Carroll, 1993; Gardner, Kornhaber & Wake, 1996; Sternberg, 1990)—are very important in school and although they continue to be important later on, they are arguably less so, as other skills come into play. It is thus unsurprising, perhaps, that conventional tests of intelligence predict school grades quite a bit better than they predict job performance (Wagner, 1997). Interestingly, these tests may not even be the best predictors of all aspects of school performance.

For example, we devised a test for college students that was quite different in kind from the *Scholastic Assessment Test* (SAT) widely used to predict college success in the United States. Our test asked students practical questions such as what teachers expect in essays, how to study effectively, and how to perform effectively in a small recitation class accompanying a large lecture course (see Sternberg, Wagner, & Okagaki, 1993). We found that scores on this test predicted college academic success at Yale as well as did the SAT, and predicted personal adjustment to the college environment much better than did the SAT.

Personal, Societal, and Cultural Values. The concept of successful intelligence explicitly acknowledges personal, societal, and cultural values, as well as their interaction. Truly, one cannot talk about adaptation, selection, or shaping outside a cultural context, any more than one can talk completely about any kind of intelligence outside a cultural context (Berry, 1974; Cole, 1996; Laboratory of Comparative Human Cognition, 1982; Sternberg, 1984). Intelligence cannot be measured in a culture free way, because intelligence occurs and is evaluated in the context of a culture. Cultures and even subcultures may differ in their concepts even of what is intelligent (Cole, Gay, Glick, & Sharp, 1971; Greenfield, 1997; Wober, 1974).

For example, in our own research, (Sternberg, Conway, Ketron, & Bernstein, 1981) we found that U.S. implicit theories or conceptions of intelligence yielded three main factors: practical problem solving, verbal ability, and social competence. But these conceptions may differ even from one occupation to another: We found that professors of art, business, philosophy, and physics had different conceptions of what would constitute an intelligent student and that their conceptions fit the adaptive requirements of their respective fields (Sternberg, 1985b).

Even within a given country, conceptions of intelligence may differ. In a study in the culturally diverse community of San Jose, California, we found that hispanic, Asian, and Anglo parents had rather different conceptions of what it means for their children to be intelligent (Okagaki & Sternberg, 1993). In particular, Asian parents heavily emphasized cognitive skills, Hispanic parents heavily emphasized social skills, and Anglo parents came in between, although closer to the Asian than to the Hispanic conception. More to the point, the school performance of the children in each group could be predicted from the match between the parental conceptions of intelligence and that of the teachers in school, who more emphasized cognitive competencies.

Once we go outside a given country, conceptions can become even much more diverse. For example, in a recent study of Taiwanese–Chinese conceptions of intelligence (Yang & Sternberg, 1997), we found five factors underlying individuals' implicit theories of intelligence: general cognitive ability, interpersonal ability, intrapersonal ability, intellectual assertiveness, and intellectual circumspection or modesty. Conventional tests of intelligence do not fully or even adequately capture any of the implicit theories of intelligence that we have studied.

It is important, as well, to take personal goals into account. In schooling, it is often assumed that the ultimate goal is to obtain the best grades possible, and grade point averages (GPA) are often used as criteria of success. But even in a school environment, practically anyone would agree that leadership roles, musical accomplishments, dramatic performances, and other forms of activities and good citizenship are part of individual success. Different students may weigh different criteria differently, much as different individuals would later in their lives. The money that is so important to one person might mean little to another, whereas the fame that one person strives for might actively be shunned by another. In measuring life success, therefore, we need to take into account not only what the society or culture values, but what the individual values as well.

In sum, successful intelligence is a broader construct than is traditional, academically defined intelligence. What are the components of successful intelligence?

Components of Successful Intelligence

Although successful intelligence is partially idiographic, there are certain broad nomothetic abilities that are relevant to the successful intelligence of virtually anyone. These are analytical, creative, and practical abilities (Sternberg, 1985a, 1988, 1996b). Analytical abilities are required to analyze and evaluate the options available in life. Creative abilities are required to generate these options in the first place, and practical abilities are required to implement the options and make them work.

Analytical Abilities

Analytical abilities are involved in analyzing, judging, evaluating, and comparing and contrasting. When, for example, a student is asked to write an essay comparing two different forms of government or to solve a mathematical word problem, the student is being asked to employ his or her analytical skills.

In our research, we have studied analytical abilities largely through methods of componential analysis (see Sternberg, 1977), whereby information processing on cognitive tasks is decomposed into its elementary components. According to the theory, there are three main kinds of components (Sternberg, 1985a). Metacomponents are used to plan, monitor, and evaluate problem solving and decision making. Performance components are used to implement the instructions of the metacomponents. Knowledge-acquisition components are used to learn how to solve the problems or make the decisions in the first place.

Metacomponents are particularly important to successful intelligence. They include (a) identifying the existence of a problem, (b) defining the nature of the problem, (c) mentally representing the problem, (d) planning a strategy for solving the problem, (e) allocating resources to solving the problem, (f) monitoring one's problem solving while it is ongoing; and (g) evaluating one's problem solving after it is done.

In our research, we found that more and less intelligent individuals (as measured by tests of fluid abilities) differ in their metacomponential functioning. For example, we found that on complex analogy tasks, the more intelligent individuals distributed their time differently from the less intelligent ones: More intelligent individuals spent relatively more time on global planning, or deciding what they were going to do before they started; less intelligent individuals spent relatively more time on local planning, or deciding what to do in the course of solving problems (Sternberg, 1981). The advantage of putting more time up front is that one is less susceptible to false paths and detours, thereby reducing overall problem-solving time. In another study (Wagner & Sternberg, 1987), we found that better readers distributed their time differently in reading multiple passages than did poorer readers. In particular, the better readers adjusted their reading speed to take into account the purpose for which they were reading, whereas the poorer readers did not.

Results such as these suggest that the traditional view of intelligence as quick thinking (Jensen, 1982; Sternberg et al., 1981; Vernon & Mori, 1992) is a fairly gross oversimplification of what is really involved in high-quality intellectual functioning. Successfully intelligent people are not necessarily faster than other people; rather, they are more effective at deciding when to be fast and when to be slow. They allocate their time more effectively. Of course, it is important sometimes to be fast, as when an automobile is coming head-on toward one's own automobile. But in the majority of real-life situations, it is knowing how much time something is worth, in addition to being able to do things in little time (or in much time, as the situation demands), that counts.

Using componential analysis, one can take a task—such as an inductive reasoning problem-analogy, classification, or series-completion problem—and break up performance on this problem into its elementary performance components, such as encoding the terms of the problem, inferring relations between the terms of the problem, and applying the inferred relation to generate a response (Sternberg & Gardner, 1982). Our models of task performance have generally accounted for 80% to 95% of the variation in latency data for solutions to the various kinds of induction problems. Correlations of components of reasoning with scores on psychometric inductive reasoning tests have generally been in the −.3 to −.6 range (negative because latencies are being correlated with percentages correct). In our work, we isolated component latencies and difficulties for individual participants, as well as the strategies they used in solving the problem. Percentages of variation accounted for in response time data of individuals are, of course, considerably lower than those for averaged data.

We used similar techniques for studying various kinds of deductive-reasoning problems (e.g., Guyote & Sternberg, 1981; Sternberg, 1980; Sternberg & Turner, 1981; Sternberg & Weil, 1980) and verbal-comprehension problems (Sternberg, 1987a, 1987b; Sternberg & Powell, 1983). Task models have typically accounted for over 80% of the variation in latency and response-choice data for the deduction tasks.

In our verbal comprehension work, we formulated a cognitive model of how people figure out meanings of words in natural contexts (see Sternberg, 1988b). The model had three major elements: contextual cues, processes of decontextualization, and textual variables that facilitate or impede decontextualization. This model accounted both for which words were easier and more difficult to learn and for which individuals were better in decontextualization than others. We also showed that the ability to figure out meanings of words from context could be taught (Sternberg, 1988a).

We believe that measures of analytical ability are improved when dynamic as well as static assessment components are considered. For example, in a collaborative effort we (Grigorenko, Sternberg, & Ehrman, 2000) devised a dynamic test of foreign-language learning ability. In this test, individuals learn an artificial language (Ursulu) at the time they take the test. Indeed, the whole test consists of performances based on one's success in learning the language. We found that the test predicts language-learning performance in the U.S. Foreign Service Institute with a validity coefficient of about 0.7, suggesting that the test is effective in accomplishing its goals.

In another context, we studied effects in Jamaica of parasitic infections on cognitive functioning (Sternberg, Powell, McGrane, & Grantham-McGregor, 1997). We found that on conventional cognitive tests, high-level functions such as complex memory and reasoning are affected by whipworm infection, but lower level functions such as selective attention are not. We did not find, however, any effect of antiparasitic treatment (albendazol) on cognitive functioning; nor did we expect to, given that higher order cognitive functions build up over a period of many years and are unlikely to recover immediately after medical treatment.

What is possible, however, is that learning abilities are improved by the treatment, although not the products and processes that have been built up by them over the course of the years. We are currently doing a study in Tanzania examining whether dynamic tests of analytical abilities may be able to pick up cognitive changes that static tests do not pick up. The study, in collaboration with Grigorenko in the United States, as well as with Nokes in England and Professor Mbise in Tanzania, may help shed light on some of the potential of dynamic tests for assessing newly gained analytical abilities.

Creative Abilities

Creative abilities are involved in creating, inventing, discovering, imagining, and going beyond the information given. A creative individual is one who generates ideas that are novel, high in quality, and task appropriate (Sternberg & Lubart, 1991, 1995, 1996).

According to our investment theory of creativity, creative individuals are ones who "buy low and sell high" in the world of ideas: They are willing to generate ideas that, like stocks with low price-earnings ratios, are unpopular and perhaps even deprecated. Creative individuals try to convince other people of the worth of these ideas. Having convinced at least some people of the value of these ideas, they then sell high, meaning that they move on to the next unpopular idea. According to this theory, creativity requires a confluence of six resources: certain cognitive processes (redefining problems and selectively encoding, combining, and comparing information), knowledge, thinking styles, personality, motivation, and the environment.

We used a variety of kinds of problems to assess various aspects of creative thinking. One kind of problem is convergent, requiring a keyed answer.

In one convergent type of problem (Sternberg, 1982, Tetewsky & Sternberg, 1986), called a conceptual-projection problem, participants are presented with novel kinds of concepts, such as *grue*—meaning green until the year 2000 and blue thereafter—and *bleen*—meaning blue until the year 2000 and green thereafter (Goodman, 1955). Or participants might be told that there is a planet, Kyron, where there are four kinds of people: plins, who are born young and die young; kwefs, who are born young and die old; balts, who are born old and die young; and prosses, who are born old and die old. Participants then have to solve induction problems, based on incomplete information. Information-processing models of task performance generally accounted for over 90% of the variation in response-latency data. The critical finding was that creative individuals are those who are more efficiently able to switch between conceptual systems, say, green-blue on the one hand and grue-bleen, on the other. In other words, they have the flexibility to alter their system of thinking without being hesitant or troubled by the switch.

Another type of item (Sternberg & Gastel, 1989a, 1989b) required participants to solve analogies and other kinds of induction problems but with either factual premises (e.g., "Birds can fly") or counterfactual premises (e.g., "Sparrows can play hopscotch"). Scores on the counterfactual items were moderately related to scores on conventional fluid-intelligence tests, and the counterfactual items seemed to be the better measures of the ability to redefine conventional ways of thinking.

The creative part of intelligence as applied to creativity also involves three knowledge-acquisition components, or processes used in learning. These three processes, in the context of creativity, are bases of insightful thinking. They are called *selective encoding*, which involves distinguishing relevant from irrelevant information; *selective combination*, which involves combining bits of relevant information in novel ways; and *selective comparison*, which involves relating new information to old information in novel ways. For example, Bohr's model of the atom as a miniature solar system was a selective comparison insight, relating the atom to the solar system, as was Freud's hydraulic model of the mind.

Sternberg and Davidson (1982; see also Davidson, 1986, 1995; Davidson & Sternberg, 1984) tested this theory of insight in a variety of studies, showing mathematical insight problems (e.g., "If you have blue socks and brown socks in a drawer mixed in a ratio of 4 to 5, how many socks do you have to take out of the drawer in order to be assured of having a pair of the same color?"). They found that the three kinds of insights could be separated via different kinds of problems, and that correlations between the insight problems and tests of fluid intelligence were moderate. In particular, the insight problems correlated .56 with a test of solving mystery problems, .53 with a classification test (letter sets), and .43 with nonsense syllogisms (a test of deductive reasoning included for discriminant-validation purposes). They also found that it was possible to teach elementary-students to improve their insightful thinking. In one study (Davidson & Sternberg, 1984) fourth-grade students (roughly 9 years old) who were labeled either as gifted or nongifted were either given training in solving insight problems or were given irrelevant training (control group). All students were given a pretest and a posttest. Experimental students improved significantly more than did controls. The training also showed transfer from the kinds of problems that were explicitly taught to related kinds of problems.

Gifted students started out at a higher level than did nongifted students, and ended up at a higher level as well. Thus, although all students improved on average, group differences were maintained. Training typically does not remove individual differences. But it can place everyone at a higher level of functioning and sometimes change rank orders of individuals.

Sternberg and Lubart (1995) tested the investment theory as a whole using divergent rather than convergent test items (see also Lubart & Sternberg, 1995; Sternberg & Lubart, 1996). They asked people to generate creative products in four domains, choosing two from among a variety of topics they were given: writing (e.g. "The Keyhole," "2983"), art (e.g., "Earth from an Insect's Point of View," "Beginning of Time"), advertising (e.g., "Brussels sprouts," "Cuff links"), and science (e.g., "How could we know if there were extraterrestrial aliens hidden among us?").

All products were rated by multiple raters. Interrater reliabilities for the four domains ranged from .81 to .89, with a median of .86. Averaging over domains, mean interrater reliability was .92. Correlations between the two products in the same domains were .63 for writing, .37 for art, .65 for advertisements, .52 for science, and .67 overall, averaging across domains.

They found only weak to moderate correlations across the four domains. In particular, correlations across domains ranged from .23 to .62, with a median of .36.

Practical Abilities

Practical abilities are involved when intelligence is applied to real-world contexts. Our notion of practical abilities hinges largely, although certainly not exclusively, on the construct of tacit knowledge.

The Nature of Tacit Knowledge. An academically intelligent individual is someone who is characterized by facile acquisition and use of *formal academic knowledge*, the kind of knowledge sampled by IQ tests and other tests of their ilk. Conversely, the hallmark of the practically intelligent individual is facile acquisition and use of tacit knowledge. Tacit knowledge refers to action-oriented knowledge, which is typically acquired without direct help from others and that allows individuals to achieve goals they personally value (Horvath et al., 1995; Sternberg & Horvath, 1999; Sternberg & Wagner, 1993; Sternberg, Wagner, Williams, & Horvath, 1995). The acquisition and use of such knowledge appears to be uniquely important to competent performance in real-world endeavors.

What, exactly, is tacit knowledge? There are three characteristic features of tacit knowledge. First, *tacit knowledge* is about knowing how—about doing. It is procedural in nature. Second, tacit knowledge is relevant to the attainment of goals people value. It is not the kind of academic material that teachers try to stuff in students' heads, where neither the students nor the teachers sometimes have the slightest idea of why the information is being imparted. Third, tacit knowledge is typically acquired with little help from others.

Knowledge with these three properties is called tacit because it often needs to be inferred from actions or statements. But although the term tacit is used to refer to this type of knowledge, the knowledge can be, and sometimes is, brought out into the open, although usually with difficulty and often with resistance. For example, there many be a big difference between what gets one a promotion according to a rule book and what gets one a promotion in reality. A company may not be eager for the true criteria—the tacit ones—to emerge. But these criteria can, and sometimes do, come to light.

Promotions are, in fact, a particularly good example of the importance of tacit knowledge to practical intelligence. When one looks at the people who get promoted within an organization, they are usually the people who have figured out how the system they are in really works, regardless of what anyone may say about how the system is supposed to work. Lawyers, for example, quickly figure out that billable hours are the key to success in a law firm, but they may also need to figure out that not all billable hours are equal—that some cases may be far better as career-builders than are others. In many fields, what matters even more than the work one does is the reputation one builds for that work and reputation is not always tantamount to the quality of the work. People are often promoted more on the grounds of the reputation they have built than for the quality of the work, resulting in the promotion of some people whose work is not, in fact, as good as that of other people who are left behind. The winners figured out what would lead to their advancement, and it was more than just the quality of the work they did.

What does tacit knowledge actually look like? Usually, it is expressed in the form of a sequence of if–then conditionals, which can be rather complex. For example,

> If (you need to deliver bad news to your boss)
>
> and
>
> If (if it is Monday morning)
>
> and
>
> If (the boss' golf game was rained out the day before)
>
> and
>
> If (the staff seems to be "walking on eggs")
> Then (wait until later to deliver the news).

What one can see from this example is that tacit knowledge is always wedded to particular uses in particular kinds of situations. People who are asked about their knowledge in practical situations will often begin by articulating general rules in roughly declarative form (e.g., "a good leader needs to know what people are like"). When such generalizations are probed, however, they often reveal themselves to be summaries of much more specific, and more useful, tacit knowledge.

Indeed, tacit knowledge is *practically useful*—it is knowledge that is instrumental to the goals people want to attain, such as how to lead, how to get promoted, or whatever. For example, knowledge about how to make subordinates feel valued is practically useful for managers or leaders who value that outcome, but is not practically useful for those who are unconcerned about making their subordinates feel valued. Thus, tacit knowledge is distinguished from knowledge, even how-to knowledge, that is irrelevant to goals that people care about personally.

An important feature of tacit knowledge is that it is usually acquired without direct help from others, and may even be acquired despite barriers to its acquisition: If everyone knew it, it would be useless. Consider, for example, how to get the next promotion. In a typical company, not everyone can get that promotion. There is knowledge about what matters to the higher ups that distinguishes those who are more likely to get that promotion from those who do not. But suppose everyone had the knowledge. Then it would not distinguish among people and it would be useless in determining who got the promotion. Very quickly, some other piece of information that some people know and some do not would become the inside information that distinguishes people who forge ahead from those who get left behind.

The implication of all this is that practically intelligent people are now those who simply try to acquire as much knowledge as they can about the system in which they are working—they are people who know that they need to acquire the information that is not readily accessible to everyone. This fact applies at any level.

Testing Tacit Knowledge. The tacit-knowledge aspect of practical intelligence can be effectively measured (see Sternberg, Wagner, & Okagaki, 1993; Sternberg, Wagner, Williams, & Horvath, 1995). The measurement instruments that were used consist of a set of work-related situations, each with between 9 and 20 response items. Each situation poses a problem for the participant to solve, and the participant indicates how he or she would solve the problem by rating the various response items. For example, in a hypothetical situation presented to a business manager, a subordinate the manager does not know well has come to him for advice on how to succeed in business. The manager is asked to rate each of several factors (usually on a 1 = low to 9 = high scale), according to the importance of each for succeeding in the given situation. In newer work, which I did in collaboration with Horvath at Yale, Forsythe of the U.S. Military Academy at West Point, and Williams at Cornell, tacit-knowledge measures for military leaders were devised. These measures have been successfully validated (Sternberg et al., 2000).

Some Findings About Tacit Knowledge. One of the first questions we asked is whether tacit knowledge predicts performance of managers. We were particularly interested in managers because they are people who are judged on their practical, not their academic intelligence. No one cares about their IQ scores, SATs, or college grades. Their superiors do care, however, about their ability to generate bottom-line revenue for the company and to enhance the company's reputation.

Does performance on measures of tacit knowledge actually predict performance in management? We found that it does. For example, in two studies (Wagner, 1987; Wagner & Sternberg, 1985), we found correlations of .2 to .4 between tacit-knowledge scores and criteria such as salary, years of management experience, and whether the manager worked for a company at the top of the Fortune 500. In another study, tacit knowledge was significantly correlated with managerial compensation (.39) and level within the company (.36). Tacit knowledge was also correlated, although more weakly, with job satisfaction (.23). These correlations were as good as or better than the .2 correlations typically found when IQ tests are used to predict managerial performance (Wigdor & Garner, 1982).

When more precise criteria were used to assess managerial performance, the tests of tacit knowledge looked even better. In a study of bank managers, for example (Wagner & Sternberg, 1985), we found correlations between tacit knowledge and average percentage of merit-based salary increase of .48 and between tacit knowledge and "generating new business for the bank" of .56.

Further support for the tacit-knowledge approach came out of a study done at a leading management training center, the Center for Creative Leadership in Greensboro, North Carolina (Wagner & Sternberg, 1990). In this study, we were able to examine correlations among a variety of measures, including an intelligence test, a well-known personality test, several tests of cognitive styles, a test of preference for innovation, a test of job satisfaction, and a test of orientation in interpersonal relations. We found the test of tacit knowledge to be the single best predictor of performance on two managerial simulations, called Earth II and Energy International. The correlation was .61. In contrast, IQ correlated only .38 with performance.

One might wonder whether that aspect of practical intelligence measured by tests of tacit knowledge is itself related to IQ. The answer, as far as we can tell, is no. We typically get correlations at the level of .1, which are not even statistically significant. In other words, contrary to the claims of Herrnstein and Murray (1994), IQ is not the only, and probably not even the best, measure of practical performance in organizations or elsewhere. In fact, we used a statistical procedure to look at the correlation of tacit knowledge with managerial performance, even after taking into account every other measure the Center for Creative Leadership used. The result: Tacit knowledge was still a significant predictor of performance, even after taking everything else into account.

The lesson of these studies is that tacit knowledge often matters as much or more than does academic intelligence for job success. It seems not to matter what the job is. Even in ivory-tower academic jobs, tacit knowledge is key. Knowing the ropes is more important than knowing the syllabus one learns in school.

Tacit knowledge comes from effective utilization of experience. In a study of 54 business managers, 51 business school students, and 22 undergraduates, we found, as one would predict, that tacit knowledge for management increases, on the average, with business experience. But IQ does not increase. Tacit knowledge is, therefore, like other aspects of practical intelligence in that it increases over the course of the life span, in contrast to academic intelligence, which may decrease. It is important to keep one additional finding in mind, however: People with more business experience did not score uniformly higher than did those with less experience. In fact, some people with many years of business experience performed quite poorly. The point here is that what matters most is not how much experience one has had but, rather, how much one has profited from the experience one has had. Some people can be in a situation for years and just do not get much out of it, because they do not learn from the mistakes, that other people make.

In a later study that focused on the development of tacit knowledge over the managerial career, Williams and I used extensive interviews and observations to construct measures of tacit knowledge for different levels of management (Williams & Sternberg, in press). We administered this measure to all executives in four high-technology manufacturing companies. We also obtained nominations from managers' superiors for outstanding and underperforming managers at the lower, middle, and upper levels. This approach enabled us to delineate the specific contents of tacit knowledge for each level of management (lower, middle, upper) by examining what experts at each level knew that their poorly performing colleagues did not.

Our results showed that there was indeed specialized tacit knowledge for each of the three management levels and that this knowledge was differentially related to success. We derived these results by comparing outstanding and underperforming managers within each management level on inventories specific for the various levels of management. For example, within the domain of knowledge about oneself, knowing how to seek out, create, and enjoy challenges is substantially more important to upper level executives than to the middle or lower level executives. Knowledge about maintaining appropriate levels of control becomes progressively more significant at higher levels of management. Knowledge about self-motivation, self-direction, self-awareness, and personal organization is roughly comparable in importance at the lower and middle levels and becomes somewhat more important at the upper level. Finally, knowledge about completing tasks and working effectively within the business environment is substantially more important at high levels. In general, the lower the level of management, the more important it is to know how to get day-to-day, operational tasks accomplished, whereas the higher the level of management, the more important it is to know how to set a vision for the company to follow.

As mentioned earlier, some psychologists believe in the importance of a general ability, roughly IQ, that they believe explains almost everything involving intelligence that can be explained about job performance (Jensen, 1993; Ree & Earles, 1993; Schmidt & Hunter, 1993). These individuals have criticized our work as ignoring this general ability. In fact, we have not ignored it, as we showed when we discussed our studies at the Center for Creative Leadership, where our measures outpredict IQ-type tests in predicting managerial skill. But it turns out that managerial ability itself shows some "g-like" qualities.

We analyzed scores from our tacit-knowledge tests and found that, in fact, people who tend to be knowledgeable about some aspects of tacit knowledge also tend to be knowledgeable about others. In other words, there was something like a general factor. Moreover, when people were tested for their tacit knowledge in two domains—business management and a field that is practically as different as one could find, academic psychology—the correlation between scores in the two domains was .58. Thus, people who are good at acquiring and using tacit knowledge do appear to have a generalizable skill. In everyday parlance, they are high in common sense. But common sense is not academic intelligence. In study after study, as mentioned earlier, we have found only trivial correlations between tacit knowledge and IQ (e.g., Wagner & Sternberg, 1985, 1990).

Our belief that tacit knowledge is not IQ was put to a rather severe test by a researcher who correlated scores on a tacit-knowledge test with scores on the Armed Services Vocational Aptitude battery (ASVAB; Eddy, 1988), which is essentially a very sophisticated and relatively broad-ranging IQ test. In a sample of 631 Air Force Recruits, of whom 29% were women and 19% members of minority groups, the median correlation between tacit-knowledge scores and ASVAB scores, on the 0 to 1 scale, was a mere .07. Statistical analysis revealed that when scores were grouped according to the underlying constructs they measured, all the *ASVAB* tests tended to cluster together, but separately from tests of tacit knowledge. Quite simply, practical and academic intelligence are not the same, never have been, and, in the foreseeable future, never will be.

Interestingly, both IQ and tacit knowledge are related to education. We have found correlations with both years of higher education (.37) and with self-reported school performance (.26). We have even found correlations with quality of college (.34). The fact that IQ also correlates with these measures tells us that tacit knowledge is predicted by educational variables, but only those aspects of education that are not correlated with IQ. In other words, it is what one gains in college that is not straight academic information that matters for tacit knowledge! Thus, from our point of view, what students learn in courses truly is only a minor part of the college or any other educational experience.

One other result stands out from the Eddy (1988) study. Scores on the ASVAB were significantly related to both sex and race, such that women and minority-group members performed more poorly than did men and majority-group members. However, tacit-knowledge scores were unrelated to either sex (correlation of .02) or race (correlation of .03). In other words, tacit knowledge, unlike IQ, is not sex- or race-loaded.

Beyond Business. Although my focus has been on business management, tacit knowledge is related to success in other domains as well. For example, in two studies of the tacit knowledge of academic psychology professors, we found correlations in the 0.4 to 0.5 range between tacit knowledge and various criteria, such as number of citations to the professors' work reported in the Social Science Citation Index (a measure of impact the field) and the rated scholarly quality of an individual's departmental faculty (see Wagner, 1987; Wagner & Sternberg, 1985).

After those studies, we examined the role of tacit knowledge in the domain of sales (see Sternberg, Wagner, & Okagaki, 1993). We found correlations in the 0.3 to 0.4 range between measures of tacit knowledge for sales and criterion measures such as sales volume and sales awards received for a sample of life insurance salespersons. In this work, we were able to express the tacit knowledge of salespeople in terms of sets of rules of thumb—rough guides to action in sales situations. Not only does knowing the rules of thumb for sales help us to assess sales tacit knowledge, it also potentially could help us in terms of devising a training program for more effective sales work.

We have also studied the role of tacit knowledge for children quite a bit younger than college students. Why? Because tacit knowledge is important at all ages. Students, as much as anyone else, need to learn about tacit knowledge as it applies to life in general and to school in particular.

In a current collaboration with Grigorenko at Yale and Moscow State, Nokes at Oxford, Geissler at the Bilharzis Institute in Copenhagen, as well as Professor Okatcha at the University of Nairobi, we are investigating the practical intelligence of young children near the village of Kisumu, Kenya. In particular, many of these children have farflung knowledge of natural herbal medicines that their society believes are useful in fighting parasitic infections. It is unclear whether these medicines actually are effective, but it is the belief in their effectiveness, rather than the effectiveness itself, that is relevant to the study. Knowledge about these natural herbal medicines is not taught in school, but is picked up in the home and in the village. The society believes the knowledge to be adaptive. Is the ability to utilize this knowledge related to g or related constructs (Steinberg et al., in press)?

We devised a test of tacit knowledge of natural herbal medicines, which we gave to children near Kisumu. We also gave these children the Mill Hill Vocabulary Scale, as well as a vocabulary tests in Luo, their home language. In a pilot study, the correlations between the tacit-knowledge test and two vocabulary tests were about the same—of the order of -0.45. In other words, children with more tacit knowledge had less formal vocabulary, perhaps because parents decided either to emphasize either more traditional or more Western education. In any case, it appears that, under some circumstances, tacit knowledge may actually be negatively correlated with more formal knowledge. We are currently examining the correlation of the tacit-knowledge test with Raven Colored Progressive Matrices.

What about practical intelligence in a school setting? Together with a team at Harvard headed by Howard Gardner, we instituted a 6-year program of research, called the Practical Intelligence for Schools (PIFS) Program (Williams et al., 1996), which involved intensive observations and interviews of students and teachers in order to determine the tacit knowledge necessary for success in school. Curricula designed to teach the essential tacit knowledge were developed and evaluated both in Connecticut and in Massachusetts, in a variety of school districts. The curriculum has been sent to hundreds of schools and is now being widely used.

The results of the curriculum evaluations have been uniformly positive. For example, students receiving PIFS showed significantly greater increases in reading, writing, homework, and test-taking ability over the school year, compared with students in the same schools not receiving the curriculum.

Furthermore, teachers, students, and administrators reported fewer behavioral problems in classes using the program (see Gardner, Krechevsky, Sternberg, & Okagaki, 1994; Sternberg, Okagaki, & Jackson, 1990; Williams et al., 1996). In other words, children can not only be assessed for tacit knowledge; they can also be taught it.

PUTTING TOGETHER THE THREE ASPECTS
OF SUCCESSFUL INTELLIGENCE

How do all of the aspects of successful intelligence fit together? And how do they matter in the school? I decided a few years ago to do a study to check out my views on the three aspects of successful intelligence and, further, to test the notion that students can succeed if they are able to capitalize on any of the three nomothetic aspects of successful intelligence, so long as they are taught and assessed in a way that enables them to capitalize on their strengths.

The goal of the study was simple. It was to see whether students would perform better in the classroom if they were taught in a way that allowed them to make use of their natural patterns of abilities. In other words, if one teaches children in a way that fits them, rather than in a one-size-fits-all way, will children learn and perform better? Here is what we did (Sternberg, 1999; Sternberg, Ferrari, Clinkenbeard, & Grigorenko, 1996):

We sent a test based on my three-part theory of successful intelligence to students all around the country. The test contained, analytical, creative, and practical items, in the verbal, quantitative, figural, and essay domains. The idea was to look in a wide variety of ways for students' patterns of abilities. We did not want to limit ourselves to the analytical kinds of items found on IQ tests; nor did we want to limit ourselves just to, say, the verbal domain or just to multiple-choice items. But testing the three aspects of my theory of successful intelligence in four different domains, we were greatly increasing the chances that, if a student had high intellectual abilities of some kind, we would be able to detect them.

What were some examples of the kinds of items that appeared on the test? In the analytical domain, for example, students had to figure out meanings or words from natural contexts, just as they did when they first learned vocabulary. In the creative domain, for example, students had to work with novel (newly invented) number operations. In the practical domain, students had to use maps to plan routes and schedules to compute time and distances, much as they do in everyday life. The practical essay required students to describe a life problem they were facing and propose practical solutions to it.

The students taking the test were high-school students from all around the country and from abroad who had been identified by their teachers or schools as potential candidates. They were not necessarily identified as conventionally gifted. We then chose students for the program who met one of five types of criteria. Either they were very high in an,lytical abilities, very high in creative abilities, very high in practical abilities, high but not necessarily very high in all three kinds of abilities, or relatively low in all three kinds of abilities. This gave us five different ability groupings.

It is worth saying right out that the groups were different from each other not only in ability, but in some other fairly obvious ways. For example, the high-analytic group was most notable for its traditional composition in terms of the usual gifted students in the United States: It was mostly white, middle- to upper-middle class, and composed of students who had been identified many times in the past as gifted in their schools. The high-creative and high-practical groups, in contrast, were much more diverse, ethnically, racially, and with respect to socioeconomic class. Many of the students in these groups had never been identified as gifted before, and they were generally not the highest achievers in their schools. The high-balanced group (who did well on all the tests) again looked more like a typical gifted group, presumably because they were high in the more conventional analytical abilities. The low-balanced group was diverse.

The students were brought to Yale to take an advanced-placement course in introductory psychology. In other words, it was a college-level course being taught to high-school students. All students received the same basic introductory psychology text (Sternberg, 1995), which is based on the three-part theory of intelligence. Students all also received identical lectures in the mornings from a star teacher at Yale who had won a teaching award.

The critical treatment distinguishing the groups occurred in the afternoon. There were four different types of afternoon instruction. One kind emphasized analytical thinking: comparing and contrasting, judging, evaluating, analyzing. A second kind of instruction emphasized creative thinking: discovering, inventing, imagining, supposing. A third kind of instruction emphasized practical thinking: using, utilizing, and applying. And the fourth kind of instruction—the so-called control group—emphasized memory, as do most introductory courses, in psychology or in other areas. Of course, these techniques are applicable not just to psychology but to other fields as well.

In science, analytical thinking is involved in, say, comparing one theory of dreaming to another; creative thinking is involved in formulating a theory or designing an experiment; practical thinking is involved in applying scientific principles to everyday life. In literature, analytical thinking is involved in analyzing plots, themes, or characters; creative thinking in writing a poem or a short story; practical thinking in applying lessons learned from literature to everyday life. In history, analytical thinking is involved in thinking about how two countries or cultures are similar and different; creative thinking in placing oneself in the position of other people of other times and places; practical thinking in applying the lessons of history to the present. In art, analytical thinking is involved in analyzing an artist's style or message; creative thinking in producing art; practical thinking in deciding what will sell, and why, in the art world. Even in sports, all three kinds of thinking are needed: analytical thinking in analyzing an opponent's strategy, creative thinking in coming up with one's own strategy, and practical thinking in psyching out the opponent.

It is important to realize one thing about the instruction. Because we were doing an experiment, we assigned students to sections that emphasized only one of analytical, creative, or practical thinking, or else memory. A good course, however, will be a combination of all of these different types of thinking. The reason is that you want to help students both to learn in ways that are comfortable to them, and to learn in ways that are not. We do not produce successfully intelligent people by coddling them—by always making things easy for them. We produce successfully intelligent people by making some things easy and others hard—by allowing students both to capitalize on strengths and to compensate for or remediate weakness.

In our summer course, we evaluated all students for four kinds of achievements: memory, analytical, creativity, and practicality. Thus, students could not just succeed by showing that they had memorized the book. They had to show different kinds of proficiencies. Teaching in analytical, creative, and practical ways is important because it actually enhances learning of material rather than detracting from it. Everyone knows that memorizing a book results in very short-term learning. Most students forget the material as soon as they take the exam, or, unfortunately, sometimes before. By thinking about the material in different ways, students are forced to process it more deeply and, thus, to learn it better. By thinking to learn, they learn to think.

When we looked at the results, they were strong and clear. Students who were placed in afternoon sections that matched their pattern of abilities performed better than did students who were placed in afternoon sections that mismatched. For example, if a creative student was given at least some chance to exercise his or her creative abilities in the course, the student's performance would be better than if not given such a chance. The same was true for analytical and practical students.

There were other results of note as well. Although overall correlations between analytical, creative, and practical scores ranged from .38 to .49, the correlations were quite a bit lower (around 0.1 to 0.2) when LISREL (confirmatory-factor) analysis controlled for mode of testing (multiple choice and essay). Furthermore, factor analysis revealed no strong general factor, confirming the view of the theory of successful intelligence that the general factor of intelligence is largely an artifact of using principal components of principal-factor analysis (which maximizes the size of the general factor) on a narrow range of tests rather than the broader range we used.

Correlations were also computed between our abilities test and more conventional tests of abilities, including the Concept Mastery Test (largely a test of crystallized abilities), the Watson-Glaser Critical Thinking Appraisal, the

Cattell Culture-Fair Test of g (Scale 3), and a homemade test consisting of insight problems. The analytical tests on our own measure correlated about .5 with these tests, as did the creative tests, but the practical tests correlated only about .3, on average. We also found, when we used stepwise multiple regression, that prediction of grades in the college-level psychology course was significantly improved by using creative and practical, as well as analytical, measures of abilities.

In a way, the results are not surprising. It makes sense that students would do better if allowed to show their strengths. But the way we teach in school, students rarely are given such a chance. We value the students with strong memory and perhaps analytical abilities and almost write off those with strong creative and practical abilities. If we want to capitalize on the gifts of our students, at any level, we need to change, teach, and assess students in ways that recognize their strengths, not just their weaknesses. One-size-fits-all teaching is a poor fit for most students. A study like this shows that we have come a long way from IQ to successful intelligence.

Of course, most teachers will complain that they do not have time to individualize their instruction and, moreover, that they need to prepare students for tests that will emphasize memory. Interactions, they may believe, are just too complicated. So in a follow-up study, students across the United States were tested for main effects (Sternberg, Torff, & Grigorenko, 1998).

In this study, two groups of children, one at the elementary level (Grade 3, or roughly 8 years of age) and one at the secondary level (Grade 8, or roughly 14 years of age) were taught a regular social-studies curriculum on communities (Grade 3) or an introductory psychology course (Grade 8). The children in the first group generally had a lower socioeconomic status (SES) and were ethnically very diverse. The children in the second group were generally middle- to upper- SES and were mostly White.

All the children were divided into three groups. In a triarchic-instruction group, they were taught the material for analytical, creative, and practical thinking, as well as for memory. In a critical-thinking instruction group, they were taught the material for analytical thinking, as well as for memory. And in a conventional-instruction group, they were taught the material in a standard way that emphasized memory. Their achievement was assessed via conventional multiple-choice, memory-based assessments and via performance assessments of analytical, creative, and practical achievements. We found that, in general, the triarchically-instructed children outperformed the other children, even on the memory-based tests. Why?

We believe that children in the triarchic group had two advantages. First, they could encode the material in multiple ways: analytically, creatively, and practically, as well as for memory. In general, people learn better when they think and learn in different ways. Second, they could both capitalize on their strengths and compensate for or remediate their weaknesses—big advantages in any learning situation. Thus, they were in a better position to learn what they needed to learn.

CONCLUSION

If we want to understand human intelligence as it is applied in life and not just in school, then we may wish to think in terms not just of g but of successful intelligence. The concept of successful intelligence is not inconsistent with g. Rather, g is seen as an element of successful intelligence, without a doubt the element most relevant for schooling. Research also shows that g is relevant in almost all aspects of life (Herrnstein & Murray, 1994). But g does not account for all of the variation between people. We believe that the augmented concept of successful intelligence, although not accounting for all of the variation, at least accounts for more. Ultimately, of course, a full picture of success in life would have to take into account many variables beyond intelligence, such as motivation, personality, and life background.

Charles Spearman is one of the greatest success stories in all of psychology. How did he become so successful? I believe the answer is to be found not in g or in any s (specific ability), but rather in something much broader and perhaps more becoming of him—successful intelligence.

REFERENCES

Berry, J. W. (1974). Radical cultural relativism and the concept of intelligence. In J. W. Berry & P. R. Dasen (Eds.), *Culture and cognition: Readings in cross-cultural psychology,* (pp. 225–229). London: Methuen.

Binet, A., & Simon, T. (1916). *The development of intelligence in children.* Baltimore: Williams & Wilkins.

Carroll, J. B. (1993). *Human cognitive abilities: A survey of factor-analytic studies.* New York: Cambridge University Press.

Cole, M. (1996). *Cultural psychology.* Cambridge, MA: Harvard University Press.

Cole, M, Gay, J., Glick, J., & Sharp, D. (1971). *The cultural context of learning and thinking.* New York: Basic Books.

Davidson, J. E. (1986). The role of insight in giftedness. In R. J. Sternberg & J. E. Davidson (Eds.), *Conceptions of giftedness* (pp. 201–222). New York: Cambridge University Press.

Davidson, J. E. (1995). The suddenness of insight. In R. J. Sternberg & J. E. Davidson (Eds.), *The nature of insight* (pp. 125–155). Cambridge, MA: MIT Press.

Davidson, J. E., & Sternberg, R. J. (1984). The role of insight in intellectual giftedness. *Gifted Child Quarterly, 28,* 58–64.

Eddy, A. S. (1988). *The relationship between the Tacit Knowledge Inventory for Managers and the Armed Services Vocational Aptitude Battery.* Unpublished master's thesis, St. Mary's University, San Antonio, TX.

Gardner, H. (1995). *Leading minds.* New York: Basic Books

Gardner, H., Krechevsky, M., Sternberg, R. J., & Okagaki, L. (1994). Intelligence in context: Enhancing students' practical intelligence for school. In K. McGilly (Ed.), *Classroom lessons: Integrating cognitive theory and classroom practice* (pp. 105–127). Cambridge, MA: Bradford Books.

Goodman, N. (1955). *Fact, fiction, and forecast.* Cambridge, MA: Harvard University Press.

Greenfield, P. M. (1997). You can't take it with you: Why assessments of abilities don't cross cultures. *American Psychologist, 52,* 1115–1124.

Grigorenko, E. L., Sternberg, R. J., & Ehrman, M. E. (1997). A theory-based approach to the measurement of foreign language learning ability: The CANAL-F theory and test. *The Modern Language Journal, 84,* 390–405.

Guyote, M. J., & Sternberg, R. J. (1981). A transitive-chain theory of syllogistic reasoning. *Cognitive Psychology, 13,* 461–525.

Herrnstein, R. J., & Murray, C. (1994). *The bell curve.* New York: Free Press.

"Intelligence and its measurement": A symposium (1921). *Journal of Educational Psychology, 12,* 123–147, 195–216, 271–275.

Jensen, A. R. (1982). The chronometry of intelligence. In R. J. Sternberg (Ed.), *Advances in the psychology of human intelligence* (Vol. 1, pp. 255–310). Hillsdale, NJ: Lawerence Erlbaum Associates.

Jensen, A. R. (1993). Test validity: *g* versus "tacit knowledge." *Current Directions in Psychological Science, 1,* 9–10.

Laboratory of Comparative Human Cognition (1982). Culture and intelligence. In R. J. Sternberg (Ed.), *Handbook of human intelligence* (pp. 642–719). New York: Cambridge University Press.

Lubart, T. I. & Sternberg, R. J. (1995). An investment approach to creativity: Theory and data. In S. M. Smith, T. B. Ward, & R. A. Finke (Eds.), *The creative cognition approach* (pp. 269–302). Cambridge, MA: MIT Press.

Okagaki, L. & Sternberg, R. J. (1993). Parental beliefs and children's school performance. *Child Development, 64*(1), 36–56.

Piaget, J. (1972). *The psychology of intelligence.* Totowa, NJ: Littlefield Adams.

Ree, M. J., & Earles, J. A. (1993). *g* is to psychology what carbon is to chemistry: A reply to Sternberg and Wagner, McClelland, and Calfee. *Current Directions in Psychological Science, 1,* 11–12.

Schmidt, F. L., & Hunter, J. E. (1993). Tacit knowledge, practical intelligence, general mental ability, and job knowledge. *Current Directions in Psychological Science, 1,* 8–9.

Spearman, C. (1927). *The abilities of man.* London: Macmillan.

Sternberg, R. J. (1977). Component processes in analogical reasoning. *Psychological Review, 84,* 353–378.

Sternberg, R. J. (1980). The development of linear syllogistic reasoning. *Journal of Experimental Child Psychology, 29,* 340–356.

Sternberg, R. J. (1981). Intelligence and nontrenchment. *Journal of Educational Psychology, 73,* 1–16.

Sternberg, R. J., Conway, B. E., Ketron, J. L., & Bernstein, M. (1981). People's conceptions of intelligence. *Journal of Personality and Social Psychology, 41,* 37–55.

Sternberg, R. J. (1982). Nontrenchment in the assessment of intellectual giftedness. *Gifted Child Quarterly, 26,* 63–67.

Sternberg, R. J. (1984). What should intelligence tests test? Implications of a triarchic theory of intelligence for intelligence testing. *Educational Researcher, 13,* 5–15.

Sternberg, R. J. (1985a). *Beyond IQ: A triarchic theory of human intelligence.* New York: Cambridge University Press.

Sternberg, R. J. (1985b). Implicit theories of intelligence, creativity, and wisdom. *Journal of Personality and Social Psychology, 49,* 607–627.

Sternberg, R. J. (1987a). Most vocabulary is learned from context. In M. G. McKeown & M. E. Curtis (Eds.), *The nature of vocabulary acquisition* (pp. 89–105). Hillsdale, NJ: Lawrence Erlbaum Associates.

Sternberg, R. J. (1987b). The psychology of verbal comprehension. In R. Glaser (Ed.), *Advances in instructional psychology* (Vol. 3, pp. 97–151). Hillsdale, NJ: Lawrence Erlbaum Associates.

Sternberg, R. J. (1988a). *The triarchic mind: A new theory of human intelligence.* New York: Viking.

Sternberg, R. J. (1988b). A triarchic view of intelligence in cross-cultural perspective. In S. H. Irvine & J. W. Berry (Eds.), *Human abilities in cultural context* (pp. 60–85). New York: Cambridge University Press.

Sternberg, R. J. (1990). *Metaphors of mind.* New York: Cambridge University Press.

Sternberg, R. J. (1994). Diversifying instruction and assessment. *The Educational Forum, 59*(1), 47–53.

Sternberg, R. J. (1995). *In search of the human mind.* Orlando: Harcourt Brace.

Sternberg, R. J. (1996a). Matching abilities, instruction, and assessment: Reawakening the sleeping giant of ATI. In I. Dennis & P. Tapsfield (Eds.), *Human abilities: Their nature and measurement* (pp. 167–181). Mahwah, NJ: Lawrence Erlbaum Associates.

Sternberg, R. J. (1996b). *Successful intelligence.* New York: Simon & Schuster.

Sternberg, R. J. (1997). What does it mean to be smart? *Educational Leadership, 54,* 20–24.

Sternberg, R. J., & Davidson, J. E. (1982, June). The mind of the puzzler. *Psychology Today, 16,* 37–44.

Sternberg, R. J., & Detterman, D. K. (Eds.). (1986). *What is intelligence? Contemporary viewpoints on its nature and definition.* Norwood, NJ: Ablex.

Sternberg, R. J., Ferrari, M., Clinkenbeard, P., & Grigorenko, E. L. (1996). Identification, instruction, and assessment of gifted children: A construct validation of a triarchic model. *Gifted Child Quarterly, 40,* 129–137.

Sternberg, R. J., Forsythe, G. B., Hedlund, J., Horvath, J., Snook, S., Williams, W. M., Wagner, R. K., & Grigorenko, E. L. (2000). *Practical intelligence in everyday life.* New York: Cambridge University Press.

Sternberg, R. J., & Gardner, M. K. (1982). A componential interpretation of the general factor in human intelligence. In H. J. Eysenck (Ed.), *A model for intelligence* (pp. 231–254). Berlin: Springer-Verlag.

Sternberg, R. J., & Gastel, J. (1989a). Coping with novelty in human intelligence: An empirical investigation. *Intelligence, 13,* 187–197.

Sternberg, R. J., & Gastel, J. (1989b). If dancers ate their shoes: Inductive reasoning with factual and counterfactual premises. *Memory and Cognition, 17,* 1–10.

Sternberg, R. J., & Horvath, J. A. (Eds.). (1999). *Tacit knowledge in professional practice.* Mahwah, NJ: Lawrence Erlbaum Associates.

Sternberg, R. J., & Lubart, T. I. (1991, April). Creating creative minds. *Phi Delta Kappan,* 608–614.

Sternberg, R. J., & Lubart, T. I. (1995). *Defying the crowd: Cultivating creativity in a culture of conformity.* New York: Free Press.

Sternberg, R. J., & Lubart, T. I. (1996). Investing in creativity. *American Psychologist, 51* (7), 677–688.

Sternberg, R. J., Nokes, K., Geissler, P. W., Prince, R., Okatcha, F., Bundy, D. A., & Grigorenke, E. L. (in press). The relationship between academic and practical intelligence: A case study in Kenya. *Intelligence.*

Sternberg, R. J., Okagaki, L., & Jackson, A. (1990). Practical intelligence for success in school. *Educational Leadership, 48,* 35–39.

Sternberg, R. J., & Powell, J. S. (1983). Comprehending verbal comprehension. *American Psychologist, 38,* 878–893.

Sternberg, R. J., Powell, C., McGrane, P. A., & Grantham-McGregor, S. (1997). Effects of a parasitic infection on cognitive functioning. *Journal of Experimental Psychology: Applied, 3,* 67–76.

Sternberg, R. J., Torff, B., & Grigorenko, E. L. (1998). Teaching triarchically improves school achievement. *Journal of Educational Psychology, 90,* 374–384.

Sternberg, R. J., & Turner, M. E. (1981). Components of syllogistic reasoning. *Acta Psychologica, 47,* 245–265.

Sternberg, R. J., & Wagner, R. K. (1993). The *g*-ocentric view of intelligence and job performance is wrong. *Current Directions in Psychological Science, 2*(1), 1–5.

Sternberg, R. J., & Wagner, R. K., & Okagaki, L. (1993). Practical intelligence: The nature and role of tacit knowledge in work and at school. In H. Reese & J. Puckett (Eds.), *Advances in lifespan development* (pp. 205–227). Hillsdale, NJ: Lawrence Erlbaum Associates.

Sternberg, R. J., Wagner, R. K., Williams, W. M., & Horvath, J. A. (1995). Testing common sense. *American Psychologist, 50*(11), 912–927.

Sternberg, R. J., & Weil, E. M. (1980). An aptitude-strategy interaction in linear syllogistic reasoning. *Journal of Educational Psychology, 72,* 226–234.

Sternberg, R. J., & Williams, W. M. (1997). Does the Graduate Record Examination predict meaningful success in psychology graduate school? A case study. *American Psychologist, 52*(6), 630–641.

Tetewsky, S. J., & Sternberg, R. J. (1986). Conceptual and lexical determinants of nontrenched thinking. *Journal of Memory and Language, 25,* 202–225.

Vernon, P. A., & Mori, M. (1992). Intelligence, reaction times, and peripheral nerve conduction velocity. *Intelligence, 8,* 273–288.

Wagner, R. K. (1987). Tacit knowledge in everyday intelligent behavior. *Journal of Personality and Social Psychology, 52,* 1236–1247.

Wagner, R. K. (1997). Intelligence, employment and training. *American Psychologist, 52,* 1059–1069.

Wagner, R. K., & Sternberg, R. J. (1985). Practical intelligence in real-world pursuits: the role of tacit knowledge. *Journal of Personality and Social Psychology, 49,* 436–458.

Wagner, R. K., & Sternberg, R. J. (1987). Executive control in reading comprehension. In B. K. Britton & S. M. Glynn (Eds.), *Executive control processes in reading* (pp. 1–21). Hillsdale, NJ: Lawrence Erlbaum Associates.

Wagner, R. K., & Sternberg, R. J. (1990). Street smarts. In K. E. Clark & M. B. Clark (Eds.), *Measures of leadership* (pp. 493–504). West Orange, NJ: Leadership Library of America.

Wigdor, A. K., & Garner, W. R. (Eds.). (1982). *Ability testing: Uses, consequences, and controversies.* Washington, D.C.: National Academy Press.

Williams, W. M., Blythe, T., White, N., Li, J., Sternberg, R. J., & Gardner, H. I. (1996). *Practical intelligence for school: A handbook for teachers of grades 5–8.* New York: Harper Collins.

Williams, W. M., & Sternberg, R. J. (in press). *Success acts for managers.* Mahwah, NJ: Lawrence Erlbuam Associates.

Wober, M. (1974). Towards an understanding of the Kiganda concept of intelligence. In J. W. Berry & P. R. Dasen (Eds.), *Culture and cognition: Readings in cross-cultural psychology* (pp. 261–80). London: Methuen.

Yang, S. Y., & Sternberg, R. J. (1997). Taiwanese Chinese conceptions of intelligence. *Intelligence, 25,* 21–36.

AUTHOR INDEX

A

Abramson, L., 290, 302
Ach, N., 139-141, 143, 159
Ackerman, P. L., 43-45, 59, 199, 201, 207, 211, 212
Adorno, T., 114, 117
Agari, T. T., 82, 96
Ahadi, S., 106, 111
Albright, L., 100, 111
Alexander, P. A., 178, 183, 186-188
Allen, R., 233, 257
Allport, G. W., 177, 188, 308, 315
Althoff, K., 182, 190
Altman, I., 322, 333
Amanti, C., 133, 138
Ames, C., 129, 136
Anastasi, A., 83, 96, 196, 211
Angleitner, A., 43, 49, 59, 66, 68, 78
APA Board of Educational Affairs, 128, 136
Arbuckle, J. L., 39-40
Arnold, C. R., 279, 286
Asher, S. R., 186, 188
Atkinson, J. W., 145, 147, 159, 164, 188
Austin, E., 23
Austin, J. T., 312, 315

B

Bacon, M., 326, 331
Baddeley, A., 302-303
Baird, W., 163, 165, 189
Bakan, D., 80, 96
Bakare, C. G. M., 276, 286
Balke, G., 29-30, 34, 41
Bandura, A., 144, 146, 156-157, 159
Bannano, G., 290, 303
Bargh, J. A., 139, 160312,315
Barker, R., 322, 331
Baron, J., 235, 242, 256
Barrett, P., 115-118, 295, 297, 303-304
Barrick, M. R., 312, 315
Barry, H., 326, 331
Bayer, U., 148, 151, 160-161
Beck, L., 105, 111

Becker, W. C., 279, 286
Beckman, J., 93, 97, 145, 149, 159, 160
Bendixon-Noe, M., 132, 136
Bennett, J., 320-322, 324, 331-332
Benware, C. A., 179, 186, 188
Bereiter, C., 124, 133, 135-136, 223, 230
Berkowitz, W., 324-325, 327, 333
Berliner, D. C., 128, 136
Berlyne, D. E., 173, 188
Bernstein, M., 43, 60, 353, 371
Berry, J. W., 274-275, 282, 286, 288, 319-320, 322-325, 330, 332, 353, 370
Biggs, J. B., 220, 222, 230
Bindra, D., 139, 159
Binet, A., 62, 77, 238, 256, 348, 351, 370
Birch, D., 145, 147, 159
Birenbaum, M., 134, 136, 298, 303, 328
Bjorklund, D. F., 186, 192
Blackman, M. C., 310, 315
Bleichrodt, N., 275-276, 287
Blinkhorn, S. F., 283, 288
Blumenfield, P. C., 129, 136, 185, 191
Boekaerts, M., 200, 211
Boldt, E. D., 325, 332
Bond, R., 326, 332
Boodoo, G., 59
Borgatta, E. F., 109, 111
Borkenau, P., 99-100, 102, 104-106, 109-111
Borkowski, J. G., 201, 211
Born, M. P., 275-276, 287, 303, 304
Bouchard, T. J., 59
Bowden, E. A. F., 276, 287
Bowers, K. S., 335, 344
Boyd, R., 324, 332
Boykin, A. W., 59
Boyle, G. J., 115, 118, 207, 211, 294, 304
Bradford, D. C., 336, 345
Bradley, A., 291, 303
Brand, C. R., 23
Brandstadter, J., 322, 332
Brandstätter, V., 150, 153-154, 159-160
Bransford, J. D., 126, 136
Brimble, A. R., 276, 288
Brody, N., 59
Brophy, J., 129, 136, 164, 188
Brown, A. L., 126, 133, 136
Brown, B., 322, 333
Brown, J., 211, 208
Brown, R., 117

Brunswik, E., 101, 111, 361
Brzozowski, P., 68, 77
Burnham, P. S., 283, 287
Burt, C., 33, 40
Bushey, B., 233-234, 257
Buss, D. M., 110, 111, 339, 344
Butcher, H. J., 82, 96

C

Cacioppo, J. T., 235, 238-239, 249-250, 255-256
Calfee, R. C., 128, 136
Calvo, M. G., 185, 189
Cameron, J., 173, 188
Camp, C. C., 313, 315
Campione, J., 126, 136
Cantor, N., 80, 83, 96, 146-146, 152, 157, 159-161, 310, 312, 315
Carey, G., 107, 111
Carli, M., 174, 190
Carnie, D., 300, 304
Carroll, J. B., 25, 27, 31-33, 35, 39-40, 84-85, 96, 114, 117, 202, 211, 250, 256, 352, 370
Carver, C. S., 139, 146-147, 159, 290, 303
Cattell, R. B., 25, 31, 33-34, 40, 71, 75, 77, 88, 96, 113-115, 117-118, 177, 188, 196, 207, 211, 294, 304
Ceci, S. J., 48, 59, 343-344
Cervone, D., 83, 96, 310, 315
Charress, M., 93, 95, 97
Chartrand, J. M., 313, 315
Cheng, H., 293, 303
Child, I., 326, 331
Church, M. A., 155, 159
Ciechanowicz, A., 67, 77
Claridge, G. S., 114, 117
Clarke, D., 291, 304
Clinkenbeard, P., 366, 372
Cohen, L, 339, 346
Cole, M., 353, 370
Collins, A. M., 90, 97, 126, 137
Colvin, C. R., 338-339, 345
Comer, J. P., 132, 136
Conway, B. E., 43, 60, 353, 371
Cooper, C., 116, 118
Cooper, L. A., 81, 96

Corno, L., 83, 94-97, 121-125, 129-131, 133, 135-136, 138-139, 161, 168, 182, 188, 193, 196, 202, 211-212, 223, 232
Costa, A. L., 252, 256
Costa, P. T., Jr., 40-41, 44, 53, 59, 114, 117, 308, 310, 316
Cotter, T., 43-44, 59, 295, 297, 300, 303
Cottrell, L. S., 111
Cox, P. W., 330, 333
Crawford, A. B., 283, 287
Cronbach, L. J., 43, 46, 59, 83, 90, 96-97, 311, 315
Crowe, E., 144, 160
Csikszentmihalyi, M., 124, 136, 165, 173-175, 188

D

D'Andrade, R. G., 108-109, 112
Daniel, M. H., 9, 23
Dantchik, A., 336, 345
Das, J. P., 263, 271
Dasen, P. R., 320, 332
Davidson, H. H., 279, 287
Davidson, J. E., 357-358, 370, 372
Davis, D. A., 276, 280, 287
Davis, J. K., 282, 287
Davis, O. L., 279, 287
Dawis, R. V., 312, 315
DeCharms, R., 173, 188
de Groat, A. A., 279, 287
De Longis, A., 339, 345
De Raad, B., 49-52, 59
Deary, I. J., 9, 23, 50, 58-59
Deci, E., 134, 136, 143, 147, 154, 159, 164-165, 168, 172-175, 178-179, 186, 188, 192
Dembo, T., 164, 190
Dennett, D. C., 82, 97
Denny, J., 327, 332
Dewey, J., 163-164, 188
Detterman, D. K., 9, 23, 351, 372
Diener, E., 106, 111, 336, 344, 346
Digman, J. M., 25, 41, 124, 136, 238, 256
Dolan, L. J., 132, 137
Dorn, L., 300, 304
Doverspike, D., 297, 304
Draycott, S., 115, 117
Drenth, P. J. D., 276, 287-288
Drewniak, U., 179, 190

Drotar, D., 15, 24
Drwal, R. L., 68, 77
Dunne, T. T., 223, 231
Dweck, C. S., 128-129, 136, 143, 155, 159, 164, 188, 339, 344
Dyk, R., 290, 304, 327, 334

E

Earles, J. A., 363, 371
Eccles, J., 164, 169, 171, 176, 188, 193
Eddy, A. S., 364, 370
Edwards, A. L., 283, 287, 310
Edwards, J. M., 336-337, 344
Egan, V., 23
Ehrman, M. E., 356, 371
Eisenberger, R., 134, 136
Eisenhardt, W. B., 179, 188
Elliot, A. J. 167
Elliott, E. S., 143, 155, 159
Emmons, R. A., 145, 157, 159-160, 168
Endler, N. S., 336-337, 344-345
English, A. C., 122, 136
English, H. B., 122, 136
Ennis, R. H., 235, 240, 252, 256
Entin, E. B., 186, 189
Entwistle, A. C., 226-231
Entwistle, N. J., 179, 189, 218, 220-223, 225-232
Ericsson, K. A., 93, 95, 97
Eysenck, H. J., 3, 10, 19, 23, 40-41, 46, 49, 59, 61-62, 64-65, 68, 76-77, 114-117, 196, 203-204, 212, 261, 264, 271, 284, 287, 295, 297, 299, 303
Eysenck, M. W., 46, 49, 61-62, 64-65, 68, 77, 185, 189, 196, 212, 312
Eysenck, S., 299, 303

F

Facione, N. C., 235, 239, 250, 256
Facione, P. A., 235, 239, 250, 256
Fagan, T. F., 15, 24
Faraday, M., 233-234, 257
Faterson, H., 290, 304, 327, 334
Feather, N. T., 171, 189
Feinstein, J. A., 235, 256
Feldman, D., 321, 333
Ferguson, G. A., 282, 287, 320, 333

Ferrara, R., 126, 136
Ferrari, J., 298, 303
Ferrari, M., 366, 372
Ferring, D., 106, 112
Festinger, L., 164, 190
Figueroa, R. A., 10, 23
Fincher-Kiefer, R., 186, 189
Fischer, B., 290, 303
Fischer, L., 290, 303
Fleeson, W., 146, 159
Folkman, S., 339, 345
Forde, A., 43, 59, 389
Forde, D., 321, 333
Forde, L., 295, 297, 300, 303
Fourie, A. B., 276, 287
Frederikson, N., 312, 315
Frearson, W. M., 19, 23
Freeman, F. S., 335, 343, 345
Frenkel-Brunswik, E., 114, 117, 264, 271
Frees, M., 139, 160
Freud, S., 114, 117
Frost, N., 81, 97
Funder, D. C., 100-102, 111, 310, 315, 338-339, 345
Furnham, A., 43, 58-59, 259, 261, 271-272, 291-293, 295, 297-301, 303, 336-337, 345
Frued, S., 118

G

Gailly, A., 130, 137
Gainen, J., 235, 239, 250, 256
Galanter, E., 139, 146, 161
Galton, F., 3, 6, 23, 109, 111
Gamble, J. J., 325, 333
Garcia, T., 223, 231
Gardner, H., 25, 41, 80, 97, 238, 250, 256, 260, 262, 271, 351-352, 355, 365-366, 370-373
Garner, W. R., 85, 98, 361, 373
Gastel, J., 357, 372
Geenen, R., 340, 345
Gibson, G. J., 23
Gibson, J. J., 89-90, 97, 131, 136
Giebelhaus, C., 132, 136
Ginsberg, P. E., 325, 333
Glavanov, D., 181, 184, 192
Goff, M., 43-45, 59, 207, 212

Goldberg, L. R., 49-52, 58-59, 62, 116-117, 297, 303, 312, 315
Goldfried, M. R., 311, 315
Goleman, D., 236, 256
Gollwitzer, P. M., 123, 126, 137, 139, 145, 147-153, 157, 159-161, 167-168, 189, 312, 315
Gomes, M., 339, 344
Gonzalez, N., 133, 138
Goodenough, D. R., 290, 304, 327, 330, 333-334
Goodman, N., 357, 371
Gorsuch, R. L., 27, 38, 41
Gottfredson, L. S., 9, 23176-177, 189
Gottfried, A. E., 166, 189
Gottschaldt, K., 151, 160
Graham, S., 133, 137, 164, 189
Granato, L., 242, 256
Grantham-McGregor, S., 356, 372
Greene, T. R., 186, 189
Greenfield, P. M., 353, 371
Greeno, J. G., 90-91, 97, 126, 137
Grigorenko, E. L., 290, 292, 294, 304, 356, 365-366, 369, 371-372
Groff, P. J., 179, 189
Grolnick, W. S., 186, 189
Gronlund, N. E., 85, 97
Gruen, R., 339, 345
Guest, A., 325, 333
Guilford, J. P., 25, 32, 41, 61, 63, 66-69, 72, 77, 118, 237, 250, 256, 283, 287, 342, 345
Guilford, J. S., 61, 77
Gustaffson, J. E., 25, 27, 29-32, 34-35, 39, 41-42
Gustafson, S. B., 313, 316
Guttman, L., 80, 97
Guyote, M. J., 355, 371

H

Hafner, J., 233, 257
Halisch, F., 139, 160
Halpern, D. F., 59
Hamutyeni, M. A., 277, 287
Harlow, R. E., 146, 160
Harman, H. H., 26, 28, 39, 41
Harris, K. R., 133, 137
Hartman, D. P., 336, 345
Hatalak, A., 179, 190

Hatfield, R., 267, 272
Hauber, K., 163, 192
Hazari, A., 114, 118
Heath, R., 218, 231
Hebb, D. O., 173, 189
Heckhausen, H., 122-124, 137, 147-150, 157, 160, 163-164, 166-168, 189, 191
Heckhausen, J., 338, 341, 344, 345
Heggestad, E. D., 43-45, 59, 199, 201, 211
Heim, A. W., 113, 118
Helmes, E., 298, 303
Hendrix, E. A., 276, 287
Henrdricks, A. A. J., 46, 49-52, 58-59, 63
Herbart, J. F., 17, 163, 189
Herrnstein, R. J., 349, 350, 362, 370-371
Hershey, L., 105, 111
Hettema, P. J., 337, 339-340, 342, 345
Hibbs, N., 295, 303
Hidi, S., 163, 165, 178, 189-191
Higgins, D. J., 339, 344
Higgins, T. E., 144, 156, 160
Hilgard, E. R., 135, 137, 195, 212
Hoare, R. M. N., 276, 287
Hodgkins, S., 158, 161
Hoehn, A. J., 279, 287
Hoepfner, R., 237, 250, 256
Hoffman, L., 170, 189
Hofstee, W. K. B., 43-45, 49-52, 59, 100, 111
Hogan, R., 110-111
Hol, D. P., 340, 345
Holden, R., 295, 298, 303
Holland, J. L., 94, 97, 163, 189, 312, 316
Holzinger, K. J., 28, 36-38, 41
Holzman, P. S., 262, 271
Horn, J. L., 26, 30, 33, 41, 237, 250, 256
Honey, P., 290, 303
Horst, P., 283, 287
Horvath, J. A., 46, 60, 359, 361, 372-373
Hough, L. M., 312, 316
Houtler, B., 267, 272
Hubbard, B., 310, 317
Humphreys, L. G., 25, 41, 200
Humphreys, M. S., 185, 189
Hunt, E., 65, 77, 81-83, 97, 187, 321, 324, 332
Hunt, J. McV., 173, 190
Hunter, J. E., 312, 317, 363, 371
Huntingdon, E., 321, 333
Hymes, C., 144, 160

I

Ickes, W., 336, 346
Irvine, S. H., 274, 276-277, 282-288, 320, 324, 332-333
Irvy, M. A., 132, 137

J

Jacklin, C. N., 176, 190
Jackson, A., 336, 372
Jackson, C., 295, 297, 303
Jackson, D. N. III, 122-125, 135, 138, 182, 193, 202, 212, 223, 232
Jackson, P., 275, 288
Jäger, A. O., 182, 190
Jahoda, G., 330, 333
James, W., 140, 142, 160
Janssen, P. J., 220, 222-223, 231
Jarman, R. F., 263, 271
Jarvis, W. B. G., 235, 256
Jaspars, J., 336-337, 345
Jaworowska, A., 67, 77
Jay, E., 223, 231
Jensen, A. R., 3, 6, 9-10, 15, 17, 20, 23-26, 41, 75, 77, 355, 363, 371
Jetton, T. L., 178, 188
John, O. P., 25, 41, 43, 59, 307, 320, 316-317
Johnson, C. E., 283, 288, 310
Johnson, J., 298, 303
Jöreskog, K. G., 39

K

Kagan, J., 76-77, 308, 316
Kagitcibasi, C., 325, 332-333
Kahneman, D., 342, 345
Kane, M. T., 86, 97
Kanfer, R., 93-94, 96, 122, 124, 126, 131, 136-137, 168, 188, 201, 212
Karp, S., 290, 304, 327, 334
Karweit, N. L., 132, 137
Kellaghan, T., 23
Kelly, G. A., 314, 316
Kenny, D.A., 100-101, 103-104, 111, 310, 316
Kenrick, D. T., 336-337, 339, 345
Kerschensteiner, G., 163, 1907
Ketron, J. L., 44, 60, 353, 371
Kihlstrom, J. F., 310, 315

Kim, U., 320 325, 333
King, L. A., 145, 160
Kinney, R. A., 149, 157, 160
Kintsch, W., 180, 182-183, 190, 193
Kirby, J. R., 263, 271
Klare, G. R., 186, 189
Klein, G. S., 262, 271
Kline, P., 113, 115-118
Klingelhofer, E. L., 276, 288
Kluckholhn, C., 319, 333
Knapp, M. S. 137
Kogan, N., 81, 97
Kohlberg, L., 176, 190
Kolar, D. C., 310, 315
Kolb, D., 290, 304
Konradt, U., 185, 192
Körkel, J., 187, 190
Krapp, A., 163, 165-166, 170, 178, 180, 182-183, 185-186, 190-192
Kraska, K., 124, 137, 197, 201, 212
Krechevsky, M., 336, 371
Kroeber, A., 321,333
Krohn, M. D., 134, 138
Kruglanski, A. W., 139, 160
Kuhl, J., 93-95, 97, 122-124, 126, 137, 139, 145, 156-157, 160, 167-168, 189-190, 197, 201, 212, 339, 343, 345
Kulikowich, J. M., 178, 183, 186-188
Külpe, O., 148, 161
Kunz, G. C., 179, 190

L

Laboratory of Comparative Human Cognition, 353, 371
Lang, G., 279, 287
Langer, E., 208, 211, 235, 251, 256
Langman, J., 132, 137
Larsen, R. J., 336, 344
Latham, G. P., 143, 154, 161, 168, 190
Lauterback, K., 339, 344
Lawty-Jones, M., 297, 303
Lazarus, R. S., 310, 316, 339, 345
Ledzubsjam, M., 65, 75, 77
Lehrke, M., 170, 189
Leidelmeijer, C., 340, 345
Leiman, J. M., 27, 30, 41
Lengfelder, A., 153, 161

Lens, W., 130, 137-138
Lent, E. B., 313, 316
Lepper, M. R., 129, 137
Leung, L., 299, 304
Levin, H. M., 132, 137
Levinson, D. J., 114, 117
Lewin, K., 139-141, 161, 164, 190
Lewowicki, T., 65, 75, 77
Liebert, R. M., 185, 190
Liebler, A., 100, 102, 104, 111
Liker, J., 343-344
Linn, R. L., 85, 97
Linton, H. B., 262, 271
Lissner, K., 141, 161
Little, B., 134, 137
Lizotte, A. J., 134, 138
Locke, E. A., 143, 154, 161, 168, 190
Loehlin, J. C., 59
Loevinger, J., 107, 111
Lofquist, L. H., 312, 315
Lohman, D. F., 79-80, 85-86, 88, 97, 210, 212
Lomax, A., 324-325, 327, 333
Long, R. I., 260, 271
Lopez, F. G., 313, 316
Lord, F. M., 91-92, 97
Lorenz, K., 177, 190
Lubart, T. I., 356, 358, 371-372
Lunneborg, C., 81, 97
Luria, A. R., 263, 271
Lynn, R., 15, 24

M

MacArthur, R. S., 288, 276
Maccoby, E. E., 176, 190
MacCullum, R., 207, 212
MacLeod, C. M., 262, 271
Madden, N. A., 132, 137
Madsen, C. H., 279, 286
Maehr, M. L., 164, 190
Magnusson, D., 307, 312, 316, 337, 345
Mahler, W., 141, 161
Malinowski, B., 319, 323, 333
Malzacher, J. T., 152, 161
Mann, J. H., 109, 111
Markus, H., 124, 135, 137
Martin, M., 291, 299, 304
Marton, F., 179, 190, 219, 228, 231
Maslow, A. H., 218, 231

Massimini, F., 174-175, 188, 190
Matarazzo, J. D., 211-212
Matczak, A., 67, 77
Matthews, G., 196, 198, 213, 300, 304
Mayr, E., 79, 84, 91-92, 97
McCauley, C., 105, 111
McCrae, R. R., 25, 40-41, 44, 53, 59, 114-117, 308, 310, 316
McCune, V., 222, 231-232
McDougall, W., 140, 142, 161
McFarland, J. H., 262, 272
McGowen, W., 298, 303
McGrane, P. A., 356, 372
McGuinness, D., 340, 342, 345
McGuire, W. J., 124, 137
McKay, B., 321, 333
McLaughlin, M., 132, 137
McNett, C. W., 325, 333
Meier, D., 132, 138
Melis, C., 342, 345
Mersman, J., 298, 304
Merten, T., 294, 296, 304
Mertin, M., 151, 161
Messick, S., 48, 58-59, 81, 97, 218, 231, 259-261, 263, 265, 269, 272-274, 276, 282, 288, 290-292, 299, 304, 313, 316
Mettam, D., 276, 283-284, 288
Metzler, J., 85-86, 97
Meyer, J. H. F., 222-223, 231
Meyer, W. J., 279, 288
Middleton, M. J., 129, 138
Midgley, C., 129, 138
Miles, D. R., 107, 111
Miller, G. A., 139, 146, 161
Miller, M., 290, 304
Mischel, W., 308, 310, 316-317, 336-337, 345-346
Mishra, R. C., 324, 333
Moll, L., 133, 138
Montag, I., 298, 303
Moran, E., 321, 333
Morgan, M., 173, 190
Morris, L. W., 185, 190
Morris, S. P., 262, 270, 278
Most, B., 205, 212
Mount, M. K., 312, 315
Mulder, G., 342, 345
Mulaik, S. A., 30, 41
Mumford, A., 290, 303

Mumford, M. D., 313, 316
Munroe, R. H., 276, 288
Munroe, R. L., 276, 288
Murdock, G. P., 326, 333
Murray, C., 349-350, 362, 370-371
Murray, H. A., 310, 312, 316, 319, 333

N

Nagieri, J. A., 15, 24, 263, 271
Napuk, S., 228, 231
Nebylitsyn, V. D., 62, 77
Neff, D., 133, 138
Neilson, I., 330, 333
Neisser, U., 49, 59, 342-343, 345
Nesselroade, J., 309, 314, 317
Newcomb, T. M., 109, 111
Nicholls, J. G., 166, 191
Nichols, R. C., 94, 97
Norris, S. P., 240, 247, 254-255, 257
Novick, M. R., 91-92, 97
Nsamenang, B., 324, 333
Nurius, P., 124, 135, 137
Nuttin, J., 130, 138

O

Okagaki, L., 353, 361, 364, 366, 371-373
Omari, I. M., 276, 287-288
Ones, D., 48, 59, 298, 304, 312, 317
Oltman, P. K., 330, 333
Orbell, S., 158, 161, 169
Osipow, S. H., 163, 193
Ostendorf, F., 43, 46, 49, 52, 58-59, 106, 109-111
Ovsiankina, M., 141, 161
Owen, A. J., 276, 280, 288
Owen, K., 15, 24

P

Pagliari, C., 9, 23
Pandey, J., 320, 332
Parsons, P., 223, 231
Pask, G., 219-220, 231, 263, 266, 272
Paul, R. W., 235, 252, 257
Paulus, D., 299, 304
Paunonen, S. V., 101, 112
Peabody, D., 58-59

Peck, V. A., 201, 211
Pekrun, R., 166-171, 191
Pelto, P., 324-325, 333
Pelletier, L. G., 178, 188
Peoples, C. E., 15, 24
Pepper, S. C., 80, 97
Perfetti, C. A., 187, 191
Perkins, D. N., 223, 231, 233-234, 236, 240, 252, 257
Perloff, R., 59
Perugini, M., 52, 59
Pervin, L. A., 139, 161, 3070-308, 311-314, 316-317
Petty, R. E., 235, 249, 256
Piaget, J., 176, 191, 351, 371
Pierce, W. D., 173, 188
Pintrich, P. R., 171, 191, 200, 211, 223, 231
Piotrowski, A., 61, 66, 68-69, 75-77
Plangger, A. B., 277, 287
Pohl, R. L., 311, 317
Pokay, P., 185, 191
Poortinga, Y. H., 320, 332
Post, T. A., 186, 189
Powell, C., 356, 372
Powell, J. S., 355, 372
Powers, W. T., 147, 161
Prenzel, M., 163, 165, 191
Pressley, M., 133, 138
Pribram, K. H., 340, 342, 345
Pribram, D. H., 139, 146, 161

R

Ramsden, P., 179, 189, 219, 231
Rand, G., 262, 272
Randi, J., 130, 136
Ratajczak, H., 123, 137, 150, 157, 160
Rawlings, D., 300, 304
Ree, M. J., 273, 288, 363, 371
Reiss, A. D., 48, 59, 298, 304
Renner, G., 339, 344
Renninger, K. A., 163, 165, 183, 186, 190-191
Resnick, L., 90, 97, 126, 137
Revelle, W., 185, 189
Reynolds, A. J, 185, 191
Rheinberg, F., 164-165, 167, 174-175, 177-178, 184-185, 187, 191-193
Rhodes, N., 124, 138
Richerson, P., 321, 332

Riemann, R., 44, 60
Riteco, C. R., 340, 346
Roberts, A. O. H., 283, 288, 310
Roberts, L. W., 325, 332-333
Roberts, M. L., 309, 317
Roberts, R. D., 76, 78, 84
Robins, R. W., 310, 316
Robinson, D. L., 64, 76-77, 83
Rocklin, T., 44-45, 60, 210, 212
Roe, A., 176, 189, 191
Rokeach, M., 114, 118, 266, 272
Romanaiah, N., 299, 304
Roney, C. J., 144, 160
Roper, B. C., 336, 345
Rorer, L. G., 86, 97
Ross, S., 267, 272
Roth, S., 339, 346
Rothbaum, F., 338, 341, 346
Ruch, W., 294, 304
Rushton, J. P.319, 333
Ryan, R. M., 134, 136, 143, 154, 159, 164-
    165, 168, 172-175, 178, 186, 188-189, 192
Ryle, G., 235, 257

S

Sabin, J., 139, 160
Saklofske, D. H., 113, 118, 195-196, 198, 204,
    213
Saklofske, R. J., 43, 60, 216, 223
Saljo, R., 179, 190, 219, 231
Salomon, G., 124, 138, 251, 257
Sanchez, C. A., 235, 239, 250, 256
Sandford, R. N., 114, 117
Sarason, S., 336, 346
Sattler, J. M., 196, 212
Scanlan, M. R., 276, 279-280
Scarr, S., 131, 138, 172, 192
Schaal, B., 139, 153, 157, 160-161
Scheier, M. F., 139, 146, 147, 159, 290, 303
Schiefele, H., 163-165, 192
Schiefele, U., 164-171, 178, 180-188, 191-192
Schleyer, E., 199, 213
Schmalhofer, F., 181, 184, 192
Schmalt, H. D., 172, 192
Schmid, J., 27, 41
Schmidt, F. L., 312, 317
Schmitt, M. J., 106, 112
Schneider, G., 163, 192

Schneider, K., 172, 175, 177, 185, 192
Schneider, W., 186-187, 190, 192
Schön, A., 179, 190
Schreyer, I., 178, 192
Schull, J., 299, 304
Schulz, R., 338, 341, 344, 345
Schulze, S. K., 183, 186, 188
Schunk, D. H., 133, 138, 144, 156, 159, 166,
    171, 191, 193
Scribner, S., 343, 346
Sears, P. S., 164, 190
Seehausen, R., 151, 161
Segal, M., 105, 111
Segall, M., 320, 332
Seligman, M., 290, 302
Shapiro, D., 259-260, 265-268, 270-272
Sheeran, P., 158, 161
Shepard, R. N., 85-86, 97
Shevrin, H., 265, 267, 272
Shields, P. M., 131, 137
Shiffrin, R. M., 263, 272
Shoda, Y., 308, 310, 316-317
Shultz, K., 298, 304
Shweder, R. A., 108-109, 112, 313, 317, 319,
    333
Sidick, J., 297, 304
Siebert, K., 294, 296, 304
Siegal, H., 235, 252, 257
Siegel, I. A. 291, 293
Siegelman, M., 176, 191
Simon, Th., 238, 256, 348-349, 351, 370
Simonton, D. K., 206, 212
Sinha, D., 324, 333
Skinner, B. F., 338, 346
Skinner, E. A., 338, 346
Skok, M., 300, 304
Slaven, R. E., 132, 137
Slobodian, J. J., 279, 287
Smith, C. A., 134, 138, 225, 231, 232
Smith, P., 326, 332
Smith, R. E., 336, 346
Smokler, I. A., 265, 267, 272
Snow, R. E., 89-92, 95, 97, 122-128, 135, 138-
    139, 161, 182, 193, 223, 232, 312, 317,
    335, 346
Snyder, M., 336, 346
Snyder, S. S., 338, 341, 346
Sörbom, D., 39, 41

Spearman, C., 4, 6-11, 13, 15, 17, 21, 24-25, 33, 41-42, 62-63, 78, 84-85, 92, 97, 135, 138, 217, 232, 237, 250, 257, 273, 276, 288, 337, 346-347, 371
Spearitt, D., 27, 31, 42
Spence, D., 262, 271
Spencer, H., 90, 97
Spranca, M., 242, 256
Stahl, P. A., 39, 41
Stanford Aptitude Seminar, 135, 138
Stankov, L., 76, 78, 115, 118, 207, 211, 294, 304
Stanovich, K. E., 235, 240, 254-255, 257
Stavridou, A., 261, 272
Steller, B., 123, 137, 149, 151, 160-161
Stephenson, W., 284, 288, 312
Sternberg, R. J., 44-46, 48, 59-60, 68, 78, 82-83, 95-96, 98, 200-201, 212, 220, 232, 238, 250, 257, 259, 271, 290, 292, 294, 304, 348, 350-359, 361-362, 364-367, 369, 370-373
Steward, J., 321, 333
Steyer, R., 106, 112
Strauss, J. P., 312, 315
Strelau, J., 61-63, 65-68, 75-78, 83
Stringfield, D. O., 336, 345
Sugar, J., 290, 303
Swanepoel, H. F., 276, 288
Swineford, F., 28, 35-38, 41
Syrad, T., 276, 283-284, 288
Szirmak, Z., 52, 59
Szustrowa, T., 67, 77

T

Tait, H., 222-223, 231-232
Taylor, S. E., 149, 157, 161, 169
Teasdale, J., 290, 302
Ten Berge, J. M. F., 51-52, 59
Teplov, B. M., 61-62, 78
Terman, L. M., 135, 138, 196, 212, 335, 346
Tetewsky, S. J., 357, 373
Teuval, E., 242, 256
Thayer, R. E., 185, 193
Thomas, D. R., 279, 286
Thompson, G., 279, 287-288
Thompson, S. U., 176, 193
Thornberry, T. P., 134, 138
Thorndike, E. L., 94-95, 98, 196, 212

Thurstone, L. L., 25-26, 31-32, 42, 61, 68, 78, 85, 98
Tiedemann, J., 290, 304
Tishman, S., 223, 231
Tobias, S., 183, 186-187, 193
Todt, E., 163, 176-177, 193
Tolman, E. C., 139, 161
Torff, B., 369, 372
Travers, R. M. W., 176, 193
Triandis, H. C., 325-326, 333
Turner, M. E., 355, 373

U

Undheim, J. O., 25, 27, 31-32, 41
Urbina, S., 59

V

Vallerand, R. J., 178, 188
van Bakel, A. P., 339, 345
van der Flier, H., 275-276, 287-288
van der Molen, M., 342, 345
van der Vijver, A. J., 342, 345
van Dijk, T. A., 180, 182-183, 186, 193
van Heck, G. L., 312, 317, 337, 345
van Zon, I., 337, 345
Vancover, J. B., 312, 315
Vayda, A. P., 321, 333
Vermunt, J. D., 223, 232
Vernon, P. A., 10, 24, 29, 33-34, 42, 355, 373
Vernon, P. E., 284, 288
Vingerhoetz, A. J., 342, 345
Viswesvaran, C., 48, 59, 298, 304
Vollmeyer, R., 184, 193
Voss, J. F., 186, 189
Vygotsky, L. S., 65, 78

W

Wachtel, P. L., 266, 272
Wagner, R. K., 46, 48, 60, 343, 346, 352, 355, 359, 361-362, 364, 372-373
Walberg, H. J., 185, 191
Wallace, J., 311, 317
Walsh, W. B., 163, 193
Wapner, S., 262, 272
Ward, K., 291, 304
Wasik, B. A., 132, 137

Watkins, D., 179, 193
Watson, D., 310, 317
Watt, H., 148, 161
Webb, E., 50, 60, 135, 138
Wechsler, D., 196, 211-212
Wegge, J., 184-185, 192-193
Weil, E. M., 355, 373
Weiner, B., 127, 138, 164, 171, 189, 193
Weintrab, J., 290, 303
Weisz, J. R., 338, 341, 346
Werner, C., 322, 333
Werner, H., 262, 272
West, R. F., 240, 254-255, 257
Whang, P. A., 20, 23
White, R. W., 173, 175, 193, 338, 346
Whitman, D., 267, 272
Wicklund, R.A., 145, 157, 161, 168
Widgor, A. K., 85, 98
Widiger, T. A., 86, 97
Wigdor, A. K., 361, 373
Wigfield, A., 129, 138, 164, 169, 188, 193
Wiggins, J., 298, 304, 328
Wijnen, W. H. F. W., 127, 138
Wild, K. –P., 170, 192
Williams, W. M., 46, 60, 351, 359, 361-362,
    365-366, 372-373
Willingham, W., 124, 138
Wilson, G., 295, 303
Wilson, J. D., 218, 231
Winteler, A., 170, 178, 192
Witkin, H. A., 151, 161, 218, 232, 290, 304,
    311, 317, 324, 327, 330, 332-334
Wober, M., 353, 373
Wonderlic, E., 302, 304
Wood, R., 283, 288
Wood, W., 124, 138
Woodworth, R. S., 94, 98
Wozniak, R. H., 163, 191
Wright, J. C.310, 317, 336, 346
Wulf, F., 289, 304
Wynn-Jones, L., 33, 42

X

Xu, J., 130, 133, 138

Y

Yang, S., 353, 373

Yuki, G. A., 143, 161

Z

Zawadski, B., 61, 67, 78
Zane, J., 267, 272
Zeidner, M., 43, 59, 68, 113, 118, 195-196,
    198-200, 204-205, 211-213
Zillmann, D., 152, 161
Zimmerman, B. J., 124, 138
Zimmerman, W. S., 61, 77
Zuckerman, M., 62, 64, 78

Subject Index

A

Abilities, 27, 41, 79–81, 87, 90–101, 109, 125, 273, 278, 324–325, 398–409
  cognitive, 34–36, 41–42
  visual-spatial, 364
Achievement motivation, 135
Action Phases, 165–168
Activitie Index, 311
Additive coaction, 204
American College Test, 183
Anxiety, 220
Armed Services Vocational Aptitude Battery (ASVAB), 364
ASSIST (Approaches and Study Skills Inventory for Students), 222, 251–256
Aptitude theory, 139–142
Attention control, 156
Availability, 102

B

Broad auditory perception, 32
Broad cognitive speediness, 33
Broad retrieval ability, 33
Broad visual perception, 32

C

California Critical Thinking Dispositions Inventory, 239
Character, 109
Classroom environment, 132
  instruction, 133
Cognition, 188, 255, 266-267, 291, 297–302
Cognitive mediators, 185
Cognitive neuroscience, 4
Cognitive style, 218, 259, 261, 271, 327–329
Cognitive teaching style, 292
Cognized environment, 321
College Characteristics Index, 311
Compartmentalization, 81
Conation, 135, 146, 196, 204, 223–225, 231–236
Consequence management, 147
Consistency, 378–380
Contextualization, 345, 351–352, 369
Control, 379–381, 384

Creative abilities, 356

Creative abilities, 356
Creativity, 149, 356
Crystallized intelligence, 30, 32
Cultural ecology, 321

D

Decontextualizaion, 369
Defensive styles, 259, 265, 269
Detection, 247
Differential Psychology, 99
Discrimination, 247
Dispositional motivational characteristics, 166
Dispositions, 263–286
Distinctive learning strategies, 220
Divergent Thinking, 72
Dweck's theory, 143
Dynamic interaction, 205

E

EPQ-R, 75, 78
Ecological anthropology, 321
Ecological approach, 362–364
Ecological psychology, 131
Elementary Cognitive Tasks (ECTs), 16, 18
Emotional control, 156
Environment, 348–351
Environmental control, 156
Essentialism, 89
  tests, 69
  typical, 48-49
Experimental cognitive psychology, 4
Expressive styles, 259
Eysenck Personality Questionaire (EPQ), 127
Eysenck Personality Profiler (EPP), 329–330

F

FCB-TI, 75–77
FFPI, 53, 55, 57
  Factor V, 56–62
Factorial invariance, 32
  Nested Factor Models (NF), 30-32, 39
  First Principal Component, 54–55
Flexibility, 66
Fluency, 66
Fluid intelligence, 32

G

g-Factor, 4, 6, 11–17
General intelligence, 217
Generalizability, 86
Global IQ, 202
Goal directed behavior, 140
Goal intention, 168
Goals, 157–165, 168, 172–176
Graduate Record Examination (GRE), 351
Guilford-Zimmerman Tempermental
    Schedule, 61

H

Hierarchical modeling, 27–29, 37
Higher order factor models (HO), 28–32, 38
Human intelligence, 195

I

IQ, 204, 233, 349, 362-363
Implementation intentions, 168
Individual motivation, 121
Information processing, 382–383
Item Response Theory (IRT), 8, 237
Interest, 185-187, 190-207
Ipsative, 313-314
Inclination, 273–277
Institute for Scientific Information
    (ISI), 6
Intelligence, 34, 51, 56, 67–68, 72–76, 91,
    196, 198, 201, 204, 223–225, 229, 231,
    236–267, 284, 319, 335-336, 341-348,
    350, 384, 391, 394–395, 410
    A, B, C, 46
    behavior, 77-78
    practical, 51-52, 385
    tests, 69
    typical, 48-49
Interests, 163-164, 176, 178, 185-187, 190-
    207
Intrinsic motivation 172-175, 177, 179
Ipsative, 313-314
Isolation, 260
Item Response Theory (IRT), 205

L

Laws of diminishing returns, 9
Learning, 135, 200-204
    environments, 121

    mastery orientation, 129
    styles, 245-251, 259
Level I-Level II theory, 10

M

Maximimal personality, 44
Mediational strategy training, 146
Memory span, 123
Mobility, 66
Modeling intelligent behavior, 237
Motivation, 123, 126-127, 147, 154, 163,
    166, 185–192, 193–195, 202
    theory, 142
Motionvational
    characteristics concepts, 168
    control, 156
    domains, 199
    factors, 182
    psychology, 201
Movement time (MT), 16–19

N

n-dimensional quadrant, 51
n-space, 49
NEO (Neuroticism, Extroversion,
    Openness), 127
Natural orthogonality, 49
Neurophysiology, 5

O

Ordinal-disordinal interactions, 205

P

p-Component, 50, 51
p-Factor, 53–54
PTS, 75, 77–78
Personality, 27, 51, 53-54, 56, 101, 109,
    118, 126–129, 203, 238, 307, 319,335-
    336, 345, 377
    development, 157
    maximal, 47–50
    traits, 53, 116
    typical, 47–50
Physical symptomatology, 145
Priming, 246
Probabilistic thinking, 90, 99
Psychology of emotion, 180
Psychometric sampling error, 17

Psychometrics, 9

R

Ratings, 110–114, 119–120,
Reaction time (RT), 16–19
Realistic Accuracy Model (RAM),
    111–112
Recognition tests, 181
Referent generality, 139
Relevance, 102
Response styles, 259

S

Salad-dressing syndrome, 43
Saliency, 246
Scanning, 260, 268, 293–299, 301
Scholastic Ability Test, 182
Scholastic Aptitude Test, 124, 352
Science Citation Index (SCI), 6
Self-concept, 305
Self-efficacy, 144, 155
Self-evaluation, 163
Sensitivity, 273–277
Social conformity, 326, 366–368
Social desirability scale, 48
Social Science Citation Index (SSCI), 6
Social size, 326, 366–368
Socio-economic status, 15
Spearman's *g*, 4
Study Interest Questionnaire (SIQ), 170-171
Style, 291–292, 296–302, 306–308, 312,
    315–317, 323–324, 326 328, 330, 370–
    371,
Styles of learning, 219
Stylistic intellect, 45
Summative effect, 204
Synergistic effects, 204

T

Taxonomic, 49
Temperament, 67–74, 76, 79–81, 82, 125
Terra firmae, 84
Terra incognita, 84
Thematic Apperception Test (TAT), 210
Thinking disposition, 234
Three-stratum model, 34–36
Thurstone Temperament Schedule, 61
Typical intelligence, 44

V

Valence belief, 169
Validity, 211
Values, 397
Visual-spatial abilities, 324
Visual-spatial studies, 323
Vocational interest, 163
Volition, 101–102, 123-124, 136–138, 147-
    148, 176, 197

W

w-Factor, 50
Wechsler Intelligence Scale for Children
    (WISC), 210
Wechsler Adult Intelligence Scale (WAIS),
    210
Weighted Average Model (WAM),
    111, 113–114
Western Academic Scientific
    Psychology (WASP), 319, 359